"David Hirsh is one of our br[...]
ists. In this excellent book of c[...]
ment, he makes an unanswerat[...]
—Anthony Julius, Professor o[...]

"For more than a decade, David Hirsh has campaigned courageously against the all-too-prevalent demonisation of Israel as the one national-ism in the world that must not only be criticised but ruled altogether illegitimate. This intellectual disgrace arouses not only his indignation but his commitment to gather evidence and to reason about it with care. What he asks of his readers is an equal commitment to plumb how it has happened that, in a world full of criminality and massacre, it is obsessed with the fundamental wrongheadedness of one and only national movement: Zionism."

—Todd Gitlin, Professor of Journalism and
Sociology, Columbia University, USA

"David Hirsh writes as a sociologist, but much of the material in his fascinating book will be of great interest to people in other disciplines as well, including political philosophers. Having participated in quite a few of the events and debates which he recounts, Hirsh has done a commendable service by deftly highlighting an ugly vein of bigotry that disfigures some substantial portions of the political left in the UK and beyond."

—Matthew H. Kramer FBA, Professor of Legal & Political
Philosophy, Cambridge University, UK

"A fierce and brilliant rebuttal of one of the Left's most pertinacious obsessions. What makes David Hirsh the perfect analyst of this disorder is his first-hand knowledge of the ideologies and dogmata that sustain it."

—Howard Jacobson, Novelist and Visiting Professor at
New College of Humanities, London, UK

"David Hirsh's new book *Contemporary Left Anti-Semitism* is an impor-tant contribution to the literature on the longest hatred. Coming at a time when there is appropriate attention to a resurgence of popu-list, classic right-wing anti-Semitism, Hirsh's work is a reminder that there is no ideological monopoly on anti-Semitism. As he delineates in detail, using Britain as a jumping off point but speaking more broadly, left-wing anti-Semitism is more challenging to identify but is no less pernicious than its right-wing counterpart. In a highly polarized world, understanding anti-Semitism from wherever it emerges is more vital than ever. Hirsh makes a large contribution toward that imperative."

—Jonathan A. Greenblatt, CEO, Anti-
Defamation League, USA

"David Hirsh has rightfully emerged as an important voice on the issue of contemporary antisemitism. He writes with passion but with balance and offers insights, to which we may have been previously oblivious, but, after reading what he has to say, seem utterly obvious. This book is not just for those who care about prejudice and antisemitism. It is also a must read for anyone who cares about the contemporary political landscape. It is a wakeup call for those who believe in the ideals and objective of leftist politics."

—Deborah Lipstadt, Dorot Professor of Modern Jewish
History and Holocaust Studies, Emory University, United States

"David Hirsh is not only one of the foremost analysts and authorities on contemporary antisemitism, he is also one of its most redoubtable opponents."

—Mark Gardener, Director of Communications, CST, UK

"David Hirsh is a relentless investigator into one of the darker corners of contemporary left discourse, always shining a probing, revealing light."

—Jonathan Freedland, Author and Journalist,
The Guardian, UK

"The rise of anti-Semitism on the British left—which reached its apex in Jeremy Corbyn's capturing the leadership of the Labour Party—is one of the most confounding, and worrisome, developments in contemporary Western politics. A man of the left himself, David Hirsh understands this phenomenon better than anyone, and has the battle scars to prove it."

—James Kirchick, Foreign Policy Analyst and Journalist, USA

CONTEMPORARY LEFT ANTISEMITISM

Today's antisemitism is difficult to recognize because it does not come dressed in a Nazi uniform and it does not openly proclaim its hatred or fear of Jews. This book looks at the kind of antisemitism which is tolerated or which goes unacknowledged in apparently democratic spaces: trade unions, churches, left-wing and liberal politics, social gatherings of the chattering classes and the seminars and journals of radical intellectuals. It analyzes how criticism of Israel can mushroom into antisemitism, and it looks at struggles over how antisemitism is defined. It focuses on ways in which those who raise the issue of antisemitism are often accused of doing so in bad faith in an attempt to silence or smear. Hostility to Israel has become a signifier of identity, connected to opposition, to imperialism, neo-liberalism and global capitalism; the 'community of the good' takes on toxic ways of imagining most living Jewish people.

Weaving together theoretical discussion with case study narrative in an engaging and interesting way, this book is a global study which is essential reading for scholars working in sociology, politics, Middle East studies, Israel studies, Jewish studies, philosophy, anthropology, journalism and history, as well as anyone interested in current affairs and politics.

David Hirsh is Senior Lecturer in Sociology at Goldsmiths University, London, UK.

CONTEMPORARY LEFT ANTISEMITISM

David Hirsh

Routledge
Taylor & Francis Group

LONDON AND NEW YORK

First published 2018
by Routledge
2 Park Square, Milton Park, Abingdon, Oxon OX14 4RN

and by Routledge
711 Third Avenue, New York, NY 10017

Routledge is an imprint of the Taylor & Francis Group, an informa business

British Library Cataloguing-in-Publication Data
A catalogue record for this book is available from the British Library

Library of Congress Cataloging-in-Publication Data
Names: Hirsh, David, author.
Title: Contemporary left antisemitism / David Hirsh. Description: Milton Park, Abingdon, Oxon ; New York, NY : Routledge, [2017] | Includes bibliographical references and index.
Identifiers: LCCN 2017016011 | ISBN 9781138235304 (hardback) | ISBN 9781138235311 (pbk.) | ISBN 9781315304311 (ebook)
Subjects: LCSH: Antisemitism—Great Britain—History—21st century. | Labour Party (Great Britain)—History—21st century. | Israel—Foreign public opinion, British. | Public opinion—Great Britain. | Zionism—Great Britain—History—21st century.
Classification: LCC DS146.G7 H57 2017 | DDC 305.892/4041—dc23
LC record available at https://lccn.loc.gov/2017016011

ISBN: 978-1-138-23530-4 (hbk)
ISBN: 978-1-138-23531-1 (pbk)
ISBN: 978-1-315-30431-1 (ebk)

Typeset in Bembo
by Apex CoVantage, LLC

Printed and bound in Great Britain by
TJ International Ltd, Padstow, Cornwall

With love to Anna, Dora, Eddie, Monique and Noa.
With honour for Mirjam, my mum.
In memory of Julian, my dad.
With thanks to Robert Fine, my teacher and friend.
For Fela, Fishel and Rushka who survived
the Nazi camps and who found asylum in Israel;
and for all their descendants.
With respect to Anne & Solomon, Hans & Rosel,
Herbert & Hildergard.
With love to Deborah & Tayip,
Judy & Saravanan and Mark & Laura.

CONTENTS

ACKNOWLEDGEMENTS

FURTHER
ACKNOWLEDGEMENTS

With acknowledgement and thanks for the help, friendship, comradeship and encouragement of:

Jane Ashworth; Sarah A Brown; Jonathan G Campbell; Kirsten Campbell; Adrian Cohen; Ben Cohen; Monique Ebell; Ronald Eissens; Robert Fine; Craig Fowlie; Claire Garbett; Mark Gardner; Eve Garrard; Norman Geras; Richard Gold; Marc Goldberg; Howard Jacobson; Alan Johnson; Anthony Julius; Wendy Kahn; Lesley Klaff; Matthias Kuentzel; Deborah Lipstadt; Eamonn MacDonagh; Jeremy Newmark; Jon Pike; Dave Rich; Jeff Samuels; Annette Seidel-Arpaci; David M Seymour; Dina Shiloh; Alexandra Simonon; Charles Small; Philip Spencer; John Strawson; David Toube; Mira Vogel; Ken Waltzer; Jeff Weintraub.

FURTHER ACKNOWLEDGEMENTS

This book is, amongst other things, a gathering together and a distillation of the work I have been doing over the last decade and more. I would like to thank, and to acknowledge the support of, those who have published and supported my work during this period. The book draws upon some of this work.

I would like to thank Charles Small, ISGAP (The Institute for the Study of Global Antisemitism and Policy) and YIISA (The Yale Initiative for the Interdisciplinary Study of Antisemitism) for giving me formal permission to draw on:

Hirsh, D. (2015) 'Anti-Zionism and Antisemitism: Cosmopolitan Reflections', in C. A. Small (ed.) *The Yale Papers: Antisemitism in Comparative Perspective*, New York: ISGAP, pp. 57–174. ISBN 9781515057796. First published as Hirsh, D. (2007) *Anti-Zionism and Antisemitism: Cosmopolitan Reflections*, *Working Paper #1*, Yale Initiative for the Interdisciplinary Study of Antisemitism, New Haven CT, Print ISSN 1940-610X; Online ISSN 1940-6118 (165 pages), http://www.yale.edu/yiisa/workingpaper/hirsh/index.htm.

This work was supported by a *Rothschilds Foundation Europe and Ford Foundation* research grant (£25,000) 'to investigate the character and dynamics of anti-Zionism as a contemporary political movement and its relationship to antisemitism', January 2007 to August 2007. It was published while I was a visiting research associate, Yale University, *Yale Initiative for the Interdisciplinary Study of Antisemitism (YIISA)*, September 2006 to June 2007.

I would also like to thank Eunice G. Pollack, for giving me permission to draw on the work I published on the 'Livingstone Formulation' in

> Hirsh, D. (2017) 'How raising the issue of antisemitism puts you outside the community of the progressive: The *Livingstone Formulation*', in E. G. Pollack (ed.) *Anti-Zionism and Antisemitism: Past & Present*, Boston: Academic Studies Press), https://engage online.wordpress.com/2016/04/29/the-livingstone-formula tion-david-hirsh-2/.

I would also like to thank Steve K Baum, editor of the *Journal for the Study of Antisemitism*. A version of my prologue has been published in this journal as 'Portia, Shylock and the exclusion of Israeli actors from the global cultural community', *JSA* vol 4, no. 2. Also some material in Chapter 9 on methodology was published in the journal as 'Hostility to Israel and Antisemitism: Toward a Sociological Approach', *JSA* vol 5, no. 1.

I would like to thank Alan Johnson, the editor of *Fathom*, and also *BICOM* (Britain Israel Communications and Research Centre). Some of the material in my Chapter 2 on the rise of Corbyn was first published in 'The Corbyn Left: The Politics of Position and the Politics of Reason', http://fathomjournal.org/the-corbyn-left-the-politics-of-position-and-the-politics-of-reason/.

Also some of the material in my Chapter 5 on defining antisemitism first appeared in Fathom in 'Defining Antisemitism Down', http://fathomjournal.org/defining-antisemitism-down/. Another version of some of this material is due to appear in

> Hirsh, D. (2016) 'Struggles over the Contemporary Definition of Antisemitism', in J. G. Campbell and L.D. Klaff (eds) *Unity & Diversity in Contemporary Antisemitism: The Bristol-Sheffield-Hallam Colloquium on Contemporary Antisemitism*, Brighton, MA: Academic Studies Press.

And some of the material in my Chapter 8 on Jewish antizionism first appeared in Fathom as a book review of 'Rebels against Zion', http://fathomjournal.org/book-review-rebels-against-zion/.

Also I would like to thank *Jewish Quarterly* for allowing me to use some of the material from: Keith Kahn-Harris, *Uncivil War: The Israel Conflict in the Jewish Community*, London: David Paul, 2014. Review: 'Civility' in Contemporary Debates about Antisemitism', *Jewish Quarterly*, Spring 2014, p. 39.

I would like to thank the *Jewish Chronicle* for publishing the following articles of mine, which I have drawn upon in this book:

> Hirsh, D. (2016) 'The Livingstone Formulation fails to rescue Livingstone', *TheJC.com*, April 28 2016, http://www.thejc.com/comment-and-debate/comment/157528/the-livingstone-formulation-finally-fails-rescue-ken-livingstone.
>
> Hirsh, D. (2015) 'Jew Hate and Today's Left', *Jewish Chronicle*, 17 March 2016, pp. 2–3, http://www.thejc.com/lifestyle/lifestyle-features/154672/jew-hate-and-today%E2%80%99s-left.
>
> Hirsh, D. (2009) 'Do not confine Jews to the couch' *Jewish Chronicle*, London, 10 April 2009, http://www.thejc.com/articles/do-not-confine-jews-couch.

I would like to thank everybody associated with the Engage network and website – much of this work was produced in early draft on the website – and more recently my Facebook community has played a role in shaping and real-time peer-reviewing my work.

This work was of course also supported by Goldsmiths, University of London, where I am a Senior Lecturer; it is the financial stability of being part of an academic institution which makes academic research and engagement possible.

PROLOGUE

A classic speaks differently to each individual and in each new context. On Monday 28 May 2012, I saw *The Merchant of Venice* performed by Habima, the Israeli National Theatre. The venue was the replica of Shakespeare's wooden, roofless, Globe Theatre. It was a hot London night, and the noise of flying machines occasionally confronted our fantasies of authenticity, if the fact that the performance was in Hebrew had not.

London is, after having been the hub of the British Empire, a multicultural world city. The Globe hosted theatre companies that summer from all over the world to perform Shakespeare in their own languages: Shakespeare from Pakistan, South Africa, Georgia, Palestine, Turkey, China and all over the world.

Since some rather nasty medieval stuff, London and Jews have got on fairly well. London stood firm against Hitler, and the local Blackshirts too; it did not mind much whether Jews stayed separate or whether they immersed themselves in its vibrancy; it did not feel threatened; it just let Jews live engaged lives. But London's very post-nationalism, and its post-colonialism, has functioned as the medium for a rather odd new kind of intolerance.

Sometimes, we define our own identities in relation to some 'other'. Early Christianity defined itself in relation to the Jews who refused to accept its gospel, and it portrayed them as Christ-killers. Some people who wanted to embrace modernity constructed their identities in relation to the image of the *traditional* Jew with his beard and coat, standing against progress. Some others who were afraid of the *new* found they could define themselves against the *modernist* Jew. Nineteenth-century nationalists often defined Jews as foreigner. Twentieth-century totalitarianisms, which had universal ambition, found their 'other' in the cosmopolitan or international Jew.

These processes created an invented image of 'the Jew', of which the antisemites portrayed themselves as victims. Antisemitism has only ever portrayed itself as defensive – never as aggressive.

Some people who love London's relaxed, diverse antiracism look for an 'other' against which to define themselves. They find Israel. They make it symbolize everything against which they define themselves: ethnic nationalism, racism, apartheid, colonialism. London's shameful past, not to mention in some ways its present, is cast out and thrust upon Israel. London has twice elected Ken Livingstone, a socialist who embraces this kind of anti-Israel scapegoating, as its Mayor.

We can tell that this hostility to Israel is as artificially constructed as any antisemitism by looking at the list of theatre groups against which the enlightened did not try to organize a boycott. Antizionists have created a whole new '-ism' around their campaign against Israel – a way of thinking about the whole world. Within this antizionist framework, a caricature of Israel is endowed with huge symbolic significance. It is a significance which relates only here and there to the actual State of Israel, to its complex conflict with the Palestinians, to its relationship with the Arab and Islamic states which neighbour it and to the diversity of existing Israeli men and women which inhabit it If the Palestinians stand, in the antizionist imagination, as symbolic of all the victims of 'the west' or 'imperialism', then Israel is thrust into the centre of the world as being symbolic of oppression everywhere. Like antisemitism, antizionism imagines Jews as being central to all that is bad in the world.

One of the sources of energy for this special focus on Israel comes from Jewish antizionists. For them, as for many other Jews, Israel is of special importance. For them, Israel's human rights abuses – real, exaggerated or imagined – are sources of particular pain, sometimes even shame.[1] Some of them take their Jewish preoccupation with Israel and try to export it into the cultural and political sphere in general, and into non-Jewish civil society spaces where a special focus on the evils of Israel takes on a new symbolic power. But the Jewish antizionists, so fond of speaking 'as a Jew', are so centred on Israel that they often fail to understand the significance of the symbolism which they so confidently normalize in the antiracist spaces of old London.

Is *The Merchant of Venice* **an antisemitic play, or is it a play which intimately depicts the anatomy of persecution, exclusion and bullying against a Jewish character?** When I see a production of *The Merchant of Venice*, it is always the audience that unsettles me. The play tells two stories which relate tangentially to each other. One is the story of Shylock, a Jewish money lender who is spat on, excluded, beaten up and, in the end, mercilessly defeated and humiliated. The other is an apparently light-hearted story about an arrogant, rich, self-absorbed young woman – clever but not wise, pretty but not beautiful – and her antisemitic friends. Shakespeare inter-cuts the gruelling, detailed scenes of the bullying of Shylock with the comedic story of Portia's love-match with a loser who has already frittered away his own inheritance.

Shakespeare offers us an intimately observed depiction of antisemitic abuse, and, each time the story reaches a new climax of cruelty, he then offers hackneyed and clichéd gags in the other story, to see if he can make us laugh. It is as if he is interested in finding out how quickly the audience forgets Shylock, off stage, and his tragedy. And the answer, in every production I have ever seen, is that the audience is happy and laughing at second-rate clowning, within seconds. And I suspect that Shakespeare means the clowning and the love story to be second rate. He is doing something more interesting than entertaining us. He is playing with our emotions in order to show us something, to make us feel something.[2]

Now, the audience at this particular performance was a strange one in any case. It felt to me like London's Jewish community out to demonstrate its solidarity with Israel and to protect the Israeli cousins from the vulgarities which they knew their city was about to inflict. The audience was uneasy because it did not know in advance what form the disruption was going to take. In the end, the atmosphere was a rather positive and happy one, like an easy home win at football against an away team which had threatened a humiliating victory. Solidarity with Israel meant something different to each person there. One man ostentatiously showed off a silky Israeli-flag tie. Others were Hebrew speakers, taking the opportunity in London to see a play in their own language. Some in the audience would have been profoundly uncomfortable with Israeli government policies but were keen to show their oneness with those parts of their families which had been expelled from Europe two or three generations ago and who were now living in a few small cities on the Eastern Mediterranean.

The audience may not have been expert either in Shakespeare or in antisemitism. Most people think of *The Merchant of Venice* as an antisemitic play. Shylock is thought to be an antisemitic stereotype, created by Shakespeare for audiences to hate. Are we supposed to enjoy the victory of the antisemites and the humiliation of the Jew? But what was this audience thinking? If it is simply an antisemitic play, why would we be watching it, and why is the Israeli National Theatre performing it? And if it is a comedy, why aren't the jokes funny, and why does Shakespeare offer us a puerile game-show?

I don't think this audience cared much. It was there to face down those who said that Israeli actors should be excluded from the global community of culture, while actors from all the other states, which had been invited to the Globe, were celebrated in a festival of the Olympic city's multiculturalism. So, the audience was happy to laugh loudly and to enjoy itself. We saw on stage how Shylock's daughter was desperate to escape from the original Ghetto, the darkness and fear of her father's house, the loneliness of being a Jew. We saw how she agreed to convert to Christianity because some little antisemitic boy said he loved her; we saw how she stole her father's money so that her new friends could spend it on drunken nights out. And we saw Shylock's despair at the loss and at the betrayal and at the intrusion. Perhaps his unbearable pain was also fuelled by guilt for having failed his daughter since her mother had died. Like the 'hunchback' in Verdi's *Rigoletto*, Shylock's humiliation and his powerlessness had rendered him incapable of navigating the responsibilities of fatherhood, both to protect but also to nurture;

he had felt forced to over-protect and had thereby been unable to nurture his daughter into self-reliant adulthood.

And then the audience laughed at silly caricatures of Moroccan and Spanish Princes, and at Portia's haughty and superior rejection of them. And now, not *representations* of antisemites but what many in the audience saw as *actual* antisemites, hiding amongst them, unfurl their banners denouncing 'Israeli apartheid', and their Palestinian flags, and they stage a performance of their own. The Palestinian people undergo the familiar indignity of being represented by those whose sympathy and friendship for them had evolved into hatred for Israel; of being represented by a movement for the silencing of Israeli actors; of being represented by those who show contempt for Jewish Londoners in the audience, who de-humanize them by refusing to refer to them as people but instead referring to them simply as 'Zionists'. And a 'Zionist' does not merit the ordinary civility with which people in a great city normally, without thinking, accord to one another.

The artistic director of the Globe had already predicted that there might be disruption. There often was, he said dryly, at this unique theatre. Pigeons flutter onto the stage but we ignore them, he said. And today, people should not get upset; they should not confront the protestors; they should allow the security guards to do their job.

One protestor shouted, 'No violence,' as the security guys made to take her away. They took a few away, the actors didn't miss a word, and the audience, largely Jewish but also English, showed its stiff upper lip and pretended that nothing had happened. Some time later, another small group of protestors, who had wanted to exclude Israelis from this festival because of their nationality, stood up and put plasters over their own mouths to dramatize their own victimhood. Antisemites always pose as victims of the Jews, or of 'Zionism', or of the 'Israel lobby'. And the claim that Jews try to silence criticism of Israel by mobilizing a dishonest accusation against them is now recognizable as one of the defining tropes of contemporary antisemitism.

Meanwhile, on stage, the antisemitic Christians are positioning themselves as the victims of Shylock. They have spat on him, stolen from him, corrupted his only daughter, libelled him, persecuted him and excluded him. Now he's angry. He's a Jew, so he can be bought off, no? They try to buy him off. But for Shylock, this is no longer about the money. It is about the desperate fury of a man whose very identity has been trampled upon throughout his life. And at that moment, I could sympathize with him more than ever. I imagined my own revenge against the articulate poseurs who were standing there pretending to have been silenced. Shylock is a flawed character; Shakespeare does not imagine him perfect. Israel is not perfect either. But how much more relevant is a play which shows the destruction of a man who is powerless to resist it? Racism does not only hurt angels; it also hurts flawed and ordinary people, and it has the power to transform good people into angry, frightened and vengeful people. Obviously, these truths can be followed around circles of violence in these contexts, from the blood libel, Christ-killing and conspiracy theory, to Nazism, to Zionism and into Palestinian nationalism and Islamism. Only the most self-righteous ones imagine that it all comes out in the end into a morality tale of good against evil.

What are they thinking, the protestors? Do they understand the play at all? Are they moved by the sensitivity of the portrayal of the anatomy of antisemitic persecution? Perhaps they are, and they think that Shylock, in our day, is a Palestinian, and Jews are the new Christian antisemites. One man exclaimed, full of thespian English diction: 'Hath not a *Palestinian* eyes?' He was referring to the moving, universalistic speech with which Shylock dismantles the racism of his persecutors. This protestor mobilized the words given by Shakespeare to the Jew, against actually existing Jews. The experience of antisemitism was totally universalized, as though the play was only about 'racism in general' and not at all about antisemitism in particular. And the point, that a longing for vengeance is destructive and self-destructive, no matter how justified it may feel, was, of course, totally missed.

Somebody replied with comedic timing: 'Piss off!' Everybody cheered. There was an understanding that the boycotters had mobilized all the disruption they had to mobilize and that they had failed really to make an impression.

Or do the protestors think that it is an antisemitic play? If so, maybe they feel that the subtext of this Israeli performance of English antisemitism is to offer a justification for everything that Israel does. Do they think the Israelis are taunting London, and by proxy the Palestinians, and trying to make them feel guilty? It is a common antizionist claim that the source of Zionist power today is a kind of moral blackmail; the accusation is one of Zionist readiness to mobilize historical Jewish victimhood as a tool, a source of Jewish power. This, again, is an old libel – that the Jews are so clever and so morally lacking, that they are able to benefit from their own persecution. When will the world forgive the Jews for antisemitism and the Holocaust?

The climax of the play sees Antonio, the smooth-tongued antisemitic merchant who has borrowed money from Shylock which he now cannot pay back, tied up in the centre of the stage like Christ on the cross. And the antisemites demand that the Jew displays Christian forgiveness. But the Jew, who has been driven half mad by antisemitic persecution, does not forgive: he wants his revenge.

Venice, for Shakespeare, is symbolic of the excitement and dynamism of the emerging modern world: a cosmopolitan world of freedom and business. Venice is strong because it has law; the powerful are prevented from stealing from the weak; contract is enforced by law; citizens are able to trade because they are able to rely on the agreements that they make. So how is the Venetian court to protect the powerful Antonio from Shylock without debasing its most valuable asset? Portia – the erudite, plausible antisemite – offers a justification, however, which both brings the desired result and also appears to protect the principle of law. And before you know it, Antonio is free, and Shylock is trussed up ready for crucifixion. And the Christians do not forgive either; they show no mercy. They humiliate Shylock, they take his money, and they force him to convert to Christianity. He ends up on his knees, bareheaded, without his daughter, without his money, without his livelihood, and he says: 'I am content.'

The day after the performance, one of the leaders of the boycott campaign, Ben White, tweeted a picture of the beautiful Jewish face of Howard Jacobson. Jacobson is a novelist who was shortly to win the *Man Booker Prize* for literature; and he is an opponent of the campaign to exclude Israeli actors from London. White added the text to his tweet of Jacobson's face: 'If you need another reason to support a boycott of Habima, I present a massive picture of Howard Jacobson's face' (Weissman 2012).

This incident later became an issue in the court case between Ronnie Fraser and the University and College Union (see Chapter 6). Jacobson wrote in his witness statement in the Fraser case:

> Had Ben White tweeted his disagreement . . . on intellectual grounds I'd have no reason to complain. But I was extremely alarmed – and I must say distressed – to see him invoking my appearance. I did not understand what my face had to do with the argument and why he used the word 'massive'.
>
> I am aware that I look Jewish. Massively Jewish. I don't know. Massively Jewish-featured I don't know. But Jewish yes. So how does the fact bear on the proposed boycott? How does it constitute a reason to support it? What does the face betoken that it might strengthen people in their commitment to boycott an Israeli theatre company?
>
> I have addressed the subject of anti-Semitism in my novels and articles; I have warned against finding prejudice where there is none; and have often spoken of how little anti-Semitism I have faced in this country. I don't go looking for it. I would rather not find it. But to see my appearance adduced as an argument to support a boycott of Habima convinced me that on this occasion anti-Semitism had found me.

It hardly seems controversial to say that while criticism of Israel may well be entirely legitimate, some forms of criticism of Israel may be antisemitic. Defining which kinds of criticism are which is a matter for judgment, and it is the subject of this book.

Notes

1 For more on 'ashamed Jews', see Jacobson (2011).
2 My reading of *The Merchant of Venice* is significantly indebted to David M. Seymour (2007).

INTRODUCTION

This book is about antisemitism in social spaces which think of themselves as antiracist and democratic. It is about antisemitism amongst people who believe that they strongly oppose antisemitism. This kind of antisemitism is usually related to hostility to Israel, but it diverges radically from rational or legitimate criticism of Israeli policy. While Israelis and Palestinians are real, localized and specific, their narratives are often appropriated, blandly simplified and woven into worldviews which serve people and purposes far away.

Ben Cohen (2014) made the distinction between *bierkeller* and *bistro* antisemitism. *Bierkeller* antisemitism is violent, abusive, vulgar and explicitly fuelled by hatred; it is easy to recognize, it comes with a Swastika on its arm and it is agreed by all decent people to be contemptible. This book is much more about *bistro* antisemitism, which is polite, civil and sophisticated; it is the antisemitism of good people. Hannah Arendt (1975) wrote about the importance of an alliance between the mob and the elite in the creation of a totalitarian movement. This book is a study of the antisemitism to be found within that part of the elite which thinks of itself as progressive. So far this elite antisemitism has failed to energize much of a mob. Antisemitism in democratic states is still largely confined to the sphere of discourse: to ways of thinking and talking.

One important exception is the danger of an antisemitic terrorist attack; and it is also true that violent antisemitic incidents, while remaining at a relatively low level, are on the rise. Although one should remain sceptical about the uniqueness of one's own time, 2016 was an extraordinary year for the success of populist political movements which mobilized mass resentments and which employed racist and xenophobic language, the like of which would, even shortly before, have seemed impossible in the political mainstream. These populist movements promise to tear everything down before it is built again. *Bistro* antisemitism is vile in itself, and it is an indicator of a profound problem in any social space which nurtures or tolerates it. But it also has the potential to find ways to manifest itself in the *bierkellers*, the streets, in mass culture and in political threat. Antisemitism is a threat to Jews. It is also a threat to democracy; to democratic institutions and to the rule of law; to the principles of equality and liberty; to democratic states; and to democratic cosmopolitan collaboration between states and between people.

This book is anchored in empirical case studies of how antisemitism emerges out of the ostensibly democratic discourse of criticism of Israel. There are lots of stories in this book: stories about things that have happened, things that people have said and done, cultures that have arisen, ways in which people have made sense of what was going on. Antisemitism is emotional, but it often dresses in the clothes of reason. Antisemitism is something which we feel we should be able to sniff out and to know, in an unmediated way; yet this is largely a book about people who are unable to do so. So as well as a book of stories and emotions, it is also a book of theory and of politics. It is an attempt to understand a complex and contradictory reality, a world in which people's self-consciousness comes into conflict with the ways in which other people interpret them and their actions.

Methodologically, it treats discourse as being related to the social movements and cultural spaces within which it develops. This work develops a sociological understanding of antisemitism as an external and objective social phenomenon rather than simply as subjective feelings of hatred or fear within individuals. There is a focus upon the United Kingdom (UK) in the case studies, but material is also gathered from further afield because antisemitism is an increasingly global phenomenon.

This contemporary variant of antisemitism is not the first radical antisemitism to position itself as siding with the oppressed against (most of) the Jews. This positioning gives it great confidence and a natural first line of defence. Those who oppose antisemitism are widely dismissed as agents of the oppressors, and they are often accused of trying to enhance Jewish victim status, and the power which is said to come with it, in attempts to silence the oppressed.

The *New Left* emerged in the 1960s in revolt against Stalinism, but the traditions which it spawned have too often tended to re-configure the old politics for a new age rather than to transcend the old politics. This book emerges from, and is part of, a left-wing and democratic response to contemporary antisemitism. As such, this book itself is as much a manifestation of a democratic left tradition as it is a critique of a totalitarian left tradition.

This book is interested in the growing ossification of a tradition of left-wing thought since the Second World War into key binary oppositions: black/white; north/south; oppressed/oppressor; imperialist/anti-imperialist; 1 per cent/99 per cent. It shows how the socialist tradition of supporting the self-liberation of the oppressed in each country is in danger of being surpassed by a new nationalist tradition of supporting whole nations which are designated as oppressed against whole nations which are designated as oppressor. It is a framework which downplays the importance of democratic values. It was within this framework that Jews, who could not have been more oppressed in 1944, can be thought of four short years later as the bearers of white European colonialism. If Jews are defined as oppressors and as white, then the assumption that antisemitism will be taken seriously in progressive movements is not necessarily correct.

This book argues that a 'politics of position' is emerging on the left in preference to a politics of reason or persuasion. This tends to solidify an essentialist notion of who belongs in the community of the oppressed and the community of the progressive. The boundaries of these communities are coming more and more to be policed by coercive discursive practices and less by democratic debate and persuasion. Hostility to Israel becomes a key marker of identity in this process. If Jews are reluctant to embrace this hostility to Israel identity, then they risk exile from what I am calling 'the community of the good'.

This book looks at radical critiques of Israel and Zionism with a focus on how they tend to free themselves from empirical, rational or comparative methodological constraints. Antizionism began as a critique of the political movement for national self-determination. After the Holocaust and the war of 1948, which radically transformed the material basis of Jewish life, antizionism became something quite new, a movement to abolish an existing nation state. It then matured into a worldview which re-positions Jewish wrongdoing at the centre of all that is problematic in the world. The critique of an idea is different from the critique of an existing nation state. Particular Jewish concern with Israel, and with its failures, takes on a new significance when it is exported into the wider institutions of civil society.

One key mechanism by which antisemitic ways of thinking graduate into concrete discrimination is in campaigns for boycotts of Israel which aim to whip up emotional support for the exclusion of Israelis, and only Israelis, from the global community of humankind. The book shows how these campaigns tend also to impact on Jews who are far from Israel but are near to such campaigns, and who often feel coerced into engaging with them.

The second key mechanism by which discourse impacts against Jews is the generalization of an assumption of bad faith against those who oppose the demonization of Israel or who oppose the antisemitism associated with it.

This book is grounded in a sociological way of thinking. This helps it step back from the Israeli and Palestinian nationalist prisms, and representations of them, which emerge far from the conflict; debates concerning antisemitism are often distorted by incorporation into these narratives. Sociology is, itself, one of the anti-hegemonic discourses which is vulnerable to antisemitic ways of thinking. Yet I argue that sociology also provides resources, methods and ways of thinking which can be mobilized for understanding and then opposing contemporary antisemitism.

Antisemitism is a threat to Jews, but it is also an indicator of a more profound and general sickness within democratic movements, institutions and cultures. The study of antisemitism is not a parochial Jewish concern; it is key to understanding what threatens the health of democratic and egalitarian cultures.

The theorists of a 'new antisemitism' (for example, Chesler 2003) have argued that hostility to Israel may be antisemitic in its motivation; or in its form; or in its disproportionate quantity or intensity; or in its effect. Each of these suggestions requires distinct analyses, and they may inter-relate back on each other in unexpected ways. This is a study of a phenomenon whose very existence is angrily contested. The book's discussion of the struggles over defining antisemitism, for example, is itself also a case study of the material in question.

This book is critical of those analyses which begin with conceptual blueprints, attempting to demonstrate from argument alone what is racist and what is antisemitic. Rather, it begins with empirical study of social movements, of debate, of discussion, of campaigns; it is concerned with how concepts arise, how they actualize and how they circulate between antisemitic and antiracist spaces.

The focus of this book is on that variant of antizionism which thinks of itself as antiracist, but this is only one tradition within global antizionism. From its roots in twentieth-century European Stalinism and at the heart of Jihadi Islamist and Arab Nationalist politics, antizionism has often been uninterested in distinguishing itself from antisemitism. Tropes, elements of rhetoric and common-sense notions migrate between antiracist and democratic spaces, nationalist and Islamist spaces, fringe and mainstream spaces, different kinds of media and the right, the left and the political centre. It is within this complex and dynamic reality that this book finds its material and moves towards its conclusions.

Today's antisemitism is difficult to recognize because it does not come dressed in a Nazi uniform and it does not openly proclaim its hatred or fear of Jews. In fact it says it has learnt the lessons of Jew-hatred *better* than most Jews have, and it says that, unlike them, it stands in the antiracist tradition. It is an antisemitism which positions Jews themselves as 'oppressors', and it positions those who develop hostile narratives about Jews as 'oppressed'.

Case studies in this book are woven together with more theoretical discussion and conceptual analysis. The first chapter looks at Ken Livingstone, one of the most popular and successful figures on the British left since the 1980s. As I write, he is suspended from Labour Party membership for comments which many have been interpreted as antisemitic. In a previous controversy over antisemitism ten years earlier, Livingstone had written: 'For far too long the accusation of antisemitism has been used against anyone who is critical of the policies of the Israeli government, as I have been' (2006). At that time, this formulation struck a chord with me; I had seen it many times. Chapter 1 describes what I have named the *Livingstone Formulation*, which has become a standard rhetorical response to accusations of antisemitism. It is a way of refusing to answer a charge of antisemitism by responding instead with a counter-charge that those who talk about antisemitism are really engaged in bad-faith efforts to silence criticism of Israel. At the time when I named it, I was a little nervous; I thought that it was, perhaps, arbitrary to associate Livingstone's name with this phenomenon. But more recently, Ken Livingstone has really made this formulation his own; he has repeatedly relied on it. He tries to change the subject when he is challenged on the topic of antisemitism. He says Jews cry 'antisemitism!' when Israel is criticized; but he cries 'Israel!' when antisemitism is criticized.

The second chapter looks at the unexpected and enduring rise of Jeremy Corbyn's faction in the Labour Party during 2015. Corbyn had been clear about his political support of Hamas and Hezbollah, saying they were dedicated to peace and justice (2015a). He had jumped to the defence of Steven Sizer, a man who had later asked in public whether Israel was responsible for 9/11, saying that he was being unfairly smeared by Zionists (Frazer 2015). He had invited Raed Salah, a man who had engaged in medieval-style blood libels against Jews, to have tea with him in the House of Commons (Johnson 2015a). Corbyn had worked for *Press TV*, the Iranian state propaganda channel (Payne 2016). He had been a patron of the *Palestine Solidarity Campaign*, an organization dedicated to the campaign to boycott Israel (Palestinian Solidarity Campaign 2016). He had been the chair of *Stop the War* (Corbyn 2015b), an organization which campaigns for war against Israel (Author unknown 2015). Corbyn had written about a meeting he had had in 2009 with Bashar Al-Assad, the dictator of Syria; in the same article he had claimed that the Israel controls the USA, writing: 'once again, the Israeli tail wags the US dog' (Bright 2012). In 2012, Corbyn had called for an inquiry into the influence of what he called 'pro-Israel lobbying groups' on UK government policy, saying that this issue went 'to the heart of what's going on in the Home Office' (Bright 2012). Chapter 2 analyzes how it is possible for a man with such a relationship to antisemitism to be elected twice to lead the Labour Party and what that tells us about recent political and cultural developments in dominant currents of the contemporary left.

Chapter 3 looks at how the issue of antisemitism in Corbyn's Labour Party emerged as an issue in the political mainstream of the UK in 2016. Antizionists, who had once been confined to extreme and doctrinaire corners of the left, were now taking leadership positions in the party, in the trade unions and in the student movement. A leading activist found it reasonable to claim that 'many Jews . . . were the chief financiers of the sugar and slave trade' and to question why Holocaust commemoration was not 'open to all peoples who've experienced Holocaust' (Gill 2016). This chapter goes on to analyze the *Chakrabarti Inquiry into Antisemitism and Other Racisms*, which was commissioned by Jeremy Corbyn to try to pull the sting of antisemitism as an issue which was hurting Labour.

With hindsight it is possible to see how the struggles within the academic unions over the boycott of Israel after 2003 prepared the ground for the crescendo of antisemitism into public discourse which are discussed in the first three chapters. So the fourth chapter steps back to the era which preceded the Corbyn leadership and focuses on the rise of the campaign to boycott Israel and, in particular, Israeli universities. It shows how the boycott campaign, which claims to have originated as a call for solidarity by Palestinians, was in fact conceived in London by a small group of British antizionist academics. It goes on to look at how that campaign succeeded within the academic trade unions in Britain and how it began to spread to other places, including the United States of America. It looks at the ways in which the boycott campaign tried to find ways of presenting itself as something other than a blacklist of individual Israeli scholars; in particular it experimented with the idea of allowing exemptions from boycott for those who passed a political test; and then it settled on the strategy of portraying itself as a boycott of institutions rather than individuals. This chapter goes on to look in detail at one of the key claims of the campaign for 'Boycott Divestment and Sanctions' (BDS) against Israel, which is to say that Israel is an 'apartheid state' like the old South Africa, and to say that the strategy of boycott is therefore appropriate.

Chapter 5 is a little more conceptual. It discusses the struggles over how antisemitism is, and should be, defined. It looks at the genealogy of the European Union Monitoring Centre (EUMC) *Working Definition of Antisemitism* which later evolved into the *International Holocaust Remembrance Association Working Definition of Antisemitism*. This definition is sometimes criticized as being political; the chapter looks at what the politics of this definition were and how it arose as a response to events at the Durban World Conference against Racism of 2001. This chapter identifies a split which appears to have developed between concern for antisemitism and concern for racism as a significant cause for concern. At Durban, the dominant faction, which thought of racism as a global structure of white power, succeeded in constructing Israel as being central to that white power; in this way it tended to trivialize antisemitism as a fake cry of legitimation made on behalf of the racist oppressors. The *Working Definition* emerged from efforts of Jewish NGOs to get a hearing for their issues in the Organization for Security and Co-operation in Europe (OSCE) and the European Union (EU). If Durban is thought of as a non-white global forum and if the OSCE and the EU are thought of as networks of white states, then the potential for antagonism between non-white antiracism and 'white' (Jewish) anxiety about antisemitism becomes clear. This diremption is then reflected in struggles over the definition of antisemitism.

Chapter 6 returns to the University and College Union (UCU) in the UK, in which struggles over boycotting Israel had been raging. Many Jews in the union as well as the spokespeople for the key institutions of the UK Jewish community were raising the alarm because they had come to the conclusion that the boycott campaign had imported antisemitic discourse and exclusions into the union. Many were alleging that a culture of institutional antisemitism had hardened within the UCU while the boycotters themselves continued to insist that this claim was a dishonest Zionist strategy aimed at unfairly de-legitimizing their campaign for an academic boycott of Israel. In 2011, matters came to a head with the passing of a motion at UCU Congress to disavow the *EUMC Working Definition*. For one activist, Ronnie Fraser, this constituted the final humiliation. He sued the union, alleging that anti-semitism in the union constituted racist harassment under the meaning of the Equality Act (2010). This chapter looks at the evidence that was presented in *Fraser v UCU*, and it analyzes the Tribunal's judgment.

In Chapter 7, the book takes a more theoretical turn again. It looks at the concepts and the discourses of antizionism itself, and it seeks to offer a critique. It seeks also to link that conceptual discussion to the ways in which it plays itself out in actual social movements. This chapter does not satisfy itself with a discussion of the ideas of antizionism; it argues that it is necessary to see how these ideas are actualized within real, complex, variegated and organic social movements. It traces ways in which the two key themes of antisemitism – blood libel and con-spiracy theory – have replicated themselves in antizionist ideas and in the way those ideas come alive in the real world.

Chapter 8 focuses on Jewish antizionism. It looks at how Jewish movements which were critical of Zionism as a strategy for dealing with antisemitism transformed, after the Holocaust and after the foun-dation of the State of Israel, into Jewish movements which were con-cerned with de-legitimizing an existing nation state. There is a great potential for specifically Jewish hostility to Israeli human rights abuses, and then to Israel itself, to take on a different character when it is exported into non-Jewish civil society. Antizionist Jews have often rhe-torically mobilized their Jewish identities in order to create an air of legitimacy to hostility to Israel. This has been an influential phenom-enon in the rise of antizionism and of antisemitism. There are Jews who have made it central to their political work to try to neutralize the issue of antisemitism when it appears in relation to struggles over Israel, its alleged wrongdoing and proposals to exclude it from the global community. This chapter goes on to look at how antizionism has sometimes evolved into even more radical and explicitly anti-Jewish movements. It looks at Gilad Atzmon, who considers himself to be an ex-Jew, and who mobilizes open antisemitic rhetoric, with its sharpest focus targeted against antizionist Jews. And then it goes on to discuss Dieudonné M'bala M'bala, who is a French comedian who has also delighted in pushing perhaps even further towards explicit antisem-itism. Dieudonné is not Jewish; he is of black African descent; but he is relevant here because his story demonstrates the further potentiality for antizionism and its ways of thinking to push on into racist territory, even while still thinking of itself as antiracist, as a way of articulating an ever more radical hostility to bourgeois norms and hegemony.

The final chapter discusses some methodological questions. It begins by looking at the development of my own social and political identities as they have related to the material in this book. I have been a key participant in many of the debates and struggles that I have described and analyzed; indeed, this book is itself part of my effort to intervene into these struggles, as well as to offer an overview of them. This chapter goes on to think about sociology. Certainly sociology, as an anti-hegemonic and sometimes radical movement, is open to the temptations of the antisemitism which we are discussing in this book; on the other hand, sociology has in some ways been steadfastly oppositional to antisemitism and has itself offered alternative worldviews, particularly to conspiracy theory. Specifically, in this book I argue that sociology offers a framework, a method and conceptual tools, which can help us to make sense of the phenomenon of contemporary antisemitism and its relationship to hostility to Israel.

Note

I write 'antisemitism', not 'anti-Semitism', because there is no 'Semitism' which antisemites oppose. Similarly, I write 'antizionism' not 'anti-Zionism' because the notion of 'Zionism' against which antizionists define themselves is self-invented. This notion of 'Zionism' is so far from actual movements and discourses which think of themselves as Zionist as to warrant the new spelling.

1

KEN LIVINGSTONE AND THE *LIVINGSTONE FORMULATION*

Many antiracist people in our time have been educated to recognize the *accusation* of antisemitism, rather than the antisemitism itself, as the dirty trick. They hear it as an attempt to smear and silence people who criticize Israel. Today's antisemitism incorporates the notion that those who complain about antisemitism are the racists. It treats the opponents of antisemitism, not the antisemites, as the cynical ones; it treats opponents of antisemitism, not the antisemites, as the powerful ones. In the wake of the Brexit and Trump movements, we are seeing opponents of other kinds of racism too being designated as the powerful ones, while racism itself is interpreted as the cry of the oppressed.

In 2006, after Ken Livingstone had been accused of antisemitism, he responded with a counter-accusation that he was being accused in this way only in order to silence his criticism of Israel. This response I named the *Livingstone Formulation*. This chapter begins by looking at Livingstone's own long career of hostility to Israel and at his relationship to antisemitism, and how in 2016 he found himself suspended from the Labour Party over the issue. The chapter goes on to look at the *Livingstone Formulation* itself and how it has become such a standard rhetorical manoeuvre. The *Livingstone Formulation* – the counter-allegation of Zionist conspiracy which treats discussion of antisemitism as though it were a vulgar, dishonest and tribal fraud – is a thread which runs throughout this form of contemporary antisemitism; and it re-appears relentlessly through the course of this book. Ken Livingstone is not responsible for the *Livingstone Formulation*, and he did not invent it; it is an honorary title rather than one which he really earned.

In May 1981, two years after Margaret Thatcher had become Prime Minister, Labour won the election for the Greater London Council (GLC). Ken Livingstone called a meeting of Labour members of the council the following day, and the left-wing Labour councillors defeated Labour leader Andrew McIntosh, putting Livingstone into place as leader of the GLC. The left was ascendant in local government in the cities, and the Campaign for Nuclear Disarmament (CND) was on the rise; the left in the Labour Party was strong; feminist, lesbian and gay and antiracist movements were seeking common cause in the 'lib-eration movements'; the miners' strike of 1984–85 posed a significant challenge to the government.

Ken Livingstone became a popular spokesperson for the radical socialist opposition to Margaret Thatcher. After the miners had been defeated, the Local Government Act was passed in 1985, which abol-ished a whole tier of institutions in which the left was strong: the met-ropolitan counties and the Greater London Council. Ken Livingstone headed a high-profile campaign to 'save the GLC'; the dying GLC put on a number of popular free concerts at which Livingstone and other figures of the left made radical speeches.

After Tony Blair's 'New Labour' took power, a London-wide elec-tion was re-instituted for the position of Mayor. Having failed to secure the Labour Party's nomination, Ken Livingstone stood as an Independ-ent in the 2000 election, and he won. He won again in 2004 as the official Labour candidate and was only defeated by the Tories in 2008 and again in 2012.

For four decades, Ken Livingstone was a celebrated and successful leading socialist in the UK; he was well known in the mainstream, and, on the left, he was widely admired.

In late April 2016, Naz Shah, the woman who had defeated George Galloway for the Parliamentary seat of Bradford West, was exposed in blogs and in the press for having published material on Facebook which could be interpreted as antisemitic. In particular, she shared an image which depicted an outline of the United States of America with, some-where near Nebraska, a small shape of Israel superimposed onto it; the caption was 're-locate Israel into the United States' (Author unknown 2016a).[1] This material was meant to be amusing and clever, but joking about the 'transportation' of five million Jews out of the Middle East was thought by many to be far from funny. A significant amount of other material shared by Naz Shah on social media emerged, most of it from the time of the Gaza war of 2014. Shah had published an image on Facebook which portrayed 'Apartheid' Israel as being similar to 'Hitler' (Author unknown 2016b). She had also warned that 'The Jews' were 'rallying' against a claim that Israel was committing war crimes (Author unknown 2016c).

Naz Shah was one of the most high profile of a number of Labour figures whose antisemitic comments were coming to light at this time, and she was formally suspended from Party membership. Usually, peo-ple on the left angrily deny all charges of antisemitism, and they accuse those making the accusations of doing so in bad faith in order to harm the left or to silence criticism of Israel. But Naz Shah made an immedi-ate and plausible apology; she promised to re-think what she had done, and she said that she wanted to understand the issues of Israel and Palestine, and antisemitism, better (Stewart, Mason and Parveen 2016). She went on to meet with a number of Jewish communal leaders and scholars of antisemitism. A few weeks later she had a meeting with Jewish congregants at her local synagogue and talked some of these issues through at length. She said there:

> It is my job in the Muslim Community to highlight the issues of anti-Semitism. Going to Auschwitz is a fantastic idea but it won't fix the problem. We need to educate the community. It's up to me to own the narrative. To have conversations with the Muslim community [about antisemitism] and that's my responsibility.
>
> *(Cohen, J. 2016)*

Justin Cohen reported that she told the gathering of 130 commu-nity members from Leeds, Bradford and York that she wanted to make a 'real apology' rather than a 'politician's apology', adding: 'I looked at myself and asked whether I had prejudice against Jewish people. But

I realised I was ignorant and I want to learn about the Jewish faith and culture. I do not have hatred for Jewish people' (2016). Naz Shah has since had her membership of the party reinstated.

Ken Livingstone, by contrast, was absolutely not in a mood to apologize for antisemitism. He took to the radio stations on 27 April in a mood to counter-attack. Defending Naz Shah, even after she herself had apologized, he said on BBC Radio London that she was a victim of a 'well-orchestrated campaign by Israel lobby'. He said:

> She's a deep critic of Israel and its policies. Her remarks were over the top but she's not anti-Semitic. I've been in the Labour party for 47 years; I've never heard anyone say anything anti-Semitic. I've heard a lot of criticism of the state of Israel and its abuse of Palestinians but I've never heard anyone say anything anti-Semitic . . . .
>
> It's completely over the top but it's not anti-Semitic. Let's remember when Hitler won his election in 1932, his policy then was that Jews should be moved to Israel. He was supporting Zionism – this before he went mad and ended up killing six million Jews. The simple fact in all of this is that Naz made these comments at a time when there was another brutal Israeli attack on the Palestinians.
>
> *(May 2016a)*[2]

Livingstone presumptuously explained Naz Shah's record by assuming that what she thinks is what he thinks; he assumed the right to explain on her behalf.

The claim from Livingstone that he had never heard anyone say anything antisemitic in his forty-seven years in the party is important. It is evidence for the view that for Livingstone there is nothing that anybody could say which – if it was said in a left-wing antiracist space, and if it related in any way to Israel – could be understood as antisemitic. In half a century of activism, he has never heard such a thing: only criticism of Israel.

And in that interview he went on to articulate a common position in one who is defending against a charge of antisemitism, which is a willingness to plead guilty to a lesser charge – to anything so long as it is not antisemitism: 'It's completely over the top but it's not anti-Semitic,' he said. For Livingstone, antisemitism on the left is close to being a contradiction in terms; he has never once seen it; it does not exist. He can plead guilty to being vulgar, stupid, rude or belligerent, but there is no guilty plea to a crime which does not, and cannot, exist.

And then Ken Livingstone turned to the claim that Naz Shah had shared on Facebook that 'apartheid Israel' was comparable to Hitler. One of the ways in which he defended the claim that Zionists were like Hitler was to re-state the old antizionist claim that Hitler was a supporter of Zionism, a claim which suggests to the listener that Zionism and Hitlerism are similar. Ken Livingstone has a particular attachment to comparing everything which he finds bad in political life to Hitler; in particular, he has a track record of comparing Israel and Jews to Nazis.

Most people know that Zionism was in fact a response to antisemitism; most people know that Hitler was not interested in responding to antisemitism because he was an antisemite. But for people from a certain current of left antizionism, comparing Zionism to Nazism is irresistible. First, Nazism is popularly understood as the supreme example of the horrors to which race-thinking can lead; and Zionism is said to embody, at its heart, the same kind of race-thinking. Second, Zionism is said to have in common with Nazism the assumption that Jews and non-Jews cannot live together in Europe; this is then portrayed as an ideological similarity, a shared critique of multiculturalism. Third, Zionism, as an ideology which is cast as being akin to Nazism, is said to have created a state and a society which is akin to that created by National Socialism. This analogy is potent on the level of emotion as well as on the level of reason. 'Scientifically' to portray Nazism and Zionism as similar is to try to make people feel towards Zionism the great loathing that good people feel towards Nazism. To say that something is like Nazism is to say that it is morally reprehensible. But to propagate the notion that Zionists – that is, the overwhelming majority of Jews – are in particular like Nazis adds a specific Jew-baiting dimension.

It is to be remembered that Ken Livingstone has been part of the hard-core antizionist movement in the UK since the days when it was a small, fringe, obsessive and eccentric clique. In 1981, when he was already leader of the GLC, Livingstone was made the figurehead editor of a left-wing newspaper called Labour Herald. It was edited by Ted Knight, a leading Workers Revolutionary Party (WRP) member. The WRP was a significant Trotskyist group in Britain which eventually broke apart when plausible allegations emerged that its leadership had been guilty of the rape and sexual abuse of younger members (Matgamna 2003). Labour Herald was also financed by the WRP, which was in turn supported by Colonel Gadafi and other Arab Nationalist dictators; the WRP spied on Arab dissidents in London too, reporting back to the murderous regimes in the Middle East (Dovkants 2008). Already in the 1980s, Livingstone's paper ran a cartoon depicting the Prime Minister of Israel, Menachem Begin, wearing a Nazi uniform, doing a straight arm salute and standing on a heap of skulls.[3]

In 1983, Lenni Brenner wrote 'Zionism in the Age of Dictators' (2014). It was an antizionist polemic and not taken seriously by mainstream scholars. Paul Bogdanor (2016) notes:

> Livingstone had written in his memoirs that Brenner's work 'helped form my view of Zionism and its history' (Livingstone 2011: 223). The book is a fixture of antizionist and antisemitic propaganda about the Holocaust on both the far left and on the far right, and Brenner has a cult following among those convinced that 'Zionists' are to blame for all evil in the world.

Jim Allen was inspired by Brenner to write *Perdition*, a play which was produced at the Royal Court Theatre in 1987. *Perdition* draws upon the story of Rudolf Kastner and the later controversies regarding later accusations that were made against him of collaboration with the Nazis during the Holocaust in Hungary. Allen takes this morally and historically complex and contested story, and he makes out of it a morality tale of Zionist collaboration with Hitler.

Bogdanor (2016)[4] writes:

> Allen characterised his play in these terms: 'Without any undue humility I'm saying that this is the most lethal attack on Zionism ever written, because it touches the heart of the most abiding myth of modern history, the Holocaust. Because it says quite

plainly that privileged Jewish leaders collaborated in the extermination of their own kind in order to help bring about a Zionist state, Israel, a state which is itself racist'.

When Ken Livingstone was asked in 2016 why he found it so compelling, he replied:

> Lenni's book shows a shared common belief between the Nazis and the Zionists in preserving their race from interracial marriage and things like that. They wanted to preserve their ethnic purity and that's why they had a working relationship.
>
> *(Bogdanor 2016)*[5]

In the 1980s there was a small clique of antizionists, many of them Jewish, who created for themselves a narrative, which became for them common sense, that Zionism was like Nazism, that it collaborated with Nazism and that it created a Nazi state. There were activists and historians who stood toe to toe with these antizionists, who followed all their polemics and their intricate and obscure sources, and who critiqued their interpretations and their conclusions.[6]

Now in 2016, these issues were moving into the mainstream. Labour MPs and activists were being scrutinized, the leader of the Party himself was accused of being an antizionist with a long history of links with antisemitic ideas and politics, and the debates were being had in the newspapers, on radio, and on television, as well as on social media and the blogs.

Ken Livingstone, for years a great communicator of socialist ideas to a general audience, suddenly found himself saying things in public which were quite normal in his own circles but which sounded eccentric on BBC Radio London. They were now to be challenged in a much more public arena. The most prominent and immediate challenge came from John Mann.

John Mann is now the Labour MP for Bassetlaw and a central driving force behind parliamentary initiatives against contemporary antisemitism both in the UK and globally. His political career began in the 1980s when he was a leader of the National Organisation of Labour Students (NOLS). Part of his own formative political education, therefore, was forged in a fight with those who were pushing these demonizing narratives about Zionism; some of the same activists were, in the early 1980s, involved in campaigns to ban student Jewish societies on the basis that they were Zionist and therefore racist and so in violation of Student Union 'no-platform' policies (Rich 2016a).

John Mann responded to Ken Livingstone's claim that 'Hitler was supporting Zionism . . . before he went mad'. Mann confronted Livingstone as he entered a BBC radio building on 28 April 2016, the same day he made the claim about Hitler. Mann managed to accuse Livingstone, loudly and clearly, in front of a TV crew, of being a 'disgusting racist', of 're-writing history', of 'lying' and of being a 'Nazi apologist'.[7] Video of the confrontation went viral on social media within an hour, and it appeared on television and radio news and in the papers the next day. In mainstream discourse, the accusation that the Jewish state had been supported by Hitler and the assertion that Hitler only 'went mad', read became genocidal, after 1932 looked eccentric in the extreme.

Ken Livingstone continued to double down and continued to insist that he was right about Hitler and Zionism. He was relying on, and distorting the purpose of, one moment of Nazi policy, the 'Haavara agreement', when there was a Nazi plan to deport Jews from Germany and make some money out of them by allowing them to move to Palestine, with German goods that they had been forced to buy. But politically, the gulf between trying to make Germany Jew-free by finding places to deport them to, on the one hand, and 'supporting Zionism', on the other, is unbridgeable. One analogy that was circulating at the time was that Livingstone's position was like somebody claiming that the Atlantic Slave Trade was 'in support of' African immigration into America. The point of all this, it is to be remembered, is to propagate the idea in the public imagination that there is something similar between Nazism and Zionism, and that that is the explanation for the collaboration between the two.

The steady build-up of stories and examples about antisemitism in the Labour Party came to a head with Ken Livingstone when Jeremy Corbyn, the leader of the Labour Party (and a close ally of Livingstone), was forced into suspending Livingstone's membership. This was when Corbyn announced the Chakrabarti Inquiry into antisemitism in the Labour Party (see subsequent chapters). This response succeeded in damping down the public scandal, which had been escalating by the day, over antisemitism in the Labour Party. John Mann was reprimanded by the Chief Whip for publicly confronting Livingstone (May 2016b). Thousands of Livingstone supporters signed a petition to have John Mann suspended from the party for 'appallingly unprofessional and toxic' behaviour (Bloom 2016). In response, a petition was circulated within the Jewish community calling for John Mann to be Knighted (Rashty 2016).

In spite of the fact that historians of the Holocaust like Yehuda Bauer lined up in the press to explain why Livingstone had got the history of this so wrong,[8] Livingstone persisted. In June, he was called as a witness to the Home Affairs Select Committee's inquiry into antisemitism. 'If I had said Hitler was a Zionist, I would apologise for that because it's rubbish,' he told *The Guardian* newspaper about his testimony, as though that would have been decisively different from saying Hitler 'was supporting' Zionism, which he admitted. 'If I'd said it, I would agree it was abhorrent. But I didn't say it' (Sherwood 2016). Notice too that Livingstone almost pleads guilty to talking 'rubbish' or saying something 'abhorrent' – but the admission that it would have been antisemitic was not forthcoming.

In 2005 I named the phenomenon of responding to an accusation of antisemitism with a counter-accusation of Zionist bad faith; I named it the *Livingstone Formulation*, after he had employed it following a row with a Jewish journalist who he accused of being 'just like a German war criminal' and after which some people accused Livingstone of antisemitism. I always worried a little that naming it after Livingstone was arbitrary and perhaps unfair, as it was a rhetorical device used by many different people. But now, in 2016, Ken Livingstone really embraced it again and made the formulation his own. Speaking after his appearance at the Select Committee, he said: 'A handful of Labour MPs used this issue, deliberately lied about what I said, and smeared me because they wished to undermine the leader of the Labour party. It's that simple. And they should be the ones who are suspended' (Sherwood 2016). And he had made the same claim in his original, unwanted defence of Naz Shah, that the issue of antisemitism had been raised only to smear the left and to silence criticism of Israel.

Antisemitism has been an issue associated with Ken Livingstone throughout his career. When Livingstone was the Mayor of London, he hosted Sheikh Yusuf al-Qaradawi at City Hall. He is pictured warmly embracing the Islamist ideologue. Livingstone insisted that Qaradawi was 'one of the leading progressive voices in the Muslim world' (James 2010). Qaradawi is the spiritual leader of the Muslim Brotherhood, of which Hamas is the Palestinian affiliate. Qaradawi speaks in favour of wife-beating, female genital mutilation and the execution of gay people (Readings 2010). He says that Hitler put the Jews in their place; he described the Holocaust both as exaggerated and as divine punishment.[9]

On 21 March 2012, a group of life-long Jewish Labour supporters sat down in a meeting with Livingstone to try to come to some agreement by which they could back him in the mayoral election. They reported that at 'various points in the discussion Ken used the words Zionist, Jewish and Israeli, interchangeably, as if they meant the same, and did so in a pejorative manner' (Gilbert *et al* 2012). They also raised the issue of Livingstone having taken money for fronting the antisemitic Iranian propaganda channel Press TV. Livingstone told the group that Jews are rich and so are not likely anyway to vote Labour (Gilbert *et al* 2012).

Ken Livingstone says antisemitic things, and he leaps to the defence of antisemites and antisemitic movements. He gave his name to a particular variant of antisemitic conspiracy theory whereby those who stand up against antisemitism are accused of doing so in bad faith. He loves getting into a fight with the Jews, those, anyway, who do not identify as antizionist. He is hungry for the spotlight in this fight.

Ken Livingstone and a significant minority of people in the UK still do not see that there is a problem of antisemitism. They see a right-wing Zionist 'witch-hunt' against good people who oppose austerity, imperialism, the Israeli occupation and Islamophobia. They are enraged by the injustice of the antisemitism 'smear'. They are entrenched in their position that the influence of Israel, as well as the Jews who support it, is toxic. They are worried how this influence seems to them to seep into the dominant ideology of the ruling class and the mainstream media. Their blood boils more and more intensely about Israel, its human rights abuses (both real and imagined), its imputed vulgarity, and the racism that is to be found there; their anger is mixed with shame at what they think of as a European colonial outpost, created under British rule. They see Islamophobia, imported from Israel and America, as the poison of post-national European hope. They feel that everybody has learnt the lessons of the Holocaust except for the Zionists, who, having rejected Christian forgiveness and love, find themselves stuck, more and more isolated, in the Nazi era.

Currently, Ken Livingstone is not suspended from the Labour Party but is prohibited from running for public office as a party candidate. In a sense this is an injustice, since Livingstone thinks the same about Israel and about antisemitism as many in the very highest positions of leadership of the party. In fact Livingstone may be ending his career as rather a pathetic figure. Every time he fails to resist the temptation to talk about Hitler in public, he makes himself look more out of touch. There is a website which tells you the number of days since Livingstone mentioned Hitler.[10] A satirical website jokingly quotes Livingstone as follows: 'Quite frankly, these constant attempts by the media to smear me are leaving a Nazi taste in my mouth' (Author unknown 2016d). On the other hand, with the Corbyn faction's consolidation of power in the Labour Party, it is possible that Livingstone may be reinstated at some point.

How raising the issue of antisemitism puts you outside the community of the progressive: the *Livingstone Formulation*

Jenny Tonge, a Liberal Democrat member of the House of Lords, said at a fringe meeting of her party's conference: 'The pro-Israeli Lobby has got its grips on the Western World, its financial grips. I think they've probably got a certain grip on our party' (Aaronvitch 2016). This seems to be an antisemitic claim because it articulates a mindset in which a Jewish conspiracy controls the western world through its financial muscle. It is a claim not about influence or lobbying but about singular and global financial control.

There is often disagreement about what is antisemitic and what is not. Spotting antisemitism requires knowledge, forensic skills, political and moral judgment, as well as a sensitive nose and a consideration of context. But the focus in this section of the book is not how to spot

antisemitism. Rather it is about a recurrent pattern of refusal even to
try. It focuses on one common response to an accusation of antisemitism. Jenny Tonge is not some kind of fascist or racist; she thinks of
herself as a liberal opponent of bigotry and antisemitism. One would
think that if Jewish individuals, Jewish communal bodies or scholars of
antisemitism told her that some of what she had said was antisemitic,
then it would worry her. You would think that she would stop, re-
consider and seek advice. But that is not what she does. Instead, she
responds like this: 'I am sick of being accused of anti-Semitism when
what I am doing is criticising Israel and the state of Israel' (Innovative
Minds 2007).

Tonge says that the people who *claim* she has said antisemitic things
do not really *believe* she has said antisemitic things. She says that these
claims are made in bad faith by people whose real concern is to silence
her criticisms of Israeli human rights abuses (Hirsh 2008a). Instead of
responding by discussing the content of what she has said, she responds
by discussing the allegedly hidden and dishonest motivation of those
who accuse her. She writes:

> They take vindictive actions against people who oppose and crit-
> icise the lobby, getting them removed from positions that they
> hold and preventing them from speaking – even on unrelated
> subjects, in my case. I understand their methods. I have many
> examples. They make constant accusations of antisemitism, when
> no such sentiment exists, to silence Israel's critics.
>
> *(Hirsh 2008a)*

Tonge does not say that people who accuse her of antisemitism are
mistaken. She says that they know they are wrong and they accuse her
in a secretly systematic and methodical way, nevertheless. Her defence
against a charge that she has employed antisemitic conspiracy theory
is to rely on antisemitic conspiracy theory: the claim that there is a
hugely powerful singular lobby which mobilizes Jewish victim-power
ruthlessly against her and other 'critics' in the interests of the state of
Israel.

Everybody agrees that criticism of Israel can be entirely legitimate and that it is open to debate, discussion and the examination of

evidence to work out which criticisms are justified and whi...
and which kinds of criticism may be bigoted or antisemitic (Hirsh
2007). But the problem with Tonge's response here is that she characterizes everything she does as 'criticism'. She is in favour of a boycott of
Israel, which some people say is antisemitic and is likely to bring antisemitic ways of thinking with it; she calls the boycott 'criticism'. When
she indulges in what appears to be antisemitic conspiracy theory, she
calls that 'criticism of Israel' too.

Tonge's response to an accusation of antisemitism is to employ the
Livingstone Formulation. The key elements of the *Livingstone Formulation*
as I characterize it are as follows:

1   To refuse to discuss the *content* of the accusation by shifting focus
     instead onto the hidden *motive* for the allegation.
2   To make a counter-accusation that the accuser is not mistaken, has
     not made an error of judgment, but is getting it wrong on purpose.
3   To collapse everything – some of which may be demonization
     of Israel, support for boycott or antisemitism – into a legitimate
     category like 'criticism'.
4   To allege that those who raise the issue of antisemitism are doing
     so as part of a common secret plan to silence such 'criticism'.

In October 2016, Jenny Tonge responded to the Home Affairs
Select Committee report on antisemitism. She wrote that it is difficult
to believe that the rise in antisemitism could be explained by people
hating Jews for no reason. She wrote that antisemitism is on the rise
because of the 'disgust amongst the general public' for 'the way the
government of Israel treats Palestinians'. For her, antisemitism is not
hating Jews for no reason; it is hating Jews for good reasons (Hirsh
2016a).

A week later, Tonge chaired an event in the House of Lords at
which a man took the floor and explained that it was a Jewish boycott
of Germany which had 'antagonized Hitler over the edge to want to
systematically kill Jews wherever he could find them'. The man was
saying that Zionist Jews, and their campaign against Nazi Germany,
were responsible for causing the Holocaust. Jenny Tonge sat respect-
fully through this speech and thanked the man warmly. Perhaps she had

only heard one word that he had said: 'boycott'. She replied by saying that the campaign for a boycott of Israel is 'very very important', but she said nothing about his antisemitic argument.

Finally, ten years after her 'financial grips' speech, this event was the last straw for the leadership of her party; they suspended her membership. She responded by resigning. She said that she had not heard the antisemitic speech. But, as though to remove all doubt anyway about the justice of her suspension, she added: 'We need an urgent definition of anti-Semitism. At the moment anyone who criticises Israel is accused of it.' She also criticised the Israeli Embassy: 'They are trying to attack the Lib Dems as they do Labour. They like to be in control of things' (Craig 2016).

In 2013, David Ward, an MP for Tonge's former party, took the opportunity of Holocaust Memorial Day to announce that he was saddened that the Jews, who suffered unbelievable levels of persecution during the Holocaust, could within a few years of liberation from the death camps be inflicting atrocities on Palestinians (Quinn 2013).

Lesley Klaff characterizes this mode of comparison as 'Holocaust Inversion': *inversion of reality* (the Israelis are cast as the 'new' Nazis, and the Palestinians as the 'new' Jews) and *inversion of morality* (the Holocaust is presented as a moral lesson for, or even a moral indictment of, 'the Jews') (2014).

David Ward responded in *The Guardian* to criticism of his remarks in terms strikingly similar to those of Jenny Tonge:

> There is a huge operation out there, a machine almost, which is designed to protect the State of Israel from criticism. And that comes into play very, very quickly and focuses intensely on anyone who's seen to criticise the State of Israel. And so I end up looking at what happened to me, whether I should use this word, whether I should use that word – and that is winning for them.
>
> *(Edemariam 2013)*

In the 1980s a certain kind of antiracism 'consciousness raising' was fashionable.[11] People would sit in a circle, and the group would begin, like a session of Alcoholics Anonymous, with each person admitting publicly that they were racist. There was a logic to proceeding in this way. We are human beings. We live and are formed within the existing social world; it is complex and contradictory, and so are we. It is impossible simply by an act of will to cleanse oneself completely of all the unwanted assumptions, feelings, unconscious motivations and linguistic vocabularies within which we exist. If we begin by admitting that we are not necessarily immune from racism simply because we decide to be antiracist, then it enables us to examine ourselves honestly, in a supportive group, without being afraid of denunciation. If we all contain some racist ways of thinking, then we can examine them and deal with them. It is the ones who claim to be pure who we need to worry about.

When Labour MP Paul Flynn was criticised for suggesting that it was inappropriate for a Jewish man to be the UK ambassador to Israel, part of his response was interesting: 'I do not have an atom of racism or anti-semitism in me' (The Board of Deputies of British Jews 2011).

Tonge says that antisemitism is a 'sentiment' which is entirely absent from her own inner life, and Flynn says that he doesn't have an atom of it in him. This subjective self-consciousness of being an opponent of antisemitism, it turns out, is no guarantee against stumbling into antisemitic ways of thinking or supporting antisemitic boycotts. This certainty about one's own political cleanliness can make one nostalgic for the 1980s consciousness raisers who remained vigilant about the possibility that racism lurked in their own inner lives, in spite of their conscious and determined wish to eradicate it.

Antisemitism is an objective social phenomenon because it resides not only inside our heads but also in the cultural spaces in between our heads and in the relationships between consciousness, culture and material reality. Antisemitism has recognizable shapes and tropes; it has been with us for a long time, and its symbols and memes are deep within us and deep within our shared cultures. So there is no contradiction when Jenny Tonge tells us that she is unaware of feeling any hostility to Jews even as she indulges in classic antisemitic conspiracy theory, or when Flynn alleges that a Jew cannot be trusted to hold a sensitive office for the British state on account of his dual loyalty, while at the same time he believes that he does not contain an atom of antisemitism.

Sometimes, it is said that hostility to Israel is a cloak which hides antisemitism. But this seems to suggest that people who are self-consciously antisemitic are adopting hostility to Israel as a way of camouflaging their real, underlying, Jew-hating motivations. Well, this may be true of David Irving, for example, whose antisemitism precedes his 'criticism of Israel'. But it is more of a puzzle when people who are aware of no antisemitic motivations, who think of themselves as implacable opponents of antisemitism, act in antisemitic ways.

Whether the hostility to Israel comes first and the antisemitism follows, or whether the antisemitism comes first, even if it is unconscious, and is a cause of the disproportionate hostility to Israel, it is difficult to know. Perhaps it makes sense to understand it as a cycle in which both antisemitism and hostility to Israel feed on each other. But in any case, the key issue here is that the antisemitism remains steadfastly unrecognized and unacknowledged by the person who has stumbled into it. This is important if we are to understand the self-righteous anger and the certainty with which such people reject any suggestion that what they have said or done is antisemitic. The indignation is genuine.

People look within themselves and find an absence of Jew-hatred. They find it difficult to understand antisemitism as an objective social fact, preferring to see it as an individual mental sentiment. Having found themselves not guilty of antisemitism, they are tempted to move quickly on to angrily counter-attacking the motives of the people who have brought up the issue.

The 1980s consciousness raisers normalized racism, understanding it as something which is common in our world and which even happens within ourselves. This way of thinking helped them to examine racism, to understand it and to oppose it. By contrast, contemporary antisemitism is often treated in the opposite way. A colleague from the Netherlands once told me that she had been invited to participate in a panel discussion in Amsterdam about a controversial play. I asked her whether she thought that the play was antisemitic. She replied: 'How can I accuse somebody of antisemitism in Holland, in the city of Anne Frank, which was occupied by the Nazis?'

I thought this answer revealed something important about the difficulty of discussing and understanding contemporary antisemitism. She told me that she thought the play was vulgar, was not a good play, was not nuanced, and did not portray Jews fairly or sensitively; but she was hugely reluctant, for reasons which had nothing to do with the play itself, even to consider whether it was antisemitic. For my colleague, the very concept of antisemitism had become unusable in any context other than that of the Nazi genocide or of its pre-history. In her mind, to say that this play was antisemitic was to say that the author was like Hitler; and since this playwright was not in any sense a Nazi, then it would have been insulting to call her play antisemitic. In this way, we deprive ourselves of the ability to interrogate our own speech or actions for antisemitism.

We need the concept 'antisemitism' to help us to understand and to oppose the phenomenon of antisemitism. But what if the term itself, and so the concept, has become unusable? What if it has become a nuclear bomb which cannot be targeted against anti-Jewish bigotry but which, instead, obliterates the whole conversation? For my Dutch colleague, it had become impossible to confront the author of the play and its audience with a reasoned and evidenced case that they had slipped into antisemitic ways of thinking. Her choice was either to dance around the issue of antisemitism using other words or to use the dreaded word, in the fear that the response of the playwright would be howling and self-righteous anger, rather than considered and sober introspection.

It suited this antizionist playwright not to have a serious discussion about her play's antisemitism just as it suited Jenny Tonge not to have to consider the antisemitic nature of her claim that the 'lobby' had its financial grips on the western world. The reason for this is not that they privately admit to producing antisemitic words but that they feel themselves to be so clean that they bitterly resent even having to consider it. Portraying the charge of antisemitism as a nuclear bomb enables them to position themselves as victims of those who they think utilize such an evil and destructive weapon.

The idea that raising the issue of antisemitism is a dirtier trick than antisemitism itself is occurring to more and more people apparently independently; each seems dazzled by their own brilliance in solving the puzzle. The insight is that the debate about contemporary antisem-itism itself should really be recognized as a manifestation of Zionist ruthlessness and duplicity. This notion, widely held, does serious dam-age to the possibility of considering antisemitism in a measured and rational way, either politically or academically.

Ken Livingstone's formulation

In February 2005, Ken Livingstone, then the Mayor of London, became involved in an apparently trivial late night argument with a reporter after a party at City Hall. Oliver Finegold asked him how the party had been. Livingstone was angry because he felt Finegold was intruding, although in fact his staff had told the reporter that he would get his quote. There was a little banter to and fro, in which the reporter said that he was only trying to do his job. Livingstone fixed on that phrase and retorted by asking him whether he had previously been a 'German war criminal'. Finegold replied that he hadn't, and that he was Jewish, and that he was offended by the suggestion. Livingstone went on to insist that Finegold was behaving just like a 'German war criminal', that his newspaper (*The Evening Standard*) 'was a load of scumbags and reactionary bigots' and that it had a record of supporting fascism (Transcript 2006).

Instead of apologizing for his comments in the sober light of day, Livingstone treated the publication of this exchange as a political opportunity rather than a gaffe. He wrote an article criticizing Ariel Sharon, then the Prime Minister of Israel. In that article he responded to charges of antisemitism which had been made in relation to the Finegold affair with the following words: 'For far too long the accusation of antisemitism has been used against anyone who is critical of the policies of the Israeli government, as I have been' (Livingstone 2006).

This is the *Livingstone Formulation*. It is a response to a charge of antisemitism. It is a rhetorical device which enables the user to refuse to engage with the charge made. It is a mirror which bounces back onto an accuser of antisemitism a counter-charge of dishonest Jewish (or 'Zionist') conspiracy.

The *Livingstone Formulation* conflates everything – criticism of Israel but also other things which do not seem to be so legitimate, such as repeatedly insulting a Jewish reporter by comparing him to a Nazi – into the category of legitimate criticism of Israel. The *Livingstone Formulation* does not simply accuse people who raise the issue of antisemitism of being wrong; it accuses them of being wrong on purpose: 'the accusation of antisemitism *has been used* against anyone who is critical' (*my italics*) – not an honest mistake, but a secret, common plan to try to de-legitimize criticism by means of the instrumental use of a charge of antisemitism; crying wolf; playing the antisemitism card. This is an allegation of malicious intent made against the (unspecified) people who raise concerns about antisemitism. It is not possible to 'use' 'the accusation of antisemitism' in order to de-legitimize criticism of Israel, without dishonest intent; it is an accusation of bad faith.

An *ad hominem* attack is one which responds to an argument by attempting to discredit the maker of the argument. Philosopher Jon Pike (2008) argues that the *Livingstone Formulation* is an *ad hominem* attack which leaves the substance of the question at issue unaddressed:

> Suppose some discussion of a 'new antisemitism' is used in an attempt to stifle strong criticism. Well, get over it. The genesis of the discussion and the motivation of the charge [don't] touch the truth or falsity of the charge. Deal with the charge, rather than indulging in some genealogical inquiry.

It is always the case that there are possible reasons for making a claim which lies beyond the truth of the claim. For example a trade union representing coal miners may want to make the case against nuclear power. It is clear enough that it has an interest in winning the argument against nuclear power. But even if instrumental self-interest is one of the reasons for miners arguing against nuclear power, it is still necessary for policy makers to come to a view about the substance of the case itself. Neither does it follow that miners do not themselves believe in the case against nuclear power or that they are making the case in bad faith.

Often, critics of Israel argue that to raise the issue of antisemitism, to launch the nuclear bomb, in relation to their criticisms of Israel is itself an *ad hominem* attack. They do this by insisting that a necessary element of antisemitism is antisemitic intent on the part of the 'critic' of Israel. In other words, to be guilty of antisemitism, a person must be aware of his or her own antisemitism; to be real, antisemitism must be a conscious motivation. The accusation of antisemitism must therefore be a charge against the person, not only against the speech or the actions of the person.

But the *Livingstone Formulation* is itself an *ad hominem* response. It is an attempt to rebut this allegedly *ad hominem* accusation of antisemitism by reference to the malicious intent of the accuser, not by reference to the content of the accusation.

So there are charges of *ad hominem* usage on both sides. On neither side can the mere making of the charge settle the argument; what is needed is an investigation into whether the charges are *true*. Do the Jews who express worry about antisemitism actually have malicious and duplicitous motives, or are there simpler ways to account for their expressions of worry? For example, perhaps the antisemitism they worry about is real, and that would account for their worrying. Or perhaps they have misjudged something legitimate to be antisemitic, and that would account for their worrying.

Alternatively, is it true that those who denounce Zionists as Nazis or as pro-apartheid, or those who call for singular punishments for Israel, are in fact behaving in a discriminatory way? If it is, then raising the issue of antisemitism is explicable in its own terms without reference to a malicious external motive.

Examples of the use of the *Livingstone Formulation*

One of the interesting things about the *Livingstone Formulation* is that it is mobilized in a similar way both by self-conscious antisemites and by people who think of themselves as opponents of antisemitism.

The former President of Iran, Mahmoud Ahmadinejad, pushed Holocaust denial and other antisemitic conspiracy theory. When he was challenged on this, he responded: 'As soon as anyone objects to the behaviour of the Zionist regime, they're accused of being anti-Semitic' (Reuters 2008). David Duke (2004), former leader of the Ku Klux Klan, wrote the following in response to an accusation of antisemitism:

> It is perfectly acceptable to criticize any nation on the earth for its errors and wrongs, but lo and behold, don't you dare criticize Israel; for if you do that, you will be accused of the most abominable sin in the modern world, the unforgivable sin of anti-Semitism!

Nick Griffin, leader of the fascistic British National Party, wrote:

> Those who claim . . . that to criticise any Jew . . . is a mortal sin against a group singled out by God or Hitler for special treatment and in consequence entitled ever-after to carry a globally valid 'Get Out of Jail Free' card, are clearly in the grip either of PC self-censorship or the last misguided upholders of the late 19th century 'Master Race' fantasy'.
>
> *(Auster 2005)*

Charles Lindbergh, the famous aviator who campaigned against the USA's entry into the Second World War under the slogan 'America First', said: 'The terms "fifth columnist," "traitor", "Nazi", "anti-Semitic" were thrown ceaselessly at any one who dared to suggest that it was not to the best interests of the United States to enter the war' (1941).

These four antisemites all respond to an accusation of antisemitism in the same way. Instead of looking at what they said which is allegedly antisemitic, they launch a counter-attack against their accusers. Instead of addressing the substance of the allegation, they seek to smear the motive of the Jewish, Zionist or antiracist accuser.

Soviet antisemitism long pre-dated Israel, but the Stalinists pioneered the strategy of demonizing Israel as 'pro-imperialist'. In 1952, Rudolph Slansky, who had himself been the General Secretary of the Communist Party of Czechoslovakia, was faced with an antisemitic purge by his 'comrades'. Slansky was removed from power, and the following 'confession' was extracted under torture:

> I deliberately shielded Zionism by publicly speaking out against the people who pointed to the hostile activities of Zionists and by describing these people as anti-Semites so that these people were in the end prosecuted and persecuted. I thus created an atmosphere in which people were afraid to oppose Zionism.
>
> *(Shindler 2011: 145–146)*

This is identical to Livingstone's formulation. The Jew confesses to (or is accused of) mobilizing a bad-faith accusation of antisemitism in order to silence opposition to Zionism.

The *Livingstone Formulation* today is commonly used by people who are avowed opponents of antisemitism when something they have said or done is challenged as antisemitic. Instead of a sober review of what was said, what was done, what the criticism was, a common response is an energetic counter-accusation of Jewish or 'Zionist' conspiracy.

The Reverend Steven Sizer – a leading supporter in the Church of England of the campaign for Boycott, Divestment and Sanctions (BDS) against Israel – wrote a letter to *The Independent* responding to an argument by the Chief Rabbi that the campaign for BDS was part of an emerging antisemitic culture in the UK (2007). The Synod of the Church, wrote Sizer, would not be intimidated by those who cry 'antisemitism' whenever Israeli human rights abuses in the occupied territories are mentioned. He went on: 'Why has the Archbishop faced a torrent of criticism over [a vote to divest from Caterpillar]? Simple: the people in the shadows know that Caterpillar is only the first [boycott]' (2007). Sizer responded to an argument that BDS was antisemitic by alleging that the argument was made in bad faith 'by the people in the shadows' (2007).

One of the people who leapt to Sizer's defence against a charge of antisemitism was Jeremy Corbyn, later to become the leader of the Labour Party in the UK. Years before he ever imagined becoming leader, Corbyn wrote a letter to the Church of England in support of Sizer, saying that he 'was under attack by a pro-Israeli smear campaign' (Wallis Simons 2015). Corbyn employed the *Livingstone Formulation*. Sizer was later banned by the Church from further participation in social media after he shared an antisemitic article on his Facebook feed entitled '9/11: Israel did it' (Bingham 2015).

Richard Ingrams, journalist and founder of *Private Eye*, wrote the following in defence of Ken Livingstone during the controversy about the Finegold affair: 'The Board [of Deputies of British Jews] . . . thinks nothing of branding journalists as racists and anti-Semites if they write disrespectfully of Mr Sharon' (2005).

The BBC news website greeted David Miliband's appointment as British Foreign Secretary in 2007 with the following comment: '[his] Jewish background will be noted particularly in the Middle East. Israel will welcome this – but equally it allows him the freedom to criticize

Israel, as he has done, without being accused of anti-Semitism' (Reynolds 2007).

Political Scientist Norman Finkelstein compressed the *Livingstone Formulation* into four words with which he headed a claim on his website that the British Parliamentary Inquiry into Antisemitism was manufactured in order to act as a smokescreen to blot out criticism of Israel's role in the war against Hezbollah in 2006: 'Kill Arabs, Cry Anti-Semitism' (2006). Finkelstein has written a whole book on 'Israel's horrendous human rights record in the Occupied Territories and the misuse of anti-Semitism to de-legitimize criticism of it' (2005).

Tariq Ali (2004), a well-known figure on the British anti-imperialist left since he was a leader of the protests in the UK against the Vietnam War, wrote:

> The campaign against the supposed new 'anti-semitism' in Europe today is basically a cynical ploy on the part of the Israeli Government to seal off the Zionist state from any criticism of its regular and consistent brutality against the Palestinians.

Ali transforms everything which worries those who argue that there is a 'new antisemitism' in Europe into 'criticism of [Israel's] regular and consistent brutality' (2004). He then states clearly that those who argue that there is a 'new antisemitism' are to be thought of as agents of the Israeli government who are engaged in carrying out its cynical ploy (Ali 2004). Ali goes on to state, as the conclusion of his article, 'To be intimidated by Zionist blackmail is to become an accomplice of war-crimes' (2004).

Sociologist Martin Shaw defended Ali's use of the *Livingstone Formulation* as follows: 'Whether this is a matter of Israeli policy, as Tariq Ali not so unreasonably suggested, I do not know: but it certainly seems to be part of Jewish-nationalist culture' (Shaw 2008a: 102). Shaw found it 'not unreasonable' of Ali to have suggested that proponents of the 'new antisemitism' thesis were cynical agents of the Israeli government. But he offered a more apparently sociological and sophisticated variant, suggesting a different interpretation of the intent of the 'new antisemitism' theorists. Instead of accusing them of being agents of a foreign government, he accused them of being (perhaps unconsciously) immersed in a Jewish nationalist culture (Shaw 2008a).

Yet later on in the same debate, Shaw was drawn back to the authentic intentionalist variant of the *Livingstone Formulation* when he wrote, in relation to Norman Geras and David Hirsh, that 'some Jewish socialists . . . use indiscriminate accusations of "anti-Semitism" to discredit the outcry against this and other policies of the Israeli state' (Shaw 2008b).

The *Livingstone Formulation* variant used by Caroline Lucas, later a Green Party Member of Parliament, also posited a strong and clear claim about intent: 'Israel has been able to act with relative immunity, hiding behind its incendiary claim that all who criticise its policies are anti Semitic' (2008). Note also the term 'incendiary', which implies that the act of making the claim that something is antisemitic is hugely damaging, powerful and malicious.

In his column in *The Independent*, Johan Hari (2009) wrote:

> For months, the opponents of Operation Cast Lead – the assault on Gaza that killed 1,434 Palestinians – have been told we are 'dupes for Islamic fundamentalists', or even anti-Semitic. The defenders of Israel's war claimed you could only believe the reports that Israeli troops were deliberately firing on civilians, scrawling 'death to Arabs' on the walls, and trashing olive groves, or using the chemical weapon white phosphorus that burns to the bone, if you were infected with the old European virus of Jew-hatred.

A group of antizionist Jews organized a pretend carol service in a London church in December 2008 to protest against Israel. There was criticism of this carol service on the basis that the changed words of the carols mirrored the blood libel and that they made use of images related to the accusation that 'the Jews' were responsible for the killing of Christ. Criticism was also made on the basis that using Christian songs and spaces for an attack on the Jewish state was inappropriate, and there was further criticism of other aspects of the content of the songs. Bruce Kent, the former Catholic priest and leader of the Campaign for Nuclear Disarmament, attempted to deflect criticism of the carol service simply by means of the *Livingstone Formulation*: 'Anyone who speaks against Zionist policies is labelled anti-Semitic' (Gledhill 2008).

In February 2009, Labour Peer Lord Nazir Ahmed was sentenced to prison. He had been texting while driving shortly before being involved in a car accident in which somebody died (Swaine 2009). In March 2009, the court of appeal released him and suspended his sentence, saying that keeping him in prison would hinder his work of 'building bridges between the Muslim world and others' (Paul 2013). In 2012, Lord Ahmed gave an interview in Urdu in Pakistan in which he claimed that a secret conspiracy of Jews in the media, the judiciary and the government had had him imprisoned, ostensibly for texting while driving, but actually because of 'his support for Palestinians in Gaza' (Paul 2013).

The Times published an English translation of Ahmed's comments. Later in the day, the Labour Party suspended Lord Ahmed's membership, saying that it 'deplores and does not tolerate any sort of racism or anti-semitism' (Paul 2013). Then there was a Twitter exchange between Daniel Finkelstein (Executive Editor of *The Times*) and Michael White (Assistant Editor of *The Guardian*). Finkelstein expressed surprise that the Lord Ahmed story had not been in the BBC radio news summaries (2013a). Michael White responded: 'I agree it's a stinker and typical of double standards. Pity about the illegal settlements though' (2013a). To which Finkelstein replies: 'What have the settlements got to do with it?' and 'Please, no. A Rotherham man is claiming the Jews helped convict him of a driving offence. What has Israel to do with it?' (2013b). And White replies with a subtle variant of the *Livingstone Formulation*: 'Danny, you're a good chap, and I know what you're doing. But it's not a healthy or wise reflex, quite the reverse' (2013b; see also Hirsh 2013a). Michael White's claim is that Finkelstein is up to something. He is ostensibly raising an issue of antisemitism, but what he is actually doing is something else, trying to deflect attention from the real issue, the 'illegal settlements'. White sees through this strategy, and he publically admonishes Finkelstein.

White's implicit charge was that Finkelstein was manufacturing a charge of antisemitism against Ahmed in order to deflect attention from Israeli human rights abuses. Well, Finkelstein's evident Jewishness was one thing; certainly, White knew that Finkelstein was also a self-confessed 'Zionist' and a defender of Israel; but how was this relevant here?

Adam Levick described it as 'a Jew-baiting tweet by *The Guardian*'s Michael White' on the 'UK Media Watch' website (2013). He said that Finkelstein is not Israeli and that to raise the issue of Israeli settlements in response to his story about Ahmed was an *ad hominem* attack relating to his Jewishness.

Finkelstein, interestingly, tried to damp down the controversy, saying publically that there was nothing antisemitic about White's response. Finkelstein evidently understood what was going on, but he went out of his way to stop the nuclear bomb of an accusation of antisemitism against a fellow senior journalist being detonated. He preferred to vouch for White's cleanliness with regard to antisemitism rather than forensically to follow through the logic of what had happened. It was as though Finkelstein understood that it would make him, not White, look bad if he was seen to go along with these accusations against White. Finkelstein had made the point clearly in his original tweet, but now he drew back from it. To make an accusation of antisemitism explicit is more vulgar than making an antisemitic connection in a tweet.

* * *

The *Livingstone Formulation* is a refusal to regard antisemitism as an objective social phenomenon, and it is a refusal to enter into reasoned discussion about what constitutes antisemitism. It is a counteraccusation of bad faith. While concern about racism in general is regarded with a presumption of seriousness, concern about antisemitism has to clear the hurdle of a presumption of Zionist bad faith.

The *Livingstone Formulation* is a discursively coercive response, which bundles the person who raises the issue of antisemitism over the boundary of legitimate discourse (Hirsh 2010a) and outside of the community of the progressive or the community of the good. It is coercive in the sense that it refuses reasoned examination, it refuses to debate the claim, it refuses to try to persuade. Instead it constructs and enforces the boundaries of the community of the good by other means: the *ad hominem* attack, the conflation of everything into 'criticism', and the refusal even to consider the possibility of antisemitism within the community of the progressive. By its accusation of silencing, it silences; by its accusation of bad faith, it refuses a hearing.

The *Livingstone Formulation* is in fact a specific instance of a wider phenomenon. Preferring to define opponents as not belonging rather than seeking to win them over is an increasingly mainstream characteristic of left-wing culture. Opponents are constructed as being outside of the community of the good or the progressive. This licenses their treatment as 'other' – impermeable to political argument, reason and evidence.

The *Livingstone Formulation* is a key element in the ascendency of the politics of position over the politics of reason and persuasion (Hirsh 2015a). Hostility to Israel is becoming more and more a marker of belonging on the contemporary left. The *Livingstone Formulation* clears the way for this kind of hostility, and it inoculates the progressive movement: not against antisemitism itself, but against having to take the issue of antisemitism seriously.

Young antiracists, both activists and scholars, are inducted into a culture where those who raise the issue of antisemitism are recognized as being reactionary, while those who are accused of being antisemitic are recognized as defenders of the oppressed and courageous opponents of imperialism.

Two things follow from this. First, in this culture, young antiracists are no longer educated to recognize or to avoid antisemitism, and they are no longer given the knowledge or the conceptual tools with which to do so. They are not taught what the *Protocols of the Elders of Zion* are, what blood libel is or how to recognize conspiracy theory; they are no longer educated in the antisemitic history of some currents of their own movement. They are taught to understand the Holocaust as a universal lesson against racism but not as a catastrophe relating to Jewish history, to antisemitism in particular and to Zionism.

The second thing that follows is that expulsion from the community of the good is normalized as a way of dealing with dissent. Expulsion does not stop with raisers of the issue of antisemitism but also comes to seem appropriate for people who raise other kinds of disagreement too. And the story of dissenters being dealt with coercively is another part of the history of the progressive movement which is not taught as thoroughly as it might be, nowadays.

Alain Badiou is a Maoist philosopher, but he is nevertheless considered legitimate in antiracist and scholarly circles; he is a celebrated and successful intellectual. He co-authored a book in 2013 called *Reflections on Antisemitism* (Badiou *et al* 2013) which, in the words of the publisher's web page, dissects 'how facile accusations of "anti-Semitism" are used to stifle dissent' (Verso 2015). Gérard Bensussan (2014) reviewed the book in *Libération*, arguing that, in making antisemitism respectable, the extreme-left had achieved what the far-right could only dream of. He argues that Badiou participates in a contemporary restoration of French antisemitism.

Badiou's first response is that there 'could be no such thing as a far-left anti-Semitism – an absurd oxymoron' (Badiou 2014). This is a clear illustration of the eclipse of the politics of reason by the politics of position. By definition, there can be no antisemitism in this place, within the community of the progressive. The suggestion that there may be such a thing as left antisemitism is not rebutted or denied; it is met with a threatening, aggressive and emotional volley of insults which effectively puts the person who made the suggestion outside the community.

Badiou proceeds to respond with the most condescending sarcasm, implying that Bensussan and his academic institution are well below his own intellectual level. He says that the accusation of antisemitism is a matter for the courts, meaning that it is a libel, but, since he places no trust in the bourgeois courts, his remedy for the libel is as follows: 'I'll simply give Professor Bensussan a smack in the face if I ever come across him, which will be a richly deserved reward for his muck-spreading rhetoric.' For more on the pleasures offered by contemporary antisemitism, see Garrard (2013).

Badiou is clear. An accusation of antisemitism, if it concerns a person on the left, if it concerns something which relates to hostility to Israel, need only be responded to by violence. Reasons, evidence or argument are appropriate for disagreements within the community of the progressive but are not appropriate for an accuser of antisemitism.

Notes

1 This material previously appeared on the website of Norman G. Finkelstein. See Stern-Weiner and Finkelstein (2016).
2 See Simons (2016) for discussion.
3 See the image on the *Workers' Liberty* website. Available: www.workersliberty.org/files/begincartoon.jpg (accessed 19 September 2016).
4 Bogdanor's reference is to David Rose, 'Rewriting the Holocaust', *The Guardian*, January 14, 1987.
5 For further discussion see also: Cohen, T. (2016).
6 For discussion see: Author unknown (2012) and Ezra (2007).
7 A video made of the confrontation is available to view on the website of the UK newspaper *The Guardian*. Available: www.theguardian.com/politics/video/2016/apr/28/john-mann-calls-ken-livingstone-a-nazi-apologist-video (accessed 19 September 2016).
8 See Frazer (2016).
9 'Al-Qaradawi Praising Hitler's Antisemitism', available: www.youtube.com/watch?v=HStliOnVl6Q (uploaded 20 February 2009) (accessed 20 September 2016).
10 Available: www.aol.co.uk/news/2016/09/08/this-website-lets-you-track-how-many-days-its-been-since-ken-livingstone-mentioned-hitler/ (accessed 20 September 2016).
11 This analogy was suggested to me by my friend and colleague Dr Ben Gidley.

2

THE RISE OF JEREMY CORBYN AND HOW TOLERANCE OF ANTISEMITISM CAME TO FUNCTION AS A MARKER OF BELONGING

In 1997 the Labour Party won the General Election with a huge 179-seat majority after having been out of power since the victory of Margaret Thatcher in 1979. Tony Blair was elected for the second time as Labour Prime Minister in 2001 with a majority only five seats fewer. It is often said that Blair's support for the war which toppled Saddam Hussein's Ba'athist regime in Iraq was politically fatal for him, but he won a third General Election two years after that war, still with a healthy majority of sixty-six seats.

Ed Miliband was elected as leader of the Labour Party in 2010 after Blair's successor, Gordon Brown, was defeated in his first General Election. Miliband received fewer votes than his brother David in the Labour Party leadership election from both Labour Members of Parliament and from members of the party, and it was support from members of the affiliated organizations, mainly trade unions, which saw him win the contest. Subsequently, Miliband may have felt himself vulnerable to the charge that he was in debt to the unions.

In 2013 there was a hard and dirty selection battle for the position of Labour's candidate in the parliamentary seat of Falkirk. The Unite union pushed to join up its members to the party in order to support its own preferred nominee. The Party brought in police to investigate alleged breaches of the rules and Ed Miliband accused Unite leader Len McCluskey of defending 'shabby practices' (Watt and Syal 2013). It was following the Falkirk skirmish that Ed Miliband pushed ahead with his reforms to the way in which union members would participate in leadership elections. The new system, whereby anybody would be able to register as a supporter of the Labour Party for £3, was supposed to diminish union influence and to open future leadership elections to a wider electorate, with a process which was envisaged as being more like a US primary. One of the safeguards built into this system was a requirement for any candidate to be nominated by 15 per cent of the Parliamentary Labour Party.

After Miliband had been defeated by the Tories in the General Election of 2015, a new leadership contest was triggered by his resignation. Jeremy Corbyn was at that time a little-known left-wing back bencher. He had never aspired to, nor been close to being offered, any kind of job in a Labour government or opposition. During the thirteen-year period of the last Labour government, Corbyn had voted against his party on 428 occasions (Cowley 2015). He was a founder and the National Chair of the *Stop the War Coalition* (Corbyn 2015b) and was a patron of the *Palestine Solidarity Campaign;*[1] he spent his political life acting as a parliamentary figurehead for left campaigns and groups, the peace movement, the Irish Republican movement (Gilligan 2015), and supporters of rhetorically anti-imperialist regimes like those of Cuba (Sommers 2016) and Iran (Corbyn 2014).

In this election, Corbyn was helped over the 15 per cent threshold for parliamentary nominations by MPs who did not want him to win but who judged that his presence in the campaign would add debate and legitimacy to the process.[2] At this time Jeremy Corbyn emerged from obscurity into a national spotlight.

The Tories were well entrenched in government, and there was little agreement in the Labour Party as to how to oppose them. In particular, there was little clarity from Labour about 'austerity' and the fiscal deficit. In 2015, Labour had been comprehensively defeated in Scotland by the Nationalists following the referendum on independence. The 'Blairites' and the 'Brownites' seemed to many in the party to be old and discredited, not least by the decadence of their own war with each other; they had not left obvious successors. Ed Miliband had been a compromise candidate who many on the broad left of the party were able to support during the election campaign.

In the 2015 leadership election, the three Labour 'establishment' candidates seemed to have little political vision, not much charisma and only an outside chance of winning a General Election. Suddenly, surprising everybody, not least Jeremy Corbyn himself and his supporters, an upsurge of support for the left began to sweep the Labour Party. Although Corbyn was a veteran of half a century of left-wing political activism, he appeared to many as new, clean, honest and interesting. In his ability to make straightforward speeches articulating standard left-wing opposition to the centre and the right, often rhetorically conflated as 'neo-liberalism', he suddenly seemed attractive to many. In this sense, his success perhaps had something in common with that of Bernie Sanders' campaign for the Democratic nomination for US President in 2016. Corbyn drew on the anti-Westminster, anti-beltway, anti-political establishment populist feeling which has also manifested itself in the rise of Donald Trump, Brexit and Scottish nationalism.

Part of Corbyn's appeal is his image as a nice and straightforward man who has not been involved in struggles for political office and power or been corrupted by personal ambition; his public image is of a person who says what he believes only because he believes it. He positions himself as a person who engages in debate over ideas and politics, who is above dirty abuse and criticism of his opponents.

On 14 August 2015, as Jeremy Corbyn emerged as a front runner in the leadership election, the *Jewish Chronicle* (JC) took the unprecedented step of giving over its front page to seven questions regarding Corbyn's record on the issue of antisemitism (*Jewish Chronicle* Editorial 2015).

It asked him about his relationship with a campaign called Deir Yassin Remembered, which was run by Paul Eisen, a man who came out publicly as a Holocaust denier. Eisen said that Corbyn had donated money and had been supportive of his campaign.

The JC asked Corbyn about his planned appearance the following week on a platform with Carlos Latuff, an antizionist cartoonist who had been awarded the second prize in President Ahmadinejad's 2006 Holocaust denial cartoon contest in Tehran. This competition had been organised as a response to the publication in Denmark of cartoons that some Islamists read as blasphemous; the idea was to answer in kind by exhibiting 'blasphemous' cartoons relating to the Holocaust. Latuff's work is filled with visual references to antisemitic conspiracy and blood libel.

The JC asked Corbyn about his defence of Steven Sizer, a Church of England vicar whose antizionism had often flirted with antisemitism and who had finally been ordered by his church to stop engaging in social media after he had shared, on Facebook, a conspiracist article entitled '9/11: Israel Did It' (Frazer 2015). The JC also asked about Corbyn's own accusation that Sizer's critics had been Zionists trying to smear him unfairly with the charge of antisemitism in order to silence his criticism of Israel.

The paper asked Corbyn about his relationship with Hamas and Hezbollah, antisemitic organizations whose spokespeople he had referred to as 'friends' and to which he offered warm political support, characterizing them as organizations which were dedicated to peace and justice in the Middle East (Corbyn 2015a). The text of part of a Corbyn speech, captured on video, is as follows:

> Tomorrow evening it will be my pleasure and my honour to host an event in parliament where our friends from Hezbollah will be speaking. I'd also invited friends from Hamas to come and speak as well. Unfortunately the Israelis would not allow them to travel here as well so it's only going to be friends from Hezbollah. So far as I'm concerned that is absolutely the right function of using parliamentary facilities to invite people from other parts of the world so that we can promote that peace, that understanding and that dialogue. And the idea that an organization that is dedicated towards the good of the Palestinian people and bringing about long term peace and social justice and political justice in the whole region should be labelled as a terrorist organization by the British Government is really a big, big historical mistake and I would invite the Government to reconsider its position on this matter and start talking directly to Hamas and Hezbollah, that is the only way forward.

> *(Corbyn 2015a)*

Hamas and Hezbollah are antisemitic and genocidal movements; they make no effort to hide this. It is unimaginable that a Labour leader would be capable of saying something similar about specific movements which were explicitly racist against, for example, black people or Muslims. If somebody claimed that such racist organizations were 'dedicated towards the good of the . . . people' or were dedicated to 'bringing about long term peace and social justice', then most Labour supporters would have little difficulty in interpreting that as political support for such racist movements. Indeed, most Labour people would characterize an individual as a racist if the individual said that he or she thought, for example, that the English Defence League or the Ku Klux Klan were dedicated to justice or peace.

Corbyn was asked by the *Jewish Chronicle* why he had never condemned the antisemitic posters and banners that dominate the annual Al-Quds Day rally, sponsored by Stop the War (when he was the National Chair) and also sponsored by a number of Islamist organizations, in particular ones which support the current regime in Iran.

Corbyn was asked why he defended Raed Salah as an 'honoured citizen'; Salah, a Palestinian leader in Israel, had explicitly employed medieval-style blood libel rhetoric in order to incite people against Jews. Corbyn defended Salah, saying that his criticism of Israel 'must be heard'; Corbyn said to Salah: 'I look forward to giving you tea on the terrace because you deserve it!' (Johnson 2015a).

Corbyn's answers to the *Jewish Chronicle* (Reporter 2015) were not convincing. He said he could not remember giving money to Eisen. He said that he had supported Eisen's campaign only before it became clear that Eisen was an antisemite, but so did a lot of other people. In truth, however, Corbyn was still attending events run by Eisen's organization as late as 2013 (Dysch 2015);[3] Eisen had begun experimenting with Holocaust denial a decade earlier (Eisen 2008).

Corbyn said that he had decided not to appear with Latuff, but he did not say why; he made no critique of Latuff, and he did not indicate why working alongside him against Israel would be problematic.

Corbyn said that he had defended Sizer in 2012 as being the victim of a Zionist smear campaign, before Sizer had become an antisemite, not after – as though his openness to 9/11 'trutherism' was not related to his particular variant of antizionism. In truth, activists within the

Christian world in particular had been exposing Sizer's antisemitism, with all their energy, for years; Corbyn lived in a political world where such exposition was de-valued, along the principle of the *Livingstone Formulation*, as Zionist machinations to silence a supporter of Palestinian rights.[4] That would explain how it was possible for Corbyn only to have discovered that Sizer was indefensible after he had been officially sanctioned by his church, and after things had changed for Corbyn by his having been elected leader of the party.

Corbyn's stock answer as to why he referred to Hamas and Hezbollah as 'friends' was that it was diplomatic language and that he was engaged in, and supportive of, the peace process. He used the same 'diplomatic language' explanation in relation to his defence of Raed Salah, the blood libeller. In truth, Corbyn has embraced the politics of Hamas and Hezbollah, he has been hosted by Hamas in Gaza a number of times, he does not take the opportunity of his contacts with them to criticize their antisemitism, and he is not worried by their links to the Iranian regime; in short, he relates to them as though they were fundamentally freedom fighters.

Corbyn answered the point that he had failed to challenge the presence of antisemitic banners and posters by saying that he opposes antisemitism.

His answers to the *Jewish Chronicle* were evasive and partial. But the answer which has real kick, the one which the Corbyn faction really relies on, is that Corbyn supports the Palestinians and that the people who accuse him of antisemitism are doing so to smear him in an effort to silence his criticism of Israel and to discredit his left-wing politics.

James Bloodworth, at the time the editor of *Left Foot Forward*, appeared on the BBC Radio 4 *Today* programme on 28 August 2015. He began with the customary throat-clearing disclaimer that nobody is saying that Corbyn is antisemitic. Bloodworth then explained why there was a problem with Corbyn's tolerance for antisemitism and his participation in, and support for, antisemitic organizations and movements.

In response, Diane Abbott, a senior left-wing Labour MP, went on the attack. This attempt to portray Corbyn as antisemitic was a sign, she said, that the 'Westminster elite' and the 'political class' were afraid of him and his anti-austerity agenda. Abbott marshalled all of her rhetorical power to make clear that such questions were impertinent and inappropriate – that they were 'personal' attacks and not political. She answered them by portraying Bloodworth as having overstepped the boundaries of political honesty and British politeness.

Early on in Corbyn's first leadership campaign, Alan Johnson, a long-time socialist and supporter of Palestinian statehood, wrote an 'open letter to Jeremy Corbyn' (Johnson 2015a). In this letter he set out the details of the Sizer story and the Salah story and Corbyn's support for Hamas and Hezbollah; he did so with evidence, quotations, references and links; he did so in a way which was explicitly friendly to Corbyn's left-wing critique of the Labour right. Johnson's letter circulated widely but did not really have any impact. Corbyn was elected in spite of it, and the evidence about his record of embracing political antisemitism was generally met with the understanding that people said hateful things about Corbyn in order to smear the left and to silence criticism of Israel.

In October 2015, Yasmin Alibhai-Brown wrote a piece in *The Independent* headed 'Fling mud if you must but don't call Jeremy Corbyn an Anti-semite':

> It is an accusation that is both absurd and menacing. The right, Blairites and hard Zionists have formed the most unholy of alliances to slay the reputation of the next likely leader of the Labour party . . . . Most depressing of all is the collusion between the powerful right and Zionists. They seem determined to crush all alternatives to neoliberal economics and Western hegemony . . . . As the forces of darkness turn on Corbyn, the leadership contest continues its descent into a passion play.
>
> *(Alibhai-Brown 2015)*

Alibhai-Brown mobilizes all of the fierce, outraged denunciation that she can muster against those who dare to raise the issue of anti-semitism. Ironically, she makes use of a number of antisemitic tropes in doing so. She employs righteous anger at the impertinence of it. There is also an appeal to the Jewish authority of antizionist Jews. 'The right, Blairites and hard Zionists' are the ones employing this dirtiest imaginable political manoeuvre, she says. The 'forces of darkness' are the 'powerful right' and 'Zionists'. Alibhai-Brown's piece is not even particularly supportive of Corbyn as a candidate for Labour leader, but what it does do is to stake out the boundaries of the community of the progressive. Blairites and the right are outside, along with 'hard Zionists' and 'Zionists'. A passion play was a traditional Easter re-telling of the suffering of Jesus on the cross; it was often antisemitic, portraying him as the victim of the Jews baying for his blood. As a metaphor for the Jewish campaign maliciously to convict the other JC of antisemitism, the picture of 'forces of darkness' as a 'passion play' could not be more inappropriate – or perhaps appropriate.

In July 2015, Corbyn was interviewed on Channel 4 News (Channel 4 News 2015). Krishnan Guru-Murthy asked him why he referred to Hamas and Hezbollah as his 'friends'. Corbyn repeated his stock answer that he is in favour of a peace process which should include Hamas. Guru-Murthy asked again why he called them 'friends'. Corbyn began to get angry and accused him of interrupting his answer. He carried on his speech about peace negotiations, and Guru-Murthy asked for a third time why he called them 'friends'. Corbyn started to raise his voice and to point, demanding to be allowed to finish. He accused Guru-Murthy of being unprepared to discuss the wider issues of the Middle East. The issue is this, he said: 'Hamas and Hezbollah are part of a peace process.' When pushed again on whether Corbyn considered Hamas and Hezbollah to be friends, he accused Guru-Murthy of 'trying to trivialise the whole discussion'. Eventually, Corbyn sat back in his chair and declared: 'Thanks for the tabloid journalism.' When cornered, Corbyn attempted to construct Guru-Murthy as profoundly and essentially hostile. No debate was possible, no reasons or answers were necessary, because he was facing somebody from outside of his own community of understanding. What could be more 'outside' to the Corbyn project than a 'tabloid' journalist?

From the beginning of his campaign for the leadership of the Labour Party, one of Jeremy Corbyn's most distinctive rhetorical stances had been: 'I don't do personal' (Hattenstone 2015). During the first leadership campaign, he responded in a speech to criticism from Tony Blair:

> What this campaign is not about, and never will be about, is personal abuse, name calling, calling into question the character

of other people, or other candidates. I believe many people, particularly young people, are totally turned off by the politics of celebrity, personality, personal abuse, name calling and all that kind of thing. Let's be adult about it. Let's have a serious debate, serious discussion, serious proposals put forward.

(Hartley 2015)

This statement by Jeremy Corbyn progressively began to look more and more problematic; it is arguably as much a profound inversion of the actual culture of his political milieu as it is a statement of his own intent. The Corbyn faction's political practice is often to avoid debate over ideas and policies. What it tends to do instead is to define itself as the community of the good, and it positions its opponents and its critics as being outside of that community. It does not do this consciously, and the suggestion that this is what happens would be angrily rejected. But this 'politics of position', as I am calling it, is a significant phenomenon which is deeply embedded in contemporary left-wing political culture. Hannah Arendt (1975: 312) argued that one of the defining features of totalitarian politics was the portrayal of political disagreements 'as invariably originating in deep natural, social, or psychological sources beyond the control of the individual and therefore beyond the power of reason'. The Corbyn left's political praxis is not quite totalitarian, but neither is it close to being confined to the democratic terrain of debate, argument and evidence. There is a totalitarian tradition in the history of left-wing politics, and the Corbyn faction draws upon the resources offered by that tradition.

The only Labour leader to have won General Elections in the era of colour television is Tony Blair. He won three. He is hated with a passion and a venom that goes beyond political disagreement. The apocryphal insult thrown back at a Labour critic of Corbyn on a Facebook thread was: 'you're a Tory'. There is a lot of this kind of rhetoric in face-to-face meetings in and around the party too. It could just as easily be 'you're a Zionist' or 'you're a Blairite'. Exiling critics outside the community of the good and punishing them for their bad faith and dishonesty is preferred to offering reasons why they may be mistaken on a matter of principle, policy or fact. Exiling critics also has the benefit of protecting the community from challenge, although it requires ever closer policing of the boundaries.

Admittedly, it is true that there is a tribalism present in all political organization: a warm camaraderie for 'us' and some degree of disrespect and resentment for 'them'. Political narrative ties ideas and policies to communities of belonging emotionally as well as intellectually. But in the Corbyn phenomenon, this process of staking out the boundaries separating the in-crowd from the out-crowd is key. The practices by which the boundaries are established and policed stand more in the Stalinist, totalitarian tradition of the left than in a left-wing democratic tradition of rational, open and comradely debate.

One aspect of this relates to the rise of identity politics on the left, which tends sometimes to compete with a conception of left politics as a programme for government or a programme for radical change. If Labour cannot win even with an Ed Miliband, and it has lost interest in winning with a Tony Blair, then perhaps it is ready to lose courageously and honestly with a Jeremy Corbyn.

In a poll carried out during Corbyn's first leadership campaign, Andy Burnham and Yvette Cooper both scored higher than Corbyn with Labour members on the question, 'Are they likely to win a General Election?' But Corbyn scored much higher on the question, 'Should they be leader?' (Dahlgreen 2015). In another poll, 'knows how to win elections' was thought to be 'among the most important leadership qualities' by only 27 per cent of voters in the leadership election (Kirkup 2015).

But there is still the rich and exciting fantasy that Corbyn can sweep to power with his radicalism and his 'new politics'; that he can enthuse masses of new people, persuade them and make them believe; that he can repeat in the country the impossible victory that he already achieved twice, and convincingly, within the party. New energy and impetus has been injected into this way of thinking by the victories of the Brexit campaign and even more by the Donald Trump victory in the US presidential election. It is being said that moderate and liberal centrist politicians like David Cameron and Hillary Clinton have lost what was perceived to be their clear advantage, which was that they were capable of winning. There is the hope that the mass uprising against the 'political class' which drove the Brexit and Trump 'revolts' can be harnessed by the Corbyn left. This left dreams of riding the tiger of populist resentment and turning it away from xenophobia and conspiracy theory, towards socialism. On the other hand, it may be that what is offered by the Corbyn left turns out to be another variant of populism rather than a democratic alternative to it. While Brexit and Trump are tolerant of xenophobia, racism and Islamophobia, the Corbyn left tends to be tolerant of antisemitism. All propagate a notion that the *status quo* is completely unbearable and needs to be torn down before it can be built anew. All have a tendency to eschew reasoned debate and respect for expertise. All have particular soft spots for undemocratic regimes abroad which combine with a certain contempt for democracy at home. All are profoundly suspicious of international reciprocal agreement to create common frameworks for free trade. All have aspects which have tendencies to skirt close to conspiracy theory.

And all rely on variants of the *Livingstone Formulation*:

> Person (a): 'Because Mr Trump's campaign (the Brexit campaign) was xenophobic, was racist and mirrored antisemitic conspiracy theory – and because these were key elements to the campaign – I'm worried about the racism which is indicated by the victory, and/or which may flow from the victory.'
>
> Person (b) responds, incandescent with rage: 'How dare you say that the American (British) electorate is racist. The American (British) electorate is good. You're just saying that Americans (Brits) are racist in order to silence their legitimate concerns about jobs, housing, social security and healthcare.'

But perhaps as significant as the hope of winning is the inward looking 'not in my name' politics which is associated with pessimism and defeat rather than with optimism and victory; this politics co-exists easily with readiness to give up on making the world better. The politics of socialism, in its best tradition a positive constructive project, lives uneasily alongside the politics of resistance, a negative symbolic enterprise concerned primarily with asserting innocence. It is also infantilizing insofar as it contents itself with opposition, often moralistic, often ineffectual. In the days following the victory of President Trump, the slogan 'Not My President' was visible on demonstrations.

The intense personal payoff of this variant of identity politics is a feeling of inner cleanliness. The world may be utterly compromised, and there may be nothing I can do about it, but it is not going to be my fault; my own soul is clean. In this sense, while the Corbyn faction loves to say that it doesn't do personal, in fact what it resists doing is 'political'.

In the same speech quoted above, eight seconds after Corbyn criticizes name calling and abuse, he says that 'the rich' and 'the powerful, that benefit so much from our political system, don't care what kind of name calling goes on, providing their tax breaks go on'. It is fine, in Corbyn's world, to make sweeping generalizations when the target is outside of the community of the 'oppressed', the 'progressive' and the 'good'.

When Corbyn is tested on his beliefs and his record, he tends to respond by characterizing a political challenge as a personal attack. He treats it as intrusive, rude and vulgar. In so doing, he accomplishes three things. He paints himself as the innocent victim of unjust aggression; he avoids responding to the detail of the challenge; and he bolsters the distinction between the good people inside his tent and the bad people outside of it. Howard Jacobson (2015) writes:

> There was something 'How very dare you', about Jeremy Corbyn's recent temper tantrum in rebuttal of the charge that the company he kept reflected badly on him. 'The idea that I'm some kind of racist or anti-Semitic person is beyond appalling, disgusting and deeply offensive', he said.

'Alarm bells ring when a politician stands haughty upon his honour,' observes Jacobson (2015). When Jeremy says he doesn't do personal, what he means is that he will not deal with criticism in the normal democratic way. He will not respond to it by means of reason or argument; he refuses to enter into serious engagement over worldviews, over ideas or over his record. He is less interested in trying to persuade than in making criticism appear as personal insult. 'Jeremy doesn't do personal' does not mean that he refrains from insulting others; it means that he refrains from responding to that which he is able to construct as insulting.

Antisemitism as a key marker of the community of the good

It is not accidental that the issue of antisemitism has become pivotal to this process of defining who is inside and who is not. In the post-war period, in democratic discourse at least, everybody recognised antisemitism as being bad, and they recognised opposition to antisemitism as an entry requirement into progressive politics. Now, just the action of initiating a discussion about what is antisemitic and what is not is suspicious to people schooled in standard progressive culture. To ask if something said or done is antisemitic is to risk placing one's own membership of the community of the good under scrutiny.

It is difficult to engage in a reasoned and evidenced discussion about contemporary antisemitism, but it is easy to mobilize the issue of antisemitism as an indicator of political cleanliness. In our time, a person who raises the issue of antisemitism is more clearly recognizable as belonging to the wrong crowd than a person who stumbles into actual antisemitism. Raising the issue becomes a marker of Blairite, Tory or Zionist obfuscation. It marks a bad-faith move designed to silence or to de-legitimize criticism of Israel, or even left politics in general. Antisemitism itself, on the other hand, when it can plausibly appear supportive of the Palestinians, does little to damage a person's reputation.

In his speech to Conservative Party Conference in October 2015, David Cameron criticised Jeremy Corbyn for having called the killing of Osama Bin Laden a tragedy. Although Cameron went on, in full Tory Party conference rhetoric mode, the points he was making were not entirely without foundation: 'My friends, we cannot let that man inflict his security-threatening, terrorist-sympathising, Britain-hating ideology on the country we love' (Wilkinson 2015).

Jeremy Corbyn is for unilateral nuclear disarmament, and he has said that, if he were Prime Minister, he would never use nuclear weapons

(Sparrow 2015). Over the years he has made clear his support for the 'Iraqi resistance', the IRA, Hamas and Hezbollah. Corbyn was the chair of 'Stop the War', which has been explicit in its support for those fighting against British and American forces.

During an appearance on Press TV, the Iranian state English-language propaganda channel, on which Corbyn has received money for hosting a show (Allegretti 2016), he did say that the killing of Bin Laden was a tragedy. The programme in question was hosted by Yvonne Ridley, a leading member of George Galloway's Respect Party. Ridley thinks that 'Israel is a vile little state' and has reassured us that Respect is a 'Zionist-free party' while the mainstream parties are 'riddled with Zionists' (Das 2012).

In this programme, Corbyn participates in a spinning swirl of conspiracy theory; perhaps Bin Laden was murdered years before; his killing is like the 'extra-judicial killing' of Adolf Eichmann by the 'Zionist state'; Charles II and Oliver Cromwell had their heads 'displayed'; there is a 'medieval triumphalism' around the death of Bin Laden; Bin Laden's killing is a 'tragedy' like 9/11 and like the attack on Afghanistan; the fact that photographs of Bin Laden's body were not published demonstrates that President Obama may be lying about the death.

So how did Corbyn respond to Cameron's attack on his nuclear unilateralism, his support for terrorism, his response to the killing of Bin Laden and his support for those attacking British forces? Corbyn has answers. His political tradition understands the key evils on the planet to be American, British and Israeli imperialism. He thinks that forces which oppose imperialism – including the Iranian state and Yvonne Ridley, Iraqi Islamist militias, Bin Laden, the IRA, Hamas and Hezbollah – are fundamentally defensive. He supports them insofar as they are 'anti-imperialist'; insofar as they are anti-democratic or terroristic, he regards them as creations of imperialism.

But Jeremy Corbyn did not engage with Cameron's criticism by defending his own record and his own beliefs. Instead, his spokesperson responded with this: 'The fact that David Cameron used his speech to make personal attacks on Jeremy Corbyn are a sure sign that he is rattled by the re-energisation of the Labour Party.'

Corbyn's official Facebook page characterised Cameron's speech as the 'most disgraceful name calling' and as 'personalised, playground attacks'. It went on:

> You'll notice the similarity between the prime minister's words and those of the tabloid press, who have smeared Jeremy Corbyn throughout the summer and beyond . . . . The motivations are the same: to drown out debate and make our arguments taboo.
>
> *(Dearden 2015)*

There is a relationship between support for totalitarian ideas and movements, on the one hand, and attraction towards the totalitarian practices, on the other. Hannah Arendt (1975: 312) wrote that a defining characteristic of the totalitarian movements of the twentieth century was

> the introduction of entirely new methods into political propaganda, and indifference to the arguments of political opponents; these movements not only placed themselves outside and against the party system as a whole, they found a membership that had never been reached, never been 'spoiled' by the party system. Therefore they did not need to refute opposing arguments and consistently preferred methods which ended in death rather than persuasion, which spelled terror rather than conviction.

For sure, the Corbyn phenomenon is not currently a physically violent movement in spite of the vicarious thrill it enjoys by embracing violent movements into its global coalition. But my argument is that there is a discursive violence present in the way in which it pushes opponents out of the room. Arendt's description (1975) of the totalitarian approach to debate and to disagreement resonates with the experiences of those from the left and from within the labour movement who have opposed the Jeremy Corbyn faction.

One experience of my own in September 2015, on Facebook, brought home to me how the issue of antisemitism was becoming a stark marker of the community of the good. I saw that somebody whom I had known decades earlier in the student movement as a serious and engaged political person had expressed support for Jeremy Corbyn. He said that one should respect Corbyn's 'massive mandate'. In reply I tried to make the point that the issue was not his mandate but his politics, not about his position but about the content of what he says. I wrote:

> It is about politics. It is about authoritarian politics. It is about antisemitism. It is about working for Press TV. It is about thinking that Hamas is dedicated to the good of the Palestinian people. It isn't about going with the majority.

The short reply which came straight back to me was: 'I stopped reading when you called JC an antisemite.' That was it; that was the end of the discussion. I had raised the un-raiseable issue and had thereby made myself into a person with whom no debate was required. This was in a relatively public forum.

Struggles over the boundaries of political discourse are often important sites of political contestation. On the contemporary left, people and ideas are more and more being bundled over the boundaries of legitimate discourse by discursive force rather than rational debate and persuasion. This is done not for good reason but in order to avoid having to give reasons. It is not the outcome of debate which positions some kinds of politics outside the community of the good; rather, the act of positioning prejudges debate itself. In the absence of reasons and discussion, the process of defining people as not belonging takes fixed and essentialist forms. That is why, although there are good reasons to worry about antisemitism on the contemporary left, those reasons are not being heard, even by people who repeat that they are opponents of antisemitism. They are silenced by the shared assumption that anyone wanting to give such reasons is really speaking in bad faith in order to collude with the oppression of the Palestinians. The totalitarians of old defined the enemies of the good in fixed categories. They were not people who said this or that; they were people who *were* this or that. It is the retreat from the politics of persuasion and discussion and its replacement with something more menacing that is at the heart of what is concerning about the rise of the Corbyn faction.

How anti-imperialism and a tolerance of antisemitism became defining characteristics of the community of the good

One element of the socialist and critical tradition, opposition to colonialism and imperialism, has been raised by increasingly influential sections of the left to a new '-ism' itself, anti-imperialism. From being one element of the tradition, anti-imperialism has more and more become fixed as an absolute principle, predominating over other left-wing and democratic principles such as self-liberation, equality, democracy, the rule of law and human rights, liberty, women's rights, lesbian and gay rights and national self-determination. This process is related to a resurgence of antisemitism on the left.

Corbyn's victory in the Labour Party is significant as an indicator of the progress of this kind of anti-imperialism from the fringes to centre stage. Characteristics that were at one time confined to the margins of the left now make a clear claim to be considered characteristics of the mainstream left. Nothing about Corbyn's record put off his supporters – not his history of support for antisemitic movements, for example; not his habit of defending antisemitic individuals or his work for *Press TV*; not his support for the IRA; not his encouragement to those fighting against British forces; not his support for Hamas and Hezbollah. None of this constituted an obstacle to supporting his leadership bid. Corbyn won a clear majority in every section of the party, amongst full members, trade union affiliated supporters and the new category of registered £3 supporters.

It is difficult to know whether people voted for Corbyn in spite of these views or because of them. Perhaps there is a huge revolt of people who think that the issues of poverty, public services and inequality in Britain are so important than these other issues are secondary; or perhaps people are excited more about appearing radical against 'the west' than they are optimistic about fighting for social change at home. And Corbyn won again inside the Labour Party in September 2016 with 61.8 per cent of the vote.

The presence of antisemitism within radical and left-wing thought and movements is not new, but in democratic countries it had died down significantly after the Holocaust, even if it always remained strong in the Soviet Bloc as well as in Arab Nationalist and Islamist circles. In 2001 the confluence of three events heralded the return of antisemitism as a temptation for progressives. At Durban there was a major UN conference at which Zionism was constructed as the most significant racism on the planet. The following Tuesday was 11 September, when the USA was attacked by Al Qaeda. In the same year, the peace process between Israel and the Palestinians collapsed, and the Second Intifada re-normalised the killing of Jewish civilians as a means of resisting oppression.

With the post-war resurgence of democratic Europe and the rise of American power, much of the left began to downplay those of its core values which did not provide a defining contrast against the newly dominant democratic ideology. Democratic values were more and more subordinated to the principle of opposition to imperialism. Struggles for equality within nations, and solidarity between the powerless across national boundaries, were sometimes sacrificed to struggles by 'oppressed' nations and peoples against imperialist states. What is meant by 'imperialist states' in the practical politics which flow from this discourse is 'democratic states' – primarily Europe and the USA. What is meant by 'oppressed nations' when this discourse is translated into worldly politics is the gangs of men who rule over them and speak in their name.

This set of developments has the potential to cause a splitting of the antiracist tradition. Any racism that was understood to be rooted in imperialism was vigorously opposed, while any racism that blurred the black/white binary was downplayed.

Some of the peoples who tended to suffer most acutely as a result of the struggle against imperialism were those who were held to be compromised by their 'collaboration' with imperialism: Tutsis, Tamils, Kurds, Baha'is, Yazidis, African Asians, Bosniaks, Armenians, Ukrainians and, of course, Jews. Some on the left are not as exercised as they might be by the oppression of these groups, because it is carried out by forces which they think of as broadly on the progressive side in the struggle against imperialism. The blood of those on the anti-imperialist left only really boils when it perceives white people, or people that it constructs as white, to be the villains. The left can be so tied to this emotional framework that it comes to feel as though all bad things in the world are the work of white people. Sometimes, other people do bad things, but, at root, it is white people who are found to be responsible. In this way, a part of the left finds itself stumbling into a worldview in which the only significant social agents are white people and all others are constructed as victims. This stripping of people who are thought of as non-white of social agency tends to infantilize them in the minds of the western left, reducing them to helpless children.

Jews seem to have the attribute, in the imagination of this current on the contemporary left, of being both white and not white; they are both 'us' and also not quite 'us'. They are sufficiently 'us' to give westerners the satisfaction of basking in the required guilt, but they are sufficiently not 'us' so that westerners can project their guilt onto them.

The Jews of the Holocaust still symbolize absolute powerlessness, the oppressed; but the Jews who survived the Holocaust, particularly those who found sanctuary in Israel or the USA, fit better into another ready-made way of thinking about Jews: disproportionate power. In the tradition of secondary antisemitism, the Holocaust itself is thought to be one significant source of that power. In the tradition of anti-capitalist antisemitism, the sale of their souls to imperialism is the other source of Jewish power. This is the old ambivalence of the left: are the Jews glamorously powerless, or are they menacingly all too powerful? Are they oppressed or oppressors?

The Corbynist worldview is one which sees some authoritarian states, some terrorist movements and some kinds of antisemitism as being objectively on our side against imperialism, as being part of the global progressive movement. Sometimes, there is an admission that the violence and the antisemitism of these 'comrades' are not quite in keeping with our own values; they are admittedly not pretty, but who are 'we' to lecture to the oppressed about values?

Alan Johnson (2015b) characterizes this worldview which raises anti-imperialism to an absolute and which places great emphasis on position rather than agency as 'campism':

> It has caused parts of the left to abandon universal progressive values rooted in the Enlightenment and sign up instead as foot soldiers in what they see as the great contest between − these terms change over time . . . − 'Progressive' versus 'Reactionary'

nations, 'Imperialism' versus 'Anti-Imperialism', 'Oppressed' versus 'Oppressor' peoples, 'The Empire' versus 'The Resistance', or simply 'Power' versus 'The Other'.

It has been steadily gaining ground on three fronts. In academia it has come to dominate disciplines such as Post-colonial Studies and Middle East Studies, and it is considered unremarkable and scholarly in a number of mainstream disciplines, including English, Sociology and Anthropology. Judith Butler, an influential and much admired philosopher and social theorist, famously said that 'understanding Hamas, Hezbollah as social movements that are progressive, that are on the left, that are part of a global left, is extremely important' (Johnson 2012).

Butler later clarified: 'They are "left" in the sense that they oppose colonialism and imperialism, but their tactics are not ones that I would ever condone' (Zimmer *et al* 2010).

Butler's distinction between their positioning within the progressive movement, on the one hand, and what they actually do and say, on the other, is significant. It is in particular this practice of positioning that is directly relevant to the argument here. Who is considered to be part of the progressive movement, and who is considered to be outside of the progressive movement is a judgment made independently of the content of what people say and how they choose to mobilize their human agency. How is it decided, and what happens to those who are placed outside?

This 'campist' worldview was marginal on the British left but has now made significant strides into the mainstream political left. The way in which positioning is taking precedence over debate in the Labour Party is indicative of its growing centrality.

And 'campism' has also been making significant inroads in public opinion and attitudes. My hypothesis is that it is becoming standard within influential liberal and left-wing sections of the elite. In this milieu it is perfectly normal to believe, for example, that Tony Bair is a war criminal, that Israel should be boycotted, that America is responsible for most of what is wrong in the Middle East and that English teenagers who go to fight for ISIS are victims of British foreign policy and were radicalized by efforts to stop them. In my trade union, in my university, in my newspaper, in my Labour Party, on BBC Radio 4, the unexamined assumptions of this variant of anti-imperialism are to be found frequently repeated without critical assessment. They constitute the warm background community-defining set of things that good people are expected to believe. There are acknowledged and unwritten boundaries which divide 'us', the 'good people', from them, the uncultured, the Tories, the Americans, the Neo-Cons, the Blairites, the Islamophobes and, in particular, the Zionists.

In October 2015, Jeremy Corbyn appointed Seumas Milne as his Chief of Communications. Milne's own political tradition is the Stalinist wing of the British Communist Party. Later he was close to George Galloway and the Respect Party. From 2001, Milne was the comment editor at *The Guardian*, and since 2007 he had been an associate editor of the whole paper. All the while he had been writing model opinion pieces and editorials demonstrating how to describe events in the world plausibly within the 'campist' and absolutist anti-imperialist paradigm.

Two days after 9/11, he wrote a piece headed: 'They can't see why they are hated' (Milne 2001), which assigned responsibility for the attack to US foreign policy. As though oblivious of the fall of the Soviet Union, Milne is still a cheerleader for Russian opposition to NATO, is still an apologist for its authoritarian leader and is still unconcerned about Ukraine's assertion of its right to self-determination (Milne 2015). There is video of Corbyn himself, two days after the tube and bus bombings in London on 7/7, with George Galloway at his shoulder, saying to an applauding crowd: 'We have to recognise that the security of this country is at risk. It's at risk because of the way we inflict an insecurity on so many other people around the world' (Corbyn and Galloway 2015).

Milne also embraces the notion that where people are situated in the spectrum of global oppression is more politically significant than what they do and what they say. In defence of a pro-Hamas column, he wrote:

> Hamas and the support it attracts is only the current expression of a spirit of Palestinian national resistance to oppression and dispossession going back decades.
>
> *(Milne in discussion with the author, Hirsh 2008b)*

Indeed, it may be unsurprising if some Palestinians respond to the everyday realities of the Israeli occupation in the language of anti-semitism. Milne himself sees it as his own job to translate antisemitic language back into the democratic language of a timeless 'spirit of Palestinian national resistance'. By doing so, he replaces what actually happens with what he wishes were happening. He tells us what Palestinians, conceived as being without significant internal diversity, really mean if they vote for Hamas. And what they really mean, according to Milne's translation, is that they want an inclusive, non-racist and democratic state.

When Milne (in discussion with the author, Hirsh 2008b) was challenged about Hamas and its antisemitic charter in 2008, he said that it was obsolete and that bringing it up in discussion was a sign of bad faith. In response to a claim that he was 'apologizing for, and denying, racism against Jews' in his support for Hamas, he responded with a venom which can only be explained by the desire to make clear that such criticism is beyond all that is appropriate within polite antiracist discourse. Milne characterized the claim as 'perverse and contemptible' on the basis that the Hamas charter of 1988 was admittedly a 'reactionary, anti-Jewish document', but it had been repeatedly disavowed by Hamas leaders, specifically in relation to the anti-Jewish tropes. It is noticeable that, even about the charter, Milne could not bring himself to use the word 'antisemitic'. Of course, the disavowal was only a rumour put around for the use of liberal apologists in democratic countries. Nine years on, we are still waiting for such a disavowal from the Hamas leadership.

The politics of position, not the politics of reason, is coming to predominate in the UK Labour movement and in the universities. It has some chance, albeit not a big chance, of forming the next government. It has clear totalitarian potential because it is more concerned with the 'objective' position of a person or a group, in a fixed and essentialist schema, than with what that person or group says or does. The twentieth-century totalitarians defined the core enemies of the good as capitalists, kulaks, Jews, Roma or gays. What capitalists, kulaks, Jews, Roma or gays said and what they did was irrelevant. They were treated as though they blocked the road of the community of the good, on its journey to the good society.

The great philosophers of modernity articulated the revolt against the divine right of kings and against the clerics who, with the authority of God, told us what to think. Descartes democratized knowledge, insisting that what was important was method, reason and evidence, not the power of the knower. Rousseau, Hobbes and Kant put the rational individual, thinking about the world and deciding what to do, at the heart of the new democratic politics. The American Declaration of Independence raised the pursuit of happiness to an inherent and inalienable right.

Then along came the social theorists who said that the ideal of the human being as an engaged, rational, autonomous subject was not exactly realized in this world. It was a world where many power structures got in the way of allowing individual human beings to know and to pursue their own rational interests. We make history, but not under the circumstances of our own choosing. We construct our world, but we are also constructed by it: we are given language, thoughts, habits, education, nation, religion, gender and race. They become part of us, part of how we relate to the world and part of how the world relates to us.

So the absolute centrality of the principle of the rational autonomous subject was eroded. Hegel founded human agency in the material world; Marx said our decisions were manifestations of social relations; sociologists said that the social world constructs us as much as we construct it; feminists said that women were excluded from the rational; Freud said that the subconscious is more telling than the conscious; Arendt said that rational critique could feed into a swirl of totalitarian rage; Said argued that colonialism clouds our thinking with racism; Foucault said that rational knowledge is still corrupted by power.

These social theorists were right to see the ways in which real human beings fell short of the ideal of the politically, ethically and legally rational and responsible subject. But many of their followers were not satisfied with that intuition. They went on to create accounts of the mass of humanity as being wholly determined by social forces. The idea of the human being as a subject with agency was ridiculed as a bourgeois and oppressive fiction. It was replaced with the division of the world into the oppressor as a rational subject, white, male, rich – and the oppressed as the irrational object, black, female, poor.

There was always, perhaps, a seed of this kind of worldview present in the social critique of bourgeois liberalism, but it has grown to dominate oppositional thinking. In March 2008, John Molyneux (2008), a leading intellectual of the Socialist Workers Party, at the time the most influential organization of the Marxist left in the UK, wrote:

> an illiterate, conservative, superstitious Muslim Palestinian peasant who supports Hamas is more progressive than an educated liberal atheist Israeli who supports Zionism (even critically).

Molyneux is clear. Who you are in the global binary of oppressor/oppressed is everything; what you think, what you say, what you do, is nothing at all.

The Enlightenment ideal was that to relate seriously to somebody was to relate seriously to the content of what they say. The 'new politics' is less interested in what you say and more interested in whether you are part of the global community of the oppressed or the global network of the oppressors. The more rational you seem, the more you're likely to be shoved into the oppressor camp. This shove is achieved by power and not by debate – not yet, in the Corbyn Labour Party, by physical violence, but by the kind of discursive violence that silences opponents and puts them out of the room.

It was the Marxists who embraced the notion of 'false consciousness'. They could see that workers were oppressed and that what they needed to do was to unite with all the other workers, the overwhelming majority of humanity, and to make a revolution. The problem was that the workers did not yet understand their own position and their own role in history. The Marxists believed that the working class would inevitably become conscious of its own role: a class not only 'in itself' but also 'for itself'.

Max Weber (1978a: 46–47) responded:

> The most classical expression of this pseudo-scientific use of concepts is the contention of a gifted writer that the individual may well mistake his own interests, but the 'class' is 'infallible' about its interests.

The contemporary version of 'false consciousness' is still more presumptuous than the Marxist one. Now, the intellectuals award themselves the role of speaking for the oppressed. They have given up hope that the oppressed will become conscious and embrace the truth as understood by the intellectuals. They think that because the oppressed are so excluded from the power discourses of rationality, they are only able to feel; thinking is too much to ask for from the oppressed. Excluded from reason, they are left with only passion. The job of the intellectuals is to interpret the passion of the oppressed into the language of reason. For example, some Palestinians may embrace Jew-hatred; they may participate in suicide bombing; they may perpetrate random knife attacks on Jews. Their role, according to their western supporters, is not to be rational, to become conscious and to develop universal socialist political forms; their role is to act through passion. The intellectuals co-opt the orientalist image of the passionate native, and they interpret this passion into whatever language and ideas is convenient to them.

Democracy itself and freedom of expression, law, truth and human rights now become suspect; they are said to hide the reality of raw power behind a facade of legitimating discourse. Costas Douzinas tells us that Spanish soldiers unfurled banners in response to the Napoleonic invasion that read 'Down With Freedom!' He suggests, and hopes, that the oppressed may soon be ready to raise the slogan 'Down With Human Rights!' (Douzinas 2000). The idea that human rights are western and imperialist is standard in contemporary progressive discourse and is routinely taught in universities. It leaves people who campaign for human rights within what is thought of as the 'community of the oppressed', entirely unsupported – not only unsupported but even constructed as opponents of the global coalition against imperialism. Campaigners for human rights, for women's rights, for lesbian and gay rights, against what are thought of as 'anti-imperialist regimes' are, themselves, in danger of being slung out of the communities both of the oppressed and of the progressive (Bennoune 2015). Yet still there is no necessary link from this radical critique of human rights into antisemitism; those who choose to take these next steps are still responsible for their own steps; Costas Douzinas himself, for example, has resisted the politics of the demonization and boycotting of Israel.

Any apparent concession won under existing conditions is considered insignificant. 'Manufactured consent' (Herman and Chomsky

1995), say the radical intellectuals, is not consent at all but false consciousness. It is this ultra-radical and one-sided critique of everything valued in bourgeois society that both Hannah Arendt (1975), and George Orwell (2004), in their distinct ways, identify as characteristically totalitarian. It is above all the 'pursuit of happiness' and personal relationships that are prohibited under totalitarianism. Everything human must be subordinated to the ultimate collective goal.

Notes

1 Palestine Solidarity Campaign, 'Our Patrons'. Available: www.palestine campaign.org/about/patrons/ (accessed 5 October 2016).
2 Margaret Beckett, a former acting leader of the party, confessed to having been a 'moron' for nominating Corbyn, saying: 'At no point did I intend to vote for Jeremy myself – nice as he is – nor advise anyone else to do it' (Beckett 2015); veteran right-winger Frank Field (2015) also nominated Corbyn. By the end of June 2016, Corbyn was to lose the confidence of all but forty of his MPs; yet he did not resign.
3 See also 'Deir Yassin Remembered'. Available: www.deiryassinremembered. org/#/2013-st-johns-wood/4576516007 (accessed 6 October 2016).
4 See, for example, the critique of Sizer by Nick Howard (2011).

3

THE CRESCENDO OF ANTISEMITISM IN CORBYN'S LABOUR PARTY AND THE CHAKRABARTI INQUIRY

In the spring of 2016, antisemitism in the Labour Party became an issue in the mainstream of British political discourse. There were two reasons for this. One was that people on the left who previously had no interest in being members of the Labour Party during the Blair, Brown and Miliband years were now rushing back to join and to try to lead the influx of energetic and enthusiastic new members. The second reason was that the Labour Party was now *led* by an antizionist, a supporter of the campaign to boycott Israel, a man who has jumped to the defence of antisemites, a man who has offered clear political support to murderous antisemitic movements and a man who employs the *Livingstone Formulation* to deflect accusations of antisemitism. Even during his first campaign for the Labour leadership in August 2015, Jeremy Corbyn was explicit about his support for BDS. At an event in Ireland he said:

> I think the boycott campaign, divestment campaign, is part and parcel of a legal process that has to be adopted . . . .

> I believe that sanctions against Israel, because of its breach of the trade agreement, are the appropriate way of promoting [the] peace process.
>
> *(Hirsh 2015b)*

The form of words by which Corbyn supports the academic boycott of Israel requires a little convolution. He says that he does not support a boycott of Israeli scholars in general but that he does support a boycott of any Israeli university which has links to arms research or to the infrastructure of occupation. It is then easy for the boycott campaign to claim that all Israeli universities are implicated in some way, to the military or to the arms industry (Winstanley 2015). Corbyn was a patron of the Palestine Solidarity Campaign, an organization entirely focused on making propaganda for a boycott of Israel.

There had always been people around the Labour movement who held antisemitic worldviews and who, on occasion, said antisemitic things. Some of them, in recent times, were committed antizionists who spent lifetimes reading and distorting historical evidence, texts and political ideas; others were much more casual and ignorant, people who just took on board antisemitic feelings and tropes in a more haphazard way, mixed up with a visceral hostility to Israel. But now there was much more of this in the Labour Party, and it was more significant to mainstream parliamentary discourse. Apparently trivial, bizarre or marginal incidents which most people could recognize as offensive or rude, even if they could not necessarily recognize them as antisemitic, were now being noticed. They were now being connected to a culture of hostility to Israel across the Labour movement and the left, and to the very leaders of that movement.

In April 2016, Malia Bouattia was elected President of the National Union of Students (NUS), one of the biggest youth movements in the world. NUS is also a key formative space where many political activists and leaders forge their ideas, their traditions and their political identities. For decades there had been antizionist factions in NUS, but now they had won the leadership of the whole movement. Bouattia referred to Birmingham University as a 'something of a Zionist outpost', saying that 'it also has the largest Jewish Society in the country, whose leadership is dominated by Zionist activists'. Bouattia has talked of 'mainstream Zionist-led media outlets' in a way which resonates with a tradition of claims that Jews have disproportional, malevolent and secret influence over the media (Weisfeld 2016). Bouattia condemned the peace process between Israel and the Palestinians as

> 'strengthening the colonial project' and added: 'To consider that Palestine will be free only by means of fundraising, non-violent protest and the boycott, divestment and sanctions movement is problematic . . . . [These] can be misunderstood as the alternative to resistance by the Palestinian people.'
>
> *(Gilligan 2016)*

The clear implication here is that she advocates a move from support of the peace process to support for violence against Israel. It is clear in the political context that this includes terrorist violence against Jewish Israeli civilians. In recent times, street violence such as stabbings and automobile killings have been embraced by some Palestinian organizations and supporters as 'resistance by the Palestinian people'.

In May 2016, Len McCluskey, the leader of Unite, the biggest union in Britain, mobilized the *Livingstone Formulation* in response to the emerging scandal of antisemitism. He said: '[t]he row over anti-Semitism within the Labour Party is nothing more than a "cynical attempt" to challenge Jeremy Corbyn's leadership' (Snowdon 2016). The allegation here is that the ostensible consensus amongst Jews and the institutions of the Jewish community that there is a problem of antisemitism in the Labour Party is a manifestation of a dishonest conspiracy to smear the left. The General Secretary of the biggest union in Britain positions those Jews who do not identify as antizionist outside of the left; he positions them as enemies of the community of the oppressed, the progressive and the good.

Antizionism used to exist in dusty, Stalinist and obsessive corners of the progressive movement. By the spring of 2016, it had taken leadership of the Labour Party, NUS and a number of the most powerful unions.

At Prime Minister's Question Time on 9 March 2016, David Cameron challenged Jeremy Corbyn over Gerry Downing, who had recently been readmitted to the Labour Party. Cameron quoted Downing's view that the 9/11 suicide bombers should not be condemned and that ISIS should be defended. 'Those are appalling views,' said the Prime Minister, 'and I hope the Leader of the Opposition will throw this person out of the party, rather than welcoming him in' (Parliament UK 2016a).

Downing is a leader of a fringe Trotskyist group named Socialist Fight. Downing has a worldview which is similar to that of many left-wing activists and intellectuals; the difference is that he articulates it in simple, straightforward and unambiguous language. He understands the world as being dominated by a rational and organized global system of oppression and killing, which is called imperialism and capitalism; this system holds billions of people in its violent and dehumanizing grip. It does so while spinning an 'imperialist ideology' of '"peace, democracy and justice" bullshit' (Downing 2016). This is the framework of understanding in which Hamas, Hezbollah, the Iranian regime and ISIS are seen as movements of resistance to the real oppressors, which are the democratic states. Downing (2016) described the 9/11 attacks as

> the justified outrage of the oppressed as opposed to the outrage of the oppressor, one violence is that of the slave and the other is that of the slave-owner. One is progressive, no matter how distorted its actions are, and must never be 'condemned', imperialism is the violence that holds the whole planet, or almost the whole planet, in thrall, and that violence can never be supported by serious Marxists in any circumstances.

While these quotes relate to antisemitism only indirectly, Gerry Downing (2015) also argues that

> Zionism is the cutting edge of bourgeois reaction today. It is not simply a Middle Eastern matter, but plays a major role in the politics of advanced capitalist countries with much larger populations and formal social and economic weight than Israel.

In this way Downing puts Jews at the very centre of this global system of oppression and murder. He argues that it is time for 'Marxists to address the Jewish Question concretely today' (Rich 2016b).

Robert Fine and Philip Spencer trace the long history of how the so-called 'Jewish Question' has always in fact been an 'antisemitism question'; there has never been a Jewish problem which requires solving; rather, the raising of the 'Jewish problem' has itself always constituted an antisemitism problem (2017).

The case of Downing illustrates one of the key problems the Labour movement has in addressing contemporary antisemitism. Many people, including Jeremy Corbyn himself, have worldviews based on the notions that Downing succinctly describes. Many people have the sense not to admit this, sometimes to themselves, sometimes to others; often, these worldviews are articulated in complex, circumlocutory or scholarly language. But they cannot be justly or effectively dealt with by expelling the likes of Downing because he only says what many other people think. And how can people be expelled for saying something similar to what the very leaders of the movement also think? There is nothing unusual about the opinions of Ken Livingstone either, that Israelis are like Nazis and that Nazis are like Zionists; but Livingstone says it more clearly and holds onto it more tenaciously.

The day before the local elections on 5 May, David Cameron again pushed Jeremy Corbyn hard at Prime Minister's Questions on the issue of antisemitism, challenging him to 'withdraw the remark' that Hamas and Hezbollah were his friends. Corbyn was unable to do so straightforwardly, without grasping for forms of words by which he would not have to admit explicitly that these organizations were antisemitic: 'Obviously, anyone who commits racist attacks or who is anti-Semitic is not a friend of mine.' David Cameron asks again: 'One more time: say you withdraw the remark about Hamas and Hezbollah being your friends!' Jeremy Corbyn responds with a counter-accusation of racism in the Tory Party. Cameron re-states his accusation, that Corbyn is a 'friend of the terrorist group Hamas'. Corbyn responds with an attack on Cameron's tax cuts for the rich (Parliament UK 2016b).

In February 2015, Alex Chalmers resigned as co-chair of Oxford University Labour Club, saying that a large proportion of club members had 'some kind of problem with Jews'. He described a culture in which those who supported a politics of peace between Israel and the Palestinians were mocked with the epithet 'Zio'; a number of student activists agreed with NUS President Malia Bouattia that supporting war against Israel was more appropriate than working for a peace between Israel and the Palestinians. The 'Zios' were routinely baited with the song 'Rockets over Tel Aviv'. 'Zio' students were treated as defenders of racism and apartheid, and attempts were made to deny 'Zio' members the right to vote in club business. Alex Chalmers (2016) wrote that the antisemitic incidents he witnessed were less troubling than the culture which allowed such behaviour to become normalized.

Jeremy Corbyn was interviewed on Sky News on 21 March. He was asked to respond to Lord Levy, who had voiced concerns about antisemitism in the party. Sky News put Levy's challenge to Corbyn to 'deliver a specific and categoric condemnation of antisemitism'. First, Corbyn responded by re-stating his opposition, in general terms, to antisemitism. He then found it necessary to condemn Islamophobia and other forms of racism, because he is not comfortable condemning antisemitism on its own. Corbyn then went on, according to the principle of the *Livingstone Formulation*, to accuse Lord Levy of bad faith. He then specified and described the kind of antisemitism he does oppose, which is that which manifests itself in the racist harassment of Jews in the street or on public transport; he remains silent on the question of political antisemitism or antizionist antisemitism. And he re-emphasized that the Labour Party is the antiracist party.

The Sky News interviewer pushed Corbyn, asking him about Vicki Kirby. In 2014, Vicki Kirby, a Labour parliamentary candidate, was warned by the party for posting antisemitic tweets. 'We invented Israel when saving them from Hitler, who now seems to be their teacher,' she wrote. She also asked why ISIS was not attacking the 'real oppressor', 'evil' Israel (Author unknown 2016e). Kirby was a party member and was active in *Momentum*, the network of Corbyn supporters in the labour movement. A picture of Kirby and Jeremy Corbyn, smiling happily together, was circulating online. Corbyn answers the Sky News interviewer by re-stating that there is no significant problem of antisemitism in the Labour Party:

> **Jeremy Corbyn**: Lord Levy clearly hasn't been listening to the seven times since I became leader I've absolutely condemned antisemitism; I've condemned Islamophobia, I've condemned

any form of racism anywhere within our society. It is absolutely something I totally passionately believe in; and I'm disappointed that Lord Levy has made these remarks.

He knows full well what my views are. He knows full well what the views of the Labour Party are. He knows full well the kind of decent inclusive society that we all want to live in. I look forward to having that discussion with him. If there is anybody behaving badly anywhere in society, any kind of racism, it has to be dealt with; it has to be investigated.

I had a long meeting with a group of women in my constituency, Muslim women, who told me the levels of abuse they receive on the buses and trains. Transport for London are dealing with that because I've asked them to. Exactly the same applies to anybody else. Jewish women or Jewish men; if they're abused on the street, deserve exactly the same protection as everybody else. We have to recognise we are a multi faith, multicultural, multi ethnic society and behave with decency and respect and inclusivity towards everyone. That is exactly what I'm doing as leader of the party; that is exactly what the Labour Party stands for.

We're the party that introduced the first Race Relations Act. We're the party that introduced the Human Rights Act. We're the party that introduced the Equalities Act. We're the party that stands up for that decent inclusive society that we all want to live in.

Sky News: But Mr Corbyn, you find yourself having to state that here on Sky News this morning, why isn't that message getting through? Why is one of your Labour Peers having to ask that question? You have got investigations going on within the Labour Party of some of your members. I use the example of Vicky Kirby who was excluded from the party over antisemitism, then included in the party then excluded again then back in. Why isn't this trickling down through the Labour Party ranks?

Jeremy Corbyn: It is very much through the Labour Party ranks, it is something which is fully throughout the Labour Party. Fully understood. And we do take action on the very,

very, very small number of cases where anything happens and if we hear any allegations they are properly and thoroughly investigated. This is a party that stands up for all the things that we as a society absolutely believe in. And if there are complaints, if anybody has, then they will be investigated as they are being investigated at the present time. But the idea that somehow or other there is a tolerance of any form of racism is wholly and totally fallacious.[1]

In March and April 2016, journalists and bloggers found that it was not difficult to trawl through the Facebook and Twitter accounts of Labour activists, councillors and parliamentary candidates to find comments and images which were easy to recognize as antisemitic. On 29 April, the local paper published an item from the Facebook page of Brent Council leader Muhammed Butt, written by somebody else, which he had shared. The text, attached to a piece of video, said that Israeli soldiers had shot a Palestinian girl. It asked why there is no outrage in the 'Western Media':

> You show videos of the #ISIS hitting women for leaving home (which is also disgusting) – but you don't condemn the terrorist state of Israel when they murder a girl in cold blood while she is on her way to college?
>
> Just because she's Muslim? Or she wears Hijab? Her life is cheap – Israel is a terrorist state like ISIS.
>
> *(King 2016)*

Butt apologized for sharing the post but was not explicit about why he was sorry; he also excused himself on the basis that it is difficult to carefully examine everything you share on Facebook.

Khadim Hussain, a Labour councillor in Bradford, shared a Facebook post claiming that pupils in schools are not taught about deaths of millions of Africans, while 'your school education system only tells you about Anne Frank and the six million Zionists that were killed by Hitler' (McSmith 2016).

Beinazir Lasharie, a Labour councillor in Kensington, posted a video on Facebook entitled 'ISIS: Israeli Intelligence Service', commenting:

'Many people know about who was behind 9/11 and also who is behind ISIS. I've nothing against Jews . . . just sharing it!' (Author unknown 2016f).

Shah Hussain, a Labour councillor in Burnley, was suspended by the Labour Party after tweeting in reference to violence against Palestinians, at Israeli footballer Yossi Benayoun, that 'you and your country' are 'doing exactly the same thing' that Hitler did (Meyjes 2016). It appears that Hussain muddled up Benayoun with another Israeli footballer, Eyal Berkovic, who he was intending to insult in that way (Agencies and Times of Israel staff 2016). By contrast to Naz Shah, who had offered apparently genuine and profound apologies, and even to those like Muhammed Butt, who had offered politicians' non-apology apologies, Shah Hussain stood his ground and insisted that he had done nothing wrong and that he was a victim of an Islamophobic witch-hunt (Sussex Friends of Israel 2016).

The political blogger who writes under the name of 'Guido Fawkes' was, during this period, busy digging up, collating and documenting examples of Labour people who had said or done antisemitic things; the accounts in the press often originated on his blog. Naively, one would imagine that an antiracist party would be grateful to somebody who had discovered and exposed a pattern of racist discourse amongst its membership, enabling it to deal with the problem. Michael White, however, assistant editor of *The Guardian* newspaper, was not grateful. He tweeted on 29 April: 'Will someone point out to the idiots that latest anti Semitism row was launched by Tory blogger, Guido Fawkes & promoted by Mail on Sunday' (2016). In this version of the *Livingstone Formulation*, White casts those who are concerned about antisemitism in the party as 'the idiots', and he constructs the whole phenomenon as a Tory plot against the party. For sure, the Tories were using the antisemitism issue to beat the left just as Labour uses the failings of the National Health Service politically against the right. Labour did not invent the deficiencies of the NHS to bash the right; Labour bashes the right because of the deficiencies of the NHS. Long ago, George Orwell found it necessary to make the rather obvious point that things that actually happened 'did not happen any the less because *The Daily Telegraph* has suddenly found out about them' (1943).

On 5 May, Facebook comments by Jacqueline Walker, a vice-chair of the Corbyn supporting *Momentum* movement, came to light. She had written:

> As I'm sure you know, millions more Africans were killed in the African holocaust and their oppression continues today on a global scale in a way it doesn't for Jews.
> ... Many Jews (my ancestors too) were the chief financiers of the sugar and slave trade which is of course why there were so many early synagogues in the Caribbean. So who are victims and what does it mean?
>
> *(Dysch 2016)*

It is a reasonable interpretation of these comments that they draw on a black nationalist antisemitic narrative that Jews were significantly responsible for, or were behind, the slave trade (Ungar-Sargon 2013; Historical Research Department of the Nation of Islam 1991). In keeping with the *Livingstone Formulation*, Walker did not simply say that the people who alleged that there was antisemitism in the party were mistaken or had judged the situation wrongly; instead, she hit back with the allegation that it was a 'lie' to suggest there was a 'major problem with antisemitism in the Labour Party' (Dysch 2016).

Walker was not finally suspended from membership of the party until 1 October, after she had been secretly filmed speaking at a training event put on by the Jewish Labour Movement for party members, which was intended to raise awareness of antisemitism. At that event, Walker implied that security at Jewish schools was more a manifestation of a Zionist campaign to make it appear that they are under threat from antisemitism than a genuine response to a real security threat.

Did Jacqueline Walker remember that in March 2012, Mohammed Merah appeared outside the Ozar Hatorah Jewish school in the city of Toulouse and murdered a rabbi and teacher, and his two sons; and then he murdered an 8-year-old girl; and he shot and injured four other people? Perhaps Walker does remember that the much respected and celebrated French intellectual Tariq Ramadan had insisted that that killer had not been 'driven by racism and anti-Semitism' (2012); notice the intellectual effort expended in the attempt to find the antisemite guilty of a lesser charge, any lesser charge, so long as it was not antisemitism. Murder, yes; disorientation, yes; pathetic, yes; but he himself was, according to Ramadan, a victim, not a perpetrator of racism. Ramadan's full paragraph:

> Religion was not Mohamed Merah's problem; nor is politics. A French citizen frustrated at being unable to find his place, to give his life dignity and meaning in his own country, he would find two political causes through which he could articulate his distress: Afghanistan and Palestine. He attacks symbols: the army, and kills Jews, Christians and Muslims without distinction. His political thought is that of a young man adrift, imbued neither with the values of Islam, or driven by racism and anti-Semitism. Young, disoriented, he shoots at targets whose prominence and meaning seem to have been chosen based on little more than their visibility. A pathetic young man, guilty and condemnable beyond the shadow of a doubt, even though he himself was the victim of a social order that had already doomed him, and millions of others like him, to a marginal existence, and to the non-recognition of his status as a citizen equal in rights and opportunities.
>
> *(Ramadan 2012)*

Jacqueline Walker also spoke about Holocaust commemoration as though it had become a Zionist-owned enterprise whose primary function is to increase the victim-power which it bestows on Jews by creating a hierarchy of victimhood and by obscuring and downplaying other 'holocausts', as she calls them: 'Wouldn't it be wonderful if Holocaust day was open to all peoples who've experienced Holocaust?' (Gill 2016). When told the day was indeed for all post–World War II genocides, she said 'in practice it is not circulated and advertised as such' (Gill 2016).

The politics of this sustained assault on Jews and Israel via the issue of Holocaust commemoration requires some unpacking; it relates to Ken Livingstone's claim that Hitler was supporting Zionism; and it relates to Ilan Pappé's claim that Israel is committing genocide like Nazis (2006); and it relates to Desmond Tutu's (2002) claim that Jews have forgotten the lessons of the Holocaust. It plays politics with the Holocaust by accusing Jews of playing politics with the Holocaust. It engages in victim competition by accusing Jews of engaging in victim competition. It obscures the actual relationship between Israel and the Holocaust by proposing all sorts of tangential, exaggerated and invented relationships between Israel and the Holocaust. Lesley Klaff (2014) names the process whereby the Jews are portrayed as the new Nazis 'Holocaust inversion'. 'The Shoa need not be denied as a historical fact, it may be invalidated as a moral truth,' writes Abram de Swaan (2004) in his paper about how 'anti-Israel enthusiasms' function as an avenue for psychological release for some people, after the general post-war repression of antisemitic urges in Europe. Secondary antisemitism is often illustrated by Zvi Rex's remark that '[t]he Germans will never forgive the Jews for Auschwitz' (cited in Broder 1986).

One of the hoped-for positive functions of publicly remembering the Holocaust is to remind us what actually happened. Sometimes, a particular image or anecdote or artefact can bring home to us, again, with a new freshness, the hugeness of what happened to the Jews of Europe. Whether we are scholars of genocide, or political activists, or people who know nothing of history, events of commemoration have the power to take us out of ourselves, our own lives, and our narrow political concerns and connect us back to the scale and depth of what the Holocaust was – and what genocide is.

In the Jewish museum in Prague, housed in four synagogues whose congregations no longer exist, there is an exhibition of drawings made by Jewish children in the ghetto and concentration camp at Terezín (Theresienstadt in German). From Terezín the children were transported to Auschwitz where they were all murdered on arrival. The website of the museum describes the exhibit:

> The story begins with reflections on the events immediately following 15 March 1939, when Bohemia and Moravia were occupied by the Nazis and transformed into a Protectorate. This is followed by a description of transports to the Terezín ghetto (starting on 24 November 1941), everyday ghetto life and the conditions in the children's homes.

There are also depictions of holiday celebrations and of the dreams that the imprisoned children had of returning home or of travelling to Palestine. This section provides a sort of poetic interlude between the brutal uprooting from their homes and deportation to Auschwitz, which is the final and most tragic chapter of the whole story.[2]

Israel is the dream of the children who were never going to have a chance of finding asylum there. All we can do now to help them is to look at their drawings in the lifeless museum. There is a connection between the Holocaust and Israel, but it is not the self-serving and trivializing one offered in the clever speeches of today's antizionist activists.

There are other senses in which Jackie Walker's rhetoric falls far short, offered with great confidence and authority, always 'as a Jew', 'as a black woman', as an antiracist hero, to people who may not have the analytic tools, the courage or the knowledge to judge whether she is right or not. She speaks as a teacher, in a broad sense, but she does not teach. Many of the pioneers of genocide studies, the people who first studied the Holocaust and then who used some of the same concepts and ideas to study other genocides, the people who pioneered the notion that genocide was not unique to the Nazis, many of these were Jewish scholars of the Holocaust. Totten and Jacobs (2013) tell the story of the 'Pioneers of Genocide Studies'. They document the remarkable contributions of Jewish scholars such as Robert Melson, Israel Charny, Irving Horowitz and Helen Fein. And in any case there was Raphael Lemkin, the man who developed the very concept of genocide and who fought a long and lonely struggle for recognition which culminated in the Genocide Convention (1948); Lemkin himself was a Polish Jew who lost forty-nine members of his family in the Holocaust. More recently, Philip Spencer has continued in that tradition with his book *Genocide since 1945* (2012). Spencer's evidence of the hollowness of the aphorism 'never again' is a challenge to Walker's *Momentum* worldview in another sense too. The story is not simply one of imperialism committing genocide against non-white people; the stories are diverse and individual. Many of them are stories of the immense failures of anti-imperialist movements and nationalisms to replace colonialism with something better – stories of people's rage against imperialism being murderously manipulated and directed against ethnic groups like Tutsi, Tamils, Armenians, African Asians and Bosniaks; mass killings in the name of anti-imperialism are as much a part of the story of human inhumanity as are the crimes of imperialism itself.

And of course Walker is not right factually about how Holocaust Memorial Days are actually organized; they are organized by people up and down the country, across the world, taking responsibility to organize days to facilitate reflection, memory and education. It is not a Zionist conspiracy; it is a story of real men and women putting time, effort and energy into doing something which they feel is important.

There is always a tension in Holocaust education. On the one hand, the Holocaust needs to be presented as something that happened specifically to the Jews, something about antisemitism in particular and something which profoundly altered the history of the Jews. On the other hand, the Holocaust needs to be taught as a lesson for humanity about racism and totalitarianism in general. It needs to remember the other victims of the Nazis and the victims of other genocides. There is a tension between the particular and the universal lessons of the Holocaust. Walker speaks as if she has no idea how people around the world agonize to create these events and to pitch them exactly right; perhaps sometimes they fail to pitch them exactly right. Walker speaks as if she has no idea how Armenians, Rwandese, Bosniaks, Darfurians, socialists, Tories and Christians are involved in these events and how Holocaust memorial strives to remember and educate about genocide in general.

Jews have reason to fear Holocaust Memorial Day (HMD). It is predictable, each year, that HMD will be seen as an appropriate occasion to mobilize the memory of the Holocaust against the Jews. An activist in Lewisham shouts at a rabbi to include Gaza in the list of genocides for which he is lighting a candle (Harris 2011); the Scottish Palestine Solidarity Campaign hosts a reading of Jim Allen's play *Perdition*, which tries to blame Zionist collaboration with the Nazis for the efficiency of the Holocaust (Rich 2015); a city in Sweden cancels its planned torch-light procession due to an intensification of conflict in Gaza (Geras 2009); the Muslim Council of Britain boycotts HMD 'in protest at the Israeli offensive in Gaza' (Mulholland 2009). An MP writes that he is 'saddened that the Jews, who suffered unbelievable levels of persecution during the Holocaust, could within a few years of liberation from the death camps be inflicting atrocities on Palestinians' (Quinn 2013). That HMD will elicit antisemitic discourse is now, shockingly, as predictable as pogroms once were at Easter.

Jackie Walker went on *Newsnight* to defend herself against charges of antisemitism. She said: 'Of course the Jewish Holocaust was an awful, extraordinary event and Jews should have a day when they celebrate that.' She repeated this obscene mistake of referring to Jewish 'celebration' of the Holocaust more than once. One can only guess as to the Freudian connections which led to her using this word in this context. It may be related to the notion that Jews feel like celebrating their success in competing with other groups for the recognition of their suffering. Feelings of envy for the Holocaust, and the immense victim-power with which it is felt by some to endow the Zionists or the Jews, may come in to play. There may be a feeling that being oppressed is connected to virtue and so worthy of celebration.[3]

After Cathy Newman, the Channel 4 News journalist, had interviewed Jacqueline Walker, Newman was sent a number of antisemitic tweets. She was denounced as a 'useless Zionist bitch' by one viewer. Newman responded: 'So people know this is what you get for asking legitimate questions about anti-semitism. Especially if your name is Newman.' Newman is, incidentally, not Jewish. Another person who describes herself as a Labour activist on her Twitter profile wrote: 'self pity won't work here. Your jewish ancestors committed an holocaust against my ancestors in the transatlantic slave trade' (*sic*) (Ridley 2016).

Walker's Labour Party membership was suspended on 30 September, and her case was discussed at a meeting of the *Momentum* Steering Committee on 3 October. The committee found Walker emphatically not guilty of antisemitism. It 'does not regard any of the comments she appears to have made, taken individually, to be anti-Semitic'. But it found her guilty of lesser charges: 'her remarks on Holocaust Memorial Day and on security of Jewish schools [were found to be] to be ill-informed, ill-judged and offensive' (Cowburn 2016). The problem is that if it was to concede that antisemitism is possible within an 'anti-racist' space, then it is conceded that one must be vigilant against antisemitism, that one must educate about antisemitism, that one must take care; that is why there is great reluctance ever to admit that anything that happens within an antiracist space is antisemitic. What is required is debate about what is antisemitic and what is not. In order to avoid such debate, it is necessary to deny that anything is antisemitic and that all such charges are made in bad faith.

Momentum removed Walker from her position as vice-chair; it kept her as a member of the steering committee, and it opposed her expulsion from the Labour Party.

The other point that *Momentum* was keen to make concerned confidentiality. In an institutionally racist institution, secrecy is taken seriously; the boundaries are policed. It is considered a breach of the community to tell tales outside the institution of what has been happening within it. A culture of institutional racism has to be protected by a culture of secrecy. '*Momentum* is concerned that footage of a training session was leaked to the press,' it announced. 'The leak is unacceptable and undermines much needed political education' (Cowburn 2016).

Yet Jacqueline Walker presents herself as a victim, and she shows no sign of contrition or regret. This is from the webpage in which she is crowdfunding so that she can pay for lawyers to sue the Labour Party for suspending her:

> On 4th May I was suspended for the alleged (subsequently cleared) charge of antisemitism. As a Jewish person, whose partner is Jewish, this was heart-breaking. Since May I have continued to be targeted by the media, in print, online and in other places. Currently I am suspended for questions asked at a training session on 'Confronting Antisemitism & Engaging Jewish Voters' at this year's Labour Conference, after being unethically filmed by a Jewish Labour Movement campaigns officer who is also a Labour councillor. It seems this training was not a 'safe space for all Jews' by any means.
>
> *(Walker 2016)*

On 1 October, the film director Ken Loach spoke at 'The People's Assembly Against Austerity' in Birmingham. He spoke from the platform:

> There have been some terrible smears in the last few weeks. One of them's the antisemitic smear. An atrocious lie if ever I heard

one. I heard Jackie speak at a meeting about this so-called . . . this lie of antisemitism. She made a thoughtful, constructive speech discussing Jewish identity. She has a Jewish identity herself. She is a decent, honourable principled woman. And we know why the smears are made. The smears are made to inhibit criticism of Israel.

(Loach 2016)

In this speech, Loach goes on to re-state his support for a boycott of Israel. In 1987, Ken Loach was the director of the Royal Court production of Jim Allen's play *Perdition*, which was based on Lenni Brenner's account of the 'Kastner affair' and which attempted to normalize the idea that Zionists collaborated with the Nazis to murder Jews because of their ideological similarity. This was the material which had influenced Ken Livingstone to claim that Hitler had 'supported' Zionism.

The Chakrabarti Inquiry

The pressure on the Labour leadership over the issue of antisemitism continued to intensify.

Baroness Jan Royall was asked in February 2016 by the Labour Party to conduct an inquiry into events at Oxford University Labour Club (OULC). Royall's report was formally adopted by the National Executive Committee (NEC) of the Labour Party in May, but only published in part; the full report was kept confidential until Royall herself later leaked it.

On 28 April, George Galloway tweeted: 'The Israel lobby has just destroyed the Labour Party. At least this Labour Party. It is an amazing achievement. They'll be dancing in Dimona.' Here, Galloway contrives to intensify the antisemitic insult of the standard *Livingstone Formulation*. Dimona is the site of the nuclear power plant in Israel and the site of nuclear weapon production. Galloway constructs this as the symbolic centre of malevolent yet super-efficient and successful global Israeli influence. No doubt to the delight of any antisemites following him, Galloway imagines celebrations at the destruction of the Labour Party being held there, in particular. Galloway's tweet is also an illustration of how the issue of antisemitism had escalated into one which really began to threaten Corbyn and his faction. It may also be an articulation of his own fantasies about being welcomed back into the fold, not of 'this Labour Party', but of the one to come.

On 29 April, at the height of the crescendo of public scandal relating to antisemitism in the Labour Party, and directly following Naz Shah's apology, and Ken Livingstone's comments that Hitler was at one time 'supporting Zionism', and John Mann's public challenge of Livingstone, Jeremy Corbyn decided that he had to act.

He appointed Shami Chakrabarti to conduct an inquiry into antisemitism and other racisms in the Labour Party – strange, since nobody was saying that there was a problem of 'other racisms' in the Labour Party. But Corbyn feels compelled never to act against antisemitism in isolation; as if there is a feeling that to do so would bestow some kind of privilege onto the Jews. Chakrabarti is one of the 'great and the good' of the British left. She is a human rights lawyer; she had been director of *Liberty*, a human rights NGO; she was known for campaigning against what she characterized as the excesses of anti-terror legislation; she was Chancellor of the University of Essex; and she was a panel member of the Leveson Inquiry in 2011 into press standards. Corbyn appointed Professor David Feldman, director of the Pears Institute for the Study of Antisemitism at Birkbeck, University of London, as vice-chair of the inquiry.

As a political move, the institution of this inquiry appeared to work well for Jeremy Corbyn. It halted the daily feed of new examples of antisemitism in the party which had been emerging in the media, and it seemed to release the relentless build-up of pressure.

Jan Royall was co-opted as a second vice-chair of the Chakrabarti Inquiry. In this way, the Royall Inquiry was rolled into the Chakrabarti Inquiry. However, Chakrabarti's report did not, in the end, draw on Jan Royall's report, nor did it explicitly mention events at Oxford University Labour Club, although Chakrabarti did outlaw the term 'Zio' as a racist epithet.

Finally, a month after Chakrabarti had published her report, Jan Royall felt forced to leak her own report in full to the press. Back on 17 May, when she had presented it to the Labour Party NEC, the headline which had resulted, for example in Jewish News, was '"No Institutional Anti-Semitism" at Oxford University Labour Club'

(Oryszczuk 2016). Jan Royall wrote a blog for the Jewish Labour Movement (JLM) which was also published in *The Guardian* under the headline 'I cleared Labour of antisemitism – but it must make Jewish people more welcome' (Royall 2016a). In this blog, she wrote that she was disappointed and frustrated that the main headline coming out of the inquiry was that there was no institutional antisemitism at Oxford University Labour Club. In the Executive Summary, right at the head of the report, Royall does explicitly clear OULC of institutional anti-semitism. But in what appears to contradict this judgment, she goes on to say in the same paragraph:

> Difficulties however, face OULC which must be addressed to ensure a safe space for all Labour students to debate and cam-paign around the great ideas of our movement.

In her JLM blog, Royall writes: 'I am clear that in the OULC there is a cultural problem which means that Jewish students do not always feel welcome.' Later in the report she adds:

> I have received no evidence that the Club is itself institution-ally antisemitic. The lack, however, of an effective complaints or disciplinary procedure and the rapid change in leadership mean that unacceptable behaviour – whether antisemitic or some other manifestation – may go unchallenged by either the victim or by those in authority. There appears to be a cultural problem in which behaviour and language that would once have been intolerable is now tolerated. Some Jewish members do not feel comfortable attending the meetings, let alone participating. It has been reported to me that this is not a situation which is experi-enced by the Jewish community alone.

Jan Royall does not specify what she means by 'institutional anti-semitism', but she says that there is none. And then she describes a situation within the institution which may well be judged to fulfil the requirements for a reasonable definition of 'institutional antisemitism'.

Both Royall and Chakrabarti discuss the Macpherson Principle, which emerged from the 1999 report into the police handling of the investigation of the 1993 racist murder of teenager Stephen Lawrence. Royall suggests that '[t]he Labour Party should consider whether adopting the Macpherson Principle that an antisemitic incident that may require investigation is any incident that is perceived to be anti-semitic by the victim' (Royall 2016b). Chakrabarti agrees, but stresses that 'it will be for the investigation and any subsequent process to determine whether [a] complaint was ultimately well-founded' (2016).

However, the Macpherson Report gives strong guidance as to what it understands by the term 'institutional racism':

> 6.34 'Institutional Racism' consists of the collective failure of an organisation to provide an appropriate and professional service to people because of their colour, culture or ethnic origin. It can be seen or detected in processes, attitudes and behaviour which amount to discrimination through unwitting prejudice, ignorance, thoughtlessness, and racist stereotyping which disad-vantage minority ethnic people.
>
> *(Macpherson 1999)*

Royall's description of the culture, norms and practices of the Oxford University Labour Club could well be judged to reach the threshold set by Macpherson for 'institutional racism'. Yet Royall clearly had some other criteria in mind, which she did not specify, by which OULC was innocent of the charge of institutional antisemitism.

The Chakrabarti Inquiry called for submissions of evidence on the question of antisemitism in the Labour Party. David Feldman arranged at least some meetings with Labour Party members who were concerned about the issue, and he heard some evidence in pri-vate one-to-one meetings. But after that, both Feldman and Royall were marginalized and contributed little to the report. It was Shami Chakrabarti who wrote the report, and she wrote it quickly, publishing it within two months. Neither Royall nor Feldman, however, criticized or distanced themselves from the report.

The report was launched at a press conference in the House of Commons. Events at the press conference itself illustrated the nature of the problem of antisemitism within in the party and the lack of serious attention which was being given to its solution.

Jeremy Corbyn spoke at the launch, and he brought with him a number of his supporters. Mark Gardner reports that a number of Corbyn's supporters present at the launch did not know what the event was or even what it was about; they were just there to support their man. 'As the room had filled up before the launch began, Corbyn's supporters were handing out leaflets against "traitors"' (2016). Marc Wadsworth, a *Momentum* activist, was handing out these leaflets, and he accused Ruth Smeeth, a Jewish Labour MP who has been involved in working against antisemitism for many years, of working 'hand in hand' with the Tory newspaper *The Daily Telegraph*. This accusation connects Smeeth's work against antisemitism and her presence at an event ostensibly dedicated to opposing antisemitism, with the disloyalty of trying to help the Tories. The context is that raising the issue of antisemitism is assumed to be a bad-faith move aimed at hurting the left and helping the right.

Smeeth was visibly upset and left the event. At the end, Wadsworth is seen on video manoeuvring himself through the crowd in order to talk to Jeremy Corbyn; Corbyn chats with him and mentions that he had sent him a text. Wadsworth is heard saying to Corbyn: 'I outed Smeeth, bloody talking to the Torygraph!' Corbyn proceeds as though he has not heard (Corbyn 2016). Ruth Smeeth issued a statement in which she called on Corbyn to resign as leader of the party:

> This morning, at the launch of the Chakrabarti Inquiry into antisemitism, I was verbally attacked by a *Momentum* activist and Jeremy Corbyn supporter who used traditional antisemitic slurs to attack me for being part of a 'media conspiracy'. It is beyond belief that someone could come to the launch of a report on antisemitism in the Labour Party and espouse such vile conspiracy theories about Jewish people, which were ironically highlighted as such in Ms Chakrabarti's report, while the leader of my own party stood by and did absolutely nothing.
>
> *(Watson 2016)*

Later, on 21 September, Ruth Smeeth talked about the volume and the intensity of the antisemitic bullying which she had subsequently been forced to endure. Charlotte Edwards (2016), who interviewed her, writes:

> 'I don't want to be known as "the Jewish MP",' says Ruth Smeeth, East End accent still audible from a childhood in London. 'I am an MP who happens to be Jewish. One of the things that makes me most angry about this whole thing is that I've ended up as the Jewish MP. Worse: a victim and a target. I should be the MP for Stoke-on-Trent North, a hard-working, lifelong member of the Labour Party.' She describes herself as 'a Labour, socialist, Jewish, woman' in that order. 'Actually, British first: British, Labour, socialist, Jewish, woman.'

Smeeth describes precisely a common experience of contemporary UK Jews. Booker Prize-winning novelist Howard Jacobson is constructed as a *Jewish* writer, not simply a writer – or a *Zionist* writer, and therefore not an artist at all, but a liar for Israel. This external construction of the Jew as Jew resonates with me personally and with my experience. I am constructed not as a sociologist but as a Jewish sociologist or a Zionist sociologist. When I am a trade unionist, because I oppose antisemitism in my union, I become a *Jewish* trade unionist or a *Zionist* trade unionist. I have no objection to being recognized as a Jew or as a Zionist, although I have very rarely identified as either in my writing or my activism. But this misses the point. The identity which is thrust upon a person who opposes antisemitism is not analogous to a positive identity which a person comes to organically, which they feel and which they embrace. It is racism which constructs race; and it does so from outside and not in warm dialogue with its victim, not in an empowering way. And it is the *Livingstone Formulation*, which allows people to relate to Jews as though they were only acting as an agent for 'the Jews', which is the racist mechanism.

Edwards (2016) writes about Ruth Smeeth that she has, since the launch of the Chakrabarti report, been called a

> 'yid c★★★' (among other racial slurs), a 'CIA/ MI5/Mossad informant', a 'dyke', and a 'f★★★ing traitor'. In all she's experienced more than 25,000 incidents of abuse, much of it racial. As

a result two people are being investigated by counter-terrorism police – one of whom penned a 1,000-word essay on how he would kill her.

And if some racist had killed Ruth Smeeth, she would not have been the first woman MP that summer to have been murdered by a racist. Jo Cox was murdered on 16 June a week before the referendum on British exit from the European Union (Brexit).

Jeremy Corbyn spoke at the launch of the Chakrabarti report, and he re-stated his opposition to antisemitism in general terms and to all forms of racism. As if to illustrate his point, he said:

> Our Jewish friends are no more responsible for the actions of Israel or the Netanyahu government than our Muslim friends are for those of various self-styled Islamic states or organisations.
>
> *(Dearden 2016)*

It is clear enough that the point he was trying to make was that hostility should not be visited upon Jews or Muslims in Britain for the actions of those who claim to act in their name abroad. But it was also predictable that people would notice that implicit within this statement is an analogy between Israel and ISIS. One of the few clear innovations in the Chakrabarti report was the recommendation that Israel should not be compared with Nazis. In introducing the report, Corbyn himself compared Israel to ISIS, which is arguably the closest contemporary equivalent to the Nazis, not least in their genocidal antisemitism. We cannot know if Corbyn and his team failed to predict that this form of words would be heard in this way – or if they decided to make this inflammatory analogy, conceivably as a nod to those who felt threatened by his general condemnation of antisemitism, albeit in a way which could be denied as accidental.

What Shami Chakrabarti did not do in her report was explain how to recognize contemporary left-wing antisemitism. She did not describe it, how it operates, how it is sometimes hidden and what its key tropes are. The inquiry was her opportunity to do this in a way which could be easily understood because her inquiry was precipitated by a number of examples of left-wing antisemitism. She could have gone through them and explained why they were antisemitic.

The Chakrabarti report did some positive things, but it did not address the key problem that it needed to address, which was the rise of political antisemitism within the Labour Party and within wider left-wing and radical culture.

It ought to have been clear that a bad-apple theory would not do as an explanation for the antisemitism on the left. It was necessary to understand what the problem was with the barrel which allowed so many apples to turn bad. Chakrabarti needed to explain the relationship between a broad culture of emotional, disproportional and irrational hostility to Israel which was accepted as legitimate in much of left politics, and the specific examples of Jew-baiting by Labour people which were the catalyst for setting up this inquiry. The inquiry report does not touch on this key relationship.

Chakrabarti needed to consider the ways in which political antisemitism had been moving into the mainstream. Previous Labour leaders had rejected one-sided hostility to Israel, and they had opposed the boycott movement. They had embraced the consensus of the Jewish community and of democratic politics in favour of peace and a two-state solution and in rejection of the demonization of Israel and its associated antisemitism. The current leader was intentionally ambivalent on these questions. Alan Johnson (2016) set it out clearly in his BICOM (British Israel Communication and Research Centre) submission:

> Everything depends on the Labour Party understanding what it is dealing with: almost never old-fashioned Jew hatred, almost always modern antisemitic anti-Zionism – a programme to abolish Israel, a movement to boycott Israel and discourse to demonise Israel. To combat it, the party needs to understand the historical roots, ideological tributaries, contemporary modes and forms of expressions of antisemitic anti-Zionism.

But there is nothing about the current political leadership of the Labour Party in the report and in particular, not a word about the way it embraced and defended antisemitic movements, antisemitic individuals and antisemitic ways of thinking.

Jane Ashworth (2016), whose experience of opposing antisemitism on the left goes back to opposition to the banning of Jewish student societies in the 1980s, described the problem as follows in her submission to the Chakrabarti Inquiry:

> Existential anti-zionism has its own gurus . . ., its own language, its own codes, its own buzz words; and it mobilises anti-Jewish motifs and legends for use against Zionists. Existential anti-zionists are driven; they behave much like the entryists of the 80's: they go hunting; and since most UK Zionists are Jews and most Jews are Zionists, Jews are their targets. The existential anti-zionists hound Jews in ways which they themselves would call racist if any other minority were involved.

In his submission to the Chakrabarti Inquiry, Richard Gold (2016), a Jewish Labour member in Manchester and a key figure in the *Engage* network, explains why there is a widespread belief within the Jewish community that Jeremy Corbyn is a supporter of Hamas and that he has a record of allying with antisemites. Gold goes on:

> In order for this enquiry to have any effect it needs to press Corbyn on the above. Corbyn has shown no remorse, he has never apologised for supporting people who want to kill Jews (not just Israeli Jews). Corbyn is a role model for many of the new members and supporters of the Labour Party. His influence is massive and so far his reaction to the problem of antisemitism in the party has been very poor.

The Chakrabarti report did make clear that that the word 'Zio' should be understood as a racial epithet and should not be used, making it analogous to 'Paki'. The report also says that 'Zionist', when used as a form of abuse, is not acceptable.

It makes clear that Nazi analogies and talk about Hitler in relation to the Israel/Palestine conflict is 'incendiary', is 'intended to be incendiary', 'brings the party into disrepute' and 'undermines the cause of peace'.

This is another example of the 'guilty of a lesser charge' syndrome; it is all these things, but it is not antisemitic. To say it is antisemitic would be to say explicitly that Ken Livingstone had done something antisemitic. To say it is antisemitic would be to admit that there is at least one practice which happens often on the left which is antisemitic. This would require explanation. And Chakrabarti was not prepared to do that.

In Richard Gold's submission (2016), he had written:

> I've picked up a new theme which has emerged. It's used by people who probably recognise the problem but are reluctant to admit it. It's the 'I wouldn't put it like that myself but it's not antisemitic' excuse. As though being unpleasant to Jews (e.g. the behaviour of the Jew-baiter Ken Livingstone) should be excused or minimised, treated merely as rudeness or bad manners, rather than racist behaviour.

The Chakrabarti report modernizes disciplinary procedure within the party. But what Chakrabarti and her team did not do was discuss why these antisemitic incidents have been bubbling up to the surface, what it is about contemporary political culture on the left, and in the leadership of the party, which relates to these incidents and which makes them possible.

In BICOM's submission, Alan Johnson (2016) raised the question of what he called 'antisemitism denial and victim-reversal', and he explained the *Livingstone Formulation* as its key mode. There is nothing in the Chakrabarti report concerning accusations of bad faith and other counter-accusations made against people who are concerned about antisemitism.

The key conclusion of my own submission to Chakrabarti was that antisemitism is a political problem, not one which could be addressed administratively. I wrote:

> The party must be clear in its choice to embrace a politics of peace, reconciliation and engagement and to reject the politics of the demonization of Israel.
>
> The politics of peace forms a virtuous circle: it mutually reinforces democratic movements on all sides of the conflict; it takes

the wind out of the sails of those who seek to mobilize hatred, racism and war.

This inquiry can and should recommend practical actions to educate the membership on the issue of antisemitism and to clamp down on people who refuse to accept the boundaries of democratic and antiracist politics. But political change is key.

If the party leadership cannot move Labour back into the mainstream democratic consensus on Israel and on antisemitism then this issue will continue to throw up crisis after crisis and it will continue to alienate most of the Jewish community; no doubt it will alienate many swing voters too.

(Hirsh 2016b)

The Chakrabarti Inquiry did not address the key issues that it needed to address, although it did address some issues of process, some issues of education and some symptomatic issues.

* * *

David Cameron resigned as Prime Minister on 24 June. On leaving office, a Prime Minister has the power to bestow 'honours' on people of his choice, including seats in the House of Lords. The Leader of the Opposition, on such an occasion, also has the opportunity to 'elevate' individuals to the House of Lords.

Shami Chakrabarti published her report on 30 June. On 4 July, Jeremy Corbyn was called to give evidence about antisemitism in front of the Home Affairs Select Committee. Shami Chakrabarti came with him and sat at his right hand a little behind him; she passed him notes, and she prompted him. She appeared to be his friend and his advocate. Indeed, on two occasions she was explicitly admonished by Keith Vaz, the chair of the committee, for trying to help Corbyn answer questions.[4] For anybody watching, it was clear that Shami Chakrabarti was not neutral or disinterested between those denying antisemitism in the Labour Party, led by Jeremy Corbyn himself, and those saying that there was a problem of antisemitism in the Labour Party. Chakrabarti showed herself clearly to be on Team Corbyn on this issue, and she did what she could to help him bat away the questioning.

On 20 July, she was interviewed by Alan Mendoza. He asked her: 'If you were offered a place in the House of Lords, would you take it?' She looked up, she gestured, she sighed, she smiled, she shook her head and she said, as though she had never in her life considered it, 'I don't know.'

'Have you been offered a place?' asks Mendoza.

She blinks, she reaches for her glass of water, and she says, 'I don't know whether I want to talk about my future ambitions at this point'.

'But have you been offered a place in the House of Lords?' asks Mendoza.

She answers: 'You can ask the question, and I'm going to evade it at this point'.

(Author unknown 2016g)

The Resignation Honours List was published on 4 August, and Chakrabarti was indeed given a peerage by Jeremy Corbyn.

On 28 September, now *Baroness* Chakrabarti gave an interview to Andrew Neil. He asked:

'When was the prospect of a peerage first discussed with you? Not the offer just the prospect'.

'After the report.'

'There was no discussion at all beforehand?'

. . . 'This particular peerage was offered to me after the report as part of the Prime Minister's resignation list'.

(Neil 2016)

By September, Shami Chakrabarti had been appointed by Corbyn as Labour's shadow Attorney General and so was a member of his shadow cabinet.

Notes

1   Transcript made by author. See Hirsh (2016b).
2   The website of the Jewish Museum in Prague, and the exhibition titled 'Children's drawings from the Terezin ghetto 1942–1944' in particular, can

be found at: www.jewishmuseum.cz/en/explore/permanent-collection/children-s-drawings-from-the-terezin-ghetto-1942-1944/ (accessed 8 October 2016).
3 See an interview with Jackie Walker conducted on 30 September 2016 by Channel 4 news at: https://vimeo.com/184913442 (accessed 8 October 2016).
4 This account is based on the author's own observation.

4

THE CAMPAIGN FOR AN ACADEMIC BOYCOTT OF ISRAEL

In medieval times, Christian authorities were often keen to keep Jews isolated from Christians. For example, there were prohibitions against Christians entering synagogues, celebrating holidays with Jews and being a guest at Jewish banquets. There were threats against Christians of excommunication if they had dealings with Jews. There were attempts to make Jews wear distinguishing badges. There were prohibitions against Jews employing Christian wet-nurses, or women servants in general. Anthony Julius writes: 'these restrictions were standard – the medieval law books were full of them' (2010: 133). There is a long Jewish memory of being boycotted, shunned and excluded by Christian society. Many people involved in contemporary boycott campaigns against Israel are not aware of this context, or of its relevance. Yet, whether the boycotters can recognize it or not, this is part of the history and of the tradition of their own discourse and practice.

According to the *Livingstone Formulation*, the real aim of Zionists when they raise the issue of antisemitism is to close down free speech.[1] Currently, there is a campaign which calls itself 'Free Speech on Israel' against those who say there is a problem of antisemitism on the left.[2] Yet antisemites have been marshalling the rhetoric of free speech for a long time; indeed, it is standard for racists and bigots of all kinds to portray themselves as victims of campaigns to prevent them speaking. They begin by demanding that it should be possible at least to discuss their issues without being silenced; people do this if their issue is immigration, or if it is whether the Holocaust really happened, or the innate intelligence of black people or women. Of course, none of this rules out the existence of genuine victims of attempts at silencing who are neither racist nor bigoted. But it is important to see that merely claiming to be the victim of silencing is not self-validating, especially when there is a long tradition of such claims being made by antisemites, which predate the existence of Israel.

In 1904, there was a boycott of Jewish businesses in the city of Limerick in Ireland organized by a Catholic priest, the Rev. Father Creagh. The *Limerick Leader* defended his right to speak, in a piece entitled 'Hear all sides':

> In another column of our issue this evening we insert Mr. Davitt's letter to the *Freeman's Journal* on the subject of the Rev. Father Creagh's recent remarks on the Jewish community in Limerick. In giving the letter publicity we are not to be taken as adopting his views, our desire being merely to show all sides fair play.
>
> *(Keogh and McCarthy 2005)*

The *Limerick Leader* warns its readership that their opponents are in the habit of exaggerating any sniff of antisemitism in order to increase the campaign of vilification against the boycotters:

> It has come to our knowledge that the Jews for the past few days have been subjected to ill-treatment and assault while passing through our public thoroughfares. We regret that such has been the case. We are living in critical times when every advantage is taken by unscrupulous opponents to misinterpret our acts and the cause of our religion. In such a crisis it is not wise to give a handle to vilification. If the people do not want the Jews, then leave them severely alone. Above all things have no recourse to violence. Such a policy only shows weakness, if not foolish vindictiveness, and will never succeed in accomplishing that which is, or may be desired.
>
> *(Keogh and McCarthy 2005)*[3]

Father Creagh was also quite 'prepared to admit that there are many [Jews] who are irreproachable'. His boycott was only aimed at those Jews who 'grind and oppress those who are unfortunate enough to get into their power' (Reverend Father Creagh, 8 February 1904, *Northern Whig*, Belfast, quoted in Keogh and McCarthy 2005). There is nothing new about boycotters relying on the rhetoric of free speech; or portraying the Jews as exaggerating and manipulating antisemitism to vilify the boycotters; or specifying that the boycott is not against all Jews; or raising the possibility of a test for 'good Jews' who may be exempted from the boycott. Such things are part of the tradition of boycotting Jews.

The Limerick boycott was organized at the height of the campaign against Jewish immigration into Britain which culminated with the passing of the Aliens Act in 1905. The British Trade Union Congress supported this act, and many unions supported an exclusion of Jews from the unions. Some on the left at that time argued for boycotts of Jewish businesses as a stand against sweatshop labour and for trade union rates of pay (Cohen 2005). This was political sentiment which is familiar again in Brexit Britain and in Trump's America.

Also, and not accidentally, a boycott of Jewish businesses was one of the tools in Hitler's armoury during the early days of Nazi rule in Germany, and it was followed by a campaign to exclude Jews from the professions, the universities and then any public or cultural space, transport, entertainment, arts, film and theatre.

A few months after the final defeat of German Nazism, on 2 December 1945, the newly formed Arab League Council declared the beginning of the Arab boycott: 'Jewish products and manufactured goods shall be considered undesirable to the Arab countries.' All Arab 'institutions, organizations, merchants, commission agents and individuals' were called upon 'to refuse to deal in, distribute, or consume Zionist products or manufactured goods' (Bard 2007). From the mid-1950s, the Arab League boycott of Israel was supported by the Soviet Union, to which many on the left around the world still looked for inspiration or for leadership.

It was some time before a boycott of Israel came to gather support on the western left, and it did so largely in happy ignorance of the context I have just sketched. Instead, the Israel boycott campaign situated itself as the heir to the anti-apartheid movement for a boycott of South

Africa. In April 2002, Steven and Hilary Rose initiated the call for a moratorium on European research collaboration with Israel, and this may be understood as the start of the current campaign for the cultural and academic boycott of Israel. The question of who initiated this call for boycott, and how, has attained a certain political significance, and so it is important for our understanding of this phenomenon.

In the 1970s and 1980s, the African National Congress (ANC) called for a boycott of South Africa. It did so in the name of the oppressed. The ANC did not speak as itself, as one political movement in debate with others, proposing a strategy and offering good reasons and arguments about why the boycott should be adopted. Rather, it insisted that it was the sole authentic voice of the whole nation. It spoke not for itself but for South Africa. It did not begin by giving reasons; it began by asserting authority.

Campaigners for the boycott of South Africa around the world positioned themselves politically as passive responders to the 'call' of the oppressed. Already in the anti-apartheid movement, this prioritization for the politics of position over the politics of reason and discussion was an indicator of a problem. A notion of a living political interaction between anti-apartheid campaigners inside and outside of South Africa was replaced by a hierarchical relationship whereby those who spoke with the authority of the oppressed were to be followed uncritically, especially by those who were not oppressed. The official anti-apartheid campaign, therefore, with its special links to the ANC, dictated strategy and tactics to those who wanted to help; it was also in control of the boycott and, in particular, exemptions from the boycott. Links of solidarity between, for example, trade unions in Britain and those in South Africa could go only through the official channels of the anti-apartheid movement. Links between political tendencies which were critical of the official movement were at risk of being defined as boycott-breaking. When musician Paul Simon collaborated with black musicians in Soweto, he was denounced as breaking the boycott. When UK academics spoke to black colleagues and students in the Bantustans, they were similarly said to be breaking the boycott.

In truth, solidarity is always political; it is always a collaboration between those 'giving' and those 'receiving' solidarity, a two-way

learning process in which decision-making is to some extent collabo-
rative. Respect for the standpoints of people who are at the centre
of the struggle is important, as is a commitment to listen seriously to
what they know; but a blank cheque to those who claim to speak for
the oppressed, as though the oppressed have only a single voice, is a
different matter. People from outside who commit themselves to the
movement have, and ought to have, some influence too.

So the politics of a 'call' from the 'oppressed' being obeyed unques-
tioningly by those in the 'oppressor' nations always indicated a certain
form of 'campist' thinking. Even in the South African case, it sometimes functioned as a factional tool for those in control of what could
be constructed as the official campaigns (Fine and Davis 1991).

The analogy between the anti-apartheid movement in South Africa
and the antizionist movement in Israel and Palestine is highly mislead-
ing in a number of ways, which I will come to later in this chapter. But
at this point, let us note that the way the movement to boycott Israel is
portrayed as having originated in Palestine is not an accurate reflection
of its actual history. This is important politically because the boycott
campaign positions itself as a passive responder around the world to the
'call' from the oppressed. It tends to present the boycott as an obligation rather than as a proposal to be debated.

That Steven and Hilary Rose initiated the 'call' was stated in Steven
Rose's profile on *The Guardian*'s 'Comment is Free' website.[4] 'More
recently,' the profile continued, 'in response to the Palestinian call for
a boycott, they [the Roses] have been involved in the establishment of
the British Committee for the Universities of Palestine' (BRICUP).

Sue Blackwell, another key boycott activist in the Association of
University Teachers (AUT), explained how the change came about
from 'initiating' to 'responding' 'to the Palestinian call for a boycott'. In
2003 she had proposed a motion at AUT Council encouraging members to sever 'any academic links they may have with official Israeli
institutions, including universities' (Woodward 2003). AUT Council
had discussed the motion, and it was comfortably defeated. When the
boycotters came back to council in 2005, Sue Blackwell explained:
'We've got to be a bit more sophisticated. We are now better organised.
One of the reasons we didn't win last time was that there was no clear

public call from Palestinians for the boycott. Now we have that, in writing' (Curtis 2005).

In May 2002, Mona Baker, a scholar at the University of Manchester Institute of Science and Technology (UMIST), fired two Israeli academics – Miriam Shlesinger from the board of her journal *The Translator*, and Gideon Toury from the board of her journal *Translation Studies Abstracts* – citing their institutional connections to Israeli universities. Both have long and distinguished records as campaigners for human rights and for peace between Israel and Palestine. Mona Baker's 'personal statement' is available on her website together with links to the correspondence she had with the woman who had been her friend (Miriam Shlesinger) and her letter to Gideon Toury.[5] She writes:

> In May 2002, following the sharp rise in the level of atrocities committed against the Palestinian population in the West Bank and Gaza, I decided to join the call to boycott Israeli academic institutions. The boycott was conceived along the same lines as the sanctions which ultimately led to the collapse of the apartheid regime in South Africa. The call was initiated by Professor Steven Rose (Physics, Open University) and Professor Hilary Rose (Bradford University) . . . . I first wrote to Miriam Shlesinger (Bar-Ilan University, Israel) on 23 May explaining my decision and asking her to resign from the Editorial Board of *The Translator*. She refused. I also wrote to Gideon Toury (Tel Aviv University, Israel) on 8 June along the same lines, asking him to resign from the panel of Consulting Editors of *Translation Studies Abstracts*. He too refused. I removed them both from the boards of the respective journals.

On 25 May 2016, there was an event at the School of Oriental and African Studies (SOAS) in London at which Ilan Pappé confirmed that the 'call' for BDS did not come originally from Palestine. The discussion was chaired by Ruba Salih, a member of the faculty at SOAS, and it was recorded on video by a Zionist activist, David Collier. Ilan Pappé, in his broad Israeli accent, is critical of Palestinian disunity, and he makes what he says is a 'desperate call for the Palestinians to lead us' – if only, wishes the Israeli antizionist, the Palestinians would do what we want them to do. Ruba Salih interrupts him, saying, 'Well, the Palestinians launched the BDS in 2005.'

> 'Yes, yes,' replies Pappé. He makes a face which shows that he knows that what is being said is not true. 'Not really, but yes. OK. For historical records, yes'.
>
> Ruba Salih then smiles, puts her hand on his shoulder and makes clear: 'That's important'.
>
> Pappé replies to her, nodding and smiling, quietly, embarrassed, patronisingly, knowingly: 'It's not true but it's important'.
>
> *(Collier 2016)*

BDS was not initiated or invented in Palestine by 'the oppressed'. It was initiated and invented in the UK, by British people who wanted to boycott Israel. They went to Palestine between 2003 and 2005, and they persuaded certain Palestinian activists that BDS would be a good strategy. They explained that the best way to put this strategy into action would be to portray the campaign as having originated in Palestine and to say that it was the authentic call from the oppressed for solidarity. Later, the same activists participated in setting up the British Campaign for the Universities of Palestine[6] and the Palestinian Campaign for the Academic and Cultural Boycott of Israel (PACBI).[7]

In June 2003, Andrew Wilkie rejected the application of an Israeli PhD student to study under his supervision at Oxford University because he had served in the Israeli armed forces. Given that such service is requirement for all Israelis, this could only have been a boycott on the basis of nationality – with, perhaps, a possible exemption for the very small number of people who refuse military service (Henry 2003).

In April 2005, after a perfunctory and truncated debate, the Association of University Teachers council voted to boycott Bar-Ilan and Haifa Universities while 'referring back' a proposal to boycott the Hebrew University, Jerusalem. Bar-Ilan was targeted on the basis that it had links with Ariel College in the occupied West Bank.

The boycotters went to AUT Council with a story from Ilan Pappé that there were serious violations of academic freedom at Haifa

University. Pappé said that the master's dissertation of Teddy Katz had been failed because the university did not like its political content; this followed controversy over a particular alleged massacre from 1948; it followed a libel trial where some of the Israeli veterans had sued Katz for accusing them of perpetrating a massacre; it followed Katz's admission that there was no massacre following the surrender of the village and Katz's retraction of this admission. The key point is that the AUT Council had no way of coming to a judgment on these complex issues; but it acted as though it was more competent to judge Katz's thesis than the historians at Haifa University and the five external examiners, who were in fact split, three to two. The AUT Council voted to boycott Haifa University on the basis that it had violated the norms of academic freedom.

The council considered a proposal to boycott Hebrew University, Jerusalem, on the basis of a claim that the university was building a new dorm block on Palestinian land. In fact the ownership of the specific plot of land on which the dorm block was being built had been contested in the Israeli courts which had decided to allow the building to go ahead. The overwhelming majority of the AUT Council certainly knew nothing of the particular history of the Hebrew University. The Mount Scopus campus had been established in the 1920s on land bought from a British land owner on the east side of Jerusalem. Albert Einstein had given the first lecture there in 1923 on relativity, the first few sentences in Hebrew. In 1948 the campus was cut off from predominantly Jewish West Jerusalem by land mine and sniper attacks. On 13 April, a convoy tried to break the siege of Hadassah hospital on the campus and was attacked. Seventy-eight people were killed in that attack, including doctors, nurses, students, patients and Israeli Haganah fighters; in addition one British soldier was killed. After the ceasefire in 1949, the campus was in Jordanian hands but was granted a special demilitarized status. After 1967 it was re-captured by Israel. The AUT Council was simply told by the boycotters that the university was occupying Palestinian land, and they were told to boycott it in response. In fact, the council referred this proposal back to the Executive Committee so that it could gather more information, although it did vote to boycott both Bar-Ilan

University and Haifa University on the basis of no more information or understanding.

About a hundred, mainly Jewish, academics resigned from AUT in protest at that time (see, for example, Lappin 2005). A network and a website named *Engage* was set up by mainly union members, to oppose the boycott campaign.[8]

Jon Pike, a founder of *Engage* and a Philosophy lecturer at Open University, read the rule book of the union and found that the union could be forced to re-call council if a requisite number of members of council asked for it. He collected the signatures, and a 'Special Council' was held to re-examine the issue of the boycotts. A number of informal debates were held up and down the country in AUT local associations in preparation for this meeting.

On 26 May 2005, there was a five-hour debate at the Special Council meeting on the issue of boycotting Israel. This meeting was better attended than any routine council meeting, and it was better connected to the opinions of members by the preceding debates, which had often functioned as part of the process of electing and mandating delegates from the branches. Special Council decided to rescind the boycotts and to set up a Special Commission to work out a coherent policy. In April 2006, AUT's Special Commission, in part directly elected by union members, proposed a thought-through policy which related to international 'greylisting' and boycotts.[9] It was a policy that left open the possibility of boycotting universities but which set forward a consistent procedure to be followed. Crucially, a university, it recommended, can be boycotted only if the academic union at that institution explicitly calls for it. The AUT Council in 2006 adopted these recommendations as policy, but the policy fell shortly afterwards, when AUT merged with the National Association of Teachers in Further and Higher Education (NATFHE) to form the new University and College Union (UCU).[10]

In May 2006, Richard Seaford of Exeter University refused to review a book for an Israeli journal, saying: 'I have, along with many other British academics, signed the academic boycott of Israel, in the face of the brutal and illegal expansionism, and the slow-motion ethnic cleansing, being practised by your government' (Traubmann 2006).

The political test and the institutional boycott

At its last conference, three days before the merger with AUT to form UCU, NATFHE voted for a boycott motion at its conference:

> Conference notes continuing Israeli apartheid policies, including construction of the exclusion wall, and discriminatory educational practices. It recalls its motion of solidarity last year for the AUT resolution to exercise moral and professional responsibility.
>
> Conference instructs the NEC to facilitate meetings in each university and college, and to circulate information to Branches, offering to fund the speakers' travel costs.
>
> Conference invites members to consider their own responsibility for ensuring equity and non-discrimination in contacts with Israeli educational institutions or individuals and to consider the appropriateness of a boycott of those that do not publicly dissociate themselves from such policies.
>
> *(Pike 2006a)*

The leadership of AUT and NATFHE responded to public concern and anger, and in particular the possibility that to implement a boycott might be a violation of the law, by saying that this policy did not stand in the new union. In any case, the motion achieved one thing for the boycott campaign, which was to finance its spokespeople to travel the country making their case.

One difficulty for the boycott campaign has been how to respond to criticism that an academic boycott would exclude opponents of Israeli human rights abuses including Palestinians who work at Israeli universities. One way of solving this problem is to propose a political test which would lead to exemption from the boycott. The 2006 NATFHE motion offered such a test when it suggested that the union should boycott members who 'do not publicly dissociate themselves' from Israel's 'apartheid policies'. The problem with this method is that the boycott campaign would then lay itself open to criticism that it undermines academic freedom with a McCarthyite test. The boycott would be targeted against people who were not ready to sign up to the required beliefs in public, and under threat. Steve Cohen argued as follows:

> Loyalty tests have a particular significance when forced on Jews. The significance is the assumption of collective responsibility, of collective guilt. Intrinsic to this is the requirement to grovel. Groveling, the humiliation of Jews, is fundamental to all anti-semitism . . . .
>
> What was important [under McCarthyism] was naming names – the degradation ceremony. Likewise the deep antisem-itism behind the NATFHE resolution is not the boycott prin-ciple. It is the loyalty test on which it is based. It is the loyalty test more than anything else which exceptionalises Israel . . . . It may be that the loyalty test was clumsily added as a 'compromise' against a blanket boycott. So what? It doesn't make it any less anti-semitic in its consequences.
>
> *(Cohen 2006)*

The boycott campaign was always reluctant to say what kind of bureaucratic machinery it proposed to set up to oversee exceptions on political grounds. In the steadfast absence of such a proposal, it is rea-sonable to assume that the idea was that the decent people who were implementing the boycott would simply know who should be made an exception to the exclusion. It seems unlikely that a boycott with a political test, therefore, would have been implemented against non-Jews or against antizionist Jews. The boundary would surely have been drawn in a haphazard way, on a case-by-case basis at a local level, and frequently by people who did not even have the political sophistication of the official boycott campaign.

The political test has echoes of the prior designations by antise-mitic movements of the 'exceptional Jew'; the Jew who converted to Christianity or the Jew who gave evidence against other Jews could be exempted from the punishment that was planned for Jews in gen-eral. Nazism was an exceptional antisemitism in the sense that it did not allow for exceptional Jews, although the practice of many previ-ous antisemitisms was less lenient to the exceptional Jew than their own rhetoric stipulated. During the Spanish Inquisition, the *conversos*,

Jews who converted to Christianity, were nevertheless subjected to ongoing scrutiny, both official and unofficial; for example, it might be deemed suspicious if smoke did not appear from a *converso* chimney on Shabbat; for example, there were obstacles to *conversos* marrying others who were not also *conversos*. The Inquisition was supposed to be religious, not racist; but it was, even then, pioneering the racialization of the Jews.

The political test would have functioned as a net with which to catch Israeli 'Zionists', if we define the term 'Zionist' as referring to people who would decline to 'publicly dissociate' from 'Israeli apartheid practices', in the required form. It would have been based on the assumption that being a 'Zionist' and an Israeli is not compatible with being a decent, ethical academic. One logical extension which the NATFHE motion allowed, although perhaps only through sloppy drafting rather than through design, was the possibility of extending the campaign against 'Zionist' academics outside of Israel. If the principle is established that we don't do business with Israeli Zionists, then some may be tempted to extend the reach of the boycott to 'Zionists' in general, defined similarly as those who refuse to dissociate, in the required way. This prospect is less remote when we remember that there had been previous campaigns in the UK to 'no platform' 'Zionists' as racists from student unions and to ban Jewish societies (Rich 2016c).

An academic who comes originally from Poland and who now lives and works in the UK said that the rhetoric of the boycotters reminded him of events in Poland in March 1968, the year following the 1967 war. Under the cover of solidarity with Palestinians and using the rhetoric of antizionism, the Polish state had purged the Jewish intelligentsia. Jewish intellectuals were challenged to declare themselves antizionist. Many of them refused, and many left the country; Poland lost a large number of its thinkers, teachers, writers and researchers. For this individual at least, the current boycott proposals resonated strongly with echoes of older antisemitic campaigns.[11] The Polish purge of 1968 was a case of antisemitism passing itself off as hostility to Israel rather than hostility to Israel having unintended antisemitic resonances or outcomes. The Polish purge was mirrored by events in Communist East Germany at the same time (Herf 2016).

The myth of the institutional boycott

The political test tends to create more problems for the boycott campaign than it solves. One way around the problem is to sacrifice the 'exceptional Israelis' – exceptional Israelis being defined by the set of Israelis who will, anyway, be happy to make the sacrifice of being boycotted – and to argue for an 'institutional boycott'.

The political advantage of such a move is that it seems to depersonalize the issue, making it harder for opponents to characterize the boycott as a blacklist of Israeli Jews or Zionists, or as an exclusion of scholars from campuses, journals or conferences. It becomes a campaign against institutions and not against individuals. Israeli individuals, says the boycott campaign, will in principle continue to be welcome members of the academic community so long as they do not appear in the name of their institutions, are not funded by their institutions and do not attempt to host events at their institutions.

Jon Pike's rebuttal of this institutional turn makes two central points (2013). Firstly, it is rare for academic institutions to produce research outputs; papers are written by individuals, presentations are made by individuals and conferences are attended by individuals. So, he argues, the reality of an institutional boycott would still be an exclusion of individuals. Further, in an argument reminiscent of one against the political test, he asks how the distinction between institutions and individuals will actually be made in practice:

> [The] covert boycott (a 'quiet stand' according to BRICUP) is, of course, denuded of a political message. But also, there is no mechanism of accountability for their actions. They claim that there is a difference between an institutional boycott and an individual boycott, and I think that there's no difference. But we won't be able to know whether or not there is an operable distinction, because the operation is now conducted in secret. We won't be able to know whether people engage in Wilkie type actions (without the incriminating email). And I guess, the boycotters who think it's OK to adopt an 'institutional' rather than an 'individual' boycott simply think we should trust them on that one.
>
> *(Pike 2013)*

It is reasonable to assume that under the influence of the campaign for an 'institutional boycott', much boycotting of individuals goes on silently and privately. It is also reasonable to assume that Israeli scholars may come to fear submitting papers to journals or conferences if they think they may be boycotted, explicitly or not; this would lead to a 'self-boycott' effect. There are anecdotal examples of the kinds of things which are likely to happen under the surface even of an institutional boycott. An Israeli colleague contacted a British academic in 2008, saying that he was in town and would like to meet for a coffee to discuss common research interests. The Israeli was told that the British colleague would be happy to meet, but he would first have to disavow Israeli apartheid.[12]

The 'PACBI call' says that Israeli institutions are guilty, Israeli intellectuals are guilty, Israeli academics who explicitly represent their institutions should be boycotted, but an affiliation in itself is not grounds for boycott.[13] The danger is that Israelis would now be asked not to disavow Israel politically but to disavow their university 'institutionally', as a pre-condition for recognition as legitimate members of the academic community. Israelis may be told that they are welcome to submit an article to a journal or to attend a seminar or a conference as an individual. For example, 'David Hirsh' is acceptable; 'David Hirsh, Tel Aviv University', is not. Some Israelis will, as a matter of principle, refuse to appear only as an individual; others may be required by the institution which pays their salary, or by the institution which funds their research, not to disavow.

Academic institutions themselves, in Israel as anywhere else, are fundamentally communities of scholars; they protect scholars, they make it possible for scholars to research and to teach, and they defend the academic freedom of scholars. The premise of the 'institutional boycott' is that, in Israel, universities are bad but scholars are (possibly, exceptionally) good, that universities are organs of the state while individual scholars are employees who may be (possibly, exceptionally) not guilty of supporting Israeli 'apartheid' or some similar formulation.

There are two fundamental elements of the 'institutional boycott' rhetoric that are contested by opponents of the boycott. First, opponents argue that academic institutions are a necessary part of the structure of academic freedom. If there were no universities, scholars would band together and invent them in order to create a framework within which they could function as professional researchers and teachers, and within which they could collectively defend their academic freedom.

Second, opponents of the boycott argue that Israeli academic institutions are not materially different from academic institutions in other free countries: they are not segregated by race, religion or gender; they have relative autonomy from the state; they defend academic freedom and freedom of criticism, not least against government and political pressure. There are of course threats to academic freedom in Israel, as there are in the US and elsewhere, but the record of Israeli institutions is a good one in defending their scholars from political interference. Neve Gordon, for example, still has tenure at Ben-Gurion University, in spite of calling for a boycott of his own institution; Ilan Pappé left Haifa voluntarily after having been protected by his institution even after travelling the world denouncing his institution and Israel in general as genocidal, Nazi and worthy of boycott.

In 2011, the University of Johannesburg decided, under pressure from the boycott campaign, to cut the institutional links it had with Ben-Gurion University for the study of irrigation techniques in arid agriculture. Logically, the cutting of links should have meant the end of the research with the Israeli scholars being boycotted as explicit representatives of their university. What in fact happened was that the boycotters had their public political victory and then the two universities quietly renegotiated their links under the radar, with the knowledge of the boycott campaign, and the agricultural research continued. The boycott campaign was able then to portray this as an institutional boycott that did not harm scientific collaboration. The risks are that such pragmatism (and hypocrisy) will not always be the outcome and that the official position of 'cutting links' will actually be implemented; in any case, the University of Johannesburg solution encourages a rhetoric of stigmatization against Israeli academics, even if it quietly neglects to act upon it.

Another problem is that the targeting of Israelis by the 'institutional boycott', or the targeting of the ones who may be expected to refuse to disavow their institutional affiliations, is likely to impact disproportionately on Jews. The ostensibly institutional boycott has the potential to become, in its actual implementation, an exclusion of Jewish Israelis; this is true in spite of the aspiration to exempt those who are considered 'good Jews' – that is to say, antizionist Jewish Israelis. The result would be a policy which harms Israeli Jews more than anybody else. Further, Jews are likely to be disproportionately represented among scholars who break the institutional boycott or who insist on arguing against it. If there are consequences which follow these activities, which some boycotters will regard as 'scabbing' or 'blacklegging', the consequences will impact most heavily on Jewish academics. Under any accepted practice of equal opportunities impact assessment, the policy of 'institutional boycott' would cross the red lines which would normally constitute warnings of institutional racism.

The reality of the 'institutional boycott' is that somebody will be in charge of judging who should be boycotted and who should be exempt. Even the official positions of PACBI seem to be contradictory; they say there will be no boycott of individuals, but they nevertheless make claims which offer justification for a boycott of individuals.

Even if nobody intends this, it is foreseeable that in practice the effects of a boycott may include exclusions, opprobrium and stigma against Jewish Israeli academics who do not pass, or who refuse to submit to, one version or another of a test of their ideological purity; similar treatment may be visited upon those non-Israeli academics who insist on working with Israeli colleagues. Palestinians who work with Israelis are of course likely to be the first academics targeted. There is a clear risk that an 'institutional boycott', if actually implemented, would in fact function as a political test.

PACBI is the 'Palestinian Campaign for the Academic and Cultural Boycott of Israel'. What it hopes to achieve is stated in its name. It hopes to institute an academic and cultural boycott of Israel. The small print concerning the distinction between institutions and individuals is contradictory, unclear and . . . small. It is likely that some people will continue to understand the term 'academic boycott of Israel' in a common-sense way to mean a boycott of Israeli academics.

In April 2007, the boycotters took forward their campaign to boycott Israeli goods as well as Israeli academics. The conference of the

National Union of Journalists (NUJ) passed a motion that instructed its executive committee to

> continue to support the work of the Palestine Solidarity Campaign including the organisation of boycotts of Israeli goods, similar to those boycotts in the struggle against apartheid South Africa.
>
> *(Fraser 2007a)*

Following that decision by NUJ conference, many journalists and institutions protested at the decision, often calling for a ballot of members: for example, the editor of *The Guardian* (Hallé 2007); the Foreign Press Association;[14] *The Guardian* leader (2007); petitions of NUJ members at BBC News and ITN (Independent Television News); Jon Snow, news anchor at Channel 4 news (Press Gazette 2007); BBC London NUJ branch (Cellan Jones 2007); NUJ chapel at Reuters; NUJ Manchester branch. But what in the end took the wind out of the sails of this campaign to reverse the boycott decision in NUJ, however, was the decision made at UCU Congress in June.

The UCU Congress of 2007 was an important moment in the struggle for and against the campaign to boycott Israel. It was the first conference of the newly merged academic union, and it was the first conference since the boycott campaign's defeat at the AUT Special Council of 2005. While many people who opposed the boycott campaign had resigned from the union, there were still at that time many people within the decision-making structures of the new union who maintained their opposition to the boycott campaign. The academic union was significant because there is a notion in the public imagination that this union speaks for the clever people, the intellectuals and the experts.

This Congress in the end voted to support the boycott campaign. It instructed the National Executive to:

- circulate the full text of the Palestinian boycott call to all branches/ LAs [Local Associations] for information and discussion
- encourage members to consider the moral implications of existing and proposed links with Israeli academic institutions

- organize a UK-wide campus tour for Palestinian academic/educational trade unionists
- issue guidance to members on appropriate forms of action.

High-profile Jewish *supporters* of the boycott campaign played an important role in the UCU. Their repeated assurances that antisemitism was not a relevant issue helped to neutralize antisemitism as a factor in the debate. From the *Independent Jewish Voices* initiative in February, to the BRICUP meeting at the UCU fringe at Bournemouth, to the debate itself at UCU Congress, respectable and senior Jewish academics, intellectuals and political activists repeated, when considering the plan to boycott Israeli academia – and only Israeli academia – that antisemitism was relevant only insofar as it was a spurious charge that 'Zionists' or the 'pro-Israel lobby' would throw at 'critics of Israel'. When well-respected and high-profile antiracist Jews reassure the British intelligentsia that there is no threat of antisemitism, they mobilize significant influence.

Many of the people who protested against the claim that the boycott was antisemitic were not themselves supporters of the boycott; but their role in legitimizing the debate was important. The role these anti-boycotters played in helping to win the UCU to support the boycott campaign was not to make the argument for a boycott; it was to help to neutralize the issue of antisemitism.

In UNISON, at the time the biggest union in the UK, the hunt to root out 'Zionism' began even before the vote to support the boycott campaign. Labourstart is an international trade union network and website which carries news and publishes calls for trade union solidarity and reports on activity. UNISON had asked Eric Lee, the editor of Labourstart, what it could do to help, so Lee asked for a donation. The international affairs committee agreed, and the decision to ratify this went to the national executive. A member of the executive posed three questions to Eric Lee: was it true that he was a Zionist? Did Labourstart censor Palestinian news? Had Lee supported the Israeli invasion of Lebanon the previous year? Eric Lee responded that it was no secret that he was a left-wing Zionist, as are many Israelis. Labourstart has links to Palestinian sites, he explained, and they take many of our news items; and Lee took the same view of Lebanon as did Tony Blair and the Labour government, he said. UNISON decided that making a donation would be too controversial (Martin 2007).

UNISON decided to make its support for the boycott campaign clear on 20 June 2007: 'Conference believes that ending the occupation demands concerted and sustained pressure upon Israel including an economic, cultural, academic and sporting boycott' (Fraser 2007b). At this time, some of those activists who had already been making the same speeches about Israel for thirty years – that Zionism was racism, that the Zionists collaborated with the Nazis, that Israel must be dismantled – suddenly found themselves being given huge standing ovations at union Conferences for speeches in favour of boycotting Israel. The process of the mainstreaming of antizionism was under way. The Transport and General Workers section of Unite also passed policy supporting the boycott campaign in July 2007.

These union conferences in the summer of 2007 may be regarded as a turning point, marking the mainstreaming and the legitimization of the boycott campaign in the UK Labour movement – in any case amongst the specific layer of activists which is delegated to attend these conferences. Things moved further away from those opposing the campaign at the end of 2008 with the outbreak of war between Israel and the Hamas regime in Gaza. The war was widely portrayed by people on the broad left of the political spectrum to be unnecessary, a war of choice by the Netanyahu government and a war of collective punishment against the civilians of Gaza. It was frequently referred to not as a war but as a 'massacre'.

By the summer of 2009, the debate was over in UCU. Mike Cushman is one of the key pro-boycott activists in the union. He reported rather breathlessly on a public email list, 'in haste from Bournemouth':

> It was brilliant. The Zionists bareley [*sic*] showed up. John Pike was totally isolated. On the first vote about invetigsting [*sic*] institutional anti-semitism in UCU he got about 6 votes out of 350.
>
> On the key motion there were only two speakers against Pike and a woman from Workers Liberty, when the president asked for other speakers against no-one put their hand up. The vote was on my estimate about 300–30 (we should have asked for a count to rub salt into the wound).

> What we must remember this was a victory built not just on hard work but even more on 1400 murders in Gaza.
>
> *(Cushman 2009)*

At the 2007 UCU Congress, the debate in and around the Congress hall itself was big, tense and hotly contested. At that time, Cushman himself proposed the motion by declaring that he was 'not going to be intimidated', and he received a huge cheer for it from delegates. What he meant, and what Congress understood, was that he was not going to be intimidated by *Zionist power*. Congress followed his lead and voted for a boycott, many delegates showing clear signs that they were collectively excited at the feeling that they were *standing up to the Zionists*. A number of witnesses who later gave evidence at the Fraser trial experienced the mood of the delegates at the 2007 Congress as a Jew-baiting mood; and it voted for a boycott motion. Those who stood up and mentioned antisemitism that day were shouted down.

At that time the boycott campaign in UCU had established an equilibrium with the union leadership. The leadership allowed them their fun with the 'Zionists' at Congress, but, in exchange, the boycott campaign understood that the union would not actually do anything at all to implement any boycott. This was all about Congress, not about Israel or Palestine; it was all about discourse in the UK, and little about actually instituting a boycott.

Two years later, however, the atmosphere was different. There was not much cheering, and there was not much howling. The reason for this was that there were no Jews left to bait. As Michael Cushman says above, 'the Zionists barely showed up.'

The chair of the Open University Branch showed up to make a case for debating whether to have a ballot of the union membership on the question of boycott. Congress, aware that the boycott campaign would have probably been defeated in a membership ballot, voted against the proposal. This may have been a tactical error by the boycott campaign. While it might well have been defeated in a membership ballot, the prize of opening up a debate amongst the 120,000 members of the union should have been a tempting one. The debate would certainly have spilled over into the media and into mainstream political and intellectual life. But the union activists preferred to win the vote at

Congress instead of taking the opportunity of opening up and legitimizing the debate in that way.

Jon Pike showed up to argue that Congress should ask the union leadership to find out why Jews are resigning from the union. Congress voted not to mandate the union to find out why Jews were resigning from the union.

Camila Bassi showed up, 'the woman from Workers' Liberty'. She was a member of the small Trotskyist group which for years in the student movement and within the far left had fought the battle against the rise of what it called 'left-antisemitism'. She made a Trotskyist speech against the boycott, critiquing it from the left: she argued for working-class unity between Israel and Palestine rather than national flag waving; she argued for solidarity rather than boycott; she argued for political engagement rather than dis-engagement; she argued for linking up with the Israeli peace movement and unions rather than boycotting them. Congress voted her down.

There were speeches against the boycott available for anyone who wanted them. But there was nobody left to make them. There were no Jews there to speak against the boycott. That was what Cushman meant when he said that '[t]he Zionists barely showed up'. True, there were a number of Jews at Congress 2009: some of them kept quiet; some of them supported the boycott.

The relatively right-wing faction of union activists, the 'reasonablists', the people who had always said they were against the boycott, remained silent, except for a procedural question from Mary Davis. Perhaps some of them had gone soft on the boycott in the aftermath of the Gaza war. Perhaps some of them were frightened of being made into pariahs in the union if they stood up against antisemitism. Not one of them spoke. Not one of them insisted on making their argument, even knowing that it was a losing argument.

In a union of 120,000 members made up of academics, teachers, librarians, technicians, and university and college support staff, one can be certain that there were a number of Jewish members. All of the survey data shows that a large proportion of Jews in the UK feel, in some sense or other, that a relationship to Israel is an important element of their identity as Jews (Graham and Boyd 2010). The fact that none of them are willing or able to speak against the boycott within the decision-making structures of the UCU is at least *prima facie* evidence of a problem of institutional antisemitism within the union.

By 2016 nothing had materially changed at UCU Congress. One observer at that Congress, Sarah Brown, recently elected onto UCU Executive, spoke against the boycott motion. Her speech was greeted with stony silence. The motion was passed overwhelmingly, with about fifteen quiet votes against.

Yet, still, it is all talk. UCU does not organize a boycott; it does not police its members' links with their Israeli colleagues; it has no machinery to exempt Israelis from boycott; it fears a political and perhaps a legal backlash.

Academic freedom

The standard liberal democratic argument against a boycott of Israeli academia is based on the principle that such a boycott would violate the norms of academic freedom. Blakemore *et al* (2003) published a general articulation of this argument against scientific boycotts in *Nature*,[15] arguing that such a boycott would be illegitimate except for in the most extreme cases. Michael Yudkin, one of the authors of the *Nature* article, updated the argument in 2007, broadening it out to cover academic boycott in general rather than just scientific, and also focusing it on the question of Israel in particular. He argues:

> The principle of the Universality of Science and Learning – that academics do not discriminate against colleagues on the basis of factors that are irrelevant to their academic work (such as race, religion, nationality etc.) – is well established and almost universally respected. To boycott academics by reason of their country of residence breaches this principle and harms the interests of the academics concerned.
>
> *(Yudkin 2007)*

In this article, Yudkin goes beyond a straightforward defence of academic freedom to challenge a number of the arguments put forward by those who support an academic boycott of Israel.

Howard Jacobson (2007) tells us that a supporter of the boycott campaign wrote to him denying that they threatened the academic freedom of Israelis. He was in favour not of gagging or silencing Israeli voices, wrote this activist, but merely of refusing to listen to them. Jacobson (2007) argues that refusing to listen, closing your ears, is not primarily an act of violence against the speaker but is in the first place an act of violence against oneself:

> To say you intend knowingly and purposefully and on principle 'not to listen' is to say you are waging a sort of war on your own faculties, because listening, if you are a reasoning person, is chief among the tools you reason with . . . . Most of what Socrates did was listen. No longer to listen is no longer to engage in the dialogue of thought. Which disqualifies you as a scholar and a teacher, for what sort of example to his pupils is a teacher who covers truth's ears and buries it under stone. A university that will not listen does far more intellectual damage to itself than to the university it has stopped listening to.

Anthony Julius and Alan Dershowitz (2007) make the same point in a different way:

> freedom of expression must incorporate freedom of address. It is not sufficient for my freedom of expression for me simply to be free to speak. What matters to me is that people should also be free to hear me. There should at least be the possibility of dialogue. Boycotts put a barrier in front of the speaker. He can speak but he is prevented from communicating. When he addresses another, that other turns away.

The point here is that the harm of the academic boycott begins at home. The boycott intends to harm Israeli universities, and it may or may not, in the end, succeed in this aspiration. But it definitely and immediately harms the universities doing the boycotting or the universities in which the campaign for the exclusion of academic colleagues rages. In normalizing the claim that Israeli universities are not genuine universities and should be shunned, British universities face the danger that their own status as universities will be degraded.

When asked why Israeli academics are singled out for punishment while academics in other human rights abusing states are not, many boycotters respond that they would also support boycotts against the other states if somebody was to organize them and if the oppressed in those states were to call for it. It is true that if there were boycotts of academics in all states which abuse human rights as much as, or more than, Israel, then the academic boycott would no longer be effectively antisemitic. It would, however, indicate the end of the academic project and the end of the university. The aspiration to international scholarly and scientific co-operation would be rendered vain – indeed international co-operation of any kind.

Judith Butler argues that a liberal abstract notion of academic freedom is not sufficient to make sense of the boycott debate. While Palestinian academics and students may enjoy an abstract right to academic freedom, the material conditions necessary for the enjoyment of those rights do not exist under occupation, she argues:

> students and faculty at institutions on the West Bank are regularly stopped at checkpoints and fail to get to class; they are often without fundamental material support for schooling, even lacking classrooms and basic supplies, and are subject to sudden closures that make the idea of a completed 'semester' almost unthinkable. Indeed, substantive notions of freedom of 'movement' and freedom of 'communication' are systematically undermined under such conditions.

(Butler 2006)

At that time, Butler opposed the boycott. She valued the principle of academic freedom and sought to extend it to people whose material conditions made it difficult for that freedom to be actualized. She wanted to extend academic freedom to those under occupation rather than to deny academic freedom to Israelis. The denial of academic freedom to Israelis would not help the campaign to extend academic freedom to Palestinians.

Many who argue for an academic boycott of Israel say that it is hypocritical for Israelis to insist on their own right to academic freedom while their state denies such freedom to Palestinians. Or as Steven Rose put it in a debate at Goldsmiths UCU branch on 27 September 2006, Israelis are hypocritical to 'squeal' about their own academic freedom while the occupation continues to deny freedom to Palestinians. It should be noted here that this way of thinking risks setting the precedent that academics should be held responsible, and punished, for the policies of the government or state in which they work. Yet Butler is right to argue that academic freedom is severely limited in the occupied territories, not by a denial of the abstract right, but by the material actualities of occupation, which renders academic freedom materially difficult to realize. This is true even if it is one-sided, since the universities of Palestine were also *founded* under Israeli occupation and did not exist *before* the Israeli occupation. There *is* a problem of academic freedom in Palestine. It is possible to respond to this by arbitrarily and artificially removing the academic freedom of Israelis, as punishment, in order to balance the situation, or in an effort to exert pressure on Israel to respect Palestinian freedom. Or it is possible to respond to this by campaigning against the occupation and against the material denials of academic freedom which come with it. Butler (2006) did not argue that abstract academic freedom may be trumped by other more important rights, but the opposite:

> I do not mean to say that we cannot invoke academic freedom in the abstract to show its absence in certain political conditions: we can and we must. But it makes no sense to value the doctrine in the abstract if we cannot call for its implementation.

Butler was not arguing that one should balance an absence of material freedom in Palestine by regarding academic freedom in Israel to be unimportant; she argued that the principle of abstract freedom must be strengthened and deepened, made material by creating the conditions for its implementation.

By 2013, Judith Butler had reversed her opposition to the BDS movement, but without ever really addressing her own previous strong arguments against it (Butler 2013).Yet she supports the boycott in a way that falls a little short of being explicit. Perhaps she feels that this kind of indirect language makes her appear more scholarly. Does she feel that appearing to stand above the fray lends her gravitas? Butler now defends every aspect of the BDS case, and she attacks a number of critics of BDS, while maintaining a rhetorical distance. Cary Nelson '[sets] aside the somewhat artificial humility front-loaded into her influential 2013 talk at Brooklyn College ("I am not even a leader of this movement") as a technical distinction'. Nelson (2014) goes on drolly:

> she's an independent advocate, not a member of the BDS governing committee. But an intellectual leader in the broader sense she surely is. Her studied denial of virtually any persuasive intent ('I am not asking anyone to join a movement this evening') I count as merely performative.

In December 2013, the council of the American Studies Association voted to support the boycott campaign. It also decided to open up the debate about whether scholars who are associated with Israeli academic institutions should be excluded from US campuses, by proposing a ballot of its membership on the question. Claire Potter, a Professor of History at The New School in New York, who blogs under the name 'tenured radical', made a standard democratic argument against the boycott:

> Scholars of any nation ought to be free to travel, publish and collaborate across borders: I consider this to be a fundamental human right, and so does the United Nations. We in the American Studies Association cannot defend some of those human rights and disregard others.

(Goldberg 2013)

This quote comes from Michelle Goldberg's piece in *The Nation*, 6 December 2013. The next day, Goldberg added an update to the online article:

> After I posted this piece, I learned that Claire Potter had changed her position on the ASA resolution and voted yes. Reached by

phone, she explained how the shift in her thinking came out. When she first expressed qualms about the academic boycott, she says, 'The response was overwhelming. There were massive numbers of people, including a lot of people I know, just writing these nasty things on my blog about what a horrible person I was.'

As the debate about BDS and academic freedom has moved forward, she looked for a way to engage in it constructively, but increasingly felt like she couldn't do so from outside. 'The problem, when you hold to a position so rigidly, you yourself become part of the polarization,' she says. 'I all of the sudden became a cause célèbre for all kinds of other people, when that is really not what I intended at all. I would like to have a conversation about academic freedom within this strategy.'

(Goldberg 2013)

Potter could not have been clearer about the true nature of her decision-making on this question. She was concerned, above all, to remain inside the community of the good. I wrote an open letter to her:

when you made clear your opposition to academic BDS, perhaps you were surprised and shocked to find yourself outside of the sphere of respect and consensus; you were treated as though you were outside of the universe of radical, counter-hegemonic and committed activism. A natural first instinct would be to step back inside the tent where you belonged. If good people, people you usually agree with, your friends and comrades, thought you had taken a position which is only held by 'horrible people', then perhaps you'd made a mistake.

It is uncomfortable to find yourself on the wrong side of a binary opposition between the radical campaign to 'do something' about Israeli human rights abuses on the one hand, and the angry, apparently conservative, often 'Zionist' opponents on the other. You say you wanted to find a middle ground, you wanted to find consensus. You had suddenly become a symbolic figure in other people's polemics and you wanted to reclaim your own actual voice. I suspect you wanted to remain on the radical,

> pro-Palestinian side, but also to think through the obvious prob-
> lems which are associated with boycotting Israel.
>
> *(Hirsh 2013b)*

In response, Potter confessed that she had only that February first heard of the BDS campaign and that her thinking was developing. Her change of mind to support the boycott campaign 'required bringing my views about academic freedom', she said, 'into alignment with anti-colonial and anti-imperial views that I have developed over a lifetime' (Potter 2013).

Potter's sudden about turn illustrates two points made in this book. First, that 'tenured radicals' of a certain type understand there to be a conflict between the principles of freedom and human rights, on the one hand, and the principle of anti-imperialism, on the other; and where there is conflict, anti-imperialism wins. Second, that 'tenured radicals' of this type take seriously their membership of the community of the good; they are sensitive to indications that they may have, by mistake, stepped over a boundary.

An old theme in radical and Marxist thought concerns how abstract rights are conceived and weighted within a system in which the concrete actualization of those rights are inconsistent. This issue may be thought of as marking the division between totalitarian politics and the politics of self-liberation. The totalitarian traditions fight for uncompromising critiques of abstract rights; they hold law, democracy, freedom of speech and human rights to be worse than useless to those disempowered by capitalism. Formal equality is, in these traditions, little more than the mechanism by which structures of power operate. It hides exploitation behind an ideology of fairness. In this tradition, men dominate women through the notion of abstract equality; the bourgeoisie exploits the poor through the equal contract; imperialist states legitimize their wars of interest with a cry of human equality.

Marx himself was explicit in his own rejection of this vulgar Marxism. In *On the Jewish Question*, he defended bourgeois rights, in this case the right to religious freedom for Jews, uncompromisingly against an argument which offered an ostensibly more radical critique of society (Marx 1994). Against Bruno Bauer, who argued that Jews did not need religious freedom but really needed to free themselves of their own religion, Marx argued for a framework which takes rights seriously; he goes on to critique their purely abstract nature in society as it exists. Rather than seeing rights as something unimportant or even danger-ous, Marx's position was that radicals should fight for rights and should fight to extend them beyond the purely abstract. His was a project of making rights real for all, not one of scoffing at those who 'squeal' about their rights.[16]

The boycott campaign sees academic freedom as being something which may be legitimately sacrificed for the greater good of ending the occupation or of defeating Zionism; academic freedom, they argue, is part of the ideological armoury brought to bear against those who fight the occupation. The opposite argument, however, is more per-suasive. The concept of academic freedom is important in itself, but it does not go far enough; a material conception of academic freedom is necessary to go beyond the critique of the boycott all the way to a fight for freedom for the Palestinians. Academic freedom is not a principle which we should reject because sometimes it fails to deliver what it promises; rather, we should fight to hold it to its promises.

When the boycott campaign raises the issue of academic freedom in Palestine, it only considers impediments created by Israel; it never considers impediments to academic freedom in Palestine caused by Palestinian movements or authorities. In particular it does not con-sider the breaches of academic freedom which result from the 'anti-normalization' campaign. This campaign threatens Palestinian academ-ics who have, or who want to make, links with Israeli colleagues for their jobs and for their physical safety. Nor does the boycott campaign ever consider the constraints of trying to organize a university under Hamas rule. Cary Nelson (2016) surveys the situation of academic freedom in Palestine, concluding:

> the most serious threats to academic freedom in Gaza and the West Bank come from Palestinian society itself. The BDS move-ment in the United States has focused its moral outrage on such matters as foreign faculty members being denied entry to teach in the West Bank, though most often they simply face delayed entry by Israeli authorities. Actual denials can easily be appealed to Israeli courts. Are not Palestinian attempts to kill Mohammed

Dajani and Abdul Sattar Qassem for their politically incorrect speech more serious? Do not the gangs of student enforcers trained by Hamas to intimidate, harass, and assault dissident faculty members represent a greater threat to academic freedom than any IDF practices? There is little hope for dialogue with those unwilling to answer these questions in the affirmative.

An attempt was made on Dajani's life after he had taken his students from Al-Quds University to Auschwitz as part of a Holocaust education programme; he was driven into exile for this act of collaboration.

Apartheid in Israel?

PACBI's 'call' for BDS begins with the claim that 'Israel's colonial oppression of the Palestinian people, which is based on Zionist ideology, comprises', among other things, '[t]he entrenched system of racial discrimination and segregation against the Palestinian citizens of Israel, which resembles the defunct apartheid system in South Africa' (PACBI 2006).

The case for boycotting Israel is frequently made in this very simple form. It is pointed out that there are different legal systems for Israelis who live in settlements in the West Bank and for Palestinians who live next door to them. Israelis are free to come and go, while Arabs are much more restricted by the infrastructure of occupation, in particular the wall and the checkpoints.

But the apartheid claim is rarely restricted to the Occupied Territories; it is usually also claimed that Israel itself, by proclaiming itself to be a Jewish state, is apartheid in its very essence. The case is generally made by listing examples of institutional, governmental or legal discrimination against Arabs in Israel; it is also made by listing examples of human rights abuses in Israel. And Israel is declared to be apartheid, and boycott is declared to be the appropriate response, and Israel is presented as being exceptional. It is never portrayed as one ethnic state amongst many ethnic states in the Middle East and beyond; that is not the function of the apartheid allegation.

We are invited by the boycotters to re-remember the narrative of how we all participated together in the boycott of South Africa and how the boycott was instrumental in ending apartheid. Other factors in the downfall of apartheid are implicitly downplayed: for example, the courage and the wisdom of those many South African people who struggled for democracy in what was a magnificent feat of self-liberation; the end of the Cold War; the stagnation of the apartheid economy for internal structural reasons.

The Israel-apartheid analogy expresses moral outrage. The analogy is also a shortcut to the political conclusion that Israel should be boycotted. Analogy and comparative study can help us to understand the world, but these aids to thinking and communication always have limits.

There may be countless analogies which can throw light onto the situation of Israel, the Israeli–Palestinian conflict and antisemitism in the Middle East. Zionism could be compared to the Black Consciousness movement or the feminist movement; Jihadi Islamism could be compared to Nazism or to Stalinism; the Israel/Palestine conflict could be compared to the conflict between the Tamils and the Sinhalese; or Bosnia, Croatia and Serbia; or the partition between India and Pakistan.

But when the political claim that Israel is like South Africa is asserted in such a way that it requires recognition by all good people, something else is happening. Then, it does not shed light, but rather it narrows the view; it is not done to offer a new angle, but it legislates the only legitimate angle.

On 3 July 2012, an Israeli academic sat down at the South African Sociological Association (SASA) Conference to give a paper on the 2011 social protest movement in Israel. He was part of a panel with other scholars giving papers about social protest movements in other places. Some minutes after the panel had been due to begin, Peter Alexander, a Professor of Sociology at the University of Johannesburg, took the floor and said: 'Who is the Israeli fellow?' The 'Israeli fellow' made himself known. Alexander, a long-time member of the Socialist Workers Party in the UK, told him that it was being made a pre-condition to his participation in the panel that he 'denounce Israeli apartheid and the treatment of the Palestinians'. The 'Israeli fellow' declined to do so. Members of the audience 'became vocal and abusive'. A board member of the South African Sociological Association was brought in to resolve the situation. His solution was that the 'Israeli fellow' should not be stopped from giving his paper, but that if the scholars present chose to leave the room and hear the other papers which were due to be given in this panel elsewhere, then that would be appropriate. That was what happened. They respected the Israeli sociologist's rights by leaving him to give a paper to an empty room while they re-constituted the panel elsewhere.[17]

After sober reflection and deliberation, the Council of the South African Sociological Association stood by its actions. Its President wrote a formal letter to the SA Jewish Board of Deputies in which he was first keen to state that 'SASA is in no way anti-Semitic and is not supporting any anti-Semitic viewpoints or sentiments'. He goes on to say that the Israeli professor

> was not prevented from presenting his paper . . . in accord with the right to free expression and speech. Had [he] not been allowed to present or prevented from presenting his paper, this would have amounted to a violation of his right to free expression of speech. By the same token, those who chose to vacate the venue and not share a platform with [him], did so in exercise of their respective right of freedom of choice and speech. Preventing them from doing so, would also have amounted to a violation of their rights in this respect. The Council is thus of the view that both parties exercised their respective rights without any hindrances.[18]

It would seem that there is no limit to the ability of some sociologists to forget the key methods and the insights of their own discipline when it comes to thinking critically about themselves, their behaviour, their norms and their explicit and their unspoken rules. Sociology, born to think about the *meaning* of social action (Weber 1978b), here contents itself with mere appearances. The meaning of the action was to leave the Israeli scholar with nobody to talk to, to boycott him and to silence him; to describe this social action in the way that SASA does is to pretend its meaning is something quite different.

The point, though, is that the apartheid analogy does not aid understanding; it lends itself rather well to becoming an inquisitorial instrument employed to illuminate the presence of evil Zionism in order that it might be separated from the community of the good.

Ronnie Kasrils, a Jewish veteran of the anti-apartheid struggle in South Africa and a leader of the South African Communist Party, wrote an opinion piece in the South African *Mail & Guardian* in 2007 in which he states that Israel is 'infinitely worse than apartheid' (2007). John Dugard, former UN special rapporteur on human rights in the Palestinian territories, employed precisely the same formulation:

> And I might add that I'm a South African who lived through apartheid. I have no hesitation in saying that Israel's crimes are infinitely worse than those committed by the apartheid regime of South Africa.
>
> *(Democracy Now! 2015)*

Desmond Tutu, another man who speaks with the battle-hardened authority of a leader of the anti-apartheid struggle in South Africa, said in March 2014: 'I associate myself with the objectives of the 10th International Israeli Apartheid Week' (Wilkins 2014). It should be noted, however, that in 2011 Tutu also characterized Jacob Zuma's government in South Africa as 'worse than apartheid' when, because of its friendship with the Chinese government, it refused to grant a visa to the Dalai Lama to visit South Africa (Lowman 2016). Desmond Tutu, a man for whom politics is fundamentally a question of morality, applies the apartheid epithet to make clear his moral indignation; and this is a pointer to what is at stake in the struggles over whether Israel is or is not an apartheid state.

Benjamin Pogrund is another veteran of the anti-apartheid struggle and now also an Israeli. He was a well-known journalist for the *Rand Daily Mail*, who reported on the lives of black people and on the sufferings apartheid caused them. He was imprisoned and 'banned' for a period of time by the apartheid regime (Fine 2014). Pogrund agrees that there are few charges graver than 'apartheid', but he disagrees with Tutu and the others about Israel's designation as such. He argues that 'there is no comparison between Israel and apartheid'. He writes:

> The Arabs of Israel are full citizens. Crucially, they have the vote and Israeli Arab MPs sit in parliament. An Arab judge sits on the country's highest court; an Arab is chief surgeon at a leading

hospital; an Arab commands a brigade of the Israeli army; others head university departments. Arab and Jewish babies are born in the same delivery rooms, attended by the same doctors and nurses, and mothers recover in adjoining beds. Jews and Arabs travel on the same trains, taxis and − yes − buses. Universities, theatres, cinemas, beaches and restaurants are open to all.

(Pogrund 2015)

In his review of Pogrund's book, Fine (2014) explains the issue as follows:

Israel is not called by its own name or understood in its own right but rather through the name of something seemingly associated in meaning with it. This rhetorical device has in turn been converted through processes of slippage into the metaphoric use of 'apartheid' in order to designate the core being of Israel . . . .

The missing term in these ideologically charged slippages − to use Ernesto Laclau's language; from contingency to essence, from contiguity to analogy, from metonymy to metaphor, from distinction to equivalence − is that of comparison. To simply say that the 'Jewish state' is like apartheid, or is apartheid, is no substitute for nuanced analysis that studies similarities and differences between the one and the other.

As John Strawson (2005) − a legal scholar who has been involved in political, scholarly and practical solidarity with the Palestinians for decades − points out:

The whole argument about South Africa in the apartheid years was that it was quite exceptional. The racial classification board declared your race at birth, which would decide where you would live, what school you would attend, what job you could have, what wages you would earn, whether you could vote and what papers you carried. This does not happen in Israel.

The apartheid analogy as used by the boycott campaign exceptionalizes Israel. Politically, it draws a clear boundary between the politics of peace between Israel and the Palestinians, on the one hand, and the politics of siding with the Palestinians in a campaign of liberation against racist Israel, on the other. To say that Israel is like apartheid South Africa is to completely de-legitimize it; it is to portray Zionism only as a racist ideology of repression and not at all as an antiracist liberation struggle of the Jewish people; it is to deny that Zionism could be understood as a response to antisemitism in Europe, Russia and the Middle East. If Israel is apartheid, it follows that it cannot be allowed to continue to exist. As the apartheid state in South Africa was dismantled and replaced with a new democratic state, so the State of Israel must also be dismantled. The apartheid analogy holds that the problem is one of imperialism, racism, and democracy, not one of national conflict. As well as de-legitimizing the Israeli state, it also de-legitimizes the Israeli nation.

The boycott campaign is involved in an ongoing political project to make people think of Israel as though it was a unique racist evil on the planet. Apartheid is lifted completely out of its African context; this discursive struggle is not only a violence against Israel, but it is also a violence to both Palestinians and South Africans too. It is a cultural appropriation of the actual anti-apartheid struggle. The real history and the real democratic victory of the anti-apartheid movement is put to work only as a founding narrative of this campaign against Israel.

One of the extraordinary things about the anti-apartheid movement was the Freedom Charter. Under the conditions of apartheid, the ANC won wide popular agreement, support and consent from many South Africans for this democratic document, whose first paragraph reads as follows:

> We, the People of South Africa, declare for all our country and the world to know: that South Africa belongs to all who live in it, black and white, and that no government can justly claim authority unless it is based on the will of all the people; that our people have been robbed of their birthright to land, liberty and peace by a form of government founded on injustice and inequality; that our country will never be prosperous or free until all our people live in brotherhood, enjoying equal rights and opportunities; that only a democratic state, based on the will of all the people, can secure to all their birthright without distinction of colour,

> race, sex or belief; And therefore, we, the people of South Africa,
> black and white together – equals, countrymen and brothers –
> adopt this Freedom Charter. And we pledge ourselves to strive
> together, sparing neither strength nor courage, until the demo-
> cratic changes here set out have been won.[19]

The Freedom Charter offered guarantees in advance that the aim of
liberation was not to reverse the racist domination of white people over
black people but to abolish race as a legal category in South Africa. The
ANC, purporting to speak not as one political faction but as the voice
of the nation, made an undertaking not to threaten or to harm or to
oppress white people in a future democratic state. The Freedom Charter
was not a black nationalist document; it was a document which aimed
to constitute a new non-racial South African nation. Precisely because
the splitting of people into races was fundamentally illegitimate, there
could be no question of self-determination for races. When it came to
the final years of the apartheid state, Nelson Mandela held onto these
guarantees and onto this political perspective tenaciously. This political
framework helped him to force a democratic end to apartheid – and
one which was significantly less violent than it might have been.

The conflict between Israel and the Palestinians is not similar to that
between white and non-white South Africa. It takes only a moment
to follow the analogy through and see where it goes. In the 1980s,
the antizionists used to squeeze the Palestinian struggle for liberation
into their own generalized template of anti-colonial nationalism. The
Palestine Liberation Organisation (PLO), it used to be insisted, was
the 'sole legitimate representative of the Palestinian People', mirror-
ing the way that the ANC positioned itself. The idea was that nations
which were oppressed by colonization resisted and opposed that colonization by creating nationalist movements which would win national
self-determination and independence. In the 1970s, the PLO's strategy
was to create a 'democratic secular' Palestinian state. Originally, this
meant driving out the Israeli colonists; later, the 'democratic secular
state' slogan developed into a programme for Palestinians and Israelis to live together within a single state. By the late 1980s, the PLO
was moving towards embracing the idea of a two-state solution by

which there would be a Palestinian state established alongside Israel. The PLO appeared to embrace the peace process, and it transformed itself into the Palestinian Authority, according to the framework of the Oslo agreement.

If Yasser Arafat, and later Mahmoud Abbas, the elected Presidents of Palestine, are considered to be the 'sole legitimate voice' of the Palestinian people, then the South Africa analogy runs into trouble. Since the 1980s, Arafat and Abbas have rejected, in rhetoric and policy at least, the aspiration to a 'democratic secular state' and have orientated themselves towards making a peace agreement with Israel, although it is true, at the same time, that they have been either unable or unwilling to follow through the logic of this position. But they have not endorsed 'boycott' or the anti-normalization politics which it reflects.

Many in the antizionist movement became impatient with the official leadership of the Palestinians. By 2009, John Pilger, for example, was ready to refer to the Palestinian President Mahmoud Abbas as a 'quisling' – a reference to the record of Vidkun Quisling, a Norwegian military officer who headed a puppet government on behalf of the Nazis during the Second World War. In this narrative, the Israelis are like the Nazis, and the Palestinian leadership are Nazi collaborators. More recently, Malia Bouattia has won the presidency of NUS arguing against the Israel/Palestinian peace process.

But the official Palestinian leadership has not openly supported either boycott or the abolition of Israel, for a generation. That is why the British scholars who initiated the contemporary boycott campaign after 2003 developed this notion of 'Palestinian civil society' which, as the voice of the oppressed, calls for boycott.

But what if Hamas – rather than the presidency, the PLO or 'civil society' – is now recognized as the sole legitimate voice of the Palestinian people? Seumas Milne described Hamas as the 'current expression of a spirit of Palestinian national resistance to oppression and dispossession going back decades' (Hirsh 2008b) What, then, would be Hamas' equivalent to the ANC's Freedom Charter? The Hamas Covenant, its founding document, expresses a profoundly antisemitic worldview. It states: 'Initiatives, and so-called peaceful solutions and international conferences, are in contradiction to the principles of the

Islamic Resistance Movement.' The Hamas Covenant offers an explicitly antisemitic account of history:

> With their money, they took control of the world media, news agencies, the press, publishing houses, broadcasting stations, and others. With their money they stirred revolutions in various parts of the world with the purpose of achieving their interests and reaping the fruit therein. They were behind the French Revolution, the Communist revolution and most of the revolutions we heard and hear about, here and there. With their money they formed secret societies, such as Freemasons, Rotary Clubs, the Lions and others in different parts of the world for the purpose of sabotaging societies and achieving Zionist interests.

And the Hamas Covenant is clear about its genocidal intent with respect to Jews:

> Allah . . . has said: 'The Day of Judgement will not come about until Moslems fight the Jews (killing the Jews), when the Jew will hide behind stones and trees. The stones and trees will say O Moslems, O Abdulla, there is a Jew behind me, come and kill him.'

The covenant is clear about the aim and intention of the organization: 'Israel will exist and will continue to exist until Islam will obliterate it.' It is difficult to see how it is possible to interpret this threat against the State of Israel, and the nation of Israel, as being in any way analogous to the ANC's aspiration for a non-racial South Africa.

The Hamas Covenant is not similar to the Freedom Charter, because the conflict in Palestine is not similar to the conflict in South Africa. Jews are not in Israel to live off and to exploit the people whom they find there; they are there because that is their home; some of them have been there since the time of the Temple; others made their home there because antisemitic movements in Europe, the Middle East and Russia were murdering, libelling, enslaving and humiliating them. Hamas taunts Israeli Jews with the same rhetoric as the movements which drove them into exile (or drove them home), and it articulates the same genocidal rhetoric from which they fled.

If there is to be peace and justice between the Israelis and the Palestinians, there will have to be a mutual recognition of their national rights and their need to defend themselves. It is not like South Africa, which was a problem of racism and a problem of democratic rights. Ironically, it turned out in the end that destroying apartheid was easier than finding peace between Israel and the Palestinians. The conflicts are not the same. Palestine cannot be 'de-colonized' as though it were occupied by a European power. Antisemitism and hatred, it turns out, is part of what perpetuates the Middle East conflict and makes it so apparently dissoluble.

Yet antizionism around the world contents itself with ever simpler and more trivial analogy politics, but the effects of that politics are far from trivial.

The Israel-Palestine conflict is a small but nasty confrontation between two communities, not a fight between good and evil. Israel does not exist to profit from Palestinians, and its oppressive policies stem from neither self-interest nor bad faith; they are products of successive failures, including by Palestinian leaders, to make peace; it is fear, not evil or greed, which fuels the violence.

But the apartheid analogy does not encourage us to think in terms of reconciliation and peace. Antisemitism has always thought of Jews as being decisive in everything bad that happens in the world. Those who insist on the appropriateness of the apartheid analogy position Israel at the centre of all that is threatening in the world, and they aim to build a global movement for its destruction. They encourage ways of thinking which see Israel as a keystone of global imperialism, as a block to world peace and even as a malicious force which controls American foreign policy.

Notes

1 For example, Jacqueline Rose *et al* (2007): 'The opponents of the boycott debate argue that a boycott is inimical to academic freedom, yet they are engaged in a campaign of vilification and intimidation in order to prevent a discussion of this issue.'

2 See the website 'Free Speech on Israel' at: http://freespeechonisrael.org.uk/category/campaign-against-antisemitism/ (accessed 17 October 2016).

3 Both this and the previous quotation are from the *Limerick Leader*, Monday evening, 18 January 1904.

4 Steven Rose was clear about this in his profile on *The Guardian*'s 'Comment is Free' website. This has since been changed, but the original profile is still available on web.archive from 29 September 2006: https://web.archive.org/web/20080127183807/http://commentisfree.guardian.co.uk/steven_rose/profile.html (accessed 8 October 2016).

5 Available: www.monabaker.com/personalstatement.htm.

6 BRICUP, British Campaign for the Universities of Palestine. See: www.bricup.org.uk/ (accessed 17 October 2016).

7 PACBI, Palestinian Campaign for the Cultural and Academic Boycott of Israel. See: www.pacbi.org/ (accessed 17 October 2016).

8 The author was one of the central activists involved in *Engage* and edited the website.

9 It was felt that the word 'blacklisting' might have racist connotations, and so the word 'greylisting' was used.

10 Jon Pike, who was a member of the Special Commission, discusses the issues underlying the debates around 'greylisting' policy and defines his distinction between boycott as solidarity and boycott as punishment, or voluntary and non-voluntary boycott (2006b).

11 Personal correspondence with the author – 13 May 2005; 16 May 2005.

12 Confidential correspondence with the author.

13 'The PACBI call for academic boycott revised: adjusting the parameters of the debate.' Available: http://pacbi.org/etemplate.php?id=1051 (accessed 17 October 2016).

14 See the website of the Foreign Press Association at: www.fpa.org.il/?categoryId=14190 (accessed 18 October 2016).

15 Two prestigious scientific journals opened debates on whether to exclude Israelis. *New Scientist* did so with an editorial on 9 June 2007 entitled 'Should scientists boycott Israel?' and the *British Medical Journal* did so with pieces for and against the boycott in its 21 July 2007 issue.

16 See Fine and Spencer (2017), who argue that those who read Marx himself as an antisemite miss both the detail and the overall structure of his work.

17 This account of what happened was given by the Israeli scholar to an official from the South African Board of Jewish Deputies and is not materially contested by the SASA, 3 August 2012.

18 This is from a letter sent to the South African Jewish Board of Deputies by Prof. J.F. Cronjé, the President of SASA, dated 20 September 2012.

19 Available: www.historicalpapers.wits.ac.za/inventories/inv_pdfo/AD1137/AD1137-Ea6-1-001-jpeg.pdf.

5

STRUGGLES OVER DEFINING ANTISEMITISM

This chapter focuses on struggles over how antisemitism is defined. These struggles over definition, over what is recognized as antisemitism, are a distillation of the wider struggles which are the subject of this book. What kinds of hostility to Israel may be understood as, or may lead to, or may be caused by, antisemitism?

In this chapter, I trace a genealogy of the EUMC (European Union Monitoring Centre on Racism and Xenophobia, now the Agency For Fundamental Rights [FRA]) *Working Definition of Antisemitism*. The definition, in a slightly evolved but functionally identical form, was later adopted by the US State Department, by the thirty-one-state International Holocaust Remembrance Alliance (IHRA) and by the UK Government.

In this chapter, I show how this definition emerged originally out of a process of splitting between the global antiracist movement on the one hand and Jewish-led opposition to antisemitism on the other. At the Durban World Conference against Racism in September 2001, there was a largely successful attempt to construct Zionism as the key form of racism on the planet. This way of thinking would encourage people to relate to the overwhelming majority of Jews, who refuse to plead not guilty to the charge of Zionism, as if they were racists.

Relating to Jews in that way has antisemitic consequences. In response, some Jewish NGOs found that they could get a hearing for their concerns within the structures of the Organization for Security and Cooperation in Europe (OSCE) and the European Union. If Durban is thought of as a non-white global forum and if the OSCE and the European Union are thought of as networks of white states, then the antagonism between non-white antiracism and white anxiety about antisemitism becomes visible and concerning. The clash between antizionism, on the one hand, and the claim that antizionism is related to antisemitism, on the other, plays out within the realm of discourse, and then it is also mirrored institutionally in these global struggles over the definition of antisemitism.

I go on to look at the specific ways in which the boycott movement in the University and College Union (UCU), at every stage, went to great lengths explicitly to insist that what it did could not be understood as antisemitic. The disavowal of the EUMC definition during the 2011 UCU Congress can be seen as the climax of this campaign to define antisemitism in such a way as the union itself was not guilty.

I then turn to look at two of the formal processes which were asked to adjudicate whether hostility to Israel had become antisemitic: the *Fraser v. UCU* case at the Employment Tribunal in 2012, and the Shami Chakrabarti *Inquiry into Antisemitism and Other Racisms* in the Labour Party in 2016.

The EUMC definition of antisemitism offers a framework for understanding the potential of certain kinds of hostility to Israel to be antisemitic. The further argument was made within the UCU, to the Employment Tribunal, and to the Chakrabarti Inquiry, that cultures of hostility to Israel and of support for boycotts tend to bring with them, into institutions which host them, cultures of antisemitism. The structures of the union, as well as the two inquiries, wholeheartedly rejected both of the claims: first, that a politics of hostility to Israel manifests itself as antisemitism in these cases; and, second, that a cultural or institutional antisemitism, analogous to institutional racism, could be identified in the UCU or the Labour Party. Where the Chakrabarti report does recognize that antisemitism has occurred, it is treated as the product of individual failings rather than a manifestation of political, cultural or institutional phenomena.

This chapter suggests that these wholehearted rejections of claims about antisemitism are themselves implicated in the functioning of contemporary antisemitism. Denial of racism is a necessary element of those kinds of racism which do not see themselves as racist. It seems clear that hostility to the EUMC definition and to arguments about cultural and institutional antisemitism are necessary components of contemporary antizionist discourse as well as the cultures and practices which flow from them.

Methodological issues concerning definitions

Defining a concept cannot be done independently of understanding that which the concept seeks to encapsulate. Defining is a process which requires us to begin by looking at the world outside of ourselves. Gold, for example, is easy to define because its properties are clearly delineated in nature. Any element with atomic number 79 is gold, and having that atomic number is enough to define it as such. That is to say that having the atomic number 79 is both necessary and sufficient for a substance to be gold. To define gold it is necessary to know something about the nature of gold.

Antisemitism, a complex and contested social phenomenon, is more difficult to define than gold, but here too the work of definition must begin with an investigation into the phenomenon itself. Antisemitism is objective, and it is external to the subjective feeling of individuals. This means that in order to shed light on debates around the definition of the concept, it is necessary to look at the actualization of the concept in the social world as well as the ways in which the processes of definition happen there.

But the procedure which is appropriate for natural concepts such as chemical elements cannot be used exactly as it stands when we want to define more complex social phenomena. One principal reason for this is that whereas a natural concept such as gold has instances which are universally agreed upon as being cases of gold, the same is not true of socially contentious phenomena such as racism, in general, and antisemitism, in particular. What counts as a case of racism is a matter of dispute; indeed, it is precisely those disputes, with all their political implications and consequences, that intensify the need for a clear definition of what it is we are disagreeing about. We need a more complex method if we are to make progress in defining the social phenomenon we are interested in. As before, we must start by looking at the world outside of us; antisemitism is not simply a matter of what is inside people's heads, either their linguistic knowledge of how the word is used or their psychological states such as feelings of hatred or contempt for Jews. Hatred may be a sufficient condition for antisemitism, but it is not at all a necessary one: antisemitism is also, and primarily, a matter of what people *do* and of what consequences their actions have. These are points which are widely accepted in the more general study of racism, but what people know about racism is sometimes forgotten when they turn their attention to antisemitism. And although there may be agreement about some cases of antisemitism, such as Nazism, other cases, especially contemporary ones, are the subject of hot political dispute. So we would need to move constantly between our emerging definition of what antisemitism is and our reflective sense of which cases are properly to be seen as constituting antisemitism, using a tentative definition to correct our intuitions about cases and our increasingly reflective sense of which cases really count as antisemitism to help us to revise and refine our definition.

This chapter is more an effort to understand what is at stake in struggles over how antisemitism should be defined than it is an attempt to come to a definition. The inbuilt methodological complexity is that analyzing and understanding the struggles around definition is also a process of analyzing and understanding the phenomenon itself of antisemitism. Observing efforts to define certain kinds of attitudes and actions as not antisemitic may at the same time also be observing the very functioning of antisemitic discourse. Observing struggles over definition in this way may require us to take sides in some of those struggles. It involves a constant interplay between our emerging definition of antisemitism and our understanding of which cases can plausibly be seen as examples of it.

So methodologically, an inquiry into defining antisemitism begins with empirical observation and analysis of cases, some hotly disputed, of the social phenomenon in question, as it is manifested in living, changing social movements, as it is produced through struggle and contestation over how things are understood and described. Analysis of the case studies leads me to suggest that the quest for an automatic and uncontested formula which can tell us what is antisemitic and what is not is going to be unsuccessful. We are not going to be able to find necessary and sufficient conditions for the presence of antisemitism. It may, however, be possible to look towards the development of a set of criteria which can help us to make, and to debate, difficult judgments regarding particular cases. This is what the *EUMC Working Definition* attempts to do. We will remain aware that any such criteria will be angrily contested.

These methodological complexities are not unique to the study of antisemitism; they also apply to attempts to define and recognize other forms of racism and bigotry. Understanding whether a comment or an institution is sexist, for example, requires a close study and an understanding of context, of the tropes and of the histories of sexism; it requires consideration of intention and of unintended consequences and of discourse and ways of thinking; it requires a consideration of norms and practices of exclusion; it requires a consideration of modes of denial. The recognition of antisemitism, similarly, requires knowledge, experience and understanding. The added complication here is that scholarly and political discussion of sexism often proceeds in social spaces in which there is a greater degree of consensus over how sexism as a phenomenon is understood, although this was not always the case. The dividing lines over the understanding of contemporary antisemitism, in contrast, tend to bisect the community of analysis and understanding.

Struggles over defining antisemitism occur in a number of different social spaces and languages. In particular, they happen within political, scholarly, legal, law-enforcement, communal and religious discourses and practices. These terrains of struggle are linked; ideas, concepts and elements of rhetoric tend to circulate from one to the other.

The case studies in this book show why there is unlikely to be even general agreement over how to define antisemitism, even amongst antiracists who broadly agree on how to recognize other forms of racism. There is a polarization around definition because the phenomenon itself is highly polarized. Some scholars and antiracists argue that hostility to Israel is related to antisemitism; others insist that relating the two is done not in error but as a malicious attempt to silence and to de-legitimize criticism of Israel.

A genealogy of the *EUMC Working Definition* of *Antisemitism*

The *EUMC Working Definition* is controversial because it states that particular kinds of hostility to Israel 'could, taking into account the overall context' be antisemitic (*EUMC Working Definition*). It offers examples: 'accusing Israel as a state of exaggerating or inventing the Holocaust' and 'accusing Jews of being more loyal to Israel than to their own nations'. It offers examples of the kinds of things which may be judged antisemitic, 'taking into account the overall context':

- denying the Jewish people their right to self-determination, e.g., by claiming that the existence of a State of Israel is a racist endeavour
- applying double standards by requiring of it a behaviour not expected or demanded of any other democratic nation
- using the symbols and images associated with classic antisemitism (e.g., claims of Jews killing Jesus or blood libel) to characterize Israel or Israelis
- drawing comparisons of contemporary Israeli policy to that of the Nazis
- holding Jews collectively responsible for actions of the State of Israel.

The definition then makes it clear that, on the other hand, 'criticism of Israel similar to that levelled against any other country cannot be regarded as antisemitic'.[1]

Mike Whine traces the pre-history of the *Working Definition* back to the immediate aftermath of the fall of Communism (2004, 2006, 2010) in Europe. The Organization for Security and Co-operation in Europe (OSCE) was a pre-existing international forum in which Europe (East and West), the USSR (later Russia and the secession states) and the USA could talk to each other. It was a forum which lent itself to the project of attempting to shape the new Europe, in particular by formulating states' commitment to the principles of human rights and democracy. At the 1990 Copenhagen Conference, commitments were made to combat all forms of racial and ethnic hatred, antisemitism, xenophobia and discrimination (Whine 2010: 92). These commitments were subsequently endorsed by heads of state in the 'Charter of Paris for a New Europe' (Organization for Security and Co-operation in Europe 1990).

It was ten years later when the peace process between Israel and the Palestinians broke down decisively in September 2000 with the outbreak of the Second Intifada and after the failure of peace talks at Taba in January 2001. The coalition of the forces arguing for a two-state solution in Israel and in Palestine collapsed into opposing national consensuses, each of which portrayed the other nation as being responsible for the renewal of conflict.

In September 2001, the United Nations (UN) World Conference against Racism (WACR) was held in the newly democratic South Africa. At that conference, there was a formidable campaign to construct Zionism as the key manifestation of racism in the world. A number of factors came together that week, in the conference venues, on the city streets and on the beachfront of Durban, which created a particular anti-Israel feeling; it was remarkable both in its intensity and in its tolerance of antisemitic content. There was a UN inter-governmental forum. There was also a parallel NGO conference, a huge event in a cricket ground, bringing together tens of thousands of activists. Something of the atmosphere can be understood from this contemporaneous account written by Ronald Eissens and published by ICARE, a European antiracist NGO which participated in the conference:

> Jews were actively discriminated [against], shouted down, meetings on Antisemitism were hijacked by Palestinian Caucus members and supporters, and people who protested against all this were branded 'Zionist pigs lovers' and 'Jewlovers'. Some NGOs were intimidated into silence. There was fear to be branded as 'Zionist'. There were NGOs and people who openly agreed with the antisemite slogans.

The big September 1st demonstration had a lot of slogans, covered a lot of issues, but one was most dominant: Free Palestine. In the march, slogans were carried like 'Kill all the Jews' and 'the good things Hitler did'. Pamphlets were handed out with a portrait of Hitler, displaying the text:

> 'What if I had won? The good things: There would be NO Israel and NO Palestinian's blood shed – the rest is your guess. The bad things: I wouldn't have allowed the making of the new beetle – the rest is your guess.'

This march ended at the Durban Jewish Club, which was another sign that the organizers not only see the state of Israel as the enemy but all Jewish people. The Jewish club had been evacuated a few hours earlier and the South African police had the building screened-off with riot police and armoured cars. A big demonstration during a World Conference Against Racism that ends as an Antisemitic rally . . .

(Eissens 2001)

There was an organized and hostile anti-Israel fervour throughout the week-long conference. Some of it was expressed in openly antisemitic forms, some was legitimate criticism of Israel expressed in antiracist forms, and some was antisemitism expressed in ostensibly democratic and antiracist language.

The Conference ended on Saturday, 8 September. Initially this meant that the Jewish organizations were unable to attend the final discussions about the text to be adopted by the conference, because it was Shabbat. But the final plenary session went on so long that they were, in the end, able to attend on Saturday evening. For some of the participants, the traumatic experience of finding that global allies in the struggle against racism were prepared to tolerate antisemitism was heightened by the attacks, three days later on 11 September, on the United States of America.

Ronald Eissens (2001) editorialized at that moment as follows:

> There is a dark cloud of hate descending upon this world. If we want to keep the dark away, we need to see clear and get rid

of the hate. Which means we have to be open and transparent about facts. We are an antiracism NGO, so it is our duty and our moral obligation to speak out against racism. Especially, I would say, when an antiracism conference becomes the scene of racism. The fact that racism was allowed to run rampant during the WCAR is astonishing. What is even more astonishing, shameful and harmful for the antiracism cause and for the victims of racism is that the majority of the organisers and participants let that happen, did nothing to stop it and did not speak out during or after the WCAR.

The collapse of the peace process, Durban and 9/11, as well as the reverberating symbolic representations of them can be understood as heralding what some (Chesler 2003) have called 'the new antisemitism'.

There were, says Whine, attempts to raise the issue of antisemitism within the European Union. A series of meetings took place between the EUMC director Beate Winkler and European Jewish Congress (EJC) officials which resulted in the commissioning of a report on antisemitism in each country. The Centre for Research on Anti-Semitism (ZfA) at Berlin's Technical University was asked to analyze the reports and publish a composite analysis. However, Whine notes, the report was badly received by the EUMC board because it apportioned much of the blame for the rise in antisemitism to Muslim communities. It was leaked to the press by the EJC in December 2003.

A second report was published side by side with the main country-by-country analysis. 'Manifestations of Anti-Semitism in the EU 2002–3' was released on 31 March 2004, and the accompanying press release said that the far right remained the main promoter of antisemitism within Europe, contradicting the body of the first report (European Monitoring Centre on Racism and Xenophobia 2004). Mike Whine (2006) writes:

> In its 2004 report on antisemitism, the EUMC noted the lack of a common definition and requested one from a small group of Jewish NGOs. This [was] intended as a template for police forces and antiracist campaigners, for use on the streets. The definition was disseminated in March 2004, and although not directed at governments for incorporation into national legislation, it [was]

nevertheless expected that it [would] seep into universal usage via adoption by the relevant parties.

This in fact happened. Delegates to the OSCE Cordoba Conference in May 2005 constantly referred to it, and the *All-Party Parliamentary Inquiry into Antisemitism* in the UK recommended its adoption,[2] as did a number of similar initiatives around the world.[3] In 2010 the US Department of State adopted a close variant as its own official definition of antisemitism (US Department of State 2010), the International Holocaust Remembrance Alliance adopted a variant later, and, in December 2016, it was formally adopted by the UK government.

The 'whitening' of Jews and the schism between anti-antisemitism and antiracism

In *Black Skin, White Masks*, Franz Fanon (1968: 122) wrote:

> At first glance it seems strange that the attitude of the anti-Semite can be equated with that of the negrophobe. It was my philosophy teacher from the Antilles who reminded me one day: 'When you hear someone insulting the Jews pay attention; he is talking about you.' And I believed at the time he was universally right, meaning that I was responsible in my body and my soul for the fate reserved for my brother. Since then, I have understood that what he meant quite simply was the anti-Semite is inevitably a negrophobe.

There is a strong tradition on the antiracist left of understanding racism and antisemitism as closely related phenomena and of opposing both equally and on a similar basis. Exemplars of this tradition include Karl Marx's critiques of antisemitism within the movement of his day (Fine and Spencer 2017), Bebel's characterization of antisemitism as the 'socialism of fools', the anti-Fascist tradition and the black/Jewish alliance during the civil rights movement in the USA. At Durban in 2001, however, racism had been defined such that 'Zionism' was its archetypal and most threatening form, and antisemitism was not only denied but also practiced with impunity. A significant number of antiracist activists and thinkers were subsequently willing to lend implicit or overt support to organizations such as Hezbollah and Hamas, either judging the antisemitism of those groups to be exaggerated or at least downplaying their political significance (for example: Judith Butler [Zimmer, Heidingsfelder and Adler 2010] and [Jeremy Corbyn 2015a]). Durban illustrated the possibility of the re-emergence of a schism between the worldviews of antiracism and anti-antisemitism.

The issue of 'whiteness' is key to the understanding of contemporary antisemitism, and it is linked to a number of developments in the twentieth-century left. The first development is a tendency for parts of the left to understand 'the oppressed', with whom it sides, more and more in terms of nations and national movements, which are fighting for liberation against the 'imperialist states' or the 'rich states', 'the West', 'the North' or the 'white' states. This is a different framework from the one in which the left thought of itself as supporting the self-liberation of the working class, of women, and of other subordinated groups within each nation and state.

Some found that the logic of their new position was to understand whites as the oppressors and non-whites as the oppressed, and to subordinate other forms of stratification to this central one. Jews occupy an ambivalent position with respect to the black/white binary. On the one hand, antisemitism is a racism, arguably the prototype of European racism, and it provides perhaps the clearest lesson about where racism can lead. On the other hand, antisemitism has often functioned, in the words of Moishe Postone, as a 'fetishized form of oppositional consciousness' through which Jews are thought of as conspiratorially powerful and lurking behind the oppression of others (2006: 99).

In the USA, Karen Brodkin's (1999) book *How Jews Became White Folks and What That Says about Race in America* presented a narrative of the 'whitening' of American Jews, and it fed into a new picture of Jews as part of a Judeo-Christian white elite. Israel – which in its early days was understood by some to be a life-raft for oppressed and stateless victims of racism (Deutscher 1981), a national liberation movement against European colonialism and a pioneer of socialist forms like the kibbutz – later came to be conceived of as a keystone of the global system of white imperialist oppression of black people. In April 2009, when President Ahmadinejad of Iran made an antisemitic speech at the UN, Seumas Milne (2009), later to become Jeremy Corbyn's Communications Chief, asked in his *Guardian* column, 'what credibility is there in Geneva's all-white boycott?'

A number of Jewish communal NGOs responded to the defeat and the trauma experienced at Durban by withdrawing into the OSCE and the European Union, where they had some success in getting a positive hearing for their concerns. In this way the ideational polarization between black and white came to be mirrored institutionally. Durban, dominated by states which thought of themselves as non-white, represented one way of defining antisemitism; the Jewish organizations retreated into the OSCE, which could be portrayed as the international coalition of white states, and won it over to quite a different way of defining antisemitism.

Opponents of the *EUMC Working Definition* have pointed to the fact that the definition was the result of purposive political action by international Jewish groups; and so it was. But this genealogy can only cast shadows over the definition if there is thought to be something inappropriate about their input. Normally, it would be unremarkable for communal groups to be involved in defining a racism of which they are the object. But in this case the Jewish groups are accused by antizionists of acting in bad faith. The accusation implicit in this understanding is that the Jewish groups are not really working in the interests of the struggle against antisemitism. Rather, they are secretly prepared to sacrifice the struggle against 'real' antisemitism by co-opting its political capital to a dishonest attempt to de-legitimize criticism of Israel.

The Jewish groups, and their *EUMC Working Definition*, are conceived of, in this antizionist narrative, as being 'white' and not antiracist; as part of the struggle of Israel against Palestine; and neither part of the struggle of Jews against antisemitism nor part of the global struggle against anti-black racism. The case study of the genealogy of the *Working Definition* illustrates the extreme polarization of efforts to define antisemitism, and it relates that polarization to problematic notions and practices of 'blackness' and 'whiteness' in contemporary antiracist thinking. It shows how the polarization in struggles over definition reflect the phenomenon itself of contemporary antisemitism.

Struggles over defining antisemitism in the University and College Union (UCU)

In May 2011, the Congress of the UCU in the UK voted overwhelmingly to pass a motion which alleged that the 'so-called' *EUMC Working Definition* is 'being used' to 'silence debate about Israel and Palestine on campus' (Hirsh 2011a). Congress resolved to make no use of the definition 'e.g. in educating members or dealing with internal complaints' and to 'dissociate itself from the EUMC definition in any public discussion'.

Representatives of the institutions of the Jewish community in Britain judged this disavowal to be the last straw, and they said that it was a manifestation of what they called 'institutional antisemitism' within the union. Jeremy Newmark, Chief Executive of the Jewish Leadership Council, said, 'After today's events, I believe the UCU is institutionally racist' (Bright 2011). His view was echoed by Jon Benjamin, the Chief Executive of the Board of Deputies of British Jews, who said that 'the UCU has ... simply redefined "antisemitism" .... The truth is apparent: whatever the motivations of its members, we believe the UCU is an institutionally racist organisation' (Paul 2011).

As we have seen, since 2003, there had been an influential campaign within the UCU to boycott Israeli universities as a protest against Israeli human rights abuses, while there had been no such campaign against the universities of any other state. Some opponents of the boycott campaign argued that this singling out of Israel was antisemitic in effect and that it brought with it into the union antisemitic ways of thinking and antisemitic exclusions (Gidley 2011). Supporters of the campaign, as well as some opponents, objected strongly to the raising of the issue of antisemitism, arguing that it constituted an *ad hominem* attack against 'critics of Israel' (see Hirsh 2010b for discussion).

From the beginning, the boycott campaign sought to protect itself against a charge of antisemitism by including clauses in its boycott motions which defined antisemitism in such a way as to make its supporters not guilty. At the Association of University Teachers (AUT) Council in 2003, Motion 54 was passed:

> Council deplores the witch-hunting of colleagues, including AUT members, who are participating in the academic boycott

of Israel. Council recognises that anti-Zionism is not anti-semitism, and resolves to give all possible support to members of AUT who are unjustly accused of anti-semitism because of their political opposition to Israeli government policy.

(UCU 2003)

A witch-hunt involves accusing individuals of witchcraft, something that could not possibly be true. To characterize an accusation of anti-semitism as a witch-hunt implies that it, similarly, could not possibly be true. The statement that 'anti-Zionism is not anti-semitism' is formally true, and nobody could argue against the resolution to support members who are unjustly accused of antisemitism. However, it is clear that the formulation, taken as a whole, functions as a way of insisting that all accusations of antisemitism which relate to Israel are unjust.

At the National Association of Teachers in Further and Higher Education (NATFHE) conference in June 2005, a motion was passed which included this text: 'To criticise Israeli policy or institutions is not anti-semitic' (see Osborn 2005). The first Congress of the newly merged UCU passed a motion which stated that 'criticism of Israel cannot be construed as anti-semitic'. While the motion supported a boycott without resolving actually to implement one, the antisemitism clause referred only to 'criticism of Israel'. The implication here is that boycott falls within the protection afforded to 'criticism'. The 'cannot be construed as' element implies that there is somebody who is trying to 'construe' criticism as antisemitic. It is an implicit allegation of the collective bad faith of those who raise the issue of antisemitism.

The ambiguity of the motion was not accidental, since Congress explicitly rejected an amendment to clarify the wording so that it would have read as follows: 'While much criticism of Israel is anti-semitic, criticism of Israeli state policy cannot necessarily be construed as anti-semitic' (see Cooke 2007 for discussion).

UCU Congress in 2008 passed a similar motion which was supportive of a boycott but which stopped short of implementing one. This time the wording on antisemitism was as follows: 'criticism of Israel or Israeli policy are [*sic*] not, as such, anti-semitic' (for discussion see Geras 2008). This form of words raised a straw man by subsuming anything which may be thought to be antisemitic into the category of 'criticism' and then legislating that, in virtue of its being 'criticism', it could not be antisemitic.

This long pre-history to the disavowal of the EUMC definition is consistent. Each new form of words refuses the straightforward, common-sense position that some kinds of hostility to Israel are anti-semitic while other kinds are not. Instead, each specifies that criticism of Israel is not antisemitic, and it implicitly subsumes all kinds of hostility and exclusions under the category of 'criticism' (Hirsh 2016a). Practically, the result has been to open up a loophole in the union's guarantees against racism and bigotry. One kind of racism is excluded from these guarantees, and that is any antisemitism which can be read as taking the form of criticism of Israel.

Instead of addressing the culture which could have been recognized by the *Working Definition* as antisemitic, the disavowal of the definition facilitated the union in continuing to treat 'Zionists' as disloyal, to single out Israel and only Israel for boycott, to hold Israeli universities and scholars responsible for their government and to allow 'Zionist' union members to be denounced and regarded as Nazis or supporters of apartheid.

Israel murders children? Israel controls US foreign policy? Star of David = Swastika stuck on your office door? Jews invent antisemitism to de-legitimize criticism of Israel? Host a man found guilty of hate speech by the South African Human Rights Commission? Exclude nobody but Israelis from the global academic community? All of these are considered, implicitly by UCU motions, and clearly by UCU norms, to constitute 'criticism of Israel' and so are in practice defined as being not antisemitic.

This narrative shows how the boycott movement sought, at each step of its campaign, to pre-empt accusations of antisemitism by con-stantly trying to develop and to refine its own critique of claims about what constitutes antisemitism. It felt the need to incorporate its claims over definition in its motions and its material; it fought for its own conception of antisemitism within its wider constituency, and it sought to inoculate itself in advance against being associated with antisem-itism. It was important to the boycott campaign to win official recog-nition for its own position within the wider social space in which it hopes to operate – but in the first instance, within the union.

In the judgment of the case Ronnie Fraser took against the UCU, which we will come to more detail in Chapter 6, the tribunal wrote the following on the question of defining antisemitism:

> the Claimant bases his case in part on the rejection by the Respondents' Congress (in 2011) of the 'Working Definition' of anti-Semitism . . . . He was content with that definition. Others disagreed, regarding it as exposing critics of Israel to the unfair accusation of anti-Semitic conduct. They pointed to the fact that the definition might be read as branding attacks on Zionism as anti-Semitic and precluding criticism of Israel save where 'similar' to that levelled against any other country. We cannot escape the gloomy thought that a definition acceptable to all interested parties may never be achieved and count ourselves fortunate that it does not fall to us to attempt to devise one.[4]

The tribunal was confident in judging that nothing that happened within the UCU constituted antisemitic harassment under the meaning of the Equality Act; this seems to be in stark contrast to its professed reluctance to come to a judgment about how antisemitism ought to be defined. The tribunal attempted to position itself neutrally between the polarized positions on what defines antisemitism, yet it judged that there was no antisemitic harassment, under the meaning of the Equality Act, within the union. In this way it threw its weight behind one of the positions on what constitutes antisemitism, and it came down strongly against the other.

The report written by Shami Chakrabarti on antisemitism in the Labour Party did not attempt either a definition of antisemitism or a description of the political problem which led to the specific scandals which triggered the inquiry. Chakrabarti did not attempt to connect the politics of hostility to Israel with antisemitism.

Both the Employment Tribunal and the Chakrabarti Inquiry were asked to adjudicate the question which had been raging amongst activists and scholars about how antisemitism should be defined. Both were positioned outside of the fray; both had the opportunity to take the time coolly to examine the arguments and the evidence which were submitted to them; both were somewhat insulated from the heated atmosphere of political debate. Both came to conclusions which were similar to those which had been arrived at within the wider social movements and which were at odds with the consensus view within the Jewish community.

★ ★ ★

The genealogy of the *EUMC Working Definition* sheds light on contemporary struggles over the definition of antisemitism and its relationship to hostility to Israel. The possibility of a departure from a standard antiracist understanding of the relationship between opposition to racism and opposition to antisemitism may be significant indeed.

Glynis Cousin and Robert Fine identify a 'methodological separatism' which has challenged, and in some quarters has had some success in supplanting, the political and conceptual unity between antiracism and anti-antisemitism (Cousin and Fine 2012). They argue that 'sociology is broken by the schism between racism and antisemitism' (Cousin and Fine 2012: 181). First, it downplays the similarity in structure and the connectedness of the histories of anti-black racism, antisemitism and Islamophobia. And, second, it brings with it temptations of competitive identity politics which may even reproduce some of the racist ways of thinking which sociology and antiracism had formerly made every effort to deconstruct and to overcome.

The genealogy of the EUMC definition is a case study of the dangers about which Cousin and Fine worry. In the 1980s, there was an antiracism which sought to build a huge rainbow alliance of everybody who suffered racism; this alliance defined itself as 'black' against a category of 'whiteness' which was understood as an identity of privilege and power. While this kind of simplification brought with it some unity and clarity, it tended to ossify; it contained within it a danger of collapse into fixed binary categories of blackness (goodness) and whiteness (badness) which did damage to the rich complexity and diversity of social and ethnic identity and conflict across the globe. This process was exacerbated by a tendency for radical thought to conceptualize the world as being more and more split between oppressor and oppressed nations and nationalisms. These tendencies created fertile conditions for the splitting off of Israel and Jews from the community of the oppressed and for conceiving of them as white, imperialist and the enemy of the oppressed.

These ways of thinking, which are replicated and reinforced by the organizational and political schisms which we have identified, contain within themselves a tendency to repeat some of the tropes and discourses of earlier antisemitisms. Insofar as we have identified these processes of splitting first in discourse and then in institutions, and then in the practice and culture, they also reproduce themselves in the actual practices of defining and understanding antisemitism.

Antisemitism must be studied empirically before it can be defined. It is necessary to see how it operates within the complexity of human and social movements, how elements of rhetoric move from one discursive field to another, how modes of denial and reassurance operate.

The week after the Chakrabarti report was published, Jeremy Corbyn appeared in front of the Home Affairs Select Committee as a witness for its investigation into antisemitism. With Chakrabarti sitting just behind him, Corbyn defined antisemitism as follows:

> Antisemitism is where you use epithets to criticize people for being Jewish, you attack Jewish people for what they are, it is completely unacceptable and I would have thought it was very obvious what antisemitism is.
>
> *(Home Affairs Committee 2016)*

This 'definition' is reminiscent of the one proposed by antizionist and pro-boycott activist Sue Blackwell in the debate in which the UCU voted to disavow the EUMC definition: 'I recommend Brian Klug's "hostility towards Jews as Jews"' (Hirsh 2011a).

Where there is great resistance to recognizing and understanding antisemitism, it would seem that there is a preference for simplistic *a priori* definitions which do not reflect a deep and detailed study of the phenomenon itself, which narrow the concept down to one single aspect of the phenomenon and which focus definition only on those manifestations on which it is easy for everybody to agree.

But antiracist NGOs, scholars and activists have studied and tried to map the features of contemporary antisemitism. Many of them have themselves experienced the shock of being summarily expelled from the antiracist and scholarly community. They have tried to set up subtle and elaborate parameters and frameworks for the understanding of this rather complex and difficult-to-encapsulate phenomenon.

Jeremy Corbyn, by contrast, invented a definition of antisemitism under cross-examination by the Select Committee; Sue Blackwell's definition is five words long; Shami Chakrabarti's account of antisemitism begins in the dictionary; the members of the Employment Tribunal say in all banality: 'we count ourselves fortunate that it does not fall to us to attempt to devise' a definition.[5]

Notes

1   Note that there are a number of US spellings in the definition and this fact was later mobilized in the UCU debate to demonstrate its illegitimacy as a European and an antiracist document. See Hirsh (2011b) for discussion.

2   See, for example: All-Party Parliamentary Group Against Antisemitism (2006) 'Report of the Parliamentary inquiry into antisemitism'. Available: www.antisemitism.org.uk/wp-content/uploads/All-Party-Parliamentary-Inquiry-into-Antisemitism-REPORT.pdf (accessed 24 August 2016).

3   See, for example: U.S. Department of State (2008) 'Contemporary global anti-semitism: a report provided to the United States Congress'. Available: www.state.gov/documents/organization/102301.pdf (accessed 21 July 2016).

4   *Judgment of the Employment Tribunal Between: Mr R Fraser v. University and College Union*, Case Numbers 2203390/2011 (25 March 2013), para. 52 (hereafter: *Judgment: Fraser v. UCU*). Available: www.judiciary.gov.uk/judgments/fraser-uni-college-union/ (accessed 21 July 2016).

5   *Judgment: Fraser v. UCU*, para. 52.

6

RONNIE FRASER V UCU

Taking the union to court for antisemitism

> When someone is honestly 55% right, that's very good and there's no use wrangling. And if someone is 60% right, it's wonderful, it's great luck, and let him thank God. But what's to be said about 75% right? Wise people say this is suspicious. Well, and what about 100% right? Whoever says he's 100% right is a fanatic, a thug, and the worst kind of rascal.
>
> (An old Jew of Galicia, from Milosz; *The Captive Mind*, 2001)

In October 2012, Ronnie Fraser sued the University and College Union (UCU). He argued that a culture of institutional antisemitism had been created and then maintained by the union; he argued that this constituted antisemitic harassment against him under the meaning of the Equality Act (2010). The environment in the UCU, he said, using the language of the act, was 'intimidating, hostile, degrading, humiliating and/or offensive to him, in respect of his Jewish identity'.[1]

After spending three weeks hearing testimony, the tribunal judged that there had been no antisemitism at all. The tribunal found against Fraser on everything: on technicalities, on legal argument and on every significant issue of substance and of fact. The tribunal found everything the UCU said in its defence to be persuasive, and it found nothing said by Fraser or any of his witnesses to have merit. The culture, the practices and the norms inside the union were found to be not anti-semitic, either in intent or in effect. Indeed, everything that Fraser and his witnesses experienced as antisemitic, the tribunal judged to have been entirely appropriate. In particular, what was appropriate was the way that union staff, rules, structures and bodies operated. Fraser said that there was a culture in which antisemitism was tolerated, but the tribunal did not accept that even one out of the many stories that it was told was an indicator of antisemitism.

Instead, the tribunal found that 'at heart' the case represented 'an impermissible attempt to achieve a political end by litigious means' (para 178). The tribunal meant that saying that the boycott campaign brought with it a culture of antisemitism was in fact a bad-faith attempt to silence criticism of Israel. The tribunal responded with a legally binding *Livingstone Formulation*.

* * *

By the time of the UCU Congress of 2011, as we have seen, opposition to the boycott campaign within the union was almost wholly silenced and defeated. The boycott campaign brought forward a motion to disa-vow the *EUMC Working Definition* of antisemitism. Rather than stop doing that which could be judged antisemitic under the definition, Congress preferred to disavow the definition. Congress is the sovereign body of the UCU; it speaks for the UCU, and it acts as the UCU.

Ronnie Fraser opposed the motion. Ronnie was an A Level maths teacher, and he ran a campaign called *Academic Friends of Israel* from his back bedroom. He had been struggling against antizionism in, first, NATFHE and then UCU since before the rise of the boycott movement. All the other activists who had been trying to oppose anti-semitism either had left the union in disgust, had been pushed out of the union, or had been silenced by the antisemitism. Ronnie kept on going, doggedly, to the end.

At the UCU Congress debate over the *Working Definition* in 2011, Ronnie Fraser took a speech against the motion. He said:

> Congress, imagine how it feels when you say that you are expe-riencing racism, and your union responds: 'Stop lying; stop trying

to play the antisemitism card' . . . . The overwhelming majority of Jews feel that there is something wrong in this union. They understand that it is legitimate to criticize Israel in a way that is, quoting from the definition, 'similar to that levelled against any other country' but they make a distinction between criticism and the kind of demonization that is considered acceptable in this union.

(Hirsh 2011a)

Congress greeted his speech in silence, and it overwhelmingly passed the motion. I was there as a visitor, reporting on proceedings for *Engage*. The delegate from my own UCU branch, now a Professor of Media and Communications, said, to warm applause: 'As a Jewish member of this union I urge you to support.' The EUMC definition, he said, conflates justified criticism of Israel with antisemitism and thereby functions to prohibit criticism as though it were antisemitism. 'Adopting the EUMC definition unnecessarily curtails our ability to intervene, to call for justice, to call for freedom for Palestinians,' he said (Hirsh 2011a).

I later wrote in my own witness statement in the *Fraser v. UCU* case:

I saw Ronnie in another room straight after this debate. While we were discussing what had happened, it became clear to me that he was very upset and on the verge of tears. He stopped speaking and walked away from me for a few moments to collect himself. I was taken aback by this because I thought of Ronnie as somebody with a very thick skin and who was very tough. I still do. But he had been hurt. I believe that he was hurting because he had just experienced an antisemitic response from a big hall of his trade union colleagues to his speech.[2]

I saw a Jewish teacher, a grandfather and a son of two Holocaust survivors experience the antisemitism which was standard and routine within the UCU; it made him cry in pain and in isolation. The union, which is ready to hear about some other racisms with compassion, listened to Fraser with a glass ear.

Later, the union was to instruct its lawyer, Antony White QC, to subject him to two days of cross-examination in which he was accused – relentlessly, articulately and professionally – of crying antisemitism for trumped-up political reasons. Fraser was courageous and tough, but he was not quick or sharp in the witness box. Ronnie did not do well under cross-examination.

The UCU disavowal of the definition was the moment at which a consensus finally crystallized in the Jewish community in the UK, which was articulated by its key institutions, that there was now a problem of institutional antisemitism within the union.

Ronnie Fraser approached lawyer Anthony Julius and asked him to represent him in a case against the union. Julius is a scholar of antisemitism, and he had represented Deborah Lipstadt in her successful defence in 2000 against a libel suit brought by Holocaust denier, David Irving. Julius was also known for representing Princess Diana against Prince Charles in their divorce. He took the case on a *pro bono* basis, out of commitment to the cause.

In July 2011, Julius sent a formal letter to the UCU (Julius 2011). It alleged a course of action by the union which amounted to institutional antisemitism, and it gave examples: annual boycott resolutions against only Israel; the conduct of these debates; the moderating of the activist list and the penalizing of anti-boycott activists; the failure to engage with people who raised concerns; the failure to address resignations; the refusal to meet the Organization for Security and Co-operation in Europe's (OSCE) special representative on antisemitism; the hosting of Bongani Masuku; the repudiation of the *EUMC Working Definition of Antisemitism*.

The UCU defended itself vigorously. It said that it was an antiracist union, that it militantly opposed antisemitism and that Fraser was illegitimately trying to frame his political defeat as a 'friend of Israel' in terms of antisemitism. The union had done nothing inappropriate, it claimed.

The tribunal sat in the autumn of 2012. It accepted evidence on behalf of Fraser from thirty-four witnesses: union activists, scientists, sociologists, historians, lawyers, philosophers, Members of Parliament, Jews, Christians, Muslims, Atheists, academic experts on antisemitism and Jewish communal leaders. Witnesses gave written statements and were subjected to cross-examination.

In her witness statement, Annette Seidel-Arpaci, a union member and at that time a visiting research fellow at Leeds University, testified:

> In my experience . . . there was an assumption that any UCU member opposing the union's stance against Israel and Israeli colleagues was Jewish. This assumption by itself appeared to me as a demonstration of UCU's intertwining of 'Israel' and 'Jews' . . . . In my experience, the conduct of UCU members campaigning for a boycott of Israel felt at all occasions like the notions of Israel and Jews were collapsed into one and the same. Moreover, as a scholar working on Holocaust memory, I felt very unsettled about the use of language by UCU activists that intertwines the experience of Jews in Europe with current Israeli politics on the occasion of events related to Jewish history.

Annette Seidel-Arpaci, who has both a Muslim and Christian family background, stated that she felt in conversations with UCU members that she was automatically expected to support a boycott of Israel. She was not cross-examined on this evidence, and so in procedural terms it stood unchallenged. The union's lawyers argued that it should be ignored because what happened in Leeds UCU to Annette Seidel-Arpaci was not relevant to this case which related to Ronnie Fraser in London; the tribunal did not refer to her evidence and appears to have accepted the union's argument on this point. But Ronnie's case was that UCU allowed and maintained a culture of antisemitism; he contested the claim that what happened in Leeds was not relevant to the culture of the organization as a whole, of which he was a member.

David Seymour, who was a lecturer in law and a union member, testified in relation to the 'activist list', the internal union email forum:

> I have observed the objective aspect of antisemitism being expressed on the Activist list many times, on familiar terms. These include, *inter alia*, that 'Zionists' or 'supporters of Israel' have access to unaccountable resources; that individuals act in concert with others (such as the suggestion that the posts of each individual are co-ordinated collectively, domestically and internationally); that those opposing the boycott are part of a larger

'lobby' . . . and that this lobby holds a dominant influence over those with whom it comes into conflict; that specific individuals (as part of the lobby) combine to undermine union democracy; that Jews remain in the background while others, non-Jews, are in the front-line; that Zionists are responsible for major catastrophes (i.e. 9.11).

. . . I was told that my identification of antisemitic tropes and imagery was a ruse either to 'deflect criticism of Israel', or to further the interests of the so-called 'Lobby' and, as such, to act to the detriment of Palestinians (and the Union). At times, I became the object of an abusive dialogue that took place between two prominent list contributors . . . . Like my communications with the list moderator, the substance of my complaints was ignored and, instead, accusations of *mal fide* were heaped upon me in this environment open to all Union members.

It was during this time that I began to feel the subjective effects of this constant stream of antisemitism. The sheer unpleasantness of having to read these comments coupled with the dismissal of my concerns by the Union and those on the activist list, left me feeling a sense of vulnerability. This sense of vulnerability and depression and feeling of isolation that gradually came to accompany it, began to spill over into other areas of my life. It was these feelings that I expressed when I formally removed myself from the activist list. Its effects linger and can be traced to my initial reluctance to recall the matters described in this statement. It is a period of my life that I did not wish to recollect. In retrospect, I believe that the negative feelings I had at the time were the result of what I can only describe as an environment of 'antisemitic bullying'.

David Seymour was cross-examined in court. The tribunal wrote the following:

> Some witnesses were most impressive. These include . . . Dr Seymour. They gave careful, thoughtful, courteous evidence and were clearly mindful of their obligations as witnesses in litigation.
>
> *(para 148)*

Having praised him, the tribunal ignored his evidence. It did not refer to Seymour's evidence at any other point in the judgment, and it appears to have given it no credence at all.

Mira Vogel, who was a member of the central support staff at Goldsmiths, University of London, wrote the following in her witness statement:

> Opposing the boycott campaign on the UCU Activists List, an email discussion group with a membership of roughly 700, was a bruising experience which left me feeling powerless.
>
> I was groundlessly accused on the Activists list of orchestrating UCU resignations . . . .
>
> I was also subjected to a diagnosis of problems with my character, which were explained in terms of flawed Jewishness on my part. This person had also addressed me with insinuating and racialized observations such as 'Apologies for my style. It is genetic you know . . .' and 'Live together is the best therapy for racism – Jews know this better than anybody'. In doing so he illustrated a troubling pair of associated assumptions which characterize UCU's boycott campaign: anti-boycotters are both Jewish and profoundly morally inferior. I am not aware of UCU moderator efforts to disrupt this association . . .
>
> While Zionism is maligned and epitomised as an evil force within UCU, I worry that my identification as a Zionist by UCU activists could become a serious problem for me at work. Ignorance about Zionism on the part of boycott campaigners is often profound . . . . Because I need to be in a position to support colleagues and students across Goldsmiths, as far as my day-to-day work is concerned it would be better for me to avoid situations where they are given to understand that I am aligned with or part of a Jewish supremacist movement which tries to manipulate world powers and plans genocide against Palestinians – particularly when colleagues are encouraged by Resolution 30's statement that 'Congress believes that in these circumstances passivity or neutrality is unacceptable'.

The tribunal did not refer to Mira Vogel's evidence anywhere in its judgment.

Duncan Bryson was a history lecturer at a college in the West Midlands. He gave evidence about the culture at UCU Congresses that he attended as a delegate:

> There was a leaflet that branded opponents of the boycott as 'apologists for massacre'. This seemed to me quite an incredible leap to make. Also, one of the stalls had a large banner above it reading 'Zionism = Racism'. This is the level of debate — it is very simplistic and does not allow for other opinions. Such sentiments made it difficult for me to express my doubts about the boycott because I felt I would be treated in a very hostile way.
>
> The debate was ill mannered, there was often loud heckling and constant interruption from the floor, speakers did not always appear in order, one speaker struggled to finish his piece amongst the noise, members of the NEC [National Executive Committee] including the chair, intervened with pro-boycott statements.
>
> In this atmosphere I did not feel comfortable contributing to the debate. I felt, rightly or wrongly, my stance on this issue would alienate me from comrades with whom I wished to make common cause on other issues. I felt that by expressing my dissenting views on the boycott I would compromise relationships within the union, that I would be seen as a 'Zionist' or an 'apologist'. To clarify, I am used to the rough and tumble of debate and I am not generally uncomfortable speaking in public. But this was beyond the usual rough and tumble.

Duncan Bryson's evidence was not referred to in the tribunal judgment.

Steve Scott, director of Trade Union Friends of Israel (TUFI), wrote in his witness statement:

> Since the 2008 conference at which TUFI exhibited, the UCU has categorically refused to allow TUFI to exhibit at its subsequent conferences, justifying its decision with the claim that they now only allow affiliated organisations . . . . TUFI formally asked the UCU if they would affiliate to TUFI, but we were told that they would not be affiliating to TUFI. No reasons were given . . . .

The UCU debate on Israel and Palestine at the national activist level has become so toxic that I believe anyone trying to promote a balanced debate is fighting a lost cause. The entrenched commitment to an aggressive anti-Israel stance and the level of anti-Israel rhetoric among conference delegates makes the UCU conference an intimidating atmosphere for voices of opposition. I can only imagine how oppressive the environment is for the UCU's Jewish membership in the context of this fierce political agenda.

Stephen Scott's evidence was not referred to in the tribunal judgment.

David-Hillel Ruben was a senior University of London Professor of philosophy. He wrote in his witness statement:

> I attended a general, London-wide meeting at SOAS [School of Oriental and African Studies] called by the union on Israel, and was laughed at and harangued. If anyone thinks these special meetings are places where open-minded discussion occurs, he should attend such a meeting in order to be disabused of this thought. They are meetings where the true believers speak to one another about Israeli imperialism and aggression. The narrative from only one side is heard. No one can seriously take these meetings to be balanced. They have in fact a threatening effect on those who have anything positive to say about Israel . . . .
>
> It was impossible for me to feel that this was any longer 'my' union, one to which I was welcome to belong. Here is what a member of the national executive committee wrote to me recently:
>
>> 'I don't want to re-enter this debate but Israel is subject to a delegitimization campaign precisely because apartheid and racism is unique to the very fabric of Israel'.
>
> If Zionism is racist, then I am being told that I, my family, my friends are racists. As Director of a small university campus from 1999–2011 (NYU [New York University] in London), I tried to encourage union membership amongst our part time academic staff. I failed. No one wanted to join. I spoke time and time again

to many, Jews and non-Jews, who had already resigned from the union out of disgust over their policies on Israel.

. . . In truth, although I resigned from the union, it felt much more like my union having been taken away from me. Over the years, I watched the anti-Israel sentiment grow. I have watched the anti-Israel sentiment in the union grow from a peculiar occupation of the union, although well within the bounds of political legitimacy, to what it is today: a fetish that has crossed the line into anti-Semitism. I appreciate that a few of the union anti-Israel activists are themselves Jewish, but the appellation of anti-Semitism is an objective one and I believe it accurately describes the union today.

Josh Robinson was a research fellow at Cambridge and a union member. He wrote in his witness statement:

From June 2007 onwards, traffic on the activists' list was dominated for several months by discussion of the motion and Israeli-Palestinian politics more generally. Opponents of Israel made countless antisemitic statements. I documented some of these in a 22-page complaint which I submitted to UCU in May 2008. The document consisted of three complaints pertaining to antisemitic conduct on the activists' list on the part of three individual members of UCU, and one pertaining to institutional antisemitism within the union as a whole.

Josh Robinson was eventually informed that the complaint would be considered by Tom Hickey, one of the leaders of the boycott campaign in the union, and Matt Waddup, who was himself responsible for monitoring the activists' list, and was now being asked to sit in judgment over his own conduct. Robinson questioned the choice of these two with a union official and was told that they were the correct and appropriate individuals to choose. Josh Robinson never received a response to his formal complaint. He goes on:

I find it difficult to draw from these events and the reaction to my complaint of institutional antisemitism any conclusion other than that those responsible for its investigation had decided in advance that there was no case to answer, and were acting (or rather: not acting) accordingly. This does strongly suggest that UCU as an organization is not committed to the establishment of an environment that is free from discrimination.

The tribunal accepted Robinson's description of these events, and it judged that the failure to deal with the complaint was 'unfortunate'; but, it went on, this failure was not 'capable of sustaining a complaint that the Respondents harassed *the Claimant*' (italics in original) (para 160). Ronnie Fraser alleged that there was an environment in the UCU that was, in the words of the act, 'intimidating, hostile, degrading, humiliating and/or offensive to him, in respect of his Jewish identity'. In plain English, he was alleging institutional antisemitism. Robinson made a formal complaint through the union structures about what he called 'institutional antisemitism'; he interpreted the union's 'unfortunate' failure to respond as further evidence of it. The tribunal judged that what happened to Robinson, and his complaint was not evidence of anything relating to Fraser.

Jon Pike was a leading activist in the *Engage* network, a Senior Lecturer in Philosophy at the Open University, and he had been elected onto the National Executive Committee (NEC) of the UCU. In relation to his experience of the activists' list, he wrote in his witness statement:

> To say discussion was bad mannered would be an understatement. It was like a cess pit. Vile accusations and comments were routinely directed at anyone who questioned the boycott policy or expressed anything but hatred for Israel.
>
> I complained formally through the complaints procedure of the union about some of these comments. I wrote a detailed complaint about three named members, whose comments seemed to me to be the most egregious. I listed other comments, and tried as best as I could to point out why they seemed out of order.
>
> One of those about whom I complained, then countercomplained by accusing me of Islamophobia. However, this complaint did not cite any evidence against me at all.

However, my complaints were quickly rejected; no reference was made to the evidence I had submitted.

I was on the NEC .... It was an unpleasant experience for me. I suffered from insomnia, and began smoking, especially around the time of NEC meetings. I can only describe it as a very hostile environment.

The way it would manifest itself would be, for example, that at meetings, and outside meetings, people would blank me and refuse to acknowledge me, including in the queues for coffee. Some people who agreed with me politically in private would refuse to talk to me in public, or on occasions when they could be seen by others ....

I felt I had to resign after [the 2009] Congress because it was such an appalling experience .... A member of the SWP [Socialist Workers Party] stood up and said 'Jon Pike has just made the worst speech ever in the history of congress'. He was applauded, until the president intervened to say that personal attacks should not be made. This indicates the level of hostility which I faced. I had experienced nothing like that in my ordinary life as an academic where it was not strange to hold the broadly liberal view that I held.

Whatever your view was on Israel, this was enough to define you politically. I was simply known as Jon Pike the 'Zionist'. It was commonly assumed that I was Jewish. 'Zionist' was uniformly seen as a term of condemnation, indeed demonization. Individuals with who I thought I had merely a nodding acquaintance, or who were near strangers would mutter under their breath when they found themselves in my proximity (for example in the gents). On one such occasion, I was told by another member of the NEC that 'if you can't take the flak you should get out of the union'.

... In the course of my involvement with the AUT and the UCU I met many Jewish academics who opposed a boycott of Israeli universities. Very few of them were able to withstand the levels of hostility and abuse that was directed against them in the union, and maintain their participation. Dozens of Jewish members have left the union, ground down by the abuse and hostility that has been directed against them. The main two exceptions are David Hirsh and Ronnie Fraser.

The tribunal, in its judgment, did not address any of this evidence given to it by Jon Pike.

Mark Osborn gave evidence about an incident which had happened in 2006 when he was a member of NATFHE, at a regional meeting. In his statement he recounts that there was a discussion about who would be delegated to national conference:

> Various speakers at this meeting objected to one proposed National Conference delegate, Ronnie Fraser. Ronnie is a religious Jew and does not attend Saturday meetings, although he is a delegate to the Region from his branch.
>
> One objection to Ronnie was that he does not attend Region meetings, and so, on these grounds, couldn't be a delegate from the Region. However, many other National Conference delegates, in the past, had not attended Region.
>
> At this point Tom Peters [name changed] from Kingsway College spoke, declaring that Ronnie should not be a delegate because he was a 'Zionist and a racist'.
>
> I interrupted, saying that calling Ronnie Fraser a racist was a disgrace, and that the remark should be withdrawn. Eventually [Tom Peters] did 'withdraw' the remark but in such a way that the allegation was both withdrawn and re-stated: TP declared Ronnie Fraser was not a racist, but that Zionists are racists and that Ronnie Fraser is a Zionist.
>
> The chair of the meeting regarded this high-volume exchange between myself and Tom Peters as an irritation. The chair (I don't know this man's name) eventually asked Tom Peters to withdraw the allegation that RF is a racist – but as a bureaucratic method of continuing the meeting, rather than as a matter of principle.
>
> Although Tom Peters' remark was awful, at least he was being honest; others were trying to edge 'the Jew' out on technical reasons of attendance – a cover for political hostility.
>
> Tom Peters then proposed a vote to elect the Region's National Conference delegates. The proposal was made – explicitly – in

order to exclude Ronnie from the delegation. There were no hustings.

The tribunal ruled that this, and a number of other pieces of evidence, were out of time. Anthony Julius had addressed this issue at the beginning of the trial as follows:

> The complainant's case is that the actions relied upon are *cumulative*: each instance of harassment has caused the evolution over time of the environment proscribed . . . .
>
> It is *continuing*: the acts complained of amounted to a series of continuing acts which contributed to the [prohibited environment] . . .
>
> . . . It is clear that these issues have been raised with UCU on numerous occasions, throughout the period complained about . . . there can clearly be a fair hearing on the issues that are raised by this claim.
>
> *(Fraser's skeleton argument, para 61.5)*

The tribunal dismissed this reasoning as follows:

> Employment tribunals exist to deliver swift, practical, economical justice in the employment field and some related areas. Narrow jurisdictional time limits are in keeping with the scheme, being designed to ensure that disputes are not allowed to fester but are promptly litigated and determined so that the parties can put their differences behind them and move on. It is for the Claimant to show a good reason to entertain a claim out of time. The length of the delay, his awareness of the tribunal's jurisdiction and his access to legal support all argue compellingly against us exercising the discretion which he invokes. Quite simply, no good reason is shown to consider this very late claim.
>
> *(para 175)*

Ronnie Fraser had been resisting what he understood to be a thickening culture of antisemitism within the union, for years. He did not go to court immediately. Members resisted antisemitism by making arguments and by persuasion, by writing articles, blogs, and papers; they did so by putting motions in branches and at Congresses; they tried to educate and to persuade; they attempted to participate in debates on the activists' list; they tried to take complaints through the formal complaints procedures of the union; they tried resigning in protest. Court was a last resort. Now the tribunal judged that anything which happened before the time limit was irrelevant. It could only do this by dismissing the argument that there was a growing problem in the union of institutional antisemitism. It first dismissed the claim that there was a relevant course of action, in order then to dismiss each instance as having occurred before the cut-off date.

There was another argument made in relation to Mark Osborn's testimony. It was said by the union that Fraser was absent when this incident occurred; he could, therefore, not possibly have been harassed by it; it was said that Annette Seidel-Arpaci's testimony could not have related to Fraser, because he was not in Leeds; it was said that things written on the activist list could not constitute harassment, because one chose to look at them. The judgment states:

> While the conduct need not be aimed at a claimant, the further he stands from it, the less likely the tribunal is to find that in fact he experienced the stated adverse effect or, if he did, that it was reasonable for the conduct to have that effect.
>
> *(para 42)*

Imagine making an analogous argument in relation to pornographic pictures on the walls of a workshop. Women could only be affected by them if somebody told them they were there; a woman in one workshop could not be affected by them if they worked in another workshop; if a woman did not look at the pictures, they could not affect her. But they would still add to an environment which constituted a violation of the act; and even if no woman employee ever saw them, or even ever heard of them, they would still relate to the possibility of women being employed in the future. The UCU relied on arguments which it would have opposed sturdily in another context; the tribunal accepted arguments which it would not have accepted in another context.

Dennis Noble was an Emeritus Professor of Physiology and a celebrated scientist; he is not Jewish. He wrote the following in his witness statement:

> In the context of UCU's insistent calls for sanctions (including boycotts) against Israel, its refusal to take the opportunity to dissociate itself from the public expression of anti-Semitic views clearly showed that the union itself is institutionally anti-Semitic.

Dennis Noble's testimony was not mentioned in the judgment.

James Mendelsohn was a Senior Lecturer in Law at the University of Huddersfield and a former union member, having resigned in protest at the antisemitism he said he suffered in the union. He testified as follows:

> I do not believe that a trade union which did in fact abhor anti-Semitism would ignore emails from its members raising concerns about issues related to anti-Semitism, as Sally Hunt did; reject calls for condemnation even of Hamas' anti-Semitic rhetoric, as Ray Lesley [name changed] and members of the Yorkshire and Humber Regional Committee had done; invite a man convicted of anti-Semitic hate speech to its premises to promote the boycott campaign, in the form of [Bongani] Masuku; or reject a definition of anti-Semitism outright, without suggesting an alternative. The UCU was an uncomfortable place for Jewish members, and I felt I had no choice but to resign.

James Mendelsohn's testimony is not addressed in the tribunal judgment.

Raphael Levy was a lecturer in Biology at Liverpool University and a union member. He wrote:

> I witnessed first with incredulity, and then with increasing anger and despair, the atmosphere of antisemitic bullying and hatred on the activist list. I was a member of that list for a period in 2008. I read comments targeting another member of the list, Mira Vogel, and implying a separation between Jewishness and humanity. There was no intervention from the moderator. I found this disturbing and decided to raise the issue on the list.

Following my post, I received unsolicited responses by email (off list), not of support, but denying that anything wrong had happened, characterizing my concerns as madness ('losing the plot'), provocations or as a dishonest attempt to silence debate, as well as a call on Jews to 'speak for themselves', i.e. declare themselves good Jews who hate Israel.

The most shocking aspect of all of this for me was not that a couple of individuals would utter racist statements, but the fact that these were tolerated. No action was ever taken by the UCU against antisemitism. On the contrary, antiracists such as David Hirsh were excluded from the list. Clearly that list was not a safe place for Jews. This was not a place for rational debate and anyone who dared challenge antisemitism or the UCU support of the boycott of Israeli colleagues was the target of abuse.

My experience of participating on the list was painful, sad, and dispiriting. The daily delivery of hate and the fact that there was never any official objection to the rabid antisemitism was probably the worst part of it.

Raphael Levy's testimony is not mentioned in the judgment. The judgment does, however, exonerate the union's management of the list:

> The List, a facility open only to members of the union who wished join it, was operated fairly and Mr Waddup's management of it was almost wholly unobjectionable. The Respondents' conduct (through him) cannot be described as 'unwanted', in the sense which we ascribe to that word. Nor is the requisite effect established. If the Claimant was upset to a significant extent by anything to do with the List, it was not Mr Waddup's management of it but the nature of the comments of pro-Palestinian contributors.
>
> *(para 160)*

Lesley Klaff was a Senior Lecturer in Law at Sheffield Hallam University and a union member. She gave evidence concerning a large number of issues which related to local union members. This is one of them:

> It was in May 2007 that I first became aware of a Sheffield Hallam University colleague, anti-Zionist and Palestine Solidarity

Campaign (PSC) activist named John Harry [name changed]. He was a UCU caseworker at Sheffield Hallam University. He was introduced to me by means of email correspondence sent to me by a Sheffield Hallam University UCU branch executive officer named Peter Smith [name changed]. Peter had apparently informed John that I was Jewish, a Zionist, and anti-boycott. John then composed an email for me, containing questions for me to answer about Israel. The email was forwarded to me by Peter Smith on 10 May 2007 . . . .

I experienced John's email as offensive. It invoked the classic trope of 'Jewish criminality' (theft of land and water) and the newer trope of 'Israel-equals-apartheid South Africa'. It also misstated the facts as I knew them to be. In fact, this was to be the first of several such distressing emails that I would receive from John Harry. They only ceased when he retired from Sheffield Hallam University . . .

There was no doubt in my mind that John's anti-Zionist on-campus activism which included his asking me questions and challenging me to a public debate, was engendered by the UCU national executive's discriminatory measures against Israel. In fact, John's initial email to me was written and sent in the context of his on-campus pro-boycott campaigning just prior to the implementation of Motion 30 at UCU Congress.

The combined effect of Motion 30 and John' simultaneous on-campus pro-boycott campaigning (in which he distributed pro-boycott leaflets) was to create a hostile working environment for me as a Jewish person with strong ties to Israel. This is because for me the boycott strategy resonated with the history of anti-Semitism, was based on false facts, and promoted a discourse which employed anti-Semitic tropes.

Lesley Klaff's evidence was not mentioned by the tribunal in its judgment. What happened at Sheffield Hallam, insisted the union's barrister, on the union's instructions, could not constitute harassment against Ronnie Fraser in London.

Eve Garrard was a research fellow in Philosophy at Manchester University and a union member. She wrote in her witness statement:

It became clear that the Union's primary concern about the charges of discrimination which some (mainly but not exclusively

Jewish) members began to raise was that such charges caused offence to pro-boycotters in the Union. The Union was anxious to protect pro-boycotters from being offended, but showed no concern for the worries of Jewish members who felt that their union was discriminating against Jews who supported Israel.

. . . Further reinforcement of my concerns was provided by the readiness of some contributors to dismiss all worries about discrimination by claiming that charges of anti-Semitism were only made in order to distract attention from Israel's crimes. This unsupported claim, each time it was made, repeated the insinuation that people concerned about the disproportionate impact of boycott proposals on Jewish members of the Union were in fact liars engaged in manipulation and deceit. The spectacle of members of my own Union engaging in all this was extremely distressing: these, after all, were my academic colleagues, whom I should have expected at the very least to be able to provide adequate arguments for their selective hostility to the Jewish state. I should also have expected them to show some attempt to understand and take seriously the concerns about discrimination which I and other anti-boycotters were expressing. The Union executive did not at any point intervene to restrain this behaviour, and indeed itself at one point declared that criticism of Israel could not be regarded as anti-Semitic.

Observing [the Congress debate in 2008 in Manchester] was an even more distressing experience than I had expected it to be. I stood in the audience and watched as motions criticising countries such as Zimbabwe and Sudan, and proposing moderate responses to them, were presented and passed by delegates who were quiet almost to the point of somnolence. But these self-same delegates became extremely alert and enthusiastic when the prospect of punishing Israel's putative crimes was put before them. I watched these people – my peers and colleagues, in effect – collectively decide not to allow this vote to go to the Union membership, presumably in case the membership refused to pass it (as indeed all the evidence suggests they would have done). As I watched the proposer of Motion 25 being given the chance to speak twice, where people who might have opposed

the Motion weren't given the opportunity to speak at all, I felt
I was in the presence of something I had never thought to find
among academic colleagues: a fixed determination to punish the
Jewish state, come what may, irrespective of considerations of
fairness or equity, or of the consequences for Jewish Colleagues.
I felt quite exceptionally lonely and isolated, watching other academics in my own Union enthusiastically pass a motion which
was bound to bear adversely on many, perhaps most, of their
Jewish colleagues.

. . . I feel I have been seriously let down by the UCU. My
Union was supposed to represent and support me; but instead
I found it to be a place where my concerns, and those of others who share them, were entirely ignored, and treated as being
of no importance. It had become for me a place in which I was
regularly faced with profoundly offensive comments and behaviour. In the end I felt that I had no choice but to leave.

None of this from Eve Garrard was mentioned in the tribunal's
judgment.

Robert Fine was an Emeritus Professor of Sociology at Warwick, a
veteran of the anti-apartheid struggle and a union member. He wrote
in his witness statement:

I consider that UCU was correct in saying that criticism of Israel
or of Israeli government policies is not *necessarily* antisemitic.
However UCU did not acknowledge that some criticisms of
Israel *may* be antiemetic, or that some members of the union
felt this to be the case. This lack of acknowledgement indicated
that antisemitism was not one of the forms of racism that UCU
took seriously.

. . . When the academic boycott motion was debated at one
Congress, opponents of the motion were given a tightly cir-
cumscribed opportunity to speak. When one opponent of the
motion used the word 'anti-Semitism' in the course of his speech,
I found it especially regrettable that he was audibly jeered and
that the organisers of the meeting, as I recollect, did nothing to
stop the jeering of the speaker (who I believe was the plaintiff

in the case, Ronnie Fraser). It went without question that other forms of racism were rejected by UCU, which sees itself as a bastion of support for academic freedom and anti-discrimination, but talk of antisemitism seems to have been treated as a ruse. It again appeared to me that UCU did not take the matter of antisemitism seriously.

Some academics from within and without the Jewish community, including myself, have felt increasingly isolated because of the UCU attitude toward the boycott of Israel and toward the issue of antisemitism. A number of colleagues resigned because of what they see as a culture of antisemitism. I myself did not do so, partly because I value very highly the role of the union, but I would certainly endorse the view that there has been a culture of neglect within the union as a result of which allegations of antisemitism have not been addressed and some members, Jewish and non-Jewish, have been significantly harmed.

Robert Fine's testimony is not mentioned in the tribunal's judgment. The tribunal did come to a judgment about the conduct of debates at UCU Congress, however:

the proceedings were well-ordered and balanced. They were carefully controlled from the Chair. They were managed in an even-handed fashion with speakers selected in turn to speak for and against the motions. On the very rare occasions when it was necessary to call Congress to order, the chairman did so and those present responded appropriately. The debates were conducted with courtesy. Speakers on both sides received applause. Despite the strength of feeling, they lightened the occasion with humour from time to time. We were quite unable to detect the atmosphere of intimidation which the written case on the Claimant's behalf attempted to convey.

Ariel Hessayon, a Senior Lecturer in History at Goldsmiths, University of London, wrote in his statement:

I ... participated in the UCU Activists' List until I had my posting rights blocked .... This followed posting a message on behalf of

Dr David Hirsh, who had himself been banned from posting on the list . . . .

I can certainly say that participating in the Activists' List was a deeply unpleasant experience: the atmosphere was frequently hostile and always intimidating. While I never personally felt humiliated I was confronted on an almost daily basis by extremists fixated on a single-minded obsession, one which constantly challenged and indeed sought to undermine my sense of my own Jewish identity.

Ariel Hessayon's evidence is not mentioned in the tribunal judgment.

A coordinated campaign by Ronnie Fraser, his lawyers and his witnesses to try to intimidate critics of Israel with a fake accusation of antisemitism would indeed be disgraceful. This is what the tribunal, in the end, concluded had been happening, and this explains the unusually intemperate and emotional language employed in its dismissal of Fraser's case. This also explains the tribunal's refusal to consider with seriousness the detailed evidence which the witnesses presented of how antisemitism functioned within the UCU.

The tribunal judged that Fraser was trying to mobilize an allegation of antisemitism in order to undermine the freedom of speech of critics of Israel. It judged: 'We are also troubled by the implications of the claim. Underlying it we sense a worrying disregard for pluralism, tolerance and freedom of expression' (para 179). The tribunal said that Fraser was trying to persuade it to outlaw criticism of Israel as antisemitic. This was in spite of the fact that Julius and a large number of witnesses had been clear about the ways they considered the distinction between criticism of Israel and antisemitism to be of key importance. There is nothing unusual about those who defend racism claiming that antiracists disregard their right to free speech. Sometimes, the tribunal appears to veer towards the view that those who complained of antisemitism were simply over-sensitive and lacking in objective judgment. But the central findings, that this was politics dressed up as litigation, and that this was an attempt to prohibit free criticism, are allegations of bad faith.

It is striking that the response that Fraser's allegation of antisemitism received in the tribunal turned out to be similar to the response which he had received within the union itself. The tribunal backed the union's way of thinking about antisemitism completely.

Fraser said that the key mode of intimidation in the UCU was the constant allegation of bad faith, the allegation that Jews who say they feel antisemitism were actually lying for Israel. The tribunal replied that Ronnie Fraser, who said that he felt antisemitism, was dressing up a political end as a problem of racist exclusion. The tribunal held that it was appropriate to make the accusation of bad faith against Jews in the union who said that they experienced antisemitism.

The Parliamentary Inquiry into Antisemitism (2006) reported that the boycott debates were likely to cause difficulties for Jewish academics and students, to exclude Jews from academic life and to have a detrimental effect on Jewish Studies. UCU responded that these allegations were made to stop people from criticizing Israel. Jon Pike explained how seventy-six members of the UCU publicly endorsed a critique of the union's response which he had written with David Hirsh, but the union took no notice. John Mann MP told the tribunal that UCU had been unique among those criticized by the inquiry in its refusal to listen.

Sean Wallis, a local UCU official, said that anti-boycott lawyers were financed by 'bank balances from Lehman Brothers that can't be tracked down' (Kovler 2009). Ronnie Fraser asked him whether he had indeed made this claim. Wallis admitted having said it. But it was Fraser who, for the crime of asking, was found to have violated union rules concerning 'rude or offensive communications' (Fraser's Witness Statement).

Gert Weisskirchen, responsible for combating antisemitism for the Organisation for Security and Co-operation in Europe, asked the union leadership for a meeting to discuss antisemitism relating to the boycott. The union did not meet with him. When thirty-nine union members protested publicly, the union ignored them. Weisskirchen provided evidence to the tribunal. He wrote:

> I can only describe the UCU's response to me as cold and dismissive. All UCU officials and representatives resolutely refused to meet with me or address any of my publicised concerns, simply stating to me that all relevant individuals were 'too busy' at all of the dates and times I had proposed.
>
> In my 40 years of trade union membership I had never encountered a response akin to the one I received from the UCU.

The union invited South African Trade Unionist Bongani Masuku to speak at a pro-boycott conference in London. Masuku was known to be under investigation by the South African Human Rights Commission (SAHRC) for antisemitic hate speech. He had written, for example, in public:

> Bongani says hi to you all as we struggle to liberate Palestine from the racists, fascists and Zionists who belong to the era of their friend Hitler! We must not apologize, every Zionist must be made to drink the bitter medicine they are feeding our brothers and sisters in Palestine.

Masuku also said that vigilante action would be taken against Jewish families suspected of having members serving in the Israeli military, and that Jews who continued to stand up for Israel should 'not just be encouraged but forced to leave South Africa'. Evidence about Masuku was presented to the tribunal by Wendy Kahn, the director of the South African Jewish Board of Deputies. She wrote in her witness statement:

> Against the backdrop of Mr Masuku's speech at the University of Witswatersrand and the complaint to the SAHRC, UCU's invitation to COSATU [Confederation of South African Trade Unions] showed very poor judgment. That UCU provided Mr Masuku with a platform to speak, after it became aware of the Finding is simply shocking. UCU has failed to apologise for the incident and has not disassociated itself from COSATU, which continues to publish a stream of anti-Semitic rhetoric. The SAJBD [South African Jewish Board of Deputies] considers that UCU's actions stand in stark contrast to its self-stated interest in confronting all forms of anti-Semitism and show a flagrant disregard for the feelings and sentiments of UCU's Jewish membership.

The union ought to have known Masuku's record. Ronnie Fraser told the union about Masuku's record. Masuku was found guilty in South Africa of hate speech before speaking as a guest of UCU. And, months later, UCU Congress explicitly rejected a motion to dissociate itself from Masuku's 'repugnant views'.

Masuku and COSATU persistently refused to recognize the SAHRC finding, and they refused to apologize for Masuku's behaviour. Eventually, the SAHRC sued Masuku and COSATU in the Equalities Court in Johannesburg. The case was heard in February 2017; the expert witness on antisemitism for the SAHRC was David Hirsh. The judgment has not yet been handed down.

On the activists' list, Ronnie Fraser responded to talk of the 'blockade of Gaza' by pointing out that there was no absolute blockade of Gaza. In response, another union member said that he was like the Nazis at Theresienstadt. In my own cross-examination, I explained to the tribunal the significance of this response. I told them that Theresienstadt was a ghetto and concentration camp in Czechoslovakia which the Nazis had dressed up as a humane home for Jews in order to show the Red Cross. I tried to help the tribunal to understand what it meant for a son of two Holocaust survivors to be denounced as being like a Nazi, in this way, in public, by his union comrades. The union found that there was nothing inappropriate about this comment which warranted union officers to step in. The tribunal found there was nothing inappropriate about the union's refusal to step in.

A significant number of union members resigned over the issue of antisemitism. Congress voted down a motion requiring the union officers to investigate these resignations. There was no mechanism for counting resignations over antisemitism, and such resignations were instead counted, according to the testimony of the union officer responsible, as being related to 'disagreements over the Middle East'.

There was an instructive exchange during the cross-examination of the general secretary of the UCU, Sally Hunt. Anthony Julius took her through a large number of examples of allegedly antisemitic things which had been said or written within union spaces – during Congress, at other meetings and on the UCU activists' email list. Hunt considered each example, and she judged each one in turn to be not antisemitic. As though rather exasperated, Julius put a hypothetical to her: 'If somebody said, "If you want to understand the Jews, read *Mein Kampf*", would *that* be antisemitic?' Hunt answered that within the union context, because the union is an antiracist union, then no, it would not necessarily be antisemitic.

This answer is an explicit endorsement of the politics of position over the politics of reason. For Hunt, what was important in judging whether a statement was antisemitic was the space in which it was made and the people who made it, not the content of the statement itself. Hunt seemed to regard antisemitism within an antiracist union to be unthinkable. Instead of coming to terms with the normalization of antisemitism in the union, Hunt *defined* the antisemitic behaviour and the antisemitic speech as being antiracist, not by virtue of its content but by virtue of its occurrence within a space which is *a priori* not antisemitic. Anybody who challenges this *a priori* truth must be cast out; anybody who tries to engage with the truth by discussion, reason, evidence or argument risks their status as part of the community.

Having presided over the relentless cross-examination of Sally Hunt, having seen her deny that each example was antisemitic, having seen her reject even that hypothetical, Judge Snelson scolded Anthony Julius in a rather condescending way and expressed the hope that Julius would soon come to discussing the evidence of the case.

Having heard all the evidence, the tribunal, like the union, judged none of them to be evidence of antisemitism. It judged:

> The Claimant is a campaigner. He chooses to engage in the politics of the union in support of Israel and in opposition to activists for the Palestinian cause. When a rugby player takes the field he must accept his fair share of minor injuries . . . . Similarly, a political activist accepts the risk of being offended or hurt on occasions by things said or done by his opponents (who themselves take on a corresponding risk).
>
> *(para 156)*

It is unimaginable that a tribunal today would say the same thing to a woman who complained of sexual harassment at work after she chose to wear a tight skirt to the office, or after she had chosen to campaign in favour of women's rights. But this is what the tribunal said to the Jewish man.

The rugby analogy demonstrates one of the central problems with the approach taken by the tribunal. The tribunal seemed unable to grasp the key distinction between criticism of Israel, on the one hand, and speech or action which could be judged to be antisemitic, on the other. In fact it said that it took the distinction seriously, and it accused Fraser of not doing so. The problem comes, however, when in practice everything is judged to be criticism and nothing is judged to be antisemitism. The result is the position that since Fraser took on the responsibility of defending Israel, then he should expect some antisemitism as part of the 'game'.

The tribunal also mentioned that it had been inappropriate to allow Tom Hickey, a union official, to sit in judgment over formal claims of antisemitism. Why? It says that the reason is that he is a 'well-known pro-Palestinian activist' (para 181). Surely, however, it is insulting to 'pro-Palestinian activists' to suggest that they are unqualified to judge what is antisemitic and what is not. Being pro-Palestine should be one thing; being antisemitic should be quite another. The tribunal found itself unable to work with the distinction. The reason why Hickey was an inappropriate judge, as the tribunal was told, was because he was not good at making the distinction between antisemitism and criticism of Israel, not because he was 'pro-Palestinian'. Fraser had offered the tribunal a video[3] to watch which showed Hickey saying that the attempt by Israeli archaeologists to write a history of Israel as something which had always existed was 'more insidious, and in some sense, almost nastier', than the Nazi genocide of Jews. Belief in this kind of bizarre and extreme position, which many would judge to be antisemitic, was the reason this man was inappropriate to judge a formal complaint of antisemitism. But the tribunal refused to watch the video, and it misconstrued the point about why he was an inappropriate judge.

Speaking for myself, I never chose to play rugby. I found that my union was considering setting up an exclusion of our Israeli colleagues from UK campuses, so I tried to make arguments against it doing so. I was, as it were, pushed onto a rugby field. There, I found myself being outnumbered and repeatedly knocked to the floor by organized opponents. I was confronted by relentless, if sometimes subtle, antisemitic rhetoric, hostility and accusations of bad faith. I appealed to the union, who was playing the part of the referee. But the referee said that it must remain neutral between the two rugby teams, and I should just get on with the game. But I was not part of a rugby team and I did not want to play. I only wanted my union to stop with the hatred of Israel and with the antisemitism which came with it. And when I tried to step outside of the rugby field and say publicly what was going on, I was punished for breaking the rules of the game. It may be appropriate to rugby-tackle somebody who has chosen to play rugby, but, when this happens outside of the rugby field, it has a different meaning.

There was a time when I and a number of others, many of whom eventually gave evidence for Ronnie in front of the tribunal, were trying to have our voices heard on the activists' list. Most of us, unlike Ronnie, were not particularly 'pro-Israel' but strong critics of Israeli policy and of the occupation. Indeed, some of my own criticism of Israel was so strong that it was read out to another witness under cross-examination as being indistinguishable from the antisemitic rhetoric of which Ronnie complained. But the witness explained to the tribunal how it was different. Nevertheless, if ever we raised the issue of anti-semitic rhetoric on the list, we would immediately be denounced for crying antisemitism in bad faith in order to silence criticism of Israel. It was a difficult time. We would try to explain what the problem was with the accusations that we supported the genocide of the Palestin-ians, or that we were racists, or that we were Nazis, and people would respond, immediately, relentlessly and in writing before hundreds of our union colleagues, that we only raised the issue of antisemitism in order to stifle their criticisms of Israel.

We appealed to the moderator of the list. We said that this was a union space and that it should not be possible to bully us out of it with antisemitic rhetoric. But the moderator acted as the referee in a tough rugby match between Israel and Palestine, rather than a union official making sure that the union was a safe place for Jewish members here in the UK. One academic who had been particularly active at that time told the tribunal that he had nearly had a nervous breakdown because of the way he was treated on the activist list.

One strategy I was minded to adopt at that time was to publish some of the antisemitic material from the list on the *Engage* website. There was a closed culture within the union in which antisemitism was never recognized and was never thought to be a problem. Institutional racism requires a heavy policing of the institutional boundaries to make sure that the values of the external world cannot intrude and the norms of the internal world cannot be seen.

In August 2007, I wrote an email on the activists' list expressing concern at the antisemitic consequences of the campaign to boycott Israel and arguing that we should be aware that it is usual for antisemitic arguments to be positioned as one side in a legitimate democratic debate. I was warned by the list moderator for the crime of saying this and told to 'be more careful in my choice of language' or otherwise I would be excluded from the discussion. I was also told not to publish anything which appeared on the list. I responded by saying that I would make no undertaking whatsoever not to publish *antisemitic* material from the list. The tribunal tells this story in its judgment, but it chooses to delete the word 'antisemitic'. In paragraph ninety-three of the judgment, it reports: 'Dr Hirsh responded, stating that he would "make no undertaking whatsoever" not to publish material from the List.' I and other critics of antisemitism were indeed excluded from the list, while nobody was ever excluded from the list for writing antisemitic things. Indeed, nothing that happened inside the union was ever judged to be antisemitic. The tribunal judge himself asked me whether I broke the rules. I told him that, as a whistleblower, I thought there were two conflicting principles. The tribunal chooses not even to consider or to describe this dilemma in its judgment.

The old Romanian Communist Party used to win elections with 100 per cent of the vote. Just this fact is enough to tell us that the process could not have been fair. The University and College Union, and now the tribunal, judged that nothing that ever happened in the union was antisemitic. Not one thing. Given the history of antisemitism in Europe and on the left, and given the hostility to Israel and to Israeli policy within the union, it is hardly plausible that hostility to Israel was never expressed in an antisemitic way. An antiracist union has a responsibility to educate against antisemitism and to guard against it. A tribunal has the responsibility to recognize antisemitism when it occurs and to protect those who are bullied by it. We live in a time and in a place where it is possible for a union and a tribunal to fail to see antisemitism, even when it is shown to them in detail and even when its significance is explained to them.

Notes

1   Claimant's skeleton argument, *Fraser v UCU*.
2   Witness statement of David Hirsh, *Fraser v UCU*.
3   Available: https://engageonline.wordpress.com/2013/04/02/antisemitism-who-gets-to-judge/.

7

ANTIZIONISM

Discourse and its actualization

The term 'antizionist' is used here to denote a variegated set of movements which coalesce not around criticism of Israeli policy or criticism of racist movements within Israel but rather around a common orientation to the existence or to the legitimacy of the State of Israel itself. This book focuses on a form of antizionism which thinks of itself as quite distinct from antisemitism, a form which claims to value highly the distinction between hostility to Zionism or Israel, on the one hand, and Jews, on the other; the relationship between this 'antiracist' antizionism and the rest of the antizionist universe is particularly important. The discussion here focuses on the hypothesis that antisemitism is a consequence, intended or not, of antizionism. It leaves to one side the complementary hypothesis that the antizionism itself is caused by an underlying antisemitism. Analysis can show what flows from antizionism; it is more difficult methodologically, as well as politically, to show how antizionism, an ostensibly democratic and antiracist discourse, flows from an underlying antisemitism.

In order to analyze the outcomes of antizionist thinking, it is necessary to examine that thinking itself. It is by beginning to make sense of antizionist discourses, what they claim, by what kind of methodologies they are produced, in what kind of political traditions they stand, that it is possible to unravel some of the elements of the central relationship between these discourses and the antisemitic ways of thinking which may be immanent within them.

It may be asked why one should focus on antizionism when many contemporary critics of Israel are not antizionists in this existential sense. Yet criticism of Israel, of this or that thing that Israel does, is not the focus of this book; its focus is antisemitism. The hypothesis is that antizionist discourse is important in shaping not only criticism of Israeli policy but also forms of hostility to Israel which constitute something more threatening, more essentializing and more demonizing than criticism; something, indeed, which cannot be properly understood as mere criticism; something which is not critical. Howard Jacobson (2007) described the distinction in this way:

> Critical – as though those who accuse Israel of every known crime against humanity, of being more Nazi than the Nazis, more fascist than the fascists, more apartheid than apartheid South Africa, are simply exercising measured argument and fine discrimination.
>
> I know a bit about being critical. It's my job. Being 'critical' is when you say that such-and-such a book works here but doesn't work there, good plot, bad characterisation, enjoyed some parts, hated others. What being critical is not, is saying this is the most evil and odious book ever written, worse than all other evil and odious books, should never have been published in the first place, was in fact published in flagrant defiance of international law, must be banned, and in the meantime should not under any circumstances be read. For that we need another word than critical.

Hostility to the idea, existence and policies of Israel comes from various sources, and it is not the same as hostility to Jews. Some manifestations of this hostility can nevertheless throw up a politics and a set of practices which create common-sense notions of Israel as a unique evil in the world; they can thereby set people up for a fight with the Jews – those Jews, anyway, who prefer not to disavow Israel by defining themselves as antizionist.

Globally, the 'antiracist' variants of antizionism constitute only one set of discourses and movements within the whole of antizionism. They are conditioned by their location within this set of different discourses and movements, through the circulation of common elements of rhetoric and of common-sense assumptions, and through explicit or tacit political alliances.

Contemporary left-wing secular 'antiracist' antizionism cannot be understood solely as an intellectual or political critique of Zionism but also needs to be understood as a movement which exists alongside a set of other antizionist movements. Methodologically, therefore, it is necessary to look at the theory, the discourses and the claims of antizionists, but it is also necessary to take into account the social reality of the ways in which these are actualized in the world. The movement is the site where the relationship between a set of shared conceptual meanings and understandings, on the one hand, and the real-world political and social actualization of those understandings and meanings, on the other, are played out.

Another sense in which contemporary antizionisms are not simply critiques of Zionism is that they are quite distinct from late nineteenth- and early twentieth-century antizionist movements. These were predominately Jewish movements which were critical of the Zionist movement and which proposed other responses to antisemitism.[1] Contemporary antizionism often tries to position itself in these older antizionist traditions, but it actually exists in a radically different world, made different by the material history of the twentieth century. It is largely the way that contemporary antizionism relates to this different world that defines it as a movement. Opposition to Israel's existence tends to try to constitute itself as a battle of ideas against an idea.

Post-1948 antizionism is not a single movement but a collection of differing currents. There is a current of Middle Eastern antizionism which was hostile to Jewish immigration into Palestine, to a Jewish presence there, and to the foundation and the continued existence of the State of Israel; in the Middle East there are both secular and Islamic antizionist traditions; in the Soviet Union and the Eastern Bloc there was a Stalinist antizionism; right-wing and neo-Nazi antisemitism is increasingly articulating its hostility to Jews in the form of antizionist rhetoric (for example, David Irving 2002; David Duke 2014); there is also a contemporary current of antizionism which toys openly with antisemitic rhetoric but which is hard to place in terms of the left/right scale and has connections with both (for example, Gilad Atzmon, Paul Eisen, Israel Shamir, Dieudonné M'bala M'bala; see the next chapter).

It is necessary to analyze the emergent properties of these ideas, discourses and narratives when they are actualized in various and diverse living movements and contexts; when elements of rhetoric which are not formally antisemitic gain a life of their own; when they escape the control and supervision of the 'antiracists' who formulate them and who put them to work in political campaigns.

If some elements of the broad antizionist movement are self-consciously antisemitic, it is necessary to analyze the ways in which those that think of themselves as antiracist relate ideologically to these other elements – to look at how concepts function in the movements which take them up, how they migrate and develop in their exposure to the public sphere, and how that actuality relates back to the development of narrative and theory. The properties which emerge, sometimes unforeseen or unintended, out of antizionist ideas and movements can be as important as the truth and coherence of the ideas themselves.

For example, antizionist discourse often challenges the claim that Zionism is a form of nationalism. Nationalism is usually understood to contain racist potentialities as well as elements which define a community of common responsibility; but Zionism is portrayed as nothing but racist exclusion. It is necessary to examine the ways that the 'Zionism = Racism' claim is actualized in the antizionist movements and in the world beyond. How do the antizionist movements actually relate to those who it says are 'Zionists' and therefore necessarily racists? How do they license or encourage others to relate to 'Zionists'? How does it, in practice, define the group, 'Zionists', which is to be treated as racist?

This is partly a question of how antizionist theorists and activists understand their own political responsibilities. Michael Neumann, a philosophy professor at Trent University in Canada, is an extreme example of one who refuses to take political responsibility for the consequences of his antizionism. He outlined his approach to the question in an email exchange with an antisemitic group, which they subsequently published (Jewish Tribal Review 2002). They asked him whether he thought that their website was antisemitic. He replied:

> Um, yes, I do, but I don't get bent out of shape about it. I know you're [*sic*] site and it's brilliantly done. Maybe I should say that I'm not quite sure whether you guys are antisemitic in the 'bad' sense or not . . . . [I]n this world, your material, and to a lesser extent mine, is a gift to neo-Nazis and racists of all sorts. Unlike most people in my political niche, this doesn't alarm me: there are far more serious problems to worry about . . . . [O]f course you are not the least bit responsible for how others use your site.[2]

This discussion occurred five months after Neumann (2002) had published a piece entitled 'What Is Antisemitism?' in which he argued that antisemitism is trivial compared to other racisms and that it is understandable that Israeli crimes result in a hatred of Jews in general. Here are some quotes from this piece by Neumann which illustrate a wilful and ostentatious refusal, by somebody who considers himself to be an antiracist, to take antisemitism seriously:

> Undoubtedly there is genuine antisemitism in the Arab world: the distribution of the Protocols of the Elders of Zion, the myths about stealing the blood of gentile babies. This is utterly inexcusable. So was your failure to answer Aunt Bee's last letter . . . . The progress of Arab antisemitism fits nicely with the progress of Jewish encroachment and Jewish atrocities. This is not to excuse genuine antisemitism; it is to trivialize it . . . . If Arab antisemitism persists after a peace agreement, we can all get together and cluck about it. But it still won't do Jews much actual harm . . . . Israel has committed war crimes. It has implicated Jews generally in these crimes, and Jews generally have hastened to implicate themselves. This has provoked hatred against Jews. Why not? Some of this hatred is racist, some isn't, but who cares? Why should we pay any attention to this issue at all?
>
> *(Neumann 2002)*

The antizionist movement has a tendency to flatten analytically important distinctions. For example, it often treats the distinction between state and civil society in Israel as being entirely absent. The idea of a unity of 'the people' with 'state' sets up a frame for doing criticism that tends to dissolve politically relevant distinctions. Antizionism tends to fuse civil society with the state; it erodes the distinction between the people in their plurality and state policy; it erases the complexities of Israeli society and history; it is often also tempted to dissolve the distinction between civilian and soldier. 'Zionism' is presented in antizionist discourse as a one-dimensional unity. There is a rejection of a methodology that is interested in development over time or in understanding the phenomenon in context or of understanding the complex and contradictory dynamics that are usually thought to characterize the development of a movement or state.

Distinctions between left and right, bigots and antiracists, one form or tradition of Zionism and another, settlers and non-settlers, occupied territories and Israel, Arab citizens and Arab non-citizens become fuzzy. The only distinction that remains clear, that dominates the discourse, is between Zionist and antizionist.

Antizionists may respond to this charge by saying that it is not the antizionists who blur distinctions but Zionism itself. It is Israel that has no separation between state and civil society; it is Israel that wants to annex the West Bank; it is Israel that subordinates politics to the imperatives of 'security'; it is Israel that singles itself out in the world. This is an illustration of the way that antizionism tends to replicate in its critique the errors and crimes of its own conception of Zionism, but not actual Zionism and not the actual practices of the State of Israel; that which it tends to replicate is the Zionism which it has itself constructed and against which it defines its own identity.

The 'Zionism' of the antizionists is a totalitarian movement which is equivalent to racism, Nazism or apartheid. The 'Zionism' that antizionist discourses depict and denounce is more a signifier of political evil than a word which depicts a real set of changing and plural beliefs and practices.

The demonization of Zionism portrays itself as rational critique and as part of a liberational worldview. But it often takes on darker and more totalitarian aspects, and it is attracted to conspiratorial thinking. The solution is conceived of not in terms of peace and reconciliation but rather in the essentialist terms of seeking and destroying the evil, wherever it is to be found.

In his critique of Zionism, Joseph Massad begins his analysis with the assertion that Zionism is a colonial movement that is 'constituted in ideology and practice by a religio-racial epistemology', adding that it is 'important also to analyze the racial dimension of Zionism' (2003). He understands Zionism to be defined by its commitment to 'building a demographically exclusive Jewish state', which he understands alongside the European colonial ideology of white supremacy over colonized people (Massad 2003). Already, we can see that Massad's notion of Zionism is, for practical purposes, homogenous; it is one 'Jewish supremacist' movement, from the 1880s to the present day. There are no significant differences between Zionism in the nineteenth and in the twenty-first century, between left and right Zionism, between religious and secular Zionism, between Labour Zionism and the Zionism of the fundamentalist settlers. Massad writes as though there was a single Israeli culture with a single ideology and a single purpose – a homogenous body of Israeli Jews. All differences are flattened out by the dominating principle of 'Jewish supremacism'. This assumption of homogeneity underpins a methodology which takes incidents and quotations from particular people, places and times to stand for and to illustrate the true nature of all Zionists in all places and throughout history. Massad does not make this assumption explicit, and he does not subject this assumption of homogeneity to the kind of critical scrutiny which would normally be deployed towards so fundamental a hypothesis.

For example, Massad tells us that the leading Russian language daily in Israel published an article in January 2002 called 'How to force them to leave' suggesting that the Israeli government should use the threat of castration to encourage Arabs to leave the country. For this, he relies on a newspaper report translated into English from Hebrew of the original newspaper article in Russian. The assumption of Zionist unity means that one opinion piece in one newspaper can be understood to illustrate the nature of Zionism as a whole. The fact that the paper reportedly received no outraged feedback from its readership should not come as a surprise, Massad tells us, since the following month the Tourism Minister Benny Elon proposed that the entire Arab population should be expelled from Israel. Elon, a far-right religious Jewish settler who is defined by his support for what he euphemistically calls 'transfer', according to the assumption of Zionist homogeneity, speaks for all 'Jewish supremacists', or Zionists. Shimon Peres, Ariel Sharon, Benny Elon, Theodor Herzl, Golda Meir and the Meretz party are all used in this piece to exemplify 'Jewish supremacism'. One piece in the Israeli newspaper *Ma'ariv* entitled 'The Jews who run Clinton's cabinet' demonstrates the 'major ideological convergence between anti-Semites and Jewish supremacists' (Massad 2003: 446).

While antiracist antizionism often claims to rest on a historical materialist methodological foundation, some of its central assumptions seem to rely more on a methodology which gives primacy to ideas in the shaping of social life than to one which focuses on material factors. Antiracist antizionism has a complex relationship to the Nazi genocide of the Jews, yet it is often more comfortable looking at cultural constructions of the Holocaust, and ways of thinking about the Holocaust, than it is thinking about the material effect of the Holocaust *itself*.

Massad's methodology starts with 'Zionist' *ideology*, and this task is much simplified by the assumption that, in all its essentials, 'Zionist' ideology is one coherent body of thought. This assumption, in turn, is justified by reference to two things in Massad's work. Firstly, Zionism is understood as part of the European colonial project. This expands the methodology of explanatory flattening globally and across five hundred years. The whole history of 'white' imperialism is understood as essentially one racist project. The Crusades, British rule in India, colonization of Australia, New Zealand, the United States, South Africa, the British Mandate in Palestine, US policy during the Cold War in South and Central America and East Asia, the wars against the Saddam regime in Iraq, Belgian rule in Congo: all are essentially the same. Particularity becomes insignificant next to the one explanatory element of European racist exploitation. And Israel is part of this wider project. Actual history, human agency and contingency constitute little but the way that the big project happens to have played itself out in different places and at different times.

The second justification for the assumption that 'Zionist' ideology is one coherent body of thought is that the 'Jewish supremacist' project is not a racist movement among Jews, in Massad's understanding, but rather it is presented as something global:

> the only way these arguments acquire any purchase is in the
> context of an international, read western, commitment to Jewish

supremacy, wherein Jews are seen as white Europeans defending white European values and civilization against the primitive Arab hordes.

(Massad 2003: 449)

'Zionists' and Israel constitute, for Massad, one central element of the larger western imperialist project.

This second element that justifies the assumption of Zionist homogeneity is definitional. What various Zionists have said and written is interpreted as coherent and unified agreement upon an essentially racist project. Zionism is defined by Massad as 'Jewish supremacism'. The essential, necessary and unchangeable character of Israel is given by definition. Actuality is construed as a manifestation of this definitional necessity. One key way of defining the difference between antizionism in the sense that we are using it here and criticism of Israeli policy is the antizionist insistence that Israel is necessarily and unchangeably unique, although this would rather contradict the narrative that Israel is only part of a much larger imperialist project. 'Zionism' is Nazism, but Israel is not like Germany; 'Zionism' carries out ethnic cleansing, but Israel is not like Croatia or Serbia; 'Zionism' settles occupied land, but Israel is not like China; 'Zionism' is a colonial settler project, but Israel is not like Australia. For antizionism, Israel is the totalitarian movement, not a nation or a state. Its policy at any particular time is understood to be a manifestation of its timeless inner essence.

This framework gives huge explanatory importance to ideas and ideology. The racist idea is held to create and define the necessarily racist state. The story, as often told by antizionists, begins with Herzl, and it picks out some racist quotes from his book; it moves on to Jabotinsky and to Ben-Gurion, picking quotes and anecdotes, before it arrives in 1948 and the *Nakba*, as the actualization of the racist idea in the world. It goes on to 1967 and shows how the inherently expansionist and colonial character of the 'Zionist idea' is manifested in the taking and settling of territory.

There is a joke from the 1920s: what is the definition of a Zionist? A Zionist is one Jew who gives money to a second Jew so that a third Jew can go to Palestine.

Contemporary antizionist discourse is comfortable on the terrain of the narrative construction of the Holocaust, but it is less comfortable with the fact of the Holocaust itself. Gillian Rose wrote about a tendency in the 1990s to treat the Holocaust as something ineffable. She criticized Habermas' implication that the Holocaust should be thought about as though it was holy, as though it was outside of history:

> It is this reference to 'the ineffable' that I would dub 'Holocaust piety' . . . . 'The ineffable' is invoked by a now wide-spread tradition of reflection on the Holocaust: by Adorno, by Holocaust theology, Christian and Jewish, more recently by Lyotard and now by Habermas. According to this view, 'Auschwitz' or 'the Holocaust' are emblems for the breakdown in divine and/or human history. The uniqueness of this break delegitimises names and narratives as such, and hence all aesthetic or apprehensive representation (Lyotard).
>
> *(Rose 1996: 41)*

In warning about Holocaust piety, Rose was perhaps prescient in understanding that what would follow piety would be Holocaust sacrilege. First, Holocaust piety was misrepresented as a wilful, self-interested and dishonest Zionist instrumentalism rather than as a healthy seriousness and respect taken too far. This made it possible for antizionists to begin to allow themselves the frisson of committing sacrilege in the cause of Palestine, which is reminiscent of Abram de Swaan's (2004) account of how anti-Israel enthusiasm is set free following its stern repression.

A clear illustration of the selective method of antizionism is its portrayal of Israel as nothing but a colonial enterprise in the image of white European settler-colonialism. It is true that some Zionists did draw inspiration from that tradition for models of how to build and settle the State of Israel. Well, Zionists drew inspiration from very many traditions. And from this kernel of partial truth, antizionism builds a whole granite edifice. The seamless insertion of the history of 'Zionism' into a schematic history of colonialism casts Jews as going to Palestine in order to get rich on the back of the people who lived there already.

It is difficult to understand how anybody could believe that Jews in the refugee camps in Europe and in British Cyprus, recovering from starvation and from existences as non-humans in concentration camps, were thinking of themselves as standard bearers of 'the European idea'. Jews are said by this element of antizionist explanation to embody a colonialist European idea of whiteness at the same moment as the Nazis throughout Europe were portraying them as rats and cockroaches constituting an existential threat to Europe. Massad (2003: 445) mentions the effect of the Holocaust in transforming 'Zionism', but he does not analyze its significance:

> Jewish antizionists continued to oppose Zionism's Jewish supremacist plans until 1948 when most of the support they had received over the decades dwindled against the reality of the holocaust and the establishment of the Jewish supremacist state.

Massad does not, however, discuss what it was about the Holocaust and the establishment of the State of Israel that changed the terms of the debate so completely. He mentions the fact that Jews did not emigrate to Palestine *en masse* due to an ideological commitment to Zionism but emigrated due to their expulsion from European and Middle Eastern countries, but he does not grasp the significance of this fact – that Zionism was not only a construction of ideology but to a significant extent the result of material circumstance. Massad is clear on the material causes of Israel:

> We have to remember that the larger segment of the Israeli Jewish population came to Israel as refugees after the war, and after 1948, from both Europe and the Arab countries, not because of the success of Zionism, but because they were refugees and had no other place to go.
>
> *(Massad in Whitehead 2002: 213)*

But he believes that this influx of refugee Jews was incorporated into the white Jewish supremacist colonialist project with unimaginable speed and efficiency:

> both Israeli Jewish society and the Israeli government, are still as Zionist as they have always been, and committed to Jewish

supremacy ... the basis of the Israeli state. This is exactly the crux of the matter.

(Massad in Whitehead 2002: 214)

Left antizionism is often adopted by people who consider them-selves to be influenced by Marxist historical materialism, yet it operates with a methodology that tends to give an overwhelming explanatory importance to *ideas*. This methodology is selective; what it leaves out is as important as what it includes. For example, it leaves out the Holo-caust, and it leaves out the ethnic cleansing of Jews from the rest of the Middle East as significant materialist transformations which under-pinned ideas of Zionist self-determination for Jews. This methodology is unable to consider the existence of the antiracist Israeli left and peace movement as anything other than a veiled form of racist belligerence. It leaves out any serious consideration of Middle Eastern antisemitism, and it is necessarily silent on the question of the influence of Nazism in the Middle East during the 1940s (Küntzel 2006; Herf 2010).

Left antizionism is often adopted by people who consider them-selves to be anti-essentialist, yet it operates with a methodology that understands events as little more than the manifestations of Israel's rac-ist, colonialist and totalitarian essences.

Left antizionism is often adopted by people who consider them-selves to be politically responsible, yet it operates in a world where, increasingly, antisemitism clothes itself in the rhetoric of antizionism (for example, Duke 2004; for example, Hamas; for example, Hezbollah). It fails to see this context as significant, and it refuses to take reasonable care in its consciousness of the boundaries between the antisemitic demonization of Israel and the legitimate criticism of particular poli-cies of the Israeli state.

An important role in fostering this approach has been played, per-haps paradoxically, by the anti-Stalinist left. Stalinists of course had been the original prime movers (on the left) of the idea that Israel was a creation of the West. But the anti-Stalinist, particularly those sec-tions which identified as Trotskyist, encountered huge difficulties in general, when faced with a post-war world in which Trotsky's global revolutionary perspective had been entirely defeated. Neither of the two possibilities which Trotsky foresaw had happened; the 'degenerated workers state' of the Soviet Union did not collapse, nor did the workers show signs of making a 'political revolution' against the 'bureaucracy'. In fact, the so-called degenerated workers state came out of the war hugely strengthened, and it replicated itself across a significant section of the world. Capitalism, also against pre-war expectations, grew and appeared to thrive. Much of the anti-Stalinist left had great difficulty coming to terms with this new world, and much of it preferred to operate by denying that there was a new situation and a new stabilization. So the antizionist denial about how the world had changed following the Second World War could be understood as only a part of a much wider failure to come to terms with a new situation.

Some on the Trotskyist left remained for decades in a state of intense political expectation, convinced that this was the moment of the final crisis of both capitalism and state 'socialism'. Others eventually embraced the new situation and became convinced that the Soviet Union, Eastern Europe and China were, after all, in some sense an advance on capitalism: they embraced one side of Trotsky's pre-war perspective, the defence of the Soviet Union against 'imperialism'. In this way, Marxist politics, for some, was radically transformed. Many now saw their immediate task not as siding with the workers, or with the oppressed in general, but as siding with what they thought of as progressive states against imperialist ones. Whereas classical internationalism was a programme of common struggle against capitalism, it now became a programme of taking sides in geopolitical power struggles.

For some, it was much more tempting to ally with some actually existing and powerful state than with a set of cosmopolitan or democratic politics; and, later, other options emerged: Cuba, Nicaragua, Venezuela. For some it mattered little that the leaders of the good 'progressive' nations wore military uniforms and had secret police forces.

Interestingly, Israel, for some, in its early days, was seen as one of these good nations. The questions that Geoffrey Wheatcroft (2006), for example, asks about Israel and the way that it is thought about in left and liberal circles in the UK are more interesting than the tentative answers that he offers. He says that people on the left used to love Israel; they were attracted to the socialist Kibbutzim, to the Labour governments, to the Jews as victims of the Holocaust, but have now reversed their position. Which is right? He is asking whether Israel is a good nation or a bad nation, a progressive nation or a threat to progress. This methodologically nationalist framework for thinking is a break from a cosmopolitan tradition of the left, which aimed to unite people in all states against the social and political structures that divided them. It did not ask which were the good nations; it asked how people within all nations could come together against their common oppressors.

What happened instead was that there was a move to substitute victim nations for good nations. Nations which were thought to have socialist or progressive regimes were, some noticed, always opposed by imperialism. So some on the left began to support any regime which mobilized an anti-imperialist rhetoric. The fallacious logic is startling: if progressive states are opposed by imperialism, it should not follow that states which oppose imperialism are therefore progressive. But it was in this way that some on the left began flying the flags of regimes which found themselves in conflict with the democratic states; this is how some people who thought of themselves as left wing turned themselves into apologists for Saddam Hussein, Slobodan Milosevic, Mahmoud Ahmadinejad, Kim Jong-il and, in the end, even Al Qaeda and ISIS.

Wheatcroft tells us that some people on the left in the 1950s had great illusory hopes in Israel as both a good nation and a victim nation and they began to wave its flag. It is sometimes these same individuals who have now swung round in disgust when it turns out that Israel is not a utopian beacon for mankind.[3] With the crumbling of their own somewhat adolescent illusions, some individuals on the left turned on Israel with a rage, a single-mindedness and an enthusiasm explainable more readily by feelings of betrayal than by looking at the actual nature of the conflict between Israel and Palestine. It is not coincidence that a number of those on the left animated by such feelings of betrayal were themselves Jewish; perhaps not only disappointed by the difference between reality and their own adolescent imaginations; perhaps also enraged by the naivety of their parents' promises about the Zionist dream.

A staple idea of antizionism is that Israel is a creature of imperialism or a client state of the USA; let us put to one side, for the moment, the opposite story that says Israel is in fact the power behind global imperialism and the USA. John Rose (2004), for example, in *The Myths of Zionism*, argued that

> Israel could play its part in helping encase the region in a military structure, which would protect Western oil supplies . . . . Within just three years of its foundation, its ideologues were ready to tie Israel's survival to the predatory intentions of the 'Western powers' . . . . Radical nationalism was poised to sweep across the Middle East. Israel's statement of intent could hardly have been more prescient. Israel would indeed become the watchdog.

Whether Israel is represented as a part of the white project of colonialism, or as America's 'strategic asset' in the Middle East, the amount of slippage required to transform Israel from an ally with America into an *essentially* imperialist entity is small but important.

There are many disconnects between the antizionist worldviews and the actual world. One problem is that Israel would not have come into existence when it did without a shift in Soviet policy on the Middle East in the mid-1940s and Soviet bloc support for partition during 1947–1948. Israel's origins are bound up in early Cold War politics and growing US–USSR rivalry. Another problem is that Israel would have been killed at birth in the war of 1948 if it had not been armed by Stalin's Soviet Union against a British and American arms embargo.[4]

The leadership of the Jews fighting for a state in Palestine was nationalist, and nationalists tend to take help from wherever they can get it. Accepting help from the imperialist Soviet Union against the British Empire and in the face of an American arms embargo was unremarkable in the context of the history of nationalist struggles for independence. In the 1950s, the USSR reconstructed its Middle East policy when it realized that it could push its own imperialist ambitions in the Middle East more effectively by backing Arab nationalist regimes against Israel; and the USA gradually came to back Israel against the Soviet-backed Arab states. This was routine bloc politics of the Cold War. What is remarkable is the widespread myth that Israel is not a nation state like others but no more than a creation of, and a creature of, the United States. The idea is that Israel was put there by Europe and America in order to facilitate the imperialist domination of the

Middle East. But this idea is at odds with the fact that the US-Israeli alliance, which began to develop in the early 1960s, was cemented only after the Six-Day War in 1967. And the idea in question is also deeply inconsistent with the fact that when the United States wants to intervene militarily in the Middle East in the contemporary period, Israel is of no use to it, and it has to rely on Egypt, Turkey, Saudi Arabia, Kuwait and other regimes for support.

Isaac Deutscher, who had lived his early political life in the Yiddish-speaking milieu of the Jewish left in Europe before the Holocaust, came later to dismiss antizionism. It does not seem to have occurred to him that a new antizionist movement might yet emerge to try to pump new life into his own antizionist political heritage, which had been destroyed, with the antizionists who embodied it, by the Nazis. Yet Deutscher still did not identify as a Zionist. He was interested in coming to a non-nationalist, cosmopolitan analysis and politics. And in response to futile arguments over who started the conflict between Jews and Arabs, he told the following story:

> A man once jumped from the top floor of a burning house in which many members of his family had already perished. He managed to save his life; but as he was falling he hit a person standing down below and broke that person's legs and arms . . . . If both behaved rationally, they would not become enemies . . . . But look what happens when these people behave irrationally. The injured man blames the other for his misery and swears to make him pay for it. The other, afraid of the crippled man's revenge, insults him, kicks him, and beats him up whenever they meet . . . . The bitter enmity, so fortuitous at first, hardens and comes to overshadow the whole existence of both men and to poison their minds.
>
> *(Deutscher 1968: 136–137, from an interview in*
> *New Left Review, 23 June 1967)*

For Deutscher, the debate was no longer about whether Zionism was the right political programme; now the debate was about different issues. How can Israeli Jews and Palestinians forge a just peace? How can the racist currents within Israel and also within Palestine be defeated politically? How can the tragic history that brought Jews and Palestinians into such a bloody conflict be transcended into the future? But even now, half a century after Deutscher, Ghada Karmi, for example, yearns 'to turn back the clock before there was a Jewish state and re-run history from there' (2007: 265). She still wishes that the 'tormented, suspicious and neurotically self-absorbed community toughened by centuries of the need to survive' had never gone to Palestine (Karmi 2007: 120).

Norman Finkelstein quotes this very passage from Deutscher, and, in his attempt to refute its relevance, he exemplifies a number of defining features of left antizionist discourse. He says:

> The Zionist denial of Palestinians' rights, culminating in their expulsion, hardly sprang from an unavoidable accident . . . . It resulted from the systematic and conscientious implementation, over many decades . . . of a political ideology the goal of which was to create a demographically Jewish state in Palestine . . . . To claim that Zionist leaders acted irrationally in refusing to 'remove or assuage the grievance' of Palestinians, then, is effectively to say that Zionism is irrational: for, given that the Palestinians' chief grievance was the denial of their homeland, were Zionists to act 'rationally' and remove it, the raison d'être of Zionism and its fundamental historic achievement in 1948 would have been nullified . . . . To suggest that Zionists had no choice – or, as Deutscher puts it elsewhere, that the Jewish state was a 'historic necessity' – is to deny the Zionist movement's massive and, in many respects, impressive exertion of will, and the moral responsibility attending the exertion of this will, in one rather than another direction.
>
> *(Finkelstein 2005: 11)*

Here, Finkelstein relies on the assumption of Zionist homogeneity. While antizionists often insist on rhetorically splitting 'the Zionist leadership' from the Jews who were cajoled, fooled and forced into following, they also tend to insist on the homogeneity of Israelis and their total incorporation into the ideology of 'Jewish supremacism'. Finkelstein bestows his enemy, now collapsed into the phrase 'the Zionist

Movement', with a satanic greatness, capable of a 'massive . . . impressive exertion of will' (2005: 11). He cannot accept Deutscher's '*ex post facto*' explanation of Zionism's transformation from a utopian movement into a state. It can only be explained by the extraordinary 'will' of Zionism, since to accept that Israel's existence is somehow connected to the Holocaust and to the plight of oppressed Jews from the Middle East and from Russia too would be to muddy the explanatory dualisms upon which antizionism relies; white/non-white; oppressor/oppressed; good nationalism/bad nationalism; colonizer/colonized.

Deutscher says that if both Israelis and Palestinians had behaved rationally, then they would have not become enemies. Finkelstein here falls back onto definitional fiat rather than sociological explanation. He replies that the only way that Israel could have made peace with Palestine would have been to dissolve itself, since it was, *by definition*, incapable of living in peace. He says that the Palestinians' chief grievance was the denial of their homeland, and he then says that 'Zionists' could only remove this grievance by nullifying the '*raison d'être* of Zionism'. Deutscher was trying to find a political orientation that could transcend both nationalisms. Finkelstein replies by saying that Israel is definitionally racist. He goes on:

> It's equally fatuous to assert that Palestinians act irrationally when they 'blame' the Zionists 'for their misery' and not accept that they were 'the victim of circumstances over which neither of them had control.' It's only irrational if Zionists bore no responsibility for what happened.
>
> *(Finkelstein 2005: 12)*

Here he tries to shift the frame of the debate. Deutscher is arguing that the foundation of Israel can only be *understood* with reference to the events in Europe that preceded it. Finkelstein reads Deutscher as using 'the Holocaust' in order to *justify* human rights abuses. And the only way that Finkelstein can frame this claim is by flattening out the complexity of the argumentative and political terrain. *Either* 'the Zionists' were responsible (hyper-agents with a 'massive' and 'impressive' will) *or* they were innocent refugees (victims), in which case they should have behaved how innocent refugees are expected (by the romantic left) to behave. Finkelstein reads Deutscher as saying that 'Zionists' bore *no* responsibility for the hurt inflicted on Palestine. But what Deutscher seems to be trying to come to terms with is that it is understandable that Jewish refugees were taught to be frightened, angry and distrustful by their experience in Europe, and later in the Middle East. Deutscher the internationalist can easily understand the attraction of nationalism to those Jews – the attraction of looking after themselves in a world which had failed to look after them. But there are significantly different political perspectives available under the umbrella of 'nationalism'; Deutscher's point is that outcomes other than ongoing war and occupation were always possible. Events were determined not by the etymological essence of 'Zionism' but rather by twentieth-century history and by political battles won and lost *amongst* Jews and *amongst* Palestinians.

Antizionism, as well as some opponents of antizionism, often constructs the struggle over ideas in such a way as to compel one to choose between competing nationalisms. Supporters of each nationalism are tempted to tell the narratives of the Middle East in such a way that we are forced to take sides. But more cosmopolitan approaches have always been possible and have always existed. There have been attempts to break from this binary, and there have always been movements which have tried to resist passive acceptance of the world as it exists. Such approaches opposed the demonization of Israel and Jews on the one hand and also rejected alternatives and explanations which demonized Muslims and Arabs on the other. A more cosmopolitan approach is compatible with enlightened Israeli and Palestinian nationalist approaches, which assume national self-interest to consist firstly in building a political framework whereby both Israel and Palestine can be guaranteed national self-determination, side by side.

It is not only Israeli nationalist imaginings of homogeneity that are accepted by left antizionism as a picture of reality but also Palestinian ones. The Palestinian population, Massad tells us, 'understood Zionism for what it was and resisted it from its inception in the late nineteenth century' (2003: 444). This view of the world as being divided into monolithic peoples, with single purposes and understandings, is recurrent in antizionist writing; it appears in some pro-Israel narratives too. And it erases from history those Palestinians, and Jews too, who felt differently, who worked and lived in peace with each other.

Massad writes: 'From the Palestinian perspective, the nature of Zionism has always been clear' (Whitehead 2002: 213). Massad writes as though there was a single Palestinian perspective. But this perspective, it seems, is not always the one of the Palestinian *leadership*, which, during the Oslo process, Massad tells us, accepted 'in many ways, *the Zionist* version, both of Jewish and Palestinian histories, and succumbed to it' (Whitehead 2002: 213). In Massad's narrative, 'the people' have always understood everything clearly; the leadership was corrupted and bought off by the enemies of the people.

He also says that he is in favour of the 'continuing resistance of Palestinians in Israel and the occupied territories to all the civil and military institutions that uphold Jewish supremacy' (Massad 2003: 450). The apparently straightforward statement of solidarity hides and glosses over the centrally important political distinctions in Palestine. Does Massad understand the suicide bombing of buses, restaurants and nightclubs to constitute 'resistance' to institutions that uphold 'Jewish supremacy'? Does he understand Hamas and Hezbollah, with their clearly antisemitic rhetoric, to be a part of that 'resistance'? Palestine is presented as a monolithic anti-colonialist nationalist struggle, although held back by corrupt leaders. It is presented as though there were no politics in Palestine, no differences of attitude amongst Palestinians to the presence of Jews and to the presence of Israel in the Middle East. There is only the authentic resistance of the Palestinian people and the pro-Zionist collaboration of their leaders. Later, Massad threw his political weight behind Hamas, and he characterized the secular nationalist tradition of the Fatah leadership in Palestine as being a 'collaborationist' one, subservient to Israeli interest (2006). Since the Hamas coup in Gaza against the Palestinian presidency, it became more common in the west, both on the far left and in mainstream liberal opinion, to treat Hamas as the single authentic voice of Palestine – and Fatah as a collaborationist or even treacherous force which failed to oppose Zionism with sufficient militancy.[5]

Massad says that if Jews were to give up their 'Jewish supremacist' ideology and allow Palestinians the 'right of return', then any threat to Jews would disappear (2003: 449). Terrorist and antisemitic threats against Jews are interpreted by antizionism as being fundamentally defensive responses to Zionism. In this paradigm, Zionism is responsible for the increase in antisemitism; antisemites are, in this way, absolved of responsibility and political agency. Other racisms are not normally analyzed by antiracists in terms of what it is that the victims of those racisms are doing to make people hate them.

Questions concerning conflicts of interest between Palestinian nationalism and Arab nationalism, or between Palestinian nationalism and Islamism, are regarded by antizionists far away from the conflict with great suspicion. One of the tropes of antizionism is a refusal to take seriously the conflicting interests of Palestinians and Arab states and an unwillingness to allow oneself to be moved by the history of exploitation, repression, killing, moving on and instrumentalization of Palestinians by Arab regimes. It is understood in antizionist circles that great suspicion should fall on anyone who asks questions about the treatment of Palestinians in Arab states. Anyone who asks how it is that Palestinians in those states have not been allowed to integrate into society but been kept separate and rightless as refugees is suspected of preparing a 'Zionist' denial which may hold Arab regimes or Arab nationalism at least partly responsible for the misery of Palestinians. While anger with Arab regimes may be appropriate in antizionist circles, it is never allowed to disrupt that which is treated as the central truth: Palestinians and Arabs in general are the victims of Israel and of America. When Palestinians have been victimized by Arab states or movements, responsibility is often allotted to imperialism as the moving force behind that victimization, either via Zionist machinations or via American-backed puppets, or as a result of the legacy of European colonialism. Hostility to Israel is such a deeply ingrained common sense for many on the left that they rarely interrogate the function that hostility to Israel and antisemitism play for the Arab ruling elites in diverting hostility away from themselves.

There are more questions which are widely understood to be forbidden in the antizionist universe, which are excluded from the narrative. We have already touched upon the ways in which certain kinds of narrative of the Holocaust are suspect if they seem to be mobilized towards justifying Israeli crimes or constructing 'Zionism' as a liberation movement. If Holocaust narratives disrupt the simple Israelis-as-oppressors, Palestinians-as-oppressed binary, then they become not quite respectable in the antizionist imagination. It is respectable to talk

about how the Holocaust is abused by Israel as a discourse of legitimation (Butler and Rose 2005). It is respectable to understand Holocaust
Memorial Day as an attack on British Muslims (Sacranie 2005). But it
is suspect in antizionist circles to argue that it was the Holocaust which
transformed the material condition of Europe such that 'Zionism' was
transformed from a utopian minority idea into a nation state.

Another unasked or unaskable question is the one which raises the
issue of how and why Jews were almost entirely pushed out of all the
Middle Eastern states in the 1950s and 1960s. For antizionism, the forced
movement of Palestinians from Israeli held territory in 1948 is the original sin which forever renders Israel uniquely illegitimate. The forced
movement of Jews from the whole of the Middle East to Israel, however,
is represented a more or less free choice; it is explained as the result of
'Zionist' agents provocateur manufacturing the antisemitism (or perhaps
the justified anger with Israel?) which forced the Jews out of the great
cosmopolitan cities of the Middle East, Baghdad, Cairo, Beirut, Damascus
and the rest. There is a right and justified concern to disallow attempts
to minimize or deny the suffering of Palestinians in 1948, and their subsequent partial exclusion from Israeli territory. Yet this concern can lead
antizionists to turn their eyes away from the wholesale expulsion of Jews
from the Middle East as part of the Arab nationalist consolidation of ethnically defined *Arab* nation states.[6] Sometimes, in blatant violation of the
assumption that people are free to define their own identities, there are
attempts to portray Jews from Arab states as being really Arabs, and so as
victims of Ashkenazi or 'white' Jewish supremacism. In this narrative, the
real history of a power divide in Israel between Jews of European and
Middle Eastern descent is fitted into a binary worldview coherent with
the assumption that the distinction between 'white' imperialism and the
rest of the world is absolute.

There is more than a touch of *orientalism* in antizionism's portrayal
of the Palestinians (Said 1978). A respectful way to relate to Palestinians
is not to pretend that they all think the same thing but to consider the
plurality of different ways of thinking and different politics and different choices which are evident amongst Palestinians. Cosmopolitan
thinking usually challenges and disrupts myths of national homogeneity (Hirsh 2003; Fine 2007) rather than offering them a left-wing
stamp of authenticity.

Nothing is gained by infantilizing Palestinians. For example, there is quite clearly a problem of antisemitism amongst Palestinians. Hamas, the most electorally popular party in Palestine, is explicitly founded on an Islamist version of the *Protocols of the Elders of Zion*. It might not seem surprising if some people who live under the occupation of an overwhelmingly Jewish army could be susceptible to antisemitism, although, even in this case, this is obviously not an automatic or a necessary response. This too needs to be placed in context rather than to be naturalized as though it were entirely unmediated by human agency or by political choices. In any case, most Arabs and Muslims do not live under occupation, and antisemitism in predominantly Arab and Muslim societies is widespread and has deep and complex roots long predating the Israel–Palestine conflict. Yet it still tends to be drastically underplayed within antizionist discourse. It is underplayed either by pretending that it is nothing but an epiphenomenon of the conflict and has no life or emergent properties independent of it or by pretending that antisemitism is a European colonialist invention and an import into the Middle East and, therefore, people in the Middle East bear no responsibility for it and are incapable of being authentically antisemitic. Other patronizing defences are attempted: for example, I have heard the argument made by a sophisticated London intellectual that Arabic is too simple a language to cope with the distinction between Israeli and Jew, and so, when people express hatred for Jews, it is only because they are not capable of the clarity required to express their hatred of Israelis.

From the idea of antizionism to its discursive actualization in antisemitism

Two themes which re-occur in discourses that demonize Jews, over the centuries, and across the globe, are the blood libel and the charge of Jewish conspiracy.

(a) Blood libel

A poster for the boycott campaign shows a wholesome Jaffa orange, cut in half, out of which blood is dripping. The slogan reads: 'Boycott

Israeli Goods: Don't squeeze a Jaffa, crush the occupation.' The combination of Jews, food and non-Jewish blood creates a graphic, emotive and powerful image. If you eat the Jaffa oranges that the Zionists are trying to sell you, you will metaphorically be drinking the blood of their victims.

How does such an image get produced with its loud echoes of the blood libel? There are three possible kinds of explanations. The first is that the similarity with the old themes is purely coincidental. We can discount this possibility because of the frequency with which this occurs. The second possible explanation for the 'blood orange' image is that the designer of the poster is a conscious antisemite who is consciously drawing on antisemitic tradition. This is unlikely and is of course strenuously denied. 'Antiracist' antizionists who campaign for a boycott of Israel say quite clearly that they are not antisemites. They do not appear to be conscious Jew-haters, and they are not knowingly drawing on older antisemitic themes.

The third possible kind of explanation is that there is some sense in which antisemitic themes are deeply embedded in the culture, and elements present themselves unconsciously to people looking for emotive images which can drive us to act against Israel. The mechanism of this cultural unconscious, how and why it works, how and why it is so often repeated, is one element of the relationship between hostility to Israel and antisemitism which requires further research and thought. But many antizionists are not prepared to think it through. Frequently, the response to the observation that some of their imagery mirrors old antisemitic themes is disdainful denial followed by a counter-allegation of bad faith.

Ariel Sharon, then the Prime Minister of Israel, was caricatured eating a baby in *The Independent* newspaper on 27 January 2003. Dave Brown, the cartoonist, won the 'political cartoon of the year award' for this image. Perhaps this image of a corrupt, violent and bullying Jew eating an innocent child is only coincidentally analogous to classic blood libel imagery. 'Brown insisted he had never intended this meaning and that his cartoon was inspired by the Goya painting Saturn Devouring one of His Children' (Byrne 2003).

Norman Finkelstein hosted an extensive gallery of cartoons on his website by the Brazilian artist 'Latuff'.[7] Latuff won second prize in Mahmoud Ahmadinejad's Tehran competition for cartoons which illustrate Holocaust denial. This, incidentally, is a clear example of the ways in which elements of rhetoric circulate around the different antizionist movements. Norman Finkelstein, who considers himself to be an antiracist and a scholar, hosts Latuff, who in turn is happy to compete in Ahmadinejad's Holocaust denial art festival. One image shows a swimming pool, the shape of the Gaza strip, filled with blood. The image shows Uncle Sam luxuriating in the blood; Ehud Olmert, the Prime Minister of Israel at the time, covered in the blood and using an Israeli flag as a towel; and a UN waiter bringing a drink of blood to the two swimmers. The world is pictured sitting in the sun, refusing to be concerned. There are a number of other images by Latuff, hosted by Finkelstein, which mirror themes of the blood libel. There is one which shows an innocent child who is either Lebanese, or who represents Lebanon itself, being doused in Israeli petrol. Another shows an Israeli soldier washing the blood off his hands using an American tap. Another image shows Ariel Sharon with vampire fangs.

The theme of Israel as a child-killing state is increasingly common. Any incident of an under-age Palestinian being killed during the conflict is liable to be understood and presented as a manifestation of Israel's essentially child-killing nature. The slippage from particular incidents to a generalized common-sense notion is a common characteristic of much antizionist discourse. The particular truth is often essentialized as the necessary truth.

Blood libel always goes hand in hand with antisemitic conspiracy theory. If 'the Jews' kill children, then certainly they conspire to hide the crime (Julius 2010: 79–105). If Israel is based on child-killing and genocide, then certainly there must be a Zionist conspiracy or an Israel Lobby which has the power to keep the fact out of the global media.

The most explicit and complete version of antisemitic conspiracy theory is the *Protocols of the Elders of Zion*, a late nineteenth-century Russian forgery which purported to constitute a report of a meeting of the Jewish conspiracy in Prague. Contemporary echoes of the old theme of Jewish conspiracy take the form of an argument that there is a Zionist lobby with such huge global influence and power that it is able to send the United States of America to war in its interests and to de-legitimize any narrative of Israel and Palestine which it does not like, as antisemitic. The *Protocols* and more contemporary charges of Zionist influence come together in the Hamas Covenant (1988), the founding document of the party which won the January 2006 election in Palestine and which then made a successful coup against the Palestinian Presidency in Gaza. The Hamas Covenant explicitly copies and endorses the original *Protocols* forgery; it holds the Jewish 'enemy' responsible for all the revolutions, wars and imperialism of the modern era.

Ilan Pappé (2006) argues that Israeli forces are committing genocide in Gaza. The charge that Israel commits genocide, in Gaza or the West Bank, or in Lebanon, is a charge commonly made by antizionists. At first sight, such a characterization would appear to be counterproductive, since while Israeli forces may have been open to allegations of specific human rights abuses, they can easily show themselves to be not guilty of genocide. When there is no genocide in Gaza, why do antizionists like Pappé continue to assert that there is? These repeated allegations have the effect of demonizing Israel, of implanting and reinforcing the notion that Israel is a unique evil. The genocide charge is a particular kind of demonization; genocide has a particular relevance to Israel, which was founded three years after the end of the Holocaust.

Pappé wrote: 'Nothing apart from pressure in the form of sanctions, boycott and divestment will stop the murdering of innocent civilians in the Gaza Strip' (2006). Perhaps his wish to advocate for this campaign is what has led him to make the claim of genocide; he does not use the term 'genocide' to describe events in 1948, which is his area of historical expertise. Yet his proposed remedy does not seem to fit the alleged disease. If there were really genocide occurring in Gaza, surely a more urgent, powerful and desperate response would be appropriate than carrying on the long, slow campaign for sanctions, boycott and divestment. Pappé finishes by exhorting the world 'not to allow the genocide of Gaza to continue' (2006). He precedes this exhortation with these words: 'in the name of the holocaust memory' (Pappé 2006). The employment of this kind of political rhetoric was unlikely to be persuasive to the majority of Israelis and Jews. But Pappé was no longer writing for Israelis; he had already given up on building a peace movement, and he had given up on Israelis as potential agents for progressive change: 'There is nothing we here in Israel can do against [the genocide in Gaza],' writes Pappé (2006). Shortly after writing this piece, Pappé accepted a chair at Exeter University in England.

(b) Conspiracy theory

Conspiracy theory is a necessary twin of blood libel; if the Jews are murdering children for their religious rituals, then for sure they are conspiring to cover it up.

In March 2006, John Mearsheimer and Stephen Walt published a paper in two different forms. 'The Israel Lobby' (2006a) was published in the *London Review of Books* and 'The Israel Lobby and US Foreign Policy' (2006b) was published as a Faculty Research Working Paper by Harvard University and the Kennedy School of Government; the book, *The Israel Lobby and U.S. Foreign Policy*, was published in 2007 (Mearsheimer and Walt 2008). The way in which the paper provided a language for the discussion of Zionist conspiracy, the way in which this language was enthusiastically, quickly and widely adopted by many who found it natural to think within this framework, is highly instructive.

Robert Fine (2006) uses the concept of 'slippage' to examine the problem. The paper itself starts with something real, and it asks answerable questions. What is the nature and influence of various lobbying and campaigning organizations which relate to Israel and Jews in the USA, such as AIPAC (American Israel Public Affairs Committee), the ADL (Anti-Defamation League) or AJC (American Jewish Committee)? How do these different organizations operate, what do they want and what effect do they have? But even within the Mearsheimer and Walt paper itself, the focus on particular and differing organizations, and concrete questions, begins to slip into a conception of 'the lobby' which is discussed as though it was a hugely powerful, coherent, covert and therefore conspiratorial political agent. The particular claim made by Mearsheimer and Walt, which shows that they were discussing what they took to be an extremely powerful and threatening world-straddling agent, is that the 'Israel Lobby' was held to be responsible for ensuring that the USA went to war against the Saddam regime in Iraq.

At a public event organized by the *London Review of Books* in New York, John Mearsheimer said: 'The Israel lobby was one of the principal driving forces behind the Iraq War, and in its absence we probably would not have had a war' (Stoll 2006). The accusation that a Jewish conspiracy pushes the world into unnecessary wars in the interest of the Jews is an old staple of antisemitic conspiracy theory. For example, Claire Hirshfield (1980: 619) tells us how some who opposed the Boer war blamed it on a Jewish diamond lobby manipulating the British Empire:

> If it could be demonstrated that the . . . government had been tricked into war by the machinations of shady Jewish capitalists and that the public had been intentionally misled by omnipotent Jewish presslords, then sufficient pressure might indeed be generated to end what its opponents considered an immoral war. That the pursuit of this worthy aim involved an appeal to a base and discreditable prejudice seems to have little troubled the various socialists, radicals and labourites who utilized the shorthand of 'Jewish finance' as a convenient means of epitomizing the dark underside of British imperialism.

Charles Lindbergh (1941), key spokesperson for 'America First', blamed un-patriotic Jewish power for trying to draw the USA into World War II against its own interests:

> I am not attacking either the Jewish or the British people. Both races, I admire. But I am saying that the leaders of both . . . for reasons which are as understandable from their viewpoint as they are inadvisable from ours, for reasons which are not American, wish to involve us in the war.

Conspiracy theories have been circulating on the internet since 11 September 2001, trying to blame 9/11 on Zionists, claiming that the Jews in the World Trade Center were warned not to go to work there that day, claiming that Israeli agents had been seen celebrating in New Jersey as the twin towers collapsed. In a notorious speech to the Reichstag, Adolf Hitler held the Jews responsible for the First World War: 'In case the Jewish financiers . . . succeed once more in hurling the peoples into a world war, the result will be . . . the annihilation of the Jewish race in Europe.'[8] Mearsheimer claimed that terrorist 'animus' against

America was the result of US policy towards Israel, which itself is a result of the machinations of the 'lobby'. He added, employing his version of the *Livingstone Formulation*, that this 'simply can't be discussed in the mainstream media' (Stoll 2006).

The tendency for this kind of slippage to occur was exacerbated when talk of the 'Israel Lobby' broke free from the control of the authors themselves and was taken up by others. Anybody who wanted to talk about Jewish or Zionist power now had a Harvard and Kennedy School stamp of respectability with which they could inoculate their own ideas against charges of antisemitism. The idea of disproportionate and dangerous Jewish power, and particularly its covert application in steering states towards war, was not new; but Mearsheimer and Walt offered a legitimate vocabulary with which to make these kinds of claims. And the offer was taken up enthusiastically by many in the summer of the Israel-Hezbollah July War which followed the publication of the 'Lobby' paper.

Of course conspiracy theory existed in Britain before Mearsheimer and Walt. For example, in May 2003, respected Labour MP Tam Dalyell accused Prime Minister Tony Blair of 'being unduly influenced by a cabal of Jewish advisers' (Brown and Hastings 2003). Dalyell had then employed the *Livingstone Formulation*: 'The trouble is that anyone who dares criticize the Zionist operation is immediately labelled anti-Semitic' (Marsden 2003). Paul Foot (2003), well-known journalist and leading member of the *Socialist Workers Party*, leapt to Dalyell's defence: 'obviously he is wrong to complain about Jewish pressure on Blair and Bush when he means Zionist pressure'. Foot knew how to interpret an antisemitic statement as an antizionist one. But after Mearsheimer and Walt came along, everybody knew how to do it, and the specific terminology of the 'Lobby' became ubiquitous in antizionist discourse.

The theoretical journal of the Socialist Workers Party, *Socialist Review*, wrote about the 2007 UCU decision to back the boycott campaign:

> A very powerful pro-Israel lobby has gone to work to denounce these decisions with the support of the pro-war 'left'. Meanwhile arch Zionist and Harvard lawyer Alan Dershowitz has threatened to 'devastate and bankrupt' any organisation which commits to a

boycott of Israel. These figures want to block discussion of Israel's actions. We must defend the right of trade unions to democratically pass resolutions and hold political debates without being subjected to such threats.

(Harman 2007)

A whole number of elements of conspiracy theory are here packed into one seemingly innocent paragraph: firstly the use of the term 'pro-Israel lobby' as a single unvariegated and therefore dishonest conspiracy; secondly its designation as 'very powerful'; thirdly the lobby's association with the 'pro-war' (pseudo) 'left', an allegation of the further dishonesty of pretending to be 'left', while not really being left, and an association of the 'pro-Israel lobby' with support for war; Alan Dershowitz, a name universally recognized by people within the community of the good to connote pure evil or 'arch' Zionism; Dershowitz's threat to 'devastate and bankrupt' resonates with the menace and power of 'the lobby'; 'these figures', Dershowitz the arch-Zionist, the Harvard lawyer, the pro-war pseudo left, the pro-Israel lobby, the sum of all that is bad in the struggle against imperialism, want to block discussion of Israel's actions. Next there is a substitution of the right to have debates for the right to support the exclusion of Israelis, then the right for trade unions to be free from criticism; and 'such threats', referring to one possibly idle threat made by Alan Dershowitz, are constructed as being something against which we must defend ourselves – something emanating from the all-powerful, dishonest, pro-war, pseudo left, lobby.

When Richard Ingrams (2007) reviewed Mearsheimer and Walt's book, he made it explicit that in his reading of the Lobby thesis, it was covert Jewish influence and not only 'pro-Israel' lobbying which was decisive in sending the mighty USA to war against its own interests:

[Mearsheimer and Walt] demonstrate that the American invasion . . . not only had the support of Israel but also that the overriding aim of those (mostly Jewish) neocons who were urging Bush to invade was to assist Israel.

Whereas Mearsheimer and Walt have repeatedly denied that their thesis has anything to do with Jews, arguing that many Jews do not support 'the lobby' and that many constituents of 'the lobby' are not Jewish, Ingrams interprets their book for a wider public in precisely the way that opponents of antisemitism had feared that it would be interpreted. In 2003 Ingrams had written in *The Observer* newspaper that he had developed a practice when 'confronted by letters to the editor in support of the Israeli government to look at the signature to see if the writer has a Jewish name'. If so, he says, he tends not to read it. Ingrams was boasting that he was in the habit of prejudging the views of people he thought were Jewish on the basis of their names; he would judge by reference to their imputed ethnicity and not to their experience, knowledge or judgment – or to the content of their character. Ingrams' writing exemplifies the process of slippage to which Mearsheimer and Walt's work lends itself. It again raises uncomfortable questions about the notion of political responsibility with which Mearsheimer and Walt operate. We should also note that it has become common and apparently normal for mainstream liberal avowedly antiracist newspapers like *The Independent*, *The Observer* and *The Guardian* to give space to people like Richard Ingrams to opine on Jews.

The Independent newspaper on 27 April 2006 carried a four-page piece by Robert Fisk (2006) headlined 'United States of Israel?' It was illustrated by a full-page, colour image of the Stars and Stripes with Stars of David replacing the usual stars. The piece profiles Stephen Walt as a hero who bravely stood up to the 'Lobby' and its malicious and dishonest accusations of antisemitism (Fisk 2006).

The image used by *The Independent* of the Jewish Stars and Stripes says that Jews control America; these are Jewish symbols, not Israeli symbols. The claim is that Jews are not patriotic Americans; they are more loyal to Jews around the world than to their country. The same device of merging Jewish stars with the American flag has long been used by neo-Nazis, conspiracy theorists and Jihadi Islamists.

The Fisk article offers no evidence for the claim that the 'Zionists' tricked or coerced the United States to risk the lives of its citizens in a war that was against its own interests. There is some rhetoric about AIPAC, 'the agent of a foreign government [that] has a stranglehold on Congress – so much so that US policy towards Israel is not debated there' (Fisk 2006). Fisk tells us that 'the lobby' monitors and condemns academics who are critical of Israel. Fisk repeats Mearsheimer and

Walt's variant of the *Livingstone Formulation* (quoted from Mearsheimer and Walt 2006b) that '[a]nyone who criticizes Israel's actions or argues that pro-Israel groups have significant influence over US Middle East policy . . . stands a good chance of being labelled an anti-semite'.

Fisk does not give an example of anyone claiming that Mearsheimer and Walt are antisemites or are motivated by antisemitism. He quotes Alan Dershowitz as saying that 'the two scholars recycled accusations that "would be seized on by bigots to promote their antisemitic agendas"' (Fisk 2006). Fisk claims that Noam Chomsky is prevented by 'the Lobby' from having a column in an American newspaper. He asserts that 'the Lobby' prevented a repeated showing of a film that Fisk had made for Channel 4. He writes that an 'Israel support group' (unnamed, although apparently part of 'the lobby') insulted Fisk. He says that 'the lobby' prevented the showing of 'I am Rachel Corrie' in New York (Fisk 2006). 'The lobby' is presented as an un-opposable, unstoppable force. It tells Presidents and members of Congress what to do and what to say. Its influence reaches into theatres, TV stations and newspapers.

On 12 October 2007 there was a conference at the University of Chicago on 'academic freedom' and in defence of Norman Finkelstein, who had failed to win tenure at De Paul University in Chicago. The assumption of the conference was that academic freedom in general and Finkelstein in particular have come under illegitimate and powerful attack by the Israel Lobby. Tony Judt (2007) spoke the following words:[9]

> If you stand up here and say, as I am saying and someone else will probably say as well, that there is an Israel lobby, that there is . . . there are a set of Jewish organizations, who do work, both in front of the scenes and behind the scenes, to prevent certain kinds of conversations, certain kinds of criticism and so on, you are coming very close to saying that there is a *de facto* conspiracy or if you like plot or collaboration to prevent public policy moving in a certain way or to push it in a certain way – and that sounds an awful lot like, you know, the Protocols of the Elders of Zion and the conspiratorial theory of the Zionist Occupational Government and so on – well if it sounds like it it's unfortunate, but that's just how it is. We cannot calibrate the truths that we're

willing to speak, if we think they're true, according to the idi-
ocies of people who happen to agree with us for their reasons.

It may well be true – I know this because I have received an
email from him – that David Duke thinks he has found allies in
John Mearsheimer or Stephen Walt or myself. But I remind you
what Arthur Koestler said in Carnegie Hall in 1948 when he
was asked, 'Why do you criticize Stalin – don't you know that
there are people in this country, Nixon and what were not yet
called McCarthyites, who also are anti-Communist and who will
use your anti-Communism to their advantage?' And Koestler's
response was the response that I think we should keep in mind
when we are faced with the charge that we are giving hostages
to crazy antisemites or whatever, and that is you can't help other
people agreeing with you for their reasons – you can't help it
if idiots once every 24 hours with their stopped political clock
are on the same time as you. You have to say what you know to
be true and be willing to defend it on your grounds and then
accept the fact that people in bad faith will accuse you of having
defended it or aligned yourself with the others on their grounds –
that's what freedom of speech means – it's very uncomfortable. It
puts you in bed sometimes with the wrong people.

Judt's response to the charge that he and Mearsheimer and Walt
provide a respectable vocabulary for the articulation of antisemitic
conspiracy theory is a surprisingly candid and flat denial of political
responsibility and an explicit refusal to 'calibrate' claims in such a way
as to make them unhelpful to antisemites. There is a number of elements to this defence which are worthy of analysis.

First, Judt admits that he comes 'very close to saying that there is
a *de facto* conspiracy or . . . plot or collaboration' and that 'that sounds
an awful lot like . . . the Protocols of the Elders of Zion and the conspiratorial theory of the Zionist Occupational Government ("ZOG")
and so on'. He then says that antisemites 'happen to agree with us'. The
difference is that 'we' think these things because they are true, and the
antisemites think these (true things) only because they hate Jews: 'you
can't help it if idiots once every 24 hours with their stopped political
clock are on the same time as you'.

Second, Judt makes an analogy with Koestler's criticisms of Stalin in 1948. Koestler thinks that the gulag exists, and he thinks that one has a responsibility to say so, even if this appears to vindicate anti-Communists who also think that the gulag exists and who say so loudly. So Judt thinks that a *de facto* Jewish conspiracy exists, and that he has a responsibility to say so even if antisemites, who also think that a Jewish conspiracy exists, are thereby apparently vindicated. The difference, however, is obvious. The gulag existed. A Jewish conspiracy, of the kind which has sufficient covert muscle to send the only super-power to war against its own interest, and to expel critics of Israel from the American academy, does not exist. Indeed, the McCarthyites were also conspiracy theorists who believed that America was falling under the spell of a Moscow plot which encompassed every liberal schoolteacher and every 'red' Hollywood actor. Koestler did not believe in the conspiracy, nor did he believe 'anything very close' nor a '*de facto* conspiracy' nor a 'plot' nor a 'collaboration'. Koestler was not like Judt. In fact, Judt's antizionism came from the political tradition of those who did remain silent about the gulag on the grounds that to speak up would play into the hands of the imperialists. The left anti-Stalinists, Trotsky, Draper, Arendt, Koestler, Orwell and the others spoke out against the left common sense of their day – that one should not criticize Stalin. Judt failed to speak out against the left common sense of his day – which holds Israel, and the Jews who 'support it', to be both uniquely evil and uniquely powerful.

Judt accuses his accusers of acting in bad faith. In this way he puts motivation at the centre of his defence. He is a good guy, he is on the left and he is motivated by the search for truth and justice (for the Palestinians). David Duke, who happens on this occasion to have stumbled onto the truth about the Israel lobby and its responsibility for war, has done so out of a malignant motivation. Those who ask why Judt and Duke have been discovered together in the bed of conspiracy theory do so, claims Judt, in bad faith.

The point about the potential danger of Judt's conspiracy theory is not an *ad hominem* point. It relies on an accusation neither of bad faith nor of malicious motivation. It does not accuse Judt of being secretly or unconsciously motivated by antisemitism. It asks why Judt is insufficiently concerned about saying the same thing, using the same language and drawing on the same images as generations of antisemitic conspiracy theorists. Judt's response is: 'it's unfortunate, but that's just how it is'. But it is not a coincidence which puts Judt in David Duke's political bed. He is there because Duke is saying the same as Judt, and Judt refuses to 'calibrate' his claims such that they become useless to Duke. If we are 'telling a truth' which puts us in bed with David Duke, then perhaps it is reasonable to conclude that we are telling it wrong – or at least in an incomplete way. Judt does not find himself in this predicament because he is, like Duke, motivated by antisemitism. Judt is not motivated by antisemitism. But this tells us that motivation is not the key here; the key is what Judt says and what he does. The danger of licensing antisemitic claims and world views, of acting as midwife to an antisemitic movement, is not neutralized by the fact that Judt was an antiracist and a respected intellectual. Indeed, the fact that Judt was widely thus recognized exacerbates the danger.

Notes

1   Miller (2007) focuses on the commonalities between non-Jewish anti-Zionism in Britain before 1948 and today; he foregrounds the similarities, 'in particular the common arguments that both current and past British antizionists have used to demonize and de-legitimize Zionism'. My argument here, in contrast, focuses on the differences between opposition to a political movement and opposition to a nation state.

2   This email exchange was published by *Jewish Tribal Review* against the wishes of Michael Neumann. I asked Neumann whether this exchange was a forgery: 'The material is not a forgery but I do not vouch for its reliability because I no longer have the original correspondence' (personal email correspondence, 5 July 2005).

3   Beller (2007) argues: 'The "It is war!" argument is really a counsel of despair, and an admission of defeat for the higher values that Israel was meant to achieve. Jews are supposed to value human life above all, not just Jewish life, human life.' Kuper (2006) says that 'Israel sees itself as a state based "on the precepts of liberty, justice and peace taught by the Hebrew Prophets". In the words of Isaiah, "We are a light unto the nations"'.

4   An article in *Haaretz*, quoted in Hirsh (2006a), gives fascinating details of the military help that flowed from Czechoslovakia to the Jews in Palestine: 'The first arms deal with Czechoslovakia was signed in January 1948 – less than two months after the UN resolution creating Israel and four months before the state was actually established. Immediately after the Partition Plan was passed, Ben-Gurion began searching for sources to supply arms to the Israeli defense forces, but found that the legal sources in the United States and most European countries were closed off to the institutions of

the Jewish state in formation. The only alternative seemed to be illegal arms acquisitions and an appeal to the Soviet bloc . . . . As part of the deal signed in January, Czechoslovakia supplied some 50,000 rifles (that remained in use in the Israeli Defence Force for around 30 years), some 6,000 machine guns and around 90 million bullets. But the most important contracts were signed in late April and early May. They promised to supply 25 Messerschmidt fighter planes and arranged for the training – on Czech soil and in Czech military facilities – of Israeli pilots and technicians who would fly and maintain them. The planes, which were disassembled and flown to Israel on large transport planes, after their reassembly played a very important role in halting the Egypt Army's advance south of Ashdod, at a place now called the Ad Halom Junction . . . . The assistance to the air force continued to flow in during the second half of 1948 – when it consisted of 56 Spitfire fighter planes. These were flown to Israel, some of them by Israeli pilots.'

5   Two examples: 'The stunning military victory by the Palestinian Hamas movement over the rival Fatah organisation in the Gaza Strip last week was a strike against imperialism in the Middle East' (Assaf 2007); 'Battered and humiliated, Abbas now needs to come up with something substantial very soon if he is not to be labelled a quisling' (O'Loughlin 2007).

6   See, for example, Shiblak (2005) on how Jews were pushed out of Iraq, and Hakakian (2004) on how Jews were pushed out of Iran.

7   This was on Finkelstein's website at: www.normanfinkelstein.com/article. php?pg=11&ar=176 (accessed 19 June 2007).

8   Adolf Hitler's announcement to the Reichstag in 1939. Available: www. nizkor.org/hweb/people/g/goebbels-joseph/goebbels-1948-excerpts-02. html (accessed 26 October 2016).

9   These words were transcribed by the author from a sound file of his speech which was posted online at the time.

8

JEWISH ANTIZIONISM

Being drawn towards the logic of antisemitism

In the first half of the twentieth century, most Jews failed to find their way to a successful strategy for dealing with the threat of antisemitism. Some individuals emigrated, for example, to Britain, the United States or Palestine. Some found their way into wider civil society, benefited from emancipation, and sometimes assimilation, and lived as citizens of European states. Some Jews found communal ways of continuing to live apart, in a changing and ever more threatening world.

There were three overlapping *political* responses to antisemitism. Universalist socialists hoped that revolution would unite workers into a new world where nations, religions and ethnic differences would, in the end, cease to be important – where Judaism itself, along with Jewish identity, would lose its significance. Bundists wanted to forge a new, modern, largely secular, Jewish identity and a set of institutions through which Jews could exist in Europe, in peace, and alongside others, and by which they could defend themselves against antisemitism if necessary. Zionists believed that Jewish national self-determination was required to ensure the endurance of Jewish life and to create a viable Jewish capacity for military self-defence.

In 2011, August Grabski edited a collection of essays, *Rebels against Zion* (2011), which outlined the arguments between Bolsheviks,

Bundists and Zionists. Roni Gechtman looked at debates within the Second International and the Bund before the First World War (2011), and Rick Kuhn focused on the debates within the Galician Socialist Movement (2011). Henry Srebrnik outlined early Soviet campaigns against Zionism and took the story into the Stalinist era, with the emergence of the characterization of Zionism as 'pro-imperialist' (2011). Bat-Ami Zucker examined the position of Jewish Communists in America, trapped between their loyalty to the increasingly totalitarian Communist Party, their disdain for the American Jewish establishment and the developing danger Nazism posed to Jews in Europe (2011). Jack Jacobs' (2011: 88) discussion of Bundist opposition to Zionism in inter-war Poland finished with a crucial and under-explored observation:

> The arguments made by the Bund between 1918 and 1939 were not wholly transferable either to the period of the Holocaust or, for that matter, the decades following the establishment of the State of Israel in 1948.

The truth, which is not sufficiently addressed in this collection, is that all the strategies adopted against antisemitism failed. Bundism was eradicated in the Nazi gas chambers. Bolshevism failed to stop the *Shoah*, and, while it did succeed in gaining state power over a third of the world, it did so not by *defeating* antisemitism but by *adopting* it, in its racist, its political and its antizionist variants. Zionism too, as was broadly predicted by both Bundists and socialists, failed to save European Jews in the necessary numbers because it had remained, until the late 1930s, a largely utopian movement.

But Israel became a reality, a nation state, not because Zionism won the debates with Bundism and Socialism, but because the material basis of Jewish life in Europe was utterly transformed. It was transformed by the 'Final Solution', by Israel's victory in the war of 1948 against the Arab Nationalist states which tried to eradicate it at birth and by Arab Nationalist and Islamist efforts to force the Jews out of the Middle East.

These profound material transformations of Jewish existence are often very much neglected by people, even those who consider themselves to be inheritors of Marxism. They are neglected by those who wish to position themselves as part of an unbroken thread of antizionist tradition from the twenty-first century back to the end of the nine-teenth. In a radical departure from the method of historical material-ism, analyses of Zionism tend to focus on Zionism as an idea, and they tend to downplay the significance of the material factors which underlay Zionism's transformation from a minority utopian project into a nation state.

In 1954 Isaac Deutscher, Trotsky's biographer, wrote that he had 'of course' abandoned his life-long antizionism. It seemed obvious to him that the world had changed, in Auschwitz and on the battle-field in the Middle East. European Jews had been murdered, and the remnants, the undead, had forged a new nation in Palestine, which Deutscher regarded as a 'historic necessity' and as a 'raft state'. Now the key questions changed. It was no longer relevant to ask whether Zionism was a winning strategy against antisemitism; the question was how would the Jewish state reach a peace with its neighbours and how it would negotiate the contradiction between its Jewishness and its democracy.

The political meaning of the term 'antizionism' could not be more different after 1948 from its meaning before 1939, yet so often peo-ple who consider themselves to be Marxists are more concerned with the continuity of *form* than with the break in *content*. Before 1939, antizionism was a position in debates amongst Jewish opponents of antisemitism. After 1948, it became a programme for the destruction of an actually existing nation state.

The conflation of 'rebels against Zion[ism]' with rebels against Israel frequently goes unexplored. Often, in fact, the dogged use of the term 'Zionism' by antizionists functions to mask the conflation itself and to deny that significant material changes had occurred. One could con-front the reality: that history had forged a Hebrew-speaking Jewish nation on the eastern shores of the Mediterranean, or one could deny it. One could come to terms with the world as it existed and start one's analysis from there, or one could cling onto the hope that the film of history could be unwound, and Israel could somehow be made to disappear. To call Israelis 'the Zionists' is to cast them as a political movement rather than as citizens of an existing state; and a political movement can be right or wrong, can be supported or opposed while a nation state can only be recognized as a reality. If 'the Zionists' are characterized as essentially 'racist' or 'apartheid' or 'Nazi', then Israeli Jews can be treated, once again, as exceptional to the human community.

Because 'Zionism' is understood by much antizionist polemic as a phenomenon of European Jewish ideational struggle, Jews from the Middle East are absent from the analysis. But in fact opposition to colonialism and to racism routinely takes a nationalist form, not only in the case of Zionism, but in the case of most anti-colonial movements. Arab Nationalism defeated and replaced colonialism throughout the Middle East. While being a strong and often successful way of mobilizing against colonialism, nationalism also contains within itself a potentiality for ethnic exclusivity. Jerusalem was by no means the only cosmopolitan city of the Middle East to come under the sovereignty of a nationalist movement. Jews, as well as other minorities, were treated as second-class citizens across the post-colonial Middle East. In Beirut, Alexandria, Cairo, Baghdad, Damascus, Tehran, Tripoli, Algiers, Tunis and many other places, Jews felt the hostility of the Arab Nationalist movements which took state power, and many left for Israel, or were driven out. In short, in the post-colonial Middle East, ethnic nationalism, with its oppressions and exclusions, was *normal* rather than exceptional. The tragedy is still playing itself out today in multi-ethnic states such as Syria, Lebanon, Iran and Iraq. But the parochialism of Jewish antizionism has little to say about the wider Middle East, except to imagine that Jewish concerns are at the centre of it all.

August Grabski (2011: 10) writes something interesting at the end of his introduction:

> Despite the current weakness of Jewish left anti-Zionist organisations, it is precisely the intellectual tradition of those organisations that has dominated the way in which the Israeli-Palestinian conflict is perceived by considerable segments of the international anti-globalisation movement and by organisations and movements to the left of the mainstream social-democratic parties.

It is understandable that many Jews have a particular interest in Israel. Many of them feel that it is only by chance that they themselves did, or did not, end up there, after the experiences of European, Russian and Middle Eastern antisemitism. Many Jews, following the failure of the international community to guarantee their safety in the twentieth century, were won over to the principle of Jewish national self-defence.

Jewish antizionists, like many other Jews, tend to have a particular, Jewish focus on Israel. They often feel especially concerned by Israeli human rights abuses, by the injustice of the Israeli occupation and by what they feel is the unthinking support offered by Jewish communal bodies around the world to Israeli governments.

Yet the particular Jewish focus on the crimes of Israel, both real and imagined, is, as Grabski observes, disproportionately influential outside of the confines of the Jewish community. The danger is that this Jewish concern is exported into secular civil society. Thus, for example, a tiny group of antizionist Jews who are for boycotting Israeli academics may have their concerns adopted by an academic trade union. Their particular Jewish concern is understandable, but when a trade union adopts this particular concern with *Jewish* human rights abuses rather than a consistent concern about human rights abuses *in general*, then there is obvious potential for the incubation of an unacknowledged antisemitic worldview.

Philip Mendes' (2011) chapter in the volume offers a closely observed and documented case study of such a transformation. He shows in detail the processes and the mechanisms by which a small Jewish antizionist group in Australia played a role in encouraging and licensing antisemitic ways of thinking.

Stan Crooke's essay is also an outstanding case study of the complex relationship between hostility to Israel and antisemitism (2011). He traces the role of Jewish antizionists as a vanguard, fighting for their own inverse Jewish nationalism in the wider labour movement. And he traces a genealogy of antizionist 'common sense' back to the Stalinist and anti-democratic traditions, in particular, of the Marxist movement.

But it is unlikely to be the chapters by Crooke and Mendes which will be remembered by most readers of this collection. Rather, it will be Jewish antizionism which (through a relentless succession of slippages, omissions and unacknowledged assumptions) will make the lasting impression – beginning with the title, which already bathes those who pick out Israel as a uniquely illegitimate state in the heroic light of minority rebellion.

★ ★ ★

One striking feature of the interactions between Jewish antizionism and the rest of the Jewish community is the heated tone of debate and the anger and conflict which it tends to generate. In 2014, Keith Kahn-Harris wrote a book, *Uncivil War: The Israel Conflict in the Jewish Community*, which looked at debates about antisemitism within the UK Jewish community; Kahn-Harris yearns for more civility in the ways in which Jews disagree with each other.

The war of words between the diverse majority of the Jewish community and its tiny but influential antizionist fringe continues to rage. Many Jews are worried that hostility to Israel is sometimes antisemitic, sometimes mirrors antisemitic forms and sometimes brings with it antisemitic exclusions or ways of thinking. The antizionist Jews tend to employ the *Livingstone Formulation* to dismiss these worries as dishonest attempts to silence criticism of Israel. We may civilly disagree about what is antisemitic and what is not; and we may argue, present evidence and discuss reasons. But the space for rational discussion is closed off in advance by accusations of bad faith. It is not said that Jews are mistaken when they think something is antisemitic; it is said that they have invented it, disgracefully, for short-term, tribal or nationalist reasons – that they are crying wolf.

This struggle happens in public, and it is influential upon the wider non-Jewish civil society. Blanket *denial* of antisemitism becomes an enabler of antisemitic discourse, boycotts and ways of thinking. What is counter-intuitive is the role played by Jews in licensing, leading and encouraging movements which single out Israel as a unique evil on the planet.

Bongani Masuku, a South African trade unionist, declares that he intends to make life hell for 'Zionists', that Zionists are like Hitler and that they should leave South Africa on an El Al plane (Pugh-Jones 2009). The Jewish antizionist fringe insists that this is only to be understood as a vulgar way of carrying on a debate about Israel and Palestine. Antizionism tends to treat talk of antisemitism as a dirty tactic in the Israel/Palestine debate.

Some people get angry and upset because they are afraid that the actions of a small minority of Jews are influential in bringing anti-semitism down on the heads of their fellow Jews, while others get equally angry and upset because they are convinced that their fellow Jews are trying to silence criticism of Israel with a dishonest accusation of antisemitism.

There is no nice way to accuse somebody of greasing the wheels of antisemitism; there is no nice way to accuse somebody of raising the issue of antisemitism dishonestly. It is the content of the claims, not their form, which is hurtful. Re-framing the issue in terms of civility does not help.

The *Livingstone Formulation*, not discussion of antisemitism, makes debate impossible. If somebody who raises the issue of antisemitism is just accused of lying, then there is no discussion which can bring us towards agreement. It silences Jewish fears, and it attempts to re-frame them as disgraceful tactics.

Because Nazism had already been defeated when we were formed politically, it was easy for us to recognize it as the enemy. Because colo-nialism and racism had been discredited, we could understand dockers who marched with Enoch Powell and racist Afrikaners as throwbacks to a disappearing age. But caricature might have been the price we paid for unanimity.

Whereas we thought of Nazism as representing the culmination of antisemitism, it was actually an *exceptional* form. We were tempted to 'other' antisemitism, to construct it as being something which could only exist outside of our own civilized sphere. But, in fact, antisemitism had always existed very much within our own spheres: within Europe, within the left, within radical philosophy, even amongst Jews.

Antisemitism has often taken political forms; it has attracted 'people like us', the good people; and it has not always been easy to recognize. It has melded with criticism of capitalism and banking, nationalism, modernity and imperialism. There have always even been some Jews who have succumbed to some of the logics of antisemitism. Max Neu-mann, for example, founded the 'Association of German National Jews' in 1921 which opposed Zionism as a racist and pro-British imperialist ideology, and it demonized Eastern European Jews as racially inferior

(Wistrich 1982: 177). Neumann's group offered Jewish support to Hitler in the following terms:

> We have always held the well-being of the German people and the fatherland, to which we feel inextricably linked, above our own well-being. Thus we greeted the results of January, 1933, even though it has brought hardship for us personally.
>
> *(1996: 315)*

Nazism itself grew partly out of radical anti-hegemonic political traditions and was attractive to some within 'our world'. But it was comfortable, afterwards, for us to imagine antisemitism only as appearing with a silly moustache and a fascist uniform, and as being permanently discredited.

The defeat of colonialism was not so straightforward either. It was defeated by nationalist movements, some of which had a tendency to succumb to the most ethnically based forms of nationalism, and some of which tended to create regimes which mirrored some of the worst race-thinking and kleptocracy of the old empires. The Soviet Cold War common sense of a world divided into imperialism and anti-imperialism gave the gloss of the 'progressive' to some of the most despotic regimes. The notion of 'progressiveness' attached itself to peoples and nations rather than to political movements or to ideas, and the violence of this black/white binary is manifested in the fate of those peoples who were constructed as falling between the two camps.

Many thought anti-Nazism was enough when they should have made more effort to understand the complexities of antisemitism, and many thought anti-colonialism and antiracism were enough when they should have made more effort to forge a positive cosmopolitan politics rather than a negative politics of opposition and resentment.

Many who think according to left orthodoxies now find themselves in a world they have trouble understanding. If Jews are thought of as white, they are therefore never thought of as potential victims of racism; nobody looks like the Nazis, so how can there be antisemitism? Israel, the refuge of the undead of Europe, is thought of as colonialist or apartheid. Jews, except for those who disavow, are conceived of as 'Zionists', which has become another word for racists or oppressors.

There is a tiny minority of Jews which leads the movement to exclude Israelis from the global community, which insists that Israel is uniquely and essentially racist, which educates people to recognize anybody who worries about antisemitism as dishonest apologists for Zionism. Hardly any Jews are antizionist, but many antizionists are Jews.

This minority often mobilizes its Jewish identity, speaking loudly 'as a Jew'. In doing so, it seeks to erode and undermine the influence of the large majority of actual Jews in the name of an authentic, radical, diasporic and ethical, but largely self-constructed Judaism. The 'as a Jew' preface is directed at non-Jews. It tempts non-Jews to suspend their own political judgment as to what is, and what is not, antisemitic. The force of the 'as a Jew' preface is to bear witness against the other Jews. It is based on the assumption that being Jewish gives you some kind of privileged insight into what is antisemitic and what is not – the claim to authority through identity substitutes for civil, rational debate. Antizionist Jews do not simply make their arguments and adduce evidence; they mobilize their Jewishness to give themselves influence. They pose as courageous dissidents who stand up against the fearsome threat of mainstream Zionist power.

Ironically, this positioning by the tiny minority tends to set the boundaries of civil discourse in such a way as to exclude and silence the legitimate concerns of the majority. It characterizes antisemitism only as a right-wing issue, and it teaches antiracists to recognize talk of antisemitism from any other source, too, as an indicator of racist apologetics.

Two Jewish antizionists who have mobilized their Jewish identity in order to bolster the credibility of their claims are Antony Lerman and Jacqueline Rose. Jacqueline Rose argued in her book *A Question of Zion* (2007) that Israel should be understood psychoanalytically. She says the trauma resulting from the Holocaust is the root cause of the difficulty Israelis seem to have in living peacefully with their neighbours. Rose also inspired Caryl Churchill to write the play *Seven Jewish Children* (2009), which portrays Jews bringing up their children in a neurotic, dishonest and dysfunctional way and which many have said is antisemitic. Rose herself discussed these issues with the actors at the theatre.

A therapist guides us on a journey to the frightening places inside ourselves and helps us to find ways to live with our demons. While we might do well to examine our own neuroses with our therapists, we do not expect to have to answer for them in public, and we expect our therapist to be on our side. Michel Foucault warned that the sciences of the mind are also techniques of power, and they have hostile as well as healing potential.

Antony Lerman, a former director of the Institute for Jewish Policy Research, also used psychology to explain current events, offering his own version of what Israeli psychologist Daniel Bar Tal reports about Israeli Jews. Lerman extrapolates the results to apply to British Jews. The consciousness of Jews 'is characterised by a sense of victimisation, a siege mentality, blind patriotism, belligerence, self-righteousness, dehumanisation of the Palestinians and insensitivity to their suffering' (Lerman 2009). Lerman writes as though it was a scientific discovery that 'the Jewish public does not want to be confused with the facts' (2009).

The picture of Jews offered by these two writers is not appetizing. If these stereotypes came from the far right, it would be easy for people to detect the antisemitic ways of thinking which are implicit within them.

Perhaps it would be better for critics of Israeli policies to make their arguments politically, and with reasons. They should avoid ascribing to Jews collectively a pathological inability to act rationally. Israel is a state and acts according to what its leaders and its electorate calculate to be its national interest. Israel may be wrong; it may sometimes seem crazy. But making peace with its neighbours is a matter for politics, not for therapy. It is a political rather than a pathological issue.

These three intellectuals — Rose, Churchill and Lerman — all imply that Jews indoctrinate their children to be indifferent to non-Jewish suffering and that this is the key factor explaining Israel's attack on targets in Gaza and on the civilians near them.

In her book, Rose argues that Zionism was from the beginning less a political movement than a messianic one, not rational but more like a religion. The trauma of the Holocaust, she thinks, rendered Zionists even more irrational. And, after Gaza, she asks how the 'most persecuted people in history', that is to say Jews, not Zionists, became 'violent oppressors' (2009). We might perhaps respond by saying that it is not 'Jews' but the occupation which is oppressive. We might contextualize the conflict historically and say that neither 'the Jews' nor Israel are more psychologically prone to oppressiveness than anyone else.

Leaving aside the implication that the Jews are now like the Nazis were, the frequently repeated idea that Jews should know better after the Holocaust is mortifying. Auschwitz was not a positive learning experience. Many Jews, traumatized perhaps, but not necessarily either mad or bad, learnt that it would be better to have a state and an army with which they could defend themselves if need be.

But Rose thinks that the Jews' inability to put the trauma behind them in a psychologically healthy way explains Israel's attack on Gaza. She does not explain how Germans have been able so successfully to recover psychologically from their part in the Holocaust and to build a peaceful and multicultural society. Can we congratulate post-national Europeans for having learnt the lessons of Auschwitz while we berate 'the Jews' for having failed to do so? And how have Rose and Lerman themselves emerged so healthily from the traumatic family history which so damaged the rest of us? In reality, of course, the splitting between neurotic Israel and healthy Europe is arbitrary; all are scarred, in their own ways, by the Holocaust; and none is rightly singled out for particular pathology.

Anthony Julius has shown that there is a long tradition of antisemites deploying Jewish witnesses against 'the Jews' (2010). These allegations about how Jews indoctrinate their children are reminiscent of this insider testimony. The problem is that they transform political questions into rather essentialized psychological diagnoses.

★ ★ ★

Neve Gordon, an Israeli political scientist at Ben-Gurion University, is another activist who has mobilized his Jewish and his Israeli identities in order to add weight to his call for a boycott of Israel. And like Judith Butler, Gordon has shifted his position from being an opponent of the campaign to boycott Israel to being a supporter of it; also like Butler, he never explicitly addressed his own arguments against boycott.

In 2003, Gordon wrote that he was being accused of treachery against Israel and antisemitism because of his vocal opposition to the occupation and because of his support for the peace process; some on the Israeli right were campaigning for him to be fired from his academic job on this basis. The fact that he was not fired from his job, argued Gordon, functioned as a 'reminder that in Israel, academic freedom still exists, much more so than in many other countries' (2003). He went on: 'Unwittingly, American and European supporters of the academic boycott against Israeli universities are aiding this attack' (Gordon 2003). While people around the world should be siding with the academics and the universities against these right-wing attacks, some of them from the government, he argued, the boycotters were in fact adding to the pressure, not helping to release it:

> To fight the anti-intellectual atmosphere within Israel, local academics need as much support as they can get from their colleagues abroad. A boycott will only weaken the elements within Israeli society that are struggling against the assault on the universities.
>
> *(Gordon 2003)*

Gordon also highlighted what he called the 'double standards' of the boycott campaign. There is pressure to boycott Israel from countries which have worse human rights records than Israel as well as from countries which are supportive of the occupation of the West Bank.

Yet by 2009, Neve Gordon was ready to write in the *LA Times*:

> It is indeed not a simple matter for me as an Israeli citizen to call on foreign governments, regional authorities, international social movements, faith-based organizations, unions and citizens to suspend cooperation with Israel. But today, as I watch my two boys playing in the yard, I am convinced that it is the only way that Israel can be saved from itself.
>
> The question that keeps me up at night, both as a parent and as a citizen, is how to ensure that my two children as well as the children of my Palestinian neighbors do not grow up in an apartheid regime.

His new position is more moralistic and emotional than it is analytic or political; in this sense it is difficult to argue with. The shift from an engagement with the politics of peace to an angry and defeated dis-engagement from it is at the heart of boycott thinking. The Israeli peace movement fought hard, and in the 1990s it gained ascendency in Israel. It won a majority of Israelis over, and it won support amongst significant numbers of Palestinians. There were, at that time, countless projects, small and large, which aimed to build links and understanding across the national divide. The Rabin government seemed serious about trying to negotiate a peace with the Palestinians.

But by 2009, the peace movement seemed to many to have been defeated. Yasser Arafat and his successor Mahmoud Abbas had both rejected Israeli proposals to end the occupation and to institute a Palestinian state. The rejectionists in both Israel and Palestine gained the ascendency, both blaming the other for having created – or perhaps for having uncovered – a new reality of permanent conflict. Hamas had taken over in Gaza and used it as a base from which to attack Israel; right-wing coalitions in Israel appeared to have created a new and enduring consensus for making the best of the *status quo* and repressing Palestinian movements rather than trying to come to an accommodation with them.

This was heart-breaking to the hard-core peace activists in Israel. A number of Israelis who had been with the peace camp in the 1990s remained critical of the ascendant right and its opposition to the peace process; but many of them began to conclude that the failure of the peace process was not Israel's responsibility alone. Palestinian, Arab, Islamist and Iranian rejectionism, belligerence and antisemitism seemed also to have been key factors.

The hard core of the peace movement, however, isolated and defeated, was in no mood to re-assess its own analysis of the situation, or to take responsibility for its own political failures. It insisted that the Israeli right alone should take the whole responsibility for the collapse of the peace process.

Gordon's response to defeat, his desperate turn to the international community, was, ironically, characteristic of one kind of Israeli parochialism. Sometimes, it is difficult to see beyond one's own exasperation with one's own immediate political foes. The small and isolated Israeli left at this time warned in more and more alarmist language of the immediate fascist threat from the Israeli right. To them, those Israelis who seemed to have defeated them must have felt more and more like the worst thing in the world. The main enemy is at home, they felt; and the global antizionist movement agreed with them: the main enemy is in Israel.

As academics and as intellectuals, the last thing they wanted was to be 'Israeli academics' or 'Israeli intellectuals'. As many on the 'global left' floated ever more free from material conditions, from their own working classes, and from a definite politics of making things better, so this part of the Israeli left yearned to be part of this intellectual and political movement. This current on the 'global left' mirrored the Israelis in their parochialism; the British became more and more one-sidedly concerned with the crimes of British colonialism; the Americans became more and more fixated on the crimes of US imperialism. And Israel has come to play an ambivalent role in this symbolic drama of good and evil. Israel is both 'us' and not quite 'us'. This tendency in the left can think of Israel as 'us' – it caricatures Israel as being financed by 'us', created by 'us', imperialist like 'us', a testbed for technologies of power and surveillance, for 'us' – and yet it can be punished and demonized and boycotted, because it is not quite 'us'.

What is the cause of Israel's inability to make peace with its neighbours? More and more people are coming to believe that Israel's problems are fundamentally self-made; and it is not the first time that people have judged Jews to have been tragically complicit in bringing disaster down upon their own heads. But maybe Israel is, as Isaac Deutscher thought, a precarious life-raft state, floating in a hostile sea and before a careless world (1968). Perhaps the pressure on Israel from outside, and the unique circumstances of its foundation and its survival, are creating too many internal contradictions and fault-lines. Whereas people used to tell the Jews of Europe to go home to Palestine, now they tell the Jews of Israel to go home to Europe.

Neve Gordon writes: 'It is . . . clear to me that the only way to counter the apartheid trend in Israel is through massive international pressure' (2009). It is as if he has given up on the task the Israeli peace movement set for itself, to win Israelis to a politics of peace. He treats his own academic colleagues and his own compatriots as though they are lost to the struggle against Israeli 'apartheid'. Only international pressure can force the Israelis to relate democratically to their neighbours, he says. He looks around the world for a new agent of progressive change, and he sees *my* colleagues in British universities, as if they're better, in some sense, or more progressive, or more antiracist, or less implicated in systems of imperialist thought, than his own colleagues.

Embracing the boycott movement feels like a way out of 'Israeli academia' and into 'global' academia – perhaps physically, perhaps psychologically in the sense of 'not in my name', perhaps intellectually.

Ilan Pappé gave up on his own colleagues at Haifa, and he found a chair in Exeter and is now celebrated and accepted as part of the global antizionist and anti-imperialist left.

In general, one should be careful not to be too judgmental about the ways in which people deal with the racism that they face. But it is worth considering the possibility that part at least of Israel's problem is caused by antisemitism; and so part of the isolation of Israelis is also caused by it. It may be an injustice that people like Neve Gordon are not allowed to be intellectuals like other intellectuals, teachers like other teachers, free to move around the world, free to do great research or free to get away with writing nonsense, in the same way that other intellectuals are. It may be an injustice that they find themselves, because of antisemitism, living in a region where they are again thought of only and essentially as foreigners and exploiters. It may be an injustice that they are living in a state which is forced to be vigilant about security and defending its citizens in a way which intellectuals in Europe and America have forgotten.

Jewish intellectuals in the UK may face an analogous kind of pressure. If they believed that they were part of an intellectual and political world in which antisemitism was significant, it would disrupt their ability to feel at home. It would tend to set them up in a fight with those around them. There is a great reward to be had for judging that there is no antisemitism in universities or in the labour movement; that reward is the ability to be an accepted or respected part of the community of the good. It is to be awarded chairs, research grants, book contracts and status. To be open to the judgment that this community is tolerant of antisemitism, and that this tolerance is an indicator of a rottenness at the core of its entire worldview, would make life more difficult for Jewish intellectuals in Britain.

Gilad Atzmon and Dieudonné M'bala M'bala: beyond antiracist antizionism

Gilad Atzmon does not think of himself as an antisemite although he is relaxed about being accused of antisemitism. Atzmon is an Israeli in London who has disavowed both his Israeli and his Jewish identities. He is self-conscious and knowing when he plays with antisemitic formulations, ideas and rhetoric. The Socialist Workers Party and the Scottish Palestine Solidarity Campaign were not put off by Atzmon's use of antisemitic language when they proudly hosted him at their events for a number of years. Atzmon is a former Israeli paratrooper, a successful jazz saxophonist, a campaigner for Palestine and someone who is comfortable employing openly anti-Jewish rhetoric. For example, he wrote: 'I would suggest that perhaps we should face it once and for all: the Jews were responsible for the killing of Jesus who, by the way, was himself a Palestinian Jew' (Atzmon 2003a). And for example:

> American Jewry makes any debate on whether the 'Protocols of the elder of Zion' are an authentic document or rather a forgery irrelevant. American Jews (in fact Zionists) do control the world. [*sic*]
>
> *(Atzmon 2003a)*

And for example:

> To regard Hitler as the ultimate evil is nothing but surrendering to the Zio-centric discourse. To regard Hitler as the wickedest man and the Third Reich as the embodiment of evilness is to let Israel off the hook. To compare Olmert to Hitler is to provide Israel and Olmert with a metaphorical moral shield. It maintains Hitler at the lead and allows Olmert to stay in the tail . . . . Israel has already established a unique interpretation of the notion of wickedness that has managed to surpass any other evil. It is about time we internalise the fact that Israel and Zionism are the ultimate Evil with no comparison . . . . Now is the time to stand up and say it, *unlike the Nazis who had respect for other national movements including Zionism*, Israel has zero respect for anyone including its next door neighbours. The Israeli behaviour should be realised as the ultimate vulgar biblical barbarism on the verge of cannibalism. Israel is nothing but evilness for the sake of evilness. It is wickedness with no comparison.
>
> *(Atzmon 2006a)*

In November 2006, Atzmon spoke and played music at an event in Edinburgh organized by the Scottish Palestine Solidarity Campaign entitled 'Zionist Control'. His argument (Atzmon 2006b) at that event was that the clean distinction which antizionists make between Zionists and Jews, antizionism and antisemitism, is largely fictional. He argued that Israel is a 'fascist state' supported by 'the vast majority of Jewish people around the world'. Antizionist Jews in the Palestine solidarity movement, therefore, play a *Jewish* role there, as gatekeepers who try to control the Palestinian narrative:

> As soon as anyone identifies the symptoms of Zionism with some fundamental or essential Jewish precepts a smear campaign is launched against that person.
>
> *(Atzmon 2006b)*

Atzmon fights for explicitly anti-Jewish politics within the Palestine solidarity movement, broadly conceived, and, in order to win, it is necessary first for him to defeat the antizionist Jews and those of their allies who consider themselves to be antiracist:

> I would use this opportunity and appeal to our friends amongst the Jewish socialists and other Jewish solidarity groups. I would ask them to clear the stage willingly, and to re-join as ordinary human beings. The Palestinian Solidarity movement is craving for a change. It needs open gates rather than gatekeepers. It yearns for an open and dynamic discourse. The Palestinians on the ground have realised it already. They democratically elected an alternative vision of their future.[1]
>
> *(Atzmon 2006b)*

Atzmon's central problem with the Jewish antizionists is that, even though they themselves treat Israel as though it was demonic, they also oppose openly antisemitic expression of that worldview. He is particularly critical of those who do this explicitly 'as Jews'. Atzmon has been trying to lead an antisemitic purge of the antizionist movement, one which would de-value the formal antiracism onto which many antizionists in the west cling so tightly. It took a long time for the opposition to Atzmon, in which antizionist Jews were active,[2] to persuade the Socialist Workers Party, as well as parts of the Palestine Solidarity Campaign,[3] not to continue to treat Atzmon as an antiracist and as a legitimate member of the antiracist movement.

The week after the Edinburgh event, Atzmon spoke at a Respect Party event entitled 'Jazz Racism and Resistance'. *Socialist Worker Online* (2006), the following week, brought us the news that Gilad Atzmon was to feature in 'one of the biggest cultural events *Socialist Worker* has put on for many a year'. The report went on: 'Gilad declared, "I will be playing at the Cultures of Resistance concert because I support the *Socialist Worker* appeal"' (*Socialist Worker Online* 2006).

Atzmon's writing regularly appeared in *Counterpunch* (for example, 2003b, 2006a), which thinks of itself as an antiracist journal. There have been links to his writing on the Palestine Solidarity Campaign (PSC) Gymru-Wales website,[4] *The Jerusalemites* website,[5] *Middle East Online* (Atzmon 2006c), *Dissident Voice* (Atzmon 2006d) and many more 'respectable' Palestine solidarity publications.

Some Jewish antizionists, as well as other antizionists for whom antiracism is an important defining value, flirt with Holocaust denial by defending the appropriateness of comparisons between Israel and Nazi Germany. Some routinely minimize antisemitism, finding excuses for the rhetoric of Jewish conspiracy, Jewish domination of the media and Jewish power. Some have found excuses for movements that wish to wipe Israel off the map. Some fight for the wide adoption of the idea that Israel is a uniquely serious human rights abuser. Some accuse those who oppose antisemitism of being part of a conspiracy to silence criticism of Israel or smear the left. Atzmon shows how a charismatic leader could harvest the antisemitic potential of these kinds of antizionist staples into a concrete and self-consciously antisemitic movement. There must be a possibility that antisemites may push the antiracist antizionist leadership out of the way to take over the antizionist movement. The antiracist antizionists are ripe for take-over if they do not understand their own part in the creation of this new current and if they do not know how to respond politically. They are being victimized by antisemites, and they do not know how to defend themselves effectively. Atzmon wrote the following to an antizionist Jewish blogger who has for years been writing articles that demonize Israel as a uniquely racist state:

> You are now presented 'as being a manifestation of Jewish exclusivity or supremacy on a par with the State of Israel' on every left and pro Palestinian site around the world . . . may I suggest that

it is never too late, you can still join humanity. Chicken soup is not a political argument.

(Hirsh 2006b)

Atzmon is not satisfied with demonizing Israel. He demands also that antizionist Jews cease to define themselves as Jews and only then may be accepted into the human community and the Palestine solidarity movement.[6] And Atzmon's antisemitism is found acceptable by people who think of themselves as antiracists. Indeed, Atzmon was given space in the website of the mainstream antiracist newspaper *The Guardian* to denounce me as an 'ultra-Zionist', as a dishonest academic, as a 'Zionist ideologist', as someone who 'needs antisemitism'. 'Antisemitism (rather than anti-Israel political reaction) exists solely in the Zionist's mind', he assured us, on *The Guardian* website (Atzmon 2006e).

In November 2007, Atzmon was quoted as follows in *The Morning Star*, a Communist newspaper in Britain which is currently hugely supportive of Jeremy Corbyn:

I know deep inside me that the Hebraic identity is the most radical version of the idea of Jewish supremacy, which is a curse for Palestine, a curse for Jews and a curse for the world. It is a major destructive force .... For an Israeli to humanise himself, he must de-zionise himself. In this way, self-hating can become a very productive power. It's the same sense of self-hating I find, too, in Jews who have given the most to humanity, like Christ, Spinoza or Marx. They bravely confronted their beast and, in doing so, they made sense to many millions.

(Searle 2007)

In 2011, I was asked by a colleague in my own department whether we should host Atzmon to talk about his new book on Jewish identity (Atzmon 2011). To my colleague, it was not clear that Atzmon's book was an inappropriate focus for a discussion on Jewish identity in a university sociology department.

Atzmon (2014) wrote the following:

maybe the time is ripe for Jewish and Zionist organisations to draw the real and most important lesson from the Holocaust

. . . . Instead of constantly blaming the *Goyim* for inflicting pain on Jews, it is time for Jews to look in the mirror and try to identify what it is in Jews and their culture that evokes so much fury.

When the right-wing Holocaust denier David Irving says such things, most people on the left are capable of interpreting them as being antisemitic. Irving is fond of saying that Jews should ask themselves the question: 'Why have they been so hated for 3000 years that there has been pogrom after pogrom in country after country?' (Barkat and Haaretz Correspondent 2006). When Atzmon says them, many people who consider themselves antiracist have more difficulty, although it is also true that even people like David Irving have been shifting their antisemitic rhetoric to the left, focusing it on Israel, and citing the usual acceptable antizionist sources. In truth Atzmon is a pioneer of an anti-imperialist, anti-bourgeois, antizionist antisemitism which is no longer in any meaningful sense on the left.

Gilad Atzmon is not just a lone antisemite of no consequence. He is a man who is widely accepted in the jazz and music world – not only as a musician but also as a political musician. He is accepted as being a cultural critic of colonialism, racism and Zionism.

Many on the left defend the Corbyn faction in the Labour Party on the basis that it came to prominence because of its opposition to austerity and because of its socialist and anti-Tory politics; they say that it was successful in spite of its association with what some concede are, and others deny are, antisemitic politics. Gilad Atzmon, on the other hand, argues the opposite: that the Corbyn faction was successful because of, and not in spite of, its antisemitism:

> Instead of telling Corbyn what to do in order to appease the Jews, Hirsh and Jewish community leaders ought to ask them-selves why the opposition to Jews is growing. If Jewish com-munity leaders fail to find the answers, I would be happy to make my way to Golders Green and give them a brief lecture in exchange for a bag of shekels.
>
> *(Atzmon 2015)*

Dieudonné and the quenelle

Dieudonné M'bala M'bala is not Jewish; he is French and of black African descent; but he is relevant here because his story demonstrates the further potentiality for antizionism and its ways of thinking to push on into racist territory, even while still thinking of itself as antiracist, as a way of articulating an ever more radical hostility to bourgeois norms and hegemony.

In January 2014, French footballer Nicholas Anelka scored an English Premier League goal for West Bromwich Albion. At that moment, when the cameras were focused upon him, he straightened his right arm as if beginning to raise it in a 'Seig Heil' Hitler salute. But his left arm went over to his right, and it appeared to suppress the gesture that his right arm was eager to make. His left arm kept his right arm safely down by his side. Like a Freudian forgetting, which protects us from saying something our unconscious feels we should not say, his left arm protected him from performing the straight armed salute. The quenelle, as the performance is known, dramatizes the censorship by which one is prevented from performing the Hitler salute in today's society. The point was not that Anelka wanted to make a Hitler salute; rather, it was that doing such a thing has been made impossible by the power of the Jews and the establishment to prevent such a gesture being made. The quenelle is a dramatized, performed, *Livingstone Formulation*. It is a protest against those who have the power to prohibit antisemitism, and it is an accusation that they do so for reasons connected to their own self-interest.

The defenders of the quenelle say that it is an anti-establishment salute, a shared expression of the impulse to kick back against all the hypocrisies of bourgeois society: like when Sid Vicious from the Sex Pistols wore a Swastika T-shirt. He was not a fascist; he was just engaging in playful blasphemy, goes the defence. The quenelle was invented by the French comedian Dieudonné M'bala M'bala. He found a sharp and succinct way of expressing the huge, complex and diverse nest of resentments he felt against the existing 'powers that be', which he associated more and more with Zionism and the official discourses and institutions of the Jewish community. He made a barbed joke out of the memory of the Holocaust; it is done to shock and to accuse. He put

together the Hebrew word often used in French to refer to the Holocaust, *Shoah*, with *Ananas*, the French word for pineapple, and he got
'Shoananas'. He dances around, singing 'Shoananas' to a catchy tune;
he has fun with the image of Zyklon B and with yellow stars; that is his
way of being anti-establishment.

Sociologist Abram de Swaan (2004) writes:

> Criticism of Israel does not come easy in Europe. There always is
> an hesitation to be overcome. But once that threshold has been
> passed, a sudden relief may take over. Then, the accusations fol-
> low one another with gusto and zest: an anti-Israeli enthusiasm
> becomes manifest. The sense of relief that so many Europeans
> experience when they raise their voice against Israel is not always
> expressed with such open, such contagious enthusiasm.

Why is it that laughing at the idea of the Holocaust works so well
as a symbolic of blasphemy against all that the powerful hold dear? The
reason is that the notion of Jewish power resonates strongly, in ways
of which we are not necessarily immediately conscious; poking at this
imagined power can be tremendously exciting and rewarding. After
decades of feeling that we are all guilty, somehow, of the *Shoah* – the
Jews of France were rounded up mainly by French people – the freedom to disobey the powerful and to release our own pent-up fears in
satirical laughter is attractive. 'Look at Palestine', people say to themselves, 'the Jews are no better than us, in fact they are worse! We in
post-national and post-colonial Europe have moved on; it is only the
Jews who are still stuck in the old racist paradigm; it is only them who
have failed to learn from Auschwitz.' Where does the guilt come from?
There is a feeling that it must be an imposition, that it is the Jews who
have the power to insist on our guilt. What if we don't feel guilty, but
we feel that they pressure us to feel guilty? According to the assumptions of secondary antisemitism, Jewish power is felt to operate through
the requirement that everybody else feels guilty, and continues to make
amends.

There is a tendency in this kind of antisemitism to associate Jews
with authority and so with grownups; in this paradigm the antisemites
thereby cast themselves as children. Remco Ensel studied antisemitic

rap music in Arabic in the Netherlands; he reports that the slang word used for 'police' is 'the Jews'; be careful while driving or the Jews will pull you over (2014).

The politics of 'not in my name' can be fundamentally self-infantilizing in that it withdraws from material responsibility for the external world into an inner moral life in which all that matters is that what happens is not our fault. Football fans grasp the opportunity to shout and sing like children once a week, and to be naughty, in a crowd, where the grown-ups cannot stop them; in itself, there is nothing wrong with this. But this is also the context in which the other team, Ajax or Tottenham, can be thought of as 'the yids' and in which fans can hiss the sound of gas at the 'Jewish' team.

And at UCU Congress, when delegates are dozing off, it is the debate about boycotting Israel, with all the opprobrium it will bring from the Jews and the grown-ups, and with all the trouble it will create for the union officials, which wakes everybody up.

Antisemitism is full of potent, half-understood symbolism, half-recognized meanings, half-confronted fears. One of the key lives of antisemitism has been as a radical, anti-hegemonic movement, a fight back of the little people. Dieudonné is a black man in France; he lives in a world where racism is one of the elements that structures people's lives; he lives in a world where Muslims can experience discrimination; he makes sense of this with a radical mix of Islamist and left-wing anti-imperialist and antiracist rhetoric. One of his starting points, no doubt, is concern for the Palestinians who suffer under occupation and who have been pushed around the Middle East for a century. Sympathy with the oppressed? Yes, but then anger with the oppressors. The Palestinians symbolize victims everywhere? Yes, but then the Israelis come to symbolize the victimizers, and Jews get constructed as being central to all that is bad in the world. Robert Fine (2011: 383) warns of the danger that

> when we view others from an exclusively victimist stance, they become ciphers of our *ressentiment* towards those perceived as their victimisers. We despise the people we charge with despising others. Our compassion for the victims becomes subordinate to our hostility to the perceived victimisers.

It can be a strangely smooth and easy journey from concern for Palestinian suffering to anger with Israel, to anger with those Jews 'here' who take Israel's side, to finding out what really works in a fight with those Jews here, to finding out what really baits Jews.

Antisemitism thinks of Jews as cunning, powerful and immoral – being both behind the powerful and in control of them. Antisemitism saw Jews behind revolutions and wars, behind Bolshevism, behind capitalism, behind imperialism, bankers, money lenders, landlords, pornographers, freemasons; today some people see Jews (or Zionists) behind the neo-cons and neo-liberalism, behind the Iraq war, as saboteurs of Middle East peace, as over-influential in academia, Hollywood, the media, the professions; Jews are the comfortable, the hypocrites, they have become 'white folk' (Brodkin 1999). For some, antizionism, anti-Americanism, anti-imperialism and antisemitism close in on each other; they share the same resonances, the same feelings, the same enemies, the same images and the same discourses.

All this is complicated, and it requires subtle arguments, difficult political judgments, historical knowledge and analytical ability. But the *Shoah* as a pineapple, and the quenelle, these are easy, cheeky and expressive.

Any antisemitism today requires some way of relating to the Holocaust. As long ago as December 2008, Dieudonné appeared on stage at one of his shows with Holocaust denier Robert Faurisson (Bosse-Platière 2012). Holocaust denial was tempting for some antisemites, but it turned out to be both too difficult to achieve (because the evidence was too clear) and unnecessarily ambitious. All that was necessary, in fact, was ostensibly subtle changes of framing in how the Holocaust is thought about. Perhaps the Holocaust is just one instance of modernity's inhumanity; perhaps Stalin was worse; perhaps the Jews (perhaps the Zionists?) use the memory of the Holocaust for their own purposes; perhaps the Holocaust is remembered only because the victims were white. And the second step on these normalization strategies is to turn anger back against the Jews by alleging that they act as if they own the Holocaust and they employ the Holocaust narrative in order to draw victim-power from that ownership.

Dieudonné and Jean Marie Le Pen, the former leader of the Front National, the father of Marine Le Pen, are friends. Le Pen is Godfather to one of Dieudonné's daughters (Zoydo 2008); but that does not mean that we can straightforwardly locate him on the far right. Dieudonné's radical politics and his attraction to antisemitism is not obviously either left or right wing. There are many possible points of agreement between the far left and the far right: a shared hostility to bourgeois culture and to democratic politics; a shared understanding of the Jews (or the Zionists) as being key to all that is wrong with the world; a shared anti-Americanism; a shared anti-imperialist rhetoric. One of the ways in which Dieudonné pushes the limits is by becoming progressively less concerned about the importance of the ostensibly antiracist distinction between hostility to 'Zionism' and hostility to Jews.

So why is a French black man and a French footballer of Muslim heritage doing the (suppressed) Nazi salute? They are not thinking about the Holocaust; they are thinking about the idea of the Holocaust, not about the thing itself but about the discourse which they say has been cultivated around it. If there was once Holocaust piety, they aim to puncture it with Holocaust blasphemy. The quenelle is not about Hitler; it does not relate directly to the Nazis; rather, it is about the way in which the Holocaust is allegedly used and policed and owned by the Jews (or by the Zionists, or by the grown-ups, or by the Americans or by the 'Murdoch Press').

The global system, the French bourgeoisie, the Americans: the question becomes, how do we hurt them: how do we puncture their po-faced hypocrisy? We rhyme *Shoah* with *Ananas*. That is all. Negative and childish resentment and Jew-baiting takes the place of a positive struggle for a better world.

Dieudonné has travelled so far down the antisemitism road that he refuses to worry any more. If a French court outlaws his antisemitic show, he says it is because the judge is a great nephew of Alfred Dreyfuss himself. He is happy to key straight into the symbolic heart of the French antisemitic tradition (Mackey 2014).

One way that the quenelle works is that it has become cool for people to be photographed doing it in naughty places; like outside the school in Toulouse where four Jews were murdered; like on the railways tracks to Auschwitz; like at the Wailing Wall in Jerusalem; like at the Holocaust memorial in Berlin. There are hundreds of such photographs circulating on social media.[7]

There are two key phenomena which come together in this form of antisemitism. One is a focus on fighting for free speech against the Jewish (establishment, Zionist, American etc.) impulse to dictate what is allowed to be said. The other is that antisemitism is not frankly admitted. The quenelle openly refers to Nazism, but its link to Nazism and antisemitism is also vigorously denied. Dieudonné comes close to openly professing antisemitism, but he never quite gets there. He plays with it, he jokes with it, he says ambiguous things and he keeps some kind of distance from it. He never steps outside of the protection that he is afforded by the anti-imperialist and the antiracist pose. Dieudonné retains his connection to the mainstream and to the left; he is regarded as a radical and challenging figure. Many still resist regarding him as an antisemite.

On 11 January 2015, two days after Amedy Coulibaly had murdered four people at the Kosher supermarket Hypercacher, in Paris, Dieudonné wrote on Facebook: 'You know that tonight as far as I'm concerned I feel like Charlie Coulibaly' (Samuel 2015). This was a parody of the 'Je Suis Charlie' meme that had been circulating on social media as a gesture of solidarity with Charlie Hebdo, following the attack there two days before in which twelve people had been murdered. Dieudonné selected the most explicitly antisemitic incident to play with. When he was put on trial for the crime of 'condoning terrorism', rowdy supporters gathered outside the court building; they sang the Marseillaise, and they chanted 'freedom of expression' and 'M'bala'; they chanted 'trash' as the prosecutors passed by.

Dieudonné's defence was that by referring to 'Charlie Coulibaly', he was aiming to find an equidistant position between *Charlie Hebdo* itself and the antisemitic killer in order to signify that he was in favour of 'the peace of Christ'. The prosecutor argued: 'To come and tell us that placing Charlie and Coulibaly back to back is a message of peace is a provocation.' She added: 'You systematically play on false ambiguity' (Samuel 2015). Dieudonné was found guilty and given a two-month suspended sentence (Agence France-Presse 2015a).

In November 2015, Dieudonné was found guilty in a Belgian court of incitement to hatred and Holocaust denial. These charges related to his show in Liège at which he had referred to Hitler as a 'sweet kid' and a 'joyful braggart', and he had called into question the existence of the

Nazi gas chambers. Dieudonné was sentenced to two months in prison in Belgium (Agence France-Presse 2015b).

The Football Association fined Nicolas Anelka £80,000 and imposed a five-match suspension. He was found to have made an 'abusive and/or indecent and/or insulting and/or improper' gesture, and it was found further that 'the misconduct was an "Aggravated Breach"' ... in that it included a reference to ethnic origin and/or race and/or religion or belief' (FA Staff 2014). Anelka had denied being antisemitic or knowing that the quenelle related to antisemitism, saying that it was only performed in solidarity with his friend Dieudonné. The regulatory commission found him guilty of performing an antisemitic gesture, but it added that it 'did not find that Nicolas Anelka is an Anti-Semite or that he intended to express or promote Anti-Semitism by his use of the quenelle' (FA Staff 2014). The antisemitic act was proven but not antisemitism as intention or 'antisemitic' as a description of the man. While the quenelle was a novelty in Britain, it was more familiar in France, whose sports minister Valerie Fourneyron described Anelka's action as 'shocking and disgusting' (BBC News 2014). The shirt sponsors of Anelka's team, 'Zoopla', ended its relationship with the team. The BBC website made a point of informing us, as though it was relevant, that Zoopla is co-owned by a Jewish businessman (BBC News 2014).

Notes

1 Presumably the 'democratically elected ... alternative vision' that he refers to is the racist antisemitism of Jihadi Islam as set out in the Hamas Covenant (1988).

2 The Jewish Socialist Group (2006) wrote an open letter in which it attempted to warn the Scottish Palestine Solidarity Campaign and the Socialist Workers Party what Atzmon was trying to do. Despite this, both of these organizations gave him a platform.

3 At least one local PSC group, the Bucks and Berks branch, sent out Atzmon's Edinburgh speech to its membership, in its mailing of 27 November, with the following introduction: 'Gilad Atzmon argues that the Palestine solidarity movement should focus soley [sic] on the Palestinian cause and urges Jewish sympathizers to support the Palestinians for what they are rather than expecting them to fit into a Jewish worldview.' Bucks and Berks PSC, here, is adopting Atzmon's antisemitic language, for example 'Jewish

worldview', relating to 'Jewish sympathisers' within the Palestine Solidarity Campaign.

4 Palestine Solidarity Campaign Gymru-Wales. Available: http://psccymru. org.uk/index.php?option=com_weblinks&catid=23&Itemid=49 (Accessed 28 February 2007).

5 *Jerusalemites*, Available: www.jerusalemites.org/articles/english/2006/ November/23.htm (Accessed 28 February 2007).

6 Atzmon is not a unique figure. He has a coterie of supporters, for example on the 'Peace Palestine' blog (available: www.peacepalestine.blogspot. com/). Also there are others in the Palestine solidarity movement who are increasingly comfortable with openly antisemitic rhetoric, such as Paul Eisen and Israel Shamir.

7 See, for example, images on the 'overblog site'. Available: http://k00ls.over blog.com/2013/12/pour-ceux-qui-pr%C3%A9tendent-que-la-quenelle-n-est-pas-un-geste-antis%C3%A9mite.html (accessed 28 October 2016).

9

SOCIOLOGICAL METHOD AND ANTISEMITISM

This work is significantly informed by participant observation. I am not a disinterested observer. I am involved in the events and the controversies analyzed in this book. This book is part of them; and it is a compilation of them.

I am resistant to discussing my own biography; in these debates, those who parade their Jewish identity tend to do so with the aim of adding weight to the evidence they give *against* the Jews. Our response has always been to make our arguments and to present the evidence; we have claimed no special authority which flows from our standpoint. Yet I think it would be a little hollow for a sociologist to claim that his social and political identity is entirely unrelated to his work.

My dad, Julian, was born into the Jewish community of the East End of London. His parents, as children, had been part of the wave of Jewish migration to the west at the time of the Kishniev Pogrom of 1903: his mother from Russia, his father from Poland. At 13, my dad won a scholarship to a public school where he was taught by the bullies how to present as a true Englishman. He became a physician, and, a twentieth-century man, he pioneered the science and the practice of geriatric medicine. He helped to develop the care of the elderly in the National Health Service, starting in wards which had once been Work Houses.

My mum was a 3-year-old child living in Germany when Hitler came to power, and she was 8 when she fled to London with her parents and her sister. Her father re-started his business, trading wholesale in fabrics, and he made some money. She never identified as a 'survivor', quite the opposite. She always says that she was immensely lucky not to have been caught up in the Holocaust.

Out of her whole extended family, three cousins from Łódź in Poland survived the concentration camp system: Fela, Fishel and Rushka. On the liberation of Auschwitz, Fishel was alone in the world. Eventually, he received a letter via the Red Cross from my grandfather telling him that two of his sisters were still alive. The letter said: 'Don't worry any more now, I will look after you.' Fela came to London and was desperate to go to Palestine; she found it intolerable to be reliant on non-Jewish authority for her security. My grandmother would not let her go until 1949, saying that she had been through enough war. After Fela arrived in Tel Aviv, she never left; she has not left Israeli sovereignty since, not even for a day. It was not exactly safety that she craved; it was the knowledge that if her safety was ever again threatened, she would be defending herself as a Jew. Fishel made his family in Haifa; Rushka made hers in Netanya.

I am a middle-class Jewish boy. I was brought up in a nice big comfortable house in North London, and I was sent to an expensive public school. I was never religious, and although I had a Bar Mitzvah at a Reform synagogue, and although I always identified without any ambiguity as Jewish, I was never particularly at home in what is known as the Jewish community.

In my teens I identified with the left, and at university I committed myself to the Marxist and anti-Stalinist politics of the tiny left group that was later to become the Alliance for Workers' Liberty (AWL). Rather than a university education, I received a Trotskyist political education about which I am now ambivalent. I am indebted to the AWL tradition and to its key theorist, Sean Matgamna, for much of the shape of the critique of orthodox left politics, including left antisemitism, which informs this book. I also learned theory and ideas in an intimate relation to practical politics in ways which seem completely alien and irrelevant to many contemporary academics. I went back to university later; much of my academic engagement with sociology was also my breaking free from the Marxist religion in which I had been educated and into which I had been socialized. For many, academia and sociology constitutes a kind of grown-up sphere in which one can earn a good living and enjoy high social status by continuing to engage with the theory and the politics of the far left. In this way one can remain within this community of the good while at the same time enjoying the benefits of middle-class success.

As students in the 1980s, we had opposed the kind of antisemitism which appears as hostility to Israel and which is the focus of this book; and we had opposed it from the left. We struggled with people who said that Jewish societies in student unions ought to be banned because they were Zionist and therefore racist; twenty years later we were up against some of the same individuals who wanted to boycott Israel in the academic trade unions.

Through the 1990s, things settled down; the assumption was widely shared that after the horse-trading was finally done, the Israelis and the Palestinians would make a deal and the virulence of the demonization of Israel and Zionism would henceforth be neutralized; it would be exiled to extreme and absurd corners of public life.

In the late 1990s, I participated in a memorable master's course on antisemitism and the Holocaust taught by Robert Fine; we studied Marx and Abram Leon, Arendt and Bauman, Adorno and Horkheimer, Primo Levi and Elie Wiesel. In the whole course, we did not look seriously at hostility to Israel; it did not seem threatening to any of us at that time. This changed profoundly in 2001, following 9/11, Durban and the failure of the peace process; or perhaps that was just when we really noticed its return.

I did not think of my PhD as being autobiographical, and I did not think of it as being about Jews or about antisemitism; with hindsight I can see that it was all of these things, but not in direct or obvious senses. My PhD was about the resurgence in the 1990s of legal ways of addressing and prosecuting ethnic cleansing and genocide. It took the Holocaust and the Nuremberg trials as a central historical foundation for contemporary thinking and emerging practice concerning crimes against humanity, and legal responses to them. My PhD looked at antisemitism, but largely as a historical phenomenon. I was interested in what could be learned from antisemitism and the Holocaust and applied to the contemporary human-authored catastrophes in Bosnia and Rwanda. Even the chapter about David Irving's libel suit against Deborah Lipstadt over her designation of him as a Holocaust denier was about the defeat of an attempt to make antisemitism come alive again.

By early 2005, I was intellectually comfortable in an academic job. Old comrades from the AWL brought it to my attention that my trade union was going to discuss a boycott of Israeli academic colleagues. I wrote a letter outlining the arguments against a boycott, and I sent it round to people I knew to see if they would put their name to it. Lots of people signed the letter, and we had it published in *The Guardian*. I was enjoying myself; the internet made political communication so much easier and more immediate than it had been; and I myself was a different person from the student activist I once was. I was confident in my ability to write, to engage and to make arguments in a way that I could only have contemplated ten years earlier as part of a group. I felt empowered by my ability to articulate what I felt needed to be articulated. I was able to have a thought in the morning and for it to be in the public domain on a blog by lunchtime. I thought that very straightforward arguments about the nature of solidarity, the principle of the university and the dangers of antisemitism would win, and win straightforwardly.

The degree of sustained hostility and ignorance that followed our opposition to the boycott – from friends, from people in my own academic discipline and from comrades in my own trade union – came as a shock, and in some ways it was a profoundly transformative experience for me.

I was a successful, confident, early career sociologist; I had written a prize-winning academic book; I had a permanent job in the coolest sociology department I knew of; I was comfortable and confident on the left; I had two decades of activism in favour of a Palestinian state and against the Israeli right under my belt. I belonged.

At a UCU event in Brighton in January 2010, I set out the story of antisemitism within the union, giving a large number of examples and quoting from many union members (Hirsh 2010b). Tom Hickey, a key leader of the boycott campaign and a member of the UCU National

Executive Committee, declared, in public, in front of my union and academic colleagues, that what I had said was

> a traducement of the truth and it's a straightforward lie and the author knows it. There has been no intimidation – the union and the chief executive would not allow it.

(Symons 2010)

He was not disagreeing with my judgment, and he did not say I was mistaken; he said that I was knowingly telling lies. He transformed me from an academic and a union activist into a person who lies for hidden reasons in defence of a foreign racist movement. He ruled out antisemitism in the union as even a possibility, saying that the union officers would never allow it.

I myself, by this time, had been banned from the internal online debate amongst union activists, for whistle-blowing. I am still banned. I am not allowed to see what people say there about me or about my work, and I have no right of reply. The level of antisemitic bullying which was occurring in that forum at the time of my ban was worrying. The union refused to take sides between those fighting antisemitism and those saying antisemitic things. But the one thing the union officials policed zealously was the prohibition against making anything public. We know that a pre-requisite for institutional racism is the policing of the boundaries of an organization or a community to make sure that the internal culture cannot leak out and that the external culture cannot shine light in.

This is how Mike Cushman, one of the leaders of the boycott campaign in the union, wrote about me in 2016: 'Colleagues have said that we should not respond to Hirsh's calumnies, suggesting that he is such a marginal and pitiful figure that he is not worth the attention.'

And what was thrown at us in the trade unions and in the field of political activism was also mobilized with little more sophistication within the academic discipline of sociology itself. I submitted a paper on sociology and antisemitism to a major European sociology journal. The paper argued that while sociology is itself not immune from the ambivalence toward antisemitism that has haunted anti-hegemonic intellectual and political traditions, the resources of sociology can also be of great value in analyzing and understanding the ways in which antisemitism is sometimes manifested in discourses and movements against Israel and Zionism, even those which think of themselves as antiracist. The paper had already been accepted by the journal after a full peer-review process. A new editor took over at the journal, however, a senior professor of the discipline, and he wrote:

> The text by Hirsh is unpublishable in a scholarly journal: it is an opinion piece, not based on any research, neither theoretical nor empirical. Even its opinions are redundant given their occurrence, in scholarly contexts, in other contributions.

The text was indeed published in a scholarly journal, but not a sociology journal: *The Journal for the Study of Antisemitism* (Hirsh 2013c).

The *Engage* website, which published thousands of blog posts and journal articles on antisemitism, which acted as a bridge between the academic study of antisemitism and public discourse, which had a significant impact in shaping practical and political responses to antisemitism and which received millions of hits over a period of more than ten years, was never valued within my university, and no pride was ever taken in it by my institution. The importance of that network, and its family of networks, shines through this book; the work of colleagues, comrades and collaborators is referred to and built upon and made use of throughout this work.[1] In order to get a hearing for this work, it was necessary to build our own intellectual and political infrastructure.

My own experience resonates with that of anybody who has spent time standing up against a culture of institutional racism. It bears down on you; it makes you doubt your own ability, your reasoning and your own senses; it makes you feel alone; it makes you feel that other people neither understand nor care; it makes you mistrust people; and it makes you wonder if what other people say is right: that you have brought all this down upon your own head, that you are really caught up in a defence of your particular nationalism or a defence of your own special privilege. I think some of the feelings mirror the experiences of women, LGBT people and ethnic minorities who have fought against institutional and cultural exclusion. But there is one key difference, I think: the world where antisemitism is strongest is precisely the world where one would expect it to have the least traction. Well, it is true that other groups fighting bigotry have experienced it in sociology departments, in the Labour Party and in the unions; there is nothing unusual about that. But there is a sense in which people fighting other forms of bigotry have had the feeling that history is on their side, that they will overcome in the end. I do not feel like that with antisemitism. I feel that things are moving away from us, slowly but consistently, one step at a time. Things that are possible today, one keeps feeling, would have been unthinkable only a couple of years ago. There is no catastrophe, no falling over the cliff; it is not 1939 again, but neither is there a feeling that we are heading, in the end, to a better place.

I cannot say how much of the analysis in this book is conditioned by my own involvement in the struggles about which I write. Of course, standpoint theory does not dictate that experience leads to a pure knowledge of truth in itself. But standpoint theory does require that the lived experience of actual human beings should be given a certain kind of epistemological weight. Experience relates to the material world. Knowing something from the inside is part of knowing it from the outside. Nancy Hartsock (1997: 159) classically argued:

> A standpoint is not simply an interested position (interpreted as bias) but is interested in the sense of being engaged . . . . A standpoint . . . carries with it the contention that there are some perspectives on society from which, however well-intentioned one may be, the real relations of humans with each other and with the natural world are not visible.

Philip Roth's 2004 novel, *The Plot against America*, was a study of an antisemitism which most people could not see. The characters who could see it clearly enough to be afraid of it were powerless and isolated. It was their position in social life, their exclusion by the antisemitism that was rife but invisible around them, which was intimately linked to their ability to understand what was going on. Of course Roth's novel is easily seen with hindsight as prescient of the rise of President Trump and his 'America First' movement. But in 2004, the novel spoke, to me anyway, about the kind of left-wing antisemitism which I was seeing first hand around me. That it was imagined on the right, I thought, was a device to allow people to look at it without instantly raising their defences against it.

A 79-year-old Arthur Miller was aware of the process of hidden and paranoid antisemitism too, in 1994, when his play *Broken Glass* was first performed. It features a woman who watches events unfold in Nazi Germany in 1938 from the safety of New York. Both her husband and her psychiatrist downplay and ridicule the threat; they tell her that it is all going to be fine; they tell her that Hitler is a passing phenomenon, that it is not her problem and that she is worrying for nothing. Her paralysis in the face of this denied antisemitic threat is dramatized in the play by the refusal of her legs to work. In both fictional accounts, we are privileged with the certainty that the antisemitic threat we are witnessing is anything but imagined; but the characters are forced to be satisfied with a much more uncertain understanding. Contemporary antisemitism fosters feelings of paranoia; those who cannot see it and those who angrily deny it are quite sure that those who can are inventing it for their own disgraceful reasons. Their certainty, and their freedom from the weight of knowledge, only serves to weigh us down more heavily.

Michael Chabon's 2007 novel, *The Yiddish Policeman's Union*, is a third fictional exploration of a Jewish American sense of dread: an effort to imagine how normal an American rejection of the Jews would look and feel. All three works are perhaps a contrast to the open and fearless Woody Allen of the 1970s, a time in which American Jews seemed able to share their own self-deprecating humour without a second thought for the hostility that it might elicit or for the unconscious memes and assumptions it might key into.

The experience of people opposing antisemitism is not decisive in understanding the phenomenon, but it would be difficult to understand antisemitism without paying close attention to the experience of those who have felt it up close. Not a single truth claim or piece of analysis in this book relies on my personal experience or identity, or on my Jewish nose for antisemitism, for its persuasiveness. Yet, I am a sociologist and I am discussing sociological method, and I am aware that identity, commitment and participation cannot be discounted as a route into understanding.

As a sociologist and as an activist, my Jewish identity has, in a sense, been thrust upon me. That is not to say that I do not have my own

Jewish identity or that I was ever ambivalent about it. But it is the nature of the *Livingstone Formulation* that the identity of the opponent of antisemitism comes under scrutiny and assumptions are made about it. Identity is thrust upon the critic of antisemitism; it is not a self-identification. Racism constructs race. Antisemitism constructs me as a *Jewish* sociologist or as a *Jewish* activist rather than as a sociologist or as an activist. I have no wish to disavow my Jewishness or, if it is thrust upon me, my Zionism either. But it is often experienced as a hostile imposition rather than as the positive identification of a free person. If you raise the issue of antisemitism, and somebody responds that you are only doing it because you are really a Jewish supremacist trying to silence solidarity with the Palestinians, then you have been constructed from outside as a Jew, rather than as an antiracist.

Guardian columnist Nick Cohen writes that he was not brought up Jewish and he did not feel Jewish. His father was Jewish in name only, and his mother not at all. Yet when Nick Cohen wrote about issues which even tangentially touched Israel, or when he opposed antisemitism, he attracted a large volume and intensity of antisemitic response, much of it relating to his Jewish name:

> I stopped [denying that I was Jewish] and accepted that racism changes your perception of the world and yourself. You become what your enemies say you are. And unless I wanted to shame myself, I had to become a Jew. A rather odd Jew, no doubt: a militant atheist who had to phone a friend to ask what on earth 'mazel tov' meant. But a Jew nonetheless.
>
> *(Cohen, N. 2016)*

I have spent a lot of time in the last ten years online. I edited and wrote for the *Engage* website; I wrote thirty-four pieces on *The Guardian's Comment Is Free*; I have had scholarly, political and journalistic pieces published online. At first arguments raged 'below the line', in the comments sections of the blogs; later these discussions largely migrated to Facebook. I am a latecomer to Twitter. Of course, it is easy to feel ashamed of being glued to your computer, as if it was some sordid addiction; and perhaps it is a bit; 'likes' and 'shares' do provide little instant injections of endorphins, of acceptance, of validation. And

there is the feeling that time spent doing what sometimes degener-
ates into online political street brawling is not befitting of one with
ambitions to intellectual gravitas. But on reflection I have come out
against Facebook-shaming. I mention this in the methodology section
of this book because it seems to me that social media has operated for
me in some ways as a research methodology. Firstly, blogs and social
media are for me something akin to a research notebook; they are
where I keep a record of material that concerns my subject matter and
thoughts or fragments that I want to remember. But it is public, and it
is open to scrutiny. This world is one where we can try out arguments,
where we can get feedback, where we can sharpen thoughts, focus on
ones that resonate, re-think ones that do not. My online communities
are mixed; there are colleagues and scholars and intellectuals from all
over the world; no longer are we forced into community with people
who happen to have offices on the same corridor; and they are plural
spaces, not limited to people who satisfy entry requirements. And ideas
and discussions and feedback bounce around quickly and unexpect-
edly; and if you get things wrong, somebody will tell you; and if others
have written things which relate to what you are thinking, you will
find out.

* * *

The research materials for this book have been gathered between 2004
and 2016, mainly in the UK, on the basis that they may be relevant
to the relationship between hostility to Israel and antisemitism. These
materials are produced by individuals, groups and institutions, including political and social movements, trades unions and churches. They
appear in many different forms: books, pamphlets, newspaper articles,
journal articles, websites, web pages, blogs, speeches, video, music and
social media. There is a focus on material which is self-defined as being
antiracist and therefore also anti-antisemitic because this material has
the greatest potential to resonate in democratic spaces.

There is a tendency in research in this area for the distinction
between primary and secondary research material to become blurred.
An academic text can also function as, or be read as, a political inter-
vention. It may itself be understood as an example of discursive antisemitism or an example of a spurious charge of antisemitism.

Materials produced within official institutional frameworks also constitute part of the terrain on which political struggles are conducted by, amongst others, academics. For example, the Report of the All-Party Parliamentary Inquiry into Antisemitism (2006), the Chakrabarti report (2016) and the Select Committee report (2016) were not simply neutral sets of findings but also attempts, in which academic scholars were participants, to institutionalize as official particular approaches to the understanding of antisemitism. The legitimacy of these official frameworks was rejected by scholars holding opposing views. The European Union Monitoring Centre *Working Definition of Antisemitism*[2] is similarly contested by some scholars, while others were actively involved in the work of drafting up the definition. The boundaries of primary materials are porous and include scholarly, political, institutional and more popular texts.

The material is qualitative, not quantitative. It never 'speaks for itself', but it always requires analysis and judgment; and it is open to different interpretations. Much of the material is gleaned from participant observation and action research. It is the fruit not of dispassionate and neutral observation but of public and contested debate and struggle.

Hostility to Israel comes from different sources and takes different forms. Tropes, elements of rhetoric and common-sense notions migrate between antiracist and democratic spaces, nationalist and Islamist spaces, fringe and mainstream spaces, different kinds of media, and the right, the left and the political centre. It is within this complex and dynamic reality that this book finds its material and moves towards specific analytical claims.

The sociological view that racism is often manifested as an unconscious, institutional or discursive cultural and political form

A key insight of sociological method is that racism, and other bigotries and exclusions, are more than a subjective feelings of hatred or fear. They are also about structures of power and ways of thinking; they are also about institutional norms and practices; they are also about cultures constituted by shared racist symbols and meanings.

In contemporary democratic societies, openly racist thought and sentiment is increasingly recognized as falling outside of the boundaries of legitimate public discourse. Racism is squeezed by legislation, legal precedent, public disapproval and institutional policy. Antiracism is, at least formally, wholly incorporated into what used to be called the 'dominant ideology'. Nevertheless, racism stubbornly persists. That which persists tends not to be conscious hatred, openly expressed, but rather unconscious institutional or discursive manifestations of racism. Racist discourse has generally shifted away from zoologically based hostilities and towards prejudicial ways of thinking more likely to be articulated in the language of culture (Barker 1981). There is also increased awareness of the complexities of racisms, and there is more unease with a simple black/white binary framework. In Britain, for example, there is a rise in bigotry and xenophobia, similar to racism in its structure, against people from Eastern Europe who would be designated as 'white' by standard critical race theory or multiculturalist assumptions (Dawney 2008).

This is still true after the Brexit summer, although maybe it is a little frayed at the edges. But even those who blame Britain's problems on foreigners, in Brussels telling us what to do, or here in Britain taking our jobs, angrily reject the charge of xenophobia or racism. Racism has not quite gone mainstream; it is more accurate to say that the *Livingstone Formulation* has been appropriated from the left and developed by the right and by the nationalists. It is almost as if the way that left antisemites angrily deflected and denied was coveted by the populist right. Anyone who raises a public concern about xenophobia in the Brexit debate is likely to be confronted with a counter-allegation of bad faith – that accusations of racism are raised in order to de-legitimize arguments for 'sovereignty', for 'taking our country back' or for 'controlling immigration'. The raising of the issue of racism in this context is portrayed as a tactic for closing down free speech. Just as some patronizingly understand Palestinian antisemitism as the cry of the oppressed, so others now interpret the xenophobia of the so-called 'white working class' in the same way. The charge is that the 'Zionists' or the 'Cosmopolitan elite' mobilize the rhetoric of antiracism as a weapon against the oppressed. Both cases, of course, lend themselves to antisemitic discourse. All of which is evidence that explicit racism remains taboo even while it endures as a significant and objectively identifiable social phenomenon. Just as antizionism and the politics of boycott was pioneered in the UK before emerging in the United States, so we saw the populist politics of xenophobic resentment being exploited with great efficiency by the Donald Trump presidential campaign.

In the 1970s, it was common for black professional footballers in England to be subjected to open, sustained and unchallenged racist abuse by crowds and opponents. But more recently, Luis Suarez, Nicolas Anelka and John Terry were quickly sanctioned by the football authorities for expressions of open racism. The tribunal which punished Suarez was careful to make a distinction between the charge that he 'was a racist' on the one hand and that he had 'done a racist thing' on the other. It de-coupled the racist *act* from an association with the quality of 'racist' which may be applied to the *person* (Reasons of the Regulatory Commission 2011). The same distinction was made in both the Anelka quenelle case and the John Terry racism case.

The public inquiry into the Metropolitan Police's mishandling of the investigation of the murder of Stephen Lawrence made use of the concept of 'institutional racism' in order to make a similar distinction between racist norms and cultures within an institution, on the one hand, and declaring police officers to be racists, on the other (Report of the Stephen Lawrence Inquiry 1999).

A clear practical benefit flows from making distinctions between racist acts and the designation of individuals as racist. It is easier in terms of natural justice for authorities to prohibit racist speech than it is to move against individuals who 'are' racist; it is easier for them to address racist norms and practices than to look into the essence of individuals. Rules can prohibit certain kinds of acts but not certain kinds of persons.

Aside from the practical issues, the question remains how scholars should analyze the relationships between racist acts, racist institutions, racist discourses, and social actors who construct, and who are constructed by, these social phenomena.

The driving of racism underground is a victory, but that which has been driven underground is not necessarily eradicated, and it may re-erupt in new and virulent forms.

Does antisemitism fit into the pattern? Following the Holocaust and the rise of the post-war antiracist movements, there was diminishing space left in public discourse for open antisemitism. Post-war Europe re-invented itself according to the narrative of the defeat of Nazism, the coming to terms with the fact of the Holocaust and the creation of a new peaceful, rights-based settlement. Overt hatred of Jews violates the norms of respectable public discourse. This book has demonstrated that antisemitism endures in more subtle ways, manifesting itself in the quality and the intensity of hostility to Israel. If contemporary anti-semitism is difficult to recognize because it is intertwined with a com-plexity of discourses, ideas, criticisms, activisms, common-sense notions and unexamined assumptions, it is not unusual amongst contemporary structures of power (Faludi 2006). Bigoted ways of thinking may have more purchase if they can be held by people who believe they oppose bigotry. This phenomenon is not as simple as people dishonestly hiding their bigotry within an ostensibly universalistic rhetoric; rather, people are unconscious of the racist memes, assumptions and outcomes which are manifested in their own thought, speech and action. It is neither pretence nor camouflage, and racism is angrily, and honestly, denied.

Emile Durkheim (1952[1897]: 43) writes the following on the notion of intent, in his landmark work on *Suicide*:

> Intent is too intimate a thing to be more than approximately interpreted by another. It even escapes self-observation. How often we mistake the true reasons for our acts! We constantly explain acts due to petty feelings or blind routine by generous passions or lofty considerations.
>
> Besides, in general, an act cannot be defined by the end sought by the actor, for an identical system of behaviour may be adjustable to too many different ends without altering its nature.

How is such unconscious racism to be recognized? One leading Israel boycotter drew attention to a case where the Commission for Racial Equality (now the Equality and Human Rights Commission) ruled that redundancies in one department of her university were racist in outcome (although not in intent) because five of the seven members made redundant in that department were from ethnic minorities. She did not follow the same logic with her proposed boycott. If a routine impact assessment study was carried out with respect to the proposal to boycott Israel, in terms of its effect against Jews, irrespective of its intent, the results would predictably show the outcome would impact disproportionately against Jews.

Antisemitism may be recognized by the replication of racist tropes and stereotypes in ostensibly non-racist discourse. For example, opponents of Israeli human rights abuses may find themselves embracing ideas reminiscent of classic antisemitic blood libels[3] or conspiracy theory.[4]

Unconscious antisemitism may manifest itself through slips or mistakes, which are otherwise difficult to explain. For example, one activist explained in a petition that the Holocaust was an event in which 'thousands of LGBT people, trade unionists and disabled people were slaughtered', forgetting to mention Jews (Bates 2008). A union official thoughtlessly made a connection between anti-boycott lawyers in Britain and 'bank balances from Lehman Brothers that can't be tracked down' (Kovler 2009).

There is anger in Britain with Israel, with its inability to make peace with its neighbours, with its continuing occupation of Palestinian territory and with its record of human rights abuses. Given the long histories of antisemitism in Europe, it would be unexpected indeed if none of this anger with Israel was ever manifested in the language, tropes or themes of antisemitism. Given the long history of antisemitism within left and radical politics, it would be surprising if antisemitic discourse did not sometimes infect or fortify left-wing and radical criticism of Israel.

Methodological tools for sociological research into contemporary antisemitism

Sociology begins as an empirical enterprise, starting with an analysis of *what is*. Our ideas about the world as it *could be* are constrained but also inspired by their relationship to the world as it is. Sociology's foundation in the social world is its materialism. Its cosmopolitanism lies in its assumption that all human beings are in some profound sense of equal worth, irrespective of those factors which divide them, such as ethnicity, gender, class and nation. Sociology's materialism keeps its cosmopolitanism from the temptation to raise universal principles to an absolute. Its cosmopolitanism keeps its materialism from the temptation to limit itself to descriptive empirical observation of what exists, to an unambitious empiricism.

For the sociological study of antisemitism and its relation to rhetoric about Israel, the objects of study are movements critical of Israel, including Palestine solidarity movements and antizionist movements. Criticism of Israeli policies and hostility to Israel come from distinct and different political traditions: liberal, democratic, post-colonial, Stalinist, socialist, nationalist, conservative, fascist, Islamist. They also come from different parts of the world, and different cultural and language traditions. These traditions are variegated and distinct, but they are also intertwined. Elements of rhetoric and common-sense notions circulate among these living spaces, evolving and moving easily from one to another, not least through the new media and social network platforms.

An understanding of contemporary antisemitism requires a methodological toolbox which draws upon a number of resources developed within sociology. For example, we need to root our understanding of Israeli and Palestinian nationalisms within the frameworks developed for the analysis of nationalism in general (for example, Anderson 1995; Hobsbawm 1995). This is a critical tradition, which has come to understand the mechanisms by which nationalist movements reproduce themselves through narratives which aspire to achieve a status which is analogous to the sacred. Through these processes events are moulded into music and movies and objects, texts which make us feel ourselves to be part of the narratives or ones which make us feel excluded. The sociological understanding of nationalism provides a framework which probes the claims of nationalists but which also understands that nationalism is fundamentally dialectical. It has the potential to construct both community and exclusion, responses to oppression but also oppressive structures. Sociological work on nationalism tends to be comparative and resistant to the representation of any particular nationalism as if it were unique, in isolation from all others. It understands nationalism as being produced and reproduced through interactions between economic, political and cultural processes. It regards nationalisms critically but looks at what is, before it moves on to consider what might be.

Sociology is full of contested terms like Zionism and antizionism, apartheid, human rights, the state, democracy, law, totalitarianism, imperialism, whiteness, genocide, ethnic cleansing. Such concepts, and the frameworks built around them, are sometimes indispensable for analysis but are also central to that which is being analyzed. Sociology understands concepts in relation to their actualization in the material world. Thus, discourse analysis addresses ways in which contested meanings are interpreted and played out, and how they solidify into distinct or opposed discursive formations. Widely different forms of hostility to Israel, embedded in distinct social movements, may host common elements of rhetoric and shared understanding, and give rise to unexpected political alliances.

Sometimes, thinking on Israel and Palestine fails to go beyond a conceptual discussion of logical principles. Some people content themselves with a demonstration that there is a contradiction between the requirements for Israel to be a democratic state for all its citizens and for Israel also to be a Jewish state. They find that contradiction to be sufficient to pronounce that Zionism is essentially a form of racism, and they understand all racism in Israel to be a manifestation of the racist essence of Zionism. Others content themselves with a demonstration that because antizionism finds Jewish self-determination to be the only illegitimate nation in the world, then antizionism is by definition antisemitic. These are conceptual frameworks which give huge explanatory weight to ideas, partially and simplistically presented.

Sociology can offer a more sophisticated framework of understanding than that which is content to show that a Jewish and democratic state is contradictory. Sociology can also offer ways of analyzing the dynamics of the contradiction and how it interacts with other contradictions. It suggests ways of exploring how the contradiction arose, how it has managed to find a material existence in a complex world, how successfully it has been able to fulfil contradictory requirements, and in which ways things might develop. Similarly, Sociology is not content to 'prove' that antizionism is antisemitic; rather, it could help us study distinct forms of antizionism and their different traditions and assumptions. Sociology offers us ways of looking at how antizionism can actualize itself in concrete political exclusions. It could explore the contradictions between the meanings social actors wish to communicate and the meanings with which their communications are heard, read and interpreted in distinct contexts.

Take for example the proposal for an academic boycott of Israel. A *sociological* analysis of the relationship between the proposal for an academic boycott and antisemitism can offer more depth than definitional and ideational claims. It can look at the ways in which the concept of an academic boycott is actually realized in a campaign. It can look at the ways in which the campaign plays itself out, say, in an academic trade union or a university. Jewish communal leaders in the UK accused the University and College Union, which represents university and college workers including academics, of being institutionally antisemitic (Davis *et al* 2011). A sociological approach to investigating this claim would be able to examine the relationship between the empirical and the conceptual. It would be able to observe union congresses and meetings employing methodological rigour from the traditions of ethnomethodology and discourse analysis. It would be able to analyze the culture, norms and practices of the union closely. It would be able to study the ways in which opponents of the campaign to boycott Israel have been isolated within the union and to look at the ways that the union leadership and structures had responded. An empirical approach would have to find ways to think about the cumulative effects which may arise from criticism of scholars who were constructed as 'Zionist' being characterized as pro-apartheid, like the Nazis, as people who are indifferent to Palestinian suffering and as people who cry wolf. It is necessary to see how concepts circulate in social situations and how concrete exclusions emerge, whether intentional or not.

Antisemitism as a social phenomenon and not just a subjective feeling

Sociology understands antisemitism as an objective social phenomenon which cannot be defined simply by reference to the subjective feelings of individuals concerned. Sociology attends to discursive and institutional forms of antisemitism and antisemitic ways of thinking, not only to conscious hostility to Jews.

Judith Butler responded to this claim made by the president of Harvard University, Lawrence Summers:

> Profoundly anti-Israel views are increasingly finding support in progressive intellectual communities. Serious and thoughtful people are advocating and taking actions that are anti-semitic in their effect if not their intent.
>
> *(cited in Butler 2003)*

Butler's (2003) response:

> When the president of Harvard University declared that to criticise Israel . . . and to call on universities to divest from Israel are 'actions that are anti-semitic in their effect, if not their intent', he introduced a distinction between effective and intentional anti-semitism that is controversial at best. The counter-charge has been that in making his statement, Summers has struck a blow against academic freedom, in effect, if not in intent. Although he insisted that he meant nothing censorious by his remarks, and that he is in favour of Israeli policy being 'debated freely and civilly', his words have had a chilling effect on political discourse. Among those actions which he called 'effectively anti-semitic' were European boycotts of Israel.

Butler takes up this same 'in effect but not intent' position in relation to freedom of speech. Although Summers insisted that he is for freedom of speech, and makes a distinction between speech and boycott (which he thinks is antisemitic), she says that his analysis is *objectively* anti-freedom in spite of his lack of intent and in spite of the explicit warning that he should not be understood in this way.

Butler is known for her pioneering work on the complex ways in which social and linguistic structures set up gendered and homophobic exclusions and how conceptual and discursive factors coalesce into systems of discrimination. According to her own theory, we are all caught up in the complexity of power relations in which our own self-consciousness is only a part of the story. But when the issue is one of antisemitism, she puts down her sophisticated social and discursive tools and argues instead that people can only be implicated in antisemitism if they are self-conscious Jew-haters. She resists the idea that the boycott campaign could have antisemitic effects even if nobody intends them. Yet when responding to Summers, she reverts to her more familiar way of thinking, emphasizing that Summers is reinforcing a power structure which chills academic freedom in spite of his declarations that he wants to find the boundary between free speech and racist discourse.

A second illustration of the complex interplay between antisemitism conceived of as a self-consciousness on the one hand or as a social structure on the other is the story of Caryl Churchill's play *Seven Jewish Children − a Play for Gaza*. This play offers an account from her imagination of the psychological dynamics within an archetypal Jewish family which have led to the situation where today's Jews are able to contemplate the suffering of the Palestinians without pity or remorse (Churchill 2009a). The author Howard Jacobson (2009) argued that Churchill's play was antisemitic, not least because it made use, in his interpretation, of themes of blood libel and, he argued, because it accused Jews of being pathologically pre-disposed to genocide.

Churchill (2009b) responded with the *Livingstone Formulation*:

> Howard Jacobson writes as if there's something new about describing critics of Israel as anti-Semitic. But it's the usual tactic.

Her letter goes on:

> When people attack English Jews in the street saying, 'This is for Gaza', they are making a terrible mistake, confusing the people who bombed Gaza with Jews in general. When Howard Jacobson confuses those who criticize Israel with anti-Semites, he is making the same mistake.
>
> *(Churchill 2009b)*

Her position is that the element of intentionality is analogous between the violent street thug and Jacobson. Jacobson's critique focuses on the distinction between criticism of Israel and antisemitism, but she accuses him simply of conflating one with the other. But then she arrives at the punchline of her letter: Jacobson is making the same mistake as the street thug, 'unless he's doing it on purpose', she adds. She ascribes malicious intent not to the violent antisemite but to the person who opposes antisemitism.

Antiracists who are accused of antisemitism in connection with their statements about Israel find themselves in an unusual position. While it is difficult to look into the heart of a person in order to discover whether they are racist, it feels easy when the person is yourself. Often, antiracists accused of antisemitism forget the importance of understanding racism objectively as something which exists outside of the individual racist. They find it easier to look within themselves and to find themselves not guilty. Intimate access to the object of inquiry yields an apparently clear result and seems to make it unnecessary to look any further at how contemporary antisemitism functions independently of the will of the social agent.

The relationship between criticism of Israel, hostility to Israel and antisemitism

Hannah Arendt must be right, that antisemitism in profoundly different times and places is bound to be significantly distinct. Antisemitism is not a timeless fact of human civilization. It exists within, not outside of, history and society. It is not a single monster across time and across the globe. Nor are manifestations of hostility to Jews isolated from other forms of racism and exclusion. The struggles against Islamophobia, antisemitism, and anti-Arab racism; the struggle against the occupation of the West Bank; and the struggle against the project to smash the state of Israel – these are all potentially democratic struggles, and, although they are distinct, they can be understood in a cosmopolitan way as belonging to the same family.

But neither is it surprising if Jews tend to experience each new hostility, which draws upon older ones for images and mythology, as just another manifestation of what Robert Wistrich called 'the longest hatred' (1994). Each antisemitism creates something enduring, which remains in the cultural reservoir ready to be drawn upon and reinvigorated. Within this cultural reservoir, two recurring motifs stand out: blood libel, which charges Jews with ethnically motivated crimes of cruelty, often against children, often involving the consumption or use of blood or body parts; and conspiracy theory, which constructs Jews, who are very small in number, as being hugely, selfishly and secretly influential on a global scale (Julius 2010).

Criticism of Israel takes many forms. One might say that the occupation of Palestinian territory is oppressive and requires a regime of racist violence and humiliation to sustain it. One might say that Israel uses targeted assassinations against its enemies and practices imprisonment of Palestinians without trial which are contrary to international human rights norms. One might say that it is an ethnically based state and not a state for all its citizens. Or it may be said that Israel was founded through a campaign of ethnic cleansing and only endures due to an ongoing campaign of ethnic exclusion. There are criticisms which have been made against Israeli policy or Israel's existence in an entirely rational way. Some of the criticisms, one may judge, are justified; others, one may judge, are not. On this level, dialogue, debate, criticism and campaigning continue.

Campaigning against Israeli human rights abuses occurs at an emotional level as well as a rational one, and it seeks to engender feelings of compassion for Palestinians and feelings of anger towards Israel and Israelis. Sometimes, antisemitic themes and images are put to work to help this process. Some antizionist movements employ antisemitic tropes to explain the behaviour of Israel, to exaggerate it, and to bind people into an emotional commitment against it. Sometimes, images and tropes which resemble those of antisemitism also appear in the anti-Israel agitation of antiracists, of people who strongly oppose antisemitism. Here, there must be an unconscious drawing upon the antisemitic motifs which reside in the collective cultural reservoir. What makes this latter hypothesis of unconscious antisemitism more puzzling still, however, is the vehemence with which antiracists who employ antisemitic tropes tend to deny that they are doing so even when it is pointed out to them – and the vehemence with which they downplay the significance of openly antisemitic agitation on the part of others, which is visible around them, against Israel.

The rational type of criticism of Israel outlined above is joined in public discourse by a swirling mass of claims which are of a different kind. Israel has a policy of killing children; Israeli lobbying is hugely powerful; Israel is responsible for the Iraq War; Israel is responsible for

ISIS; Israel is responsible for instability throughout the Middle East; Israel destroys the reputation of anybody in public life who criticizes it; Israel has huge influence over the media; Israel exaggerates the Holocaust and manipulates its memory for its own instrumental purposes; Israel steals the body parts of its enemies; Israel poisons Palestinian water supplies; Israel is genocidal; Israel is apartheid; Israel is essentially racist; Israel is colonialist; Israel is the testing ground and the prototype for 'western' techniques of power and surveillance.

The border between rational criticism and irrational claim is contested and difficult to define; sometimes, the same claim may be either a rational criticism or a blunt weapon, depending on how it is mobilized and in what combination; sometimes, rational criticisms and irrational libels combine in toxic, angry swirls which are difficult to de-couple and which have emergent properties which were not present before their release and combination.

A common feature of diverse antisemitisms has been that they construct 'the Jews' as centrally important to everything that is wrong with the world. Jews have usually been portrayed by antisemites as having a universal importance for humankind. Christian antisemitism pioneered this view. It said that that the Jews murdered God. They watched him suffer on the cross, suffer for the universal benefit of all mankind, yet they still refused his love. In so doing, they not only condemned themselves to damnation; they also stood between humanity as a whole and blissful redemption. Bauman wrote that the Jews became 'a ubiquitous and constant concomitant of Christianity', whose overcoming is necessary for the accomplishment of the Christian mission (1993: 37). Left antisemitism, which Bebel called 'the socialism of fools', said that Jewish bankers, capitalists and the cosmopolitan elite in general sucked the productive capital from the capitalist system for their own benefit. Modernist antisemitism held Jews responsible for resisting modernity; anti-modernist antisemitism said that Jews were responsible for modernity's assault on traditional values and institutions. Nazi antisemitism said that Jews were like an infection which made the whole of society sick. In all cases 'the Jews', who are very small in number, are afforded universal significance.

It is often the case that Israel or Zionism is constructed by critics of Israel or by antizionists as being globally important: Israel is the keystone of the whole edifice of imperialism; Israel prevents peace and democracy across the Middle East; the Israel Lobby is responsible for war; Israel shows us all our future because 'American power' may be undergoing a process of 'Israelization'; Zionism is responsible for re-importing Islamophobia into Europe.

There is a tendency for the Israel/Palestine conflict to attain a place of great symbolic importance. In this way the Palestinians come to symbolize victims everywhere, and then it follows that Israelis tend to become symbolic representatives of all oppressors. In this context, discussion about Israel and Palestine sometimes functions less as a way of understanding a small if intractable conflict on the eastern shores of the Mediterranean and more as a symbolic narrative with global reso-nance. The conflict becomes an empty vessel into which we can pour our own concerns: British concerns over the colonial legacy; European concerns about the Holocaust; American concerns about the frontier; Irish concerns about Unionism and Republicanism; South African concerns about overcoming apartheid. Apart from putting Jews back at the centre of the world, this tendency is also disrespectful to the suffering of the Palestinians. By constructing Palestinians as universally symbolic, their existence as actual people goes largely un-considered. Rather than human beings finding a multiplicity of ways to live and to struggle in difficult circumstances, the Palestinians find themselves portrayed as one single heroic victim of the ubiquitous Zionist evil.

In these ways of thinking, the usual sociological approaches to nationalism are reversed, when looking at the Israel/Palestine conflict and at its related antisemitism. Nationalisms are usually looked at in sociology critically and comparatively, but Israeli nationalism is often singled out as unique and essentially racist. Narratives of nationhood are usually not examined only for their truth or falsity but understood also as social phenomena with particular trajectories and functions, while Israeli nationalism is often denounced in simplistic binary terms as artificial, as though all the other nations were in some sense authen-tic. Palestinians are constructed as indigenous and Israelis as settlers, while notions of authentic ties to pieces of land are normally chal-lenged by a sociological approach. Contradictions are usually exam-ined and their consequences traced, but regarding Israel they are often employed to construct essentialist patterns of thinking to denounce the idea and reality of a Jewish state. Sociology itself is not immune to forms of antisemitism that claim to speak for the oppressed and to confront the powerful (Postone 2006). Antisemitism, after all, can be attractive to radical people who look at the world that exists and find everything wrong with it. However, Sociology also holds an important key to understanding antisemitism and the world that produces it.

Notes

1 Paul Berman (2006): 'If I had a million dollars, which I don't, I would give it to a little cluster of political and intellectual projects in Britain whose purpose is to renovate the liberal left with new ideas. The people working on these projects are best known for having produced a document called the Euston Manifesto, which was composed in a bar near the Euston station of the London metro. (If these people had a million dollars, they wouldn't have to compose their manifestos in bars – they would be able to rent a proper office for themselves.) Their online journal, Democratiya, has become, by my lights, the liveliest and most stimulating new intellectual journal on political themes in the English-speaking world – certainly the liveliest new thing to appear on the English-speaking left in a good long time. Their project Engage has rather bravely taken up the challenge of arguing against the slightly demented anti-Zionism that appears to have apparently overrun whole regions of British intellectual life. And people from the same group put out a couple of vigorous blogs as well: Harry's Place and Normblog.'

2 European Union EUMC *Working Definition of Antisemitism*. Available: http://fra.europa.eu/fra/material/pub/AS/AS-WorkingDefinition-draft. pdf (accessed 8 November 2007).

3 From the *Daily Mirror*: 'We looked away as Israel bombed the crap out of Gaza. When the 1,314 dead Palestinians temporarily sated Tel Aviv's blood-lust' (Reade 2009).

4 John Mearsheimer: 'The Israel lobby was one of the principal driving forces behind the Iraq War, and in its absence we probably would not have had a war' (Stoll 2006).

EPILOGUE

Written after the 8 June General Election 2017

There are three central claims made in this book. The first is that a specific form of left wing antisemitism has been moving into the mainstream. The second is that this antisemitism is carried by people and movements which consider themselves to be wholly hostile to antisemitism. The third is that this antisemitism is insulated by a layer of discourse that casts suspicion against anybody who experiences it, analyses it or opposes it; it casts them out of the community of the oppressed and of the progressive. In this way the Jewish community as a whole, when it raises the issue of this type of antisemitism, is cast out of the community of the oppressed and of the progressive.

Unhappily, the result of the General Election of June 2017 does nothing to falsify these three hypotheses.

While the Labour Party, led by the Corbyn faction, did not win, it did do well enough to damage the Tory Government seriously and to put itself into a position where it appears possible that Jeremy Corbyn could be elected as Prime Minister.

The most common critique of Jeremy Corbyn had been that he was unelectable. With his Stalinist political biography, his commitment to the politics of Israel-demonization, his decades-long association with antisemitic politics and terrorist movements, and his softness toward any movement which positioned itself as anti-imperialist, many people believed that the electorate would never vote for him and that he would lead Labour to disaster. That was the calculation made by Theresa May, and it was not correct.

May made what seemed to be a perfectly logical political assessment. To understand the background to her decision to call an election for 8 June, it is useful to go back to the referendum on the UK's membership of the European Union the previous June. The mainstream of the Tory Party had, since the 1970s, clearly understood that membership of the European Union coincided with a Tory notion of British national interest; it was good for trade, for stability, for peace and for business. David Cameron had felt forced by pressure from the populist right to promise the EU referendum, but he was confident of winning it. Yet, within hours of losing the referendum, the Tory Party found its way to an apparently brilliant and audacious strategy of transforming the whole narrative of British patriotism.

Even the majority of Tory erstwhile 'remainers' were immediately on board with the new Brexit Britishness. They said that 'the people' had spoken and that any second thoughts would inflame the kind of extremist opinion which already claimed that democracy was merely a sham and that the political class just did what it wanted in any case.

With immense speed, it became backward-looking and undemocratic – rather absurd in fact – to be in favour of Britain's continued membership of the European Union. The term 'remoaner' was mobilized to ridicule those who were so un-English as to be bad losers. 'Enemy of the People' was screamed at judges or politicians who were thought not to be on board with the new thinking. Anybody who worried about the economic damage that Brexit would do was treated as if they were 'talking down' Britain. Those who expressed concern about the mainstreaming of racism and xenophobia were told that they were elitists who did not care about the suffering of the 'white working class'. If anyone worried that the EU might follow its own interests in negotiations to the detriment of the United Kingdom, this observation was adduced as evidence that Britain was right to leave such a petty and vindictive organisation. The left of the Tory Party resolved to implement Brexit in a way which minimized its damage while the right gloried in its vindication. Some Tories were beside themselves with satisfaction, hoping that, with the help of Corbyn, they had out-manoeuvred the Labour Party for a generation.

Theresa May asked the electorate for a resounding personal mandate to implement Brexit. But there turned out to be a profound incoherence at the heart of her platform. She promised 'strong and stable' government. She said 'Brexit is Brexit' and she proposed to carry out the 'will of the people' in a rational way which would minimise harm.

But the electorate laughed at her. Those who wanted 'strong and stable' had not wanted Brexit, and those who wanted Brexit had not wanted 'strong and stable'.

Brexit had been a cypher for a populist politics of resentment. It was a codeword, but a plastic one, meaning all things to all people. Some had voted Brexit because they thought the EU was socialist and it prevented Britain from following a free market agenda; others had voted Brexit because they thought the EU was 'neoliberal' and it stopped Britain from following a socialist agenda. Some voted Brexit because they felt out of control and they imagined it would help them regain it. Some did so because they did not like foreigners living in Britain; some felt a special resentment towards the Poles, Latvians and Romanians who were working hard, educating their children and making lives for themselves in difficult circumstances. Some voted Brexit because they believed that the EU took all our money, but they did not understand that the burgeoning Brexit bureaucracy, the new ministries, experts, lawyers and negotiators would be much more expensive and wasteful than the fabled Brussels bureaucracy.

The electorate was not focused on the messy business of implementing Brexit; that was last year's cry of resentment. This year's conduit for the politics of resentment was Jeremy Corbyn. May promised to transform the cypher of Brexit into a concrete programme but by doing this, she stripped it of its cypher-magic, its rebelliousness and its excitement; the electorate turned away.

This book shows that Jeremy Corbyn has, for his whole career, embraced or tolerated certain kinds of antisemitic and totalitarian politics. It also demonstrates that these positions are broadly acceptable within the milieu around him, a milieu that was once confined to the fringes of the far left but which now stands on the threshold of number 10 Downing Street.

There were those who believed that Corbyn's work for the Iranian propaganda TV station alone disqualified him from leadership. For others, it was the fact that he had quite deliberately claimed that Hamas and Hezbollah were dedicated to peace and justice and to the good of the Palestinian people, or that he supported a boycott of Israel but of nowhere else on the planet. Any one of a hundred things that he has done were thought to make him unsuitable to lead the Labour Party, let alone to be Prime Minister.

But we need to stop being surprised. I was shocked when my academic colleagues voted to boycott Israel; and again when they failed to understand how this was dangerous in terms of antisemitism; and again when anti-boycott activists were pushed out of the discussion in the University and College Union; and when the Employment Tribunal listened to the evidence about antisemitism for three weeks and then responded that it all amounted to a dirty trick to silence criticism of Israel; and again when Jeremy Corbyn was elected leader; and then a second time; and when Shami Chakrabarti whitewashed the Labour Party inquiry into antisemitism; and then when Corbyn came within a sniff of number 10. I keep entreating myself to stop being surprised.

There are many people for whom belonging in the Labour Party is important. For some, it constitutes a key aspect of their identity; it constitutes a kind of family; it is important in their own understanding of who they are, and also of who they are not. For others, councillors, MPs and party workers, as well as layers of people who work in trade unions and in the voluntary sector, Labour Party success is a requirement for professional advancement, or at least for their social status. Many people opposed Corbyn because they thought he would lose – and they thought he would take them down with him. Now, when it looks like he might be a winner, much of this opposition has melted away. Parliamentary opponents have been queuing up to declare their loyalty and in some cases, to make abject apologies. They used to say that Corbyn was a loser because he embraced anti-democratic politics; now that he is a winner, they seem much less concerned about his anti-democratic politics.

It turned out that there were only four constituencies where Labour may have been punished for its attitude to antisemitism and all four are home to significant Jewish populations. Although they are exactly the kinds of constituencies that Labour won from the Tories in this election, and while the vote was very close in all four, the swing to Labour was lower than in comparable London constituencies. Antisemitism did not seem to be an issue anywhere else. As I watched the TV coverage through the night of the election, flicking from channel to channel, I did not see antisemitism being mentioned at all.

Activists who have been analysing and opposing left antisemitism throughout its twenty-first century renaissance feel exasperated and afraid, as does much of the Jewish community. How could the electorate still not know, or care?

Some respond that the millions who are excited about Corbyn's radical and socialist agenda simply do not know about the dark side of his politics. It is said that that the little Stalinist bloc around Corbyn will be made insignificant by the influx of fresh and young activists, infused with anger, energy and hope; it is said that the antisemitism and common cause with totalitarian movements will be swept away by this new movement.

So if it is true that Corbyn voters do not know, and it is not the case that they do not want to know, what follows?

How do voters know about things? They know via layers of journalists, activists, intellectuals, researchers and people in public life. Increasingly, these layers are much more organic and diffuse than they used to be, consisting of gradations of smaller opinion-formers all over social media. If the voters do not know about the issue of Corbyn and antisemitism, then it is because each of these layers have not communicated their alarm and their knowledge to those who rely on them for information and for understanding.

Of course if Corbyn had a career-long association with anti-black racists or with misogynist movements, first he would never have become leader of the Labour Party; second, everybody would know about it. That is, assuming that the racist or misogynist movements were not regarded as 'anti-imperialist'.

But contemporary antisemitism comes packaged with its own self-inoculation. Many people at every opinion-forming level have learnt to mis-recognize talk about left wing antisemitism as smears and as lies.

They don't repeat the knowledge and they don't believe what they hear.

Instead of the fresh and energetic influx extinguishing the old anti-semitic core, the worry is that the cadres of antizionist activists within the existing movement will socialize the new young people into the exiting culture, that activists will quickly be educated to understand that the issues of Israel and antisemitism are important signifiers of the boundaries of the community of the good, and that tolerance of antisemitism will play the role of an initiation rite for the new society.

It is difficult to tell how many people are attracted to the movement in spite of the antisemitism and totalitarian thinking and how many are attracted because of it. There is a need for empirical quantitative research on this question.

Corbyn, no less than Brexit, is also a cypher, a blank populist canvas onto which everybody is free to paint their own fantasy.

Many Brexit supporters in the old Labour heartlands abandoned their flirtation with the UK Independence Party and came back to Labour. But many London 'remainers' also voted Labour. People who opposed the notorious Tory policy of subjecting disabled social security claimants to 'Work Capability Assessments' voted for Corbyn. People who felt that the National Health Service was being starved of money voted for Corbyn. People who could not or who did not want to help pay for their children to go to university voted for Corbyn. People who worked hard but still could not afford decent housing voted for him. People who blamed British foreign policy for terrorism and people who imagined that if we were nicer, the terrorists would leave us alone; people who admired Hamas, the IRA, Hezbollah, Chavez, Castro and Putin voted for Corbyn as did people who blamed bankers, the Rothchilds and the 'Davosocracy' for all our problems. People who liked Corbyns refusal to step into line voted for him. People who hated Corbyn but liked Labour voted for him. People who hated Labour but liked Corbyn voted for him.

In this election the choice was between the immediate implemen-tation of Brexit by a Tory government committed to the politics of austerity on the one hand, and the Jeremy Corbyn cypher on the other. The electorate was split – as though reluctant to commit to either.

It is difficult to see how the next election, which might come soon, can be anything other than a straight choice between two variants of populist, angry, hollow and resentful politics.

In this context, of course, it is quite legitimate to prefer Labour populism to Tory populism while at the same time recognising with great clarity that Labour has an antisemitism problem. But it is rare that people are prepared to embrace this position openly.

Many people are more attracted to rationalizations and to accommodations which permit them fully to take their place in the movement. This is a moment in which nobody wants to be left behind. The excitement which so many people are experiencing at the prospect of the vindication of oppositionist or socialist politics should not be under-estimated; neither should the rapidity or the ferocity of the response against those who are thought of as being disloyal to the movement in its moment of possibility. The other significant danger is the potential fury of the populism of the far right when it is confronted by the prospect of the Corbyn faction taking governmental power in Britain.

Some say that Corbyn's antisemitism is only a kind of abstract antisemitism; that he would not want to enact laws or policies against Jews; that only a practical and immediate threat is genuine antisemitism. Others say that Corbyn has changed, that he no longer speaks at the annual Al Quds demonstration in London, with its Hezbollah flags and its antisemitic rhetoric; he now supports a two-state solution; he would no longer dare to jump to the defence of antisemites as he did when he was an unimportant back bencher.

It is difficult to know exactly what the consequences would be of having a Prime Minister who has for so long been connected to antisemitic ways of thinking and antisemitic movements. The threat is amorphous. One might assume that there will be no laws or policies against Jews from the antiracists who believe that they abhor the very idea of antisemitism.

Britain's voice in international institutions may become stridently anti-Israel. The denouncing of most Jews as pro-apartheid or as defenders of racism and neoliberalism might increase as it is legitimized by the known politics of the Prime Minister himself. If Jewish children in schools are picked out for denunciation as Zionists and Islamophobes, where will they go for help? The bullies will say they're only repeating what the Prime Minister himself thinks; the teachers will check their union policy and may have trouble making the Jewish kids feel safe. Jewish parents may be pushed back into Jewish schools; the funding for 'elitist', 'Zionist' and 'religious' Jewish schools may be brought into question by the left.British citizens with Israeli citizenship may find themselves under threat for having served in the Israeli army.

But the measure of the real threat is more than the sum of these various practical threats. The real threat is the mainstreaming and the normalization of antisemitic politics in ways which are as yet difficult precisely to predict. Britain may be approaching a period of significant and dangerous insecurity and turmoil.

Democracy itself is under assault from a number of different directions; the distinct and opposing critiques of democracy have more in common with each other than their apparently distinct proponents are aware of. The far left, the radical intellectuals, the antisemites, the xenophobic and Islamophobic right, the radical Islamists, the Trumpists and the Brexiters share a number of perspectives. They have a tendency to embrace discourses in which contempt for democratic states and cultures, for (neo-)liberals, for the liberty and equality of human beings are key elements. Profound suspicion of international co-operation and institutions is on the rise. Scepticism extends to the rule of law, science and knowledge, international trade, the very idea of the market. It is now common to encounter those who believe that these elements are mere facades which hide the old power structures in order to subordinate the many to the few.

It is not yet clear how antisemitism might play out in the coming years. But the emotional appeal of the populist movements requires enemies: enemies which are to be found at the centre of dangerous, global and powerful conspiracies.

Antisemitism has never been just an isolated eccentricity. It has always also been an indicator of a profound political sickness. To tolerate this as a symptom and to miss the fatal disease which causes it may prove to be an error.

REFERENCES

Aaronvitch, D. (2016) 'Tonge's obnoxious ideas on Jews set a terrible example', *The Times*. Available: www.thetimes.co.uk/article/tonges-obnoxious-ideas-on-jews-set-a-terrible-example-pbvgl9nrg (accessed 12 November 2016).

Agence France-Presse (2015a) 'French comedian found guilty of "condoning terrorism" in Facebook post', *The Guardian*. Available: www.theguardian.com/world/2015/mar/18/french-comedian-dieudonne-mbala-mbala-guilty-condoning-terrorism (accessed 28 October 2016).

Agence France-Presse (2015b) 'French comedian Dieudonné given prison sentence for hate speech', *The Guardian*. Available: www.theguardian.com/world/2015/nov/25/french-comedian-dieudonne-prison-sentence-hate-speech (accessed 28 October 2016).

Agencies and Times of Israel Staff (2016) 'Third labour official in day suspended for anti-Israel remarks', *The Times of Israel*. Available: www.timesofisrael.com/third-uk-labour-official-in-day-suspended-for-anti-israel-remarks/ (accessed 7 October 2016).

Ali, T. (2004) 'To be intimidated is to be an accomplice: notes on anti-semitism, Zionism and Palestine', *Counterpunch*. Available: www.counterpunch.org/2004/03/04/notes-on-anti-semitism-zionism-and-palestine/ (accessed 27 November 2015).

Alibhai-Brown, Y. (2015) 'Stop lying about Jeremy Corbyn', *The Independent*. Available: https://archive.is/pqExP (accessed 12 November 2016).

Allegretti, A. (2016) 'Jeremy Corbyn Press TV: Labour leader defends taking money from Iranian state broadcaster appearances', *Huffington Post*.

Available: www.huffingtonpost.co.uk/entry/jeremy-corbyn-defends-taking-money-from-iranian-state-broadcaster-press-tv-appearances_uk_57c705b7e4b01e359229a9be (accessed 11 November 2016).

All-Party Parliamentary Group Against Antisemitism (2006) 'Report of the Parliamentary inquiry into antisemitism'. Available: www.antisemitism.org.uk/wp-content/uploads/All-Party-Parliamentary-Inquiry-into-Antisemitism-REPORT.pdf (accessed 24 August 2016).

Anderson, B. (1995) *Imagined Communities*, London: Verso.

Arendt, H. (1975) *The Origins of Totalitarianism*, San Diego: Harvest.

Ashworth, J. (2016) 'Jane Ashworth's submissions to the Chakrabarti inquiry into antisemitism', *Engage*. Available: https://engageonline.wordpress.com/2016/07/02/jane-ashworths-submission-to-the-chakrabarti-inquiry-into-antisemitism/ (accessed 12 November 2016).

Assaf, S. (2007) 'Hamas's victory in Gaza is a blow to Bush's plans', *Socialist Worker*. Available: https://socialistworker.co.uk/art/11874/Hamass+victory+in+Gaza++is+a++blow+to+Bushs+plans (accessed 26 October 2016).

Atzmon, G. (2003a) 'On antisemitism', *www.Gilad.co.uk*. Available: www.gilad.co.uk/html%20files/onanti.html (accessed 30 November 2006).

Atzmon, G. (2003b) 'The most common mistakes of Israelis', *Counterpunch*. Available: www.counterpunch.org/2003/08/28/the-most-common-mistakes-of-israelis/ (accessed 28 October 2016).

Atzmon, G. (2006a) 'Beyond comparison', *PeacePalestine*. Available: http://peacepalestine.blogspot.co.uk/2006/08/gilad-atzmon-beyond-comparison.html (accessed 28 October 2016).

Atzmon, G. (2006b) 'What is to be done?', *Counterpunch*. Available: www.gilad.co.uk/writings/palestinian-solidarity-discourse-and-zionist-hegemony-gilad.html (accessed 12 November 2016).

Atzmon, G. (2006c) 'Pre-traumatic stress disorder: a glimpse into Israeli collective psychosis', *Middle East Online*. Available: www.middle-east-online.com/english/?id=17604 (accessed 28 October 2016).

Atzmon, G. (2006d) 'Jewish secular fundamentalism', *Dissident Voice*. Available: www.dissidentvoice.org/Feb06/Atzmon07.htm (accessed 28 October 2016).

Atzmon, G. (2006e) 'A response to David Hirsh', *The Guardian*. Available: www.theguardian.com/commentisfree/2006/dec/12/giladatzmonrespondstodavid (accessed 28 October 2016).

Atzmon, G. (2011) *The Wandering Who? A Study of Jewish Identity Politics*, Hants: Zero Books.

Atzmon, G. (2014) 'Holocaust day: the time is ripe for an apology', *www.Gilad.co.uk*. Available: www.gilad.co.uk/writings/holocaust-day-the-time-is-ripe-for-a-jewish-apology.html (accessed 30 October 2016).

Atzmon, G. (2015) 'Hirsh v. Corbyn', *www.Gilad.co.uk*. Available: www.gilad. co.uk/writings/2015/9/19/hirsh-vs-corbyn (accessed 28 October 2016).

Auster, L. (2005) 'BNP leader criticizes antisemitism', *View from the Right*. Available: www.amnation.com/vfr/archives/004615.html (accessed 27 November 2015).

Author unknown (2012) 'The "Perdition" affair', *Workers' Liberty*. Available: www.workersliberty.org/story/2012/05/10/perdition-affair (accessed 19 September 2016).

Author unknown (2015) 'Stop the war deleted controversial articles including one advocating war with Israel', *Jewish News Online*. Available: http:// jewishnews.timesofisrael.com/stop-the-war-deleted-controversial-articles-including-one-advocating-war-with-israel/ (accessed 4 November 2016).

Author unknown (2016a) 'Labour MP: Israelis should face "transportation" out of Middle East', *Guido Fawkes*. Available: http://order-order. com/2016/04/26/labour-mp-israelis-should-face-transportation-out-of-middle-east/ (accessed 19 September 2016).

Author unknown (2016b) 'Naz Shah compared Israel's to Hitler', *Guido Fawkes*. Available: http://order-order.com/2016/04/26/naz-shah-compared-israe lis-to-hitler/ (accessed 19 September 2016).

Author unknown (2016c) 'Naz Shah: "the Jews are rallying"', *Guido Fawkes*. Available: http://order-order.com/2016/04/26/naz-shah-the-jews-are-rallying/ (accessed 19 September 2016).

Author unknown (2016d) 'Hitler, insists Ken Livingstone', *Newsthump*. Available: http://newsthump.com/2016/09/07/hitler-insists-ken-livingstone/ (accessed 20 September 2016).

Author unknown (2016e) 'Candidate who suggested that ISIS should attack Israel readmitted to Labour', *Guido Fawkes*. Available: http://order-order. com/2016/03/14/candidate-who-suggested-isis-should-attack-israel-readmitted-to-labour/ (accessed 7 October 2016).

Author unknown (2016f) 'Labour reinstates suspended Corbynista who said "Jews" behind ISIS and 9/11', *Guido Fawkes*. Available: http://order-order. com/2016/03/23/labour-reinstates-suspended-corbynista-who-said-jews-behind-isis-and-911/ (accessed 7 October 2016).

Author unknown (2016g) 'Highlights: Shami Chakrabarti grilled on Labour Party antisemitism', *YouTube*, Online Posting. Available: www.youtube. com/watch?v=A_ZRtoR32NU (accessed 9 October 2016).

Badiou, A. (2014) 'Alain Badiou's "anti-Semitism": Badiou, Segré, and winter respond to the current accusations in France', *Versobooks.com*. Available: www.versobooks.com/blogs/1688-alain-badiou-s-anti-semitism-badiou-segre-and-winter-respond-to-the-current-accusations-in-france (accessed 26 October 2015).

Badiou, A., Hazan, E., and Segré, I. (2013) *Reflections on Antisemitism*, London: Verso.

Bard, M. (2007) 'The Arab boycott', *Jewish Virtual Library*. Available: http://dev. jewishvirtuallibrary.org/cgi-bin/itemPrintMode.pl?Id=11241 (accessed 17 October 2016).

Barkat, A., and Haaretz Correspondent (2006) 'David Irving: Jews should ask themselves why they are hated', *Haaretz*. Available: www.haaretz.com/news/ david-irving-jews-should-ask-themselves-why-they-are-hated-1.207968 (accessed 28 October 2016).

Barker, M. (1981) *The New Racism: Conservatives and the Ideology of the Tribe*, London: Junction Books.

Bates, G. (2008) 'Has the SWP discovered a "Jew-free" Holocaust?', *Workers' Liberty*. Available: www.workersliberty.org/story/2008/08/18/has-swp-discovered-jew-free-holocaust (accessed 30 October 2016).

Bauman, Z. (1993) *Modernity and the Holocaust*, London: Polity.

BBC News (2014) 'Nicolas Anelka banned and fined £80,000 for "quenelle" gesture'. Available: www.bbc.co.uk/sport/football/26326484 (accessed 28 October 2016).

Beckett, M. (2015) 'I was a moron to nominate Jeremy Corbyn', *BBC News*. Available: www.bbc.co.uk/news/uk-politics-33625612 (accessed 5 October 2016).

Beller, S. (2007) 'In Zion's hall of mirrors: a comment on *neuer Antisemitismus*?', *Patterns of Prejudice*, 41(2): 215–238.

Bennoune, K. (2015) *Your Fatwa Doesn't Apply Here – Untold Stories from the Fight against Muslim Fundamentalism*, New York: W.W. Norton & Company, Inc.

Bensussan, G. (2014) 'L'extrême droite en a rêvé, l'extrême gauche l'a fait', *Libération*. Available: http://www.liberation.fr/france/2014/07/22/l-extre me-droite-en-a-reve-l-extreme-gauche-l-a-fait_1068401 (accessed 15 May 2017).

Berman, P. (2006) 'How to give away a million dollars', *Slate*. Available: www. slate.com/articles/life/philanthropy/2006/11/how_to_give_away_a_mil lion_dollars.html (accessed 30 March 2017).

Bingham, J. (2015) 'Vicar investigated over "9/11 Israel did it" posting', *The Telegraph*. Available: www.telegraph.co.uk/news/religion/11378475/Vicar-investigated-over-911-Israel-did-it-posting.html (accessed 27 November 2015).

Blakemore, C., Dawkins, R., Noble, D., and Yudkin, M. (2003) 'Is a scientific boycott ever justified?', *Nature*, 421: 314.

Bloom, D. (2016) 'Thousands sign petition demanding John Mann is disciplined for rant at Ken Livingstone', *Mirror*. Available: www.mirror.co.uk/ news/uk-news/thousands-sign-petition-demanding-john-7857921 (accessed 19 September 2016).

The Board of Deputies of British Jews (2011) 'Flynn apologises for comments', *The Board of Deputies of British Jews*. Available: www.bod.org.uk/live/con tent.php?Item_ID=287 (accessed 16 November 2013).

Bogdanor, P. (2016) 'An antisemitic hoax: Lenni Brenner on Zionist "collaboration" with the Nazis', *Fathom*. Available: http://fathomjournal.org/an-antisemitic-hoax-lenni-brenner-on-zionist-collaboration-with-the-nazis/ (accessed 19 September 2016).

Bosse-Platière, R. (2012) 'Dieudonné: La Rochelle doit lui verser 40.000 euros', *Le Figaro*. Available: www.lefigaro.fr/theatre/2012/09/05/03003-20120905ARTFIG00579-dieudonne-la-rochelle-doit-lui-verser-40000-euros.php (accessed 28 October 2016).

Brenner, L. (2014) *Zionism in the Age of the Dictators*, New York: Lawrence Hill & Co.

Bright, M. (2011) 'UCU 'antisemitism motion passes', *The Jewish Chronicle*. Available: www.thejc.com/news/uk-news/49660/ucu-antisemitism-motion-passes (accessed 16 November 2015).

Bright, M. (2012) 'Jeremy Corbyn calls for inquiry on "pro-Israel lobby"', *The Jewish Chronicle Online*. Available: www.thejc.com/news/uk-news/66606/jeremy-corbyn-calls-inquiry-pro-israel-lobby (accessed 4 November 2016).

Broder, H. (1986) *Der Ewige Antisemit*, Frankfurt am Main: S. Fischer Verlag.

Brodkin, K. (1999) *How Jews Became White Folks and What That Says About Race in America*, New Brunswick: Rutgers University Press.

Brown, C., and Hastings, C. (2003) 'Fury as Dalyell attacks Blair's "Jewish Cabal"', *Daily Telegraph*. Available: www.telegraph.co.uk/news/uknews/1429114/Fury-as-Dalyell-attacks-Blairs-Jewish-cabal.html (accessed 27 November 2015).

Bulman, M. (2016) 'Shami Chakrabarti appointed shadow Attorney General by Jeremy Corbyn', *The Independent*. Available: www.independent.co.uk/news/uk/politics/shami-chakrabarti-attorney-general-shadow-cabinet-jeremy-corbyn-appointed-labour-party-reshuffle-a7349471.html (accessed 8 October 2016).

Butler, J. (2003) 'No, it's not antisemitic', *London Review of Books*. Available: www.lrb.co.uk/v25/n16/butl02_.html (accessed 30 October 2016).

Butler, J. (2006) 'Israel/Palestine and the paradoxes of academic freedom', *Radical Philosophy*. Available: www.radicalphilosophy.com/article/israelpalestine-and-the-paradoxes-of-academic-freedom (accessed 18 October 2016).

Butler, J. (2013) 'Judith Butler's remarks to Brooklyn College on BDS', *The Nation*. Available: www.thenation.com/article/judith-butlers-remarks-brooklyn-college-bds/ (accessed 18 October 2016).

Butler, J. in conversation with Rose, J. (2005). 'Holocaust premises: political implications of the traumatic frame' at Senate House, London, 22 September.

Byrne, C. (2003) 'Independent cartoon cleared of antisemitism', *The Guardian*. Available: www.theguardian.com/media/2003/may/22/theindependent. pressandpublishing (accessed 26 October 2016).

Cellan Jones, R. (2007) 'London branch calls for ballot', *Stop the NUJ Boycott*. Available: http://stopnujboycott.blogspot.co.uk/2007/05/london-branch-calls-for-ballot.html (accessed 18 October 2016).

Chabon, M. (2007) *The Yiddish Policeman's Union*, New York: Harper Torch.

Chakrabarti, S. (2016) 'Report: the Shami Chakrabarti Inquiry'. Available: www.labour.org.uk/page/-/party-documents/ChakrabartiInquiry.pdf (accessed 21 July 2016).

Chalmers, A. (2016) 'Antisemitic anti-Zionism and the scandal of Oxford University Labour Club', *Fathom*, Spring. Available: http://fathomjournal.org/antisemitic-anti-zionism-and-the-scandal-of-oxford-university-labour-club/ (accessed 7 October 2016).

Channel 4 News (2015) 'Jeremy Corbyn on Hamas, the Middle East and the super-rich', *YouTube*, Online Posting. Available: www.youtube.com/watch?v=QZAn7ZEvwek (uploaded 13 July 2015) (accessed 11 November 2016).

Chesler, P. (2003) *The New Antisemitism*, San Francisco: Jossey-Bass.

Churchill, C. (2009a) *Seven Jewish Children: A Play for Gaza*, London: Royal Court.

Churchill, C. (2009b) 'My play is not antisemitic', Letters, *The Independent*. Available: www.independent.co.uk/opinion/letters/letters-jacobson-on-gaza-1628191.html (accessed 30 October 2016).

Cohen, B. (2014) *Some of My Best Friends: A Journey Through Twenty-First Century Antisemitism*, Berlin: Edition Critic.

Cohen, J. (2016) 'Suspended MP Naz Shah tells synagogue: "I was ignorant about Judaism"', *Jewish News Online*. Available: http://jewishnews.timesofisrael.com/suspended-mp-naz-shah-tells-synagogue-i-was-ignorant-about-judaism/ (accessed 19 September 2016).

Cohen, N. (2016) 'Why I'm becoming Jewish and why you should, too', *The Guardian*. Available: www.theguardian.com/commentisfree/2016/mar/19/why-i-am-becoming-a-jew-and-you-should-too (accessed 30 October 2016).

Cohen, S. (2005) 'That's funny, you don't look antisemitic', *Engage*. Available: https://engageonline.wordpress.com/thats-funny-you-dont-look-antisemitic-steve-cohen/ (accessed 17 October 2016).

Cohen, S. (2006) 'I would hate myself in the morning', *That's Funny, You Don't Look Anti-semitic*. Available: http://you-dont-look-anti-semitic.blogspot.co.uk/2006/05/i-would-hate-myself-in-morning.html (accessed 17 October 2016).

Cohen, T. (2016) 'Livingstone says Labour should reinstate him', *Sky News*. Available: http://news.sky.com/story/livingstone-says-labour-should-reinstate-him-10262440 (accessed 19 September 2016).

Collier, D. (2016) 'Its' not true but it's important', *David-collier.com*. Available: http://david-collier.com/?p=2229 (accessed 17 October 2016).

Cooke, S. (2007) 'Boycott "apartheid Israel"?', *Workers' Liberty*. Available: www.workersliberty.org/story/2007/10/27/boycott-apartheid-israel (accessed 21 July 2016).

Corbyn, J. (2014) 'The 35th anniversary of the Islamic revolution in Iran – the all-encompassing revolution', *YouTube*, Online Posting. Available: www.youtube.com/watch?v=8aL947jPaSU&feature=youtu.be&t=4522 (uploaded 10 February 2014) (accessed 5 October 2016).

Corbyn, J. (2015a) 'Jeremy Corbyn on Hamas and Hezbollah', *YouTube*, Online Posting. Available: www.youtube.com/watch?v=pGj1PheWiFQ (uploaded 15 June 2015) (accessed 24 August 2016).

Corbyn, J. (2015b) 'Why I'm standing down as chair of stop the war coalition', *Stop the War Coalition*. Available: http://stopwar.org.uk/index.php/news/702-think-before-you-fisk-10-things-the-economist-got-wrong-on-ukraine (accessed 5 October 2016).

Corbyn, J. (2016) 'UK: Corbyn shakes head at suggestion he compared actions of IS and Israel', *YouTube*, Online Posting. Available: www.youtube.com/watch?v=U9XfYwetHXw (uploaded 30 June 2016) (accessed 9 October 2016).

Corbyn, J., and Galloway, G. (2015) 'Jeremy Corbyn and George Galloway after the 7/7 bombings', *YouTube*, Online Posting. Available: www.youtube.com/watch?v=iP3df8SH_W4 (uploaded 15 September 2015) (accessed 28 October 2016).

Cousin, G., and Fine, R. (2012) 'A common cause: reconnecting the study of racism and antisemitism', *European Societies*, 14(2): 166–185.

Cowburn, A. (2016) 'Momentum vice-chair Jackie Walker removed from position over Holocaust comments', *The Independent*. Available: www.independent.co.uk/news/uk/politics/momentum-vice-chair-jackie-walker-removed-after-holocaust-comments-a7343226.html (accessed 8 October 2016).

Cowley, P. (2015) 'Corbyn and the whip', *Revolts*. Available: http://revolts.co.uk/?p=914 (accessed 5 October 2016).

Craig, J. (2016) 'Baroness Tonge resigns from the Liberal Democrat party in anti-semitic row', *Sky News*. Available: http://news.sky.com/story/baroness-tonge-resigns-from-the-liberal-democrats-in-anti-semitic-row-10634539 (accessed 28 October 2016).

Crooke, S. (2011) 'Boycott Apartheid Israel', in A. Grabski (ed.) *Rebels against Zion: Studies on the Jewish Left Anti-Zionism*, Warsaw: Jewish Historical Institute, pp. 259–286.

Curtis, P. (2005) 'Boycott call resurfaces', *The Guardian*. Available: www.theguardian.com/education/2005/apr/05/internationaleducationnews.highereducation (accessed 17 October 2016).

Cushman, M. (2009) 'No title', UCU Congress endorses boycotts, divestment and sanctions against Israel despite legal warning, Online posting. Available: https://groups.yahoo.com/neo/groups/JustPeaceUK/conversations/topics/26407 (accessed 18 October 2016).

Cushman, M. (2016) 'The wrong sort of Jews', *Free Speech on Israel*. Available: http://freespeechonisrael.org.uk/wrong-sort-jews/ (accessed 29 October 2016).

Dahlgreen, W. (2015) 'With one month to go, Corbyn's lead increases', *Yougov*. Available: https://yougov.co.uk/news/2015/08/10/corbyn-pull-ahead/ (accessed 16 October 2016).

Das, S. (2012) 'Yvonne Ridley: says Zionists should be "hunted down", "loathes" Israel; Supports Hamas . . . ', *Left Foot Forward*. Available: http://leftfootforward.org/2012/11/yvonne-ridley-respect-rotherham-hamas/ (accessed 6 October 2016).

Davis, M., Ronson, G.M., Wineman, V., and Chinn, T. (2011) 'Letter to UCU general secretary Sally Hunt', *The Jewish Chronicle Online*. Available: www.thejc.com/news/uk-news/49573/letter-ucu-general-secretary-sally-hunt (accessed 30 October 2016).

Dawney, L. (2008) 'Racialisation of Central and East European migrants in Herefordshire', *Sussex Centre for Migration Research Working Paper no 53*. Available: www.sussex.ac.uk/migration/documents/mwp53.pdf (accessed 30 October 2016).

De Swaan, A. (2004) 'Anti-Israeli enthusiasms and the tragedy of blind process'. Available: http://deswaan.com/wp-content/uploads/2015/07/anti-israeli-enthusiasms-eng-long.pdf (accessed 8 October 2016). Published in French as: 'Les enthousiasmes anti-israéliens: la tragédie d'un aveugle', *Raisons Politiques*, November 2004: 105–124.

Dearden, L. (2016) 'Jeremy Corbyn speech: Labour leader accused of comparing Israel to "Islamic states" in antisemitism report response', *The Independent*. Available: www.independent.co.uk/news/uk/politics/jeremy-corbyn-antisemitism-labour-row-report-compares-israel-government-isis-islamic-states-a7110931.html (accessed 9 October 2016).

Dearden, L. (2015) 'Jeremy Corbyn says David Cameron's conference speech attack shows Conservatives are "rattled"', *The Independent*. Available: www.independent.co.uk/news/uk/politics/jeremy-corbyn-says-david-camerons-conference-speech-attack-shows-conservatives-are-rattled-a6684806.html (accessed 6 October 2016).

Democracy Now! (2015) 'Ex-U.N. official John Dugard: Israel's crimes are "infinitely worse" than in apartheid South Africa', *Democracy Now!* Available: www.democracynow.org/2015/5/6/ex_un_official_john_dugard_israel (accessed 25 October 2016).

Deutscher, I. (1968) *The Non-Jewish Jew and Other Essays*, London: Oxford University Press.

Deutscher, I. (1981) *The Non-Jewish Jew and Other Essays*, London: The Merlin Press.

Douzinas, C. (2000) *The End of Human Rights*, Oxford: Hart.

Dovkants, K. (2008) 'Anti-semitism – and a timely question for Ken', *Evening Standard*. Available: www.standard.co.uk/news/mayor/anti-semitism-and-a-timely-question-for-ken-6626642.html (accessed 19 September 2016).

Downing, G. (2015) 'Why Marxists must address the Jewish Question concretely today', *Socialist Fight*. Available: https://socialistfight.com/2015/08/22/why-marxists-must-address-the-jewish-question-concretely-today/ (accessed 7 October 2016).

Downing, G. (2016) 'The social and political meaning of 9/11 conspiracy theory', *Socialist Fight*. Available: https://socialistfight.com/2016/01/24/the-social-and-political-meaning-of-911-conspiracy-theory/ (accessed 7 October 2016).

Duke, David (2004) 'What is antisemitism?' Available: http://www.David Duke.com (24 March 2004), http://www.davidduke.com/date/2004/03/ (accessed 24 February 2007).

Duke, D. (2014) 'Jerusalem killings: Zionist terror comes home to roost'. Available: http://davidduke.com/jerusalem-killings-zionist-terror-comes-home-roost/ (accessed 12 November 2016).

Durkheim, E. (1952 [1897]) *Suicide*, London: Routledge and Kegan Paul.

Dysch, M. (2015) 'Revealed: Jeremy Corbyn attended hosted by Holocaust denier's group in 2013', *The Jewish Chronicle*. Available: www.thejc.com/news/uk-news/142555/revealed-jeremy-corbyn-attended-event-hosted-holocaust-deniers-group-2013 (accessed 6 October 2016).

Dysch, M. (2016) 'Labour suspends Momentum supporter who claimed Jews caused "an African holocaust"', *The Jewish Chronicle*. Available: www.thejc.com/news/uk-news/157709/labour-suspends-momentum-supporter-who-claimed-jews-caused-african-holocaust%E2%80%99 (accessed 7 October 2016).

Edemariam, A. (2013) 'The solid ground I stand on is that I am not a racist', *The Guardian*. Available: www.theguardian.com/politics/2013/feb/06/david-ward-not-racist (accessed 4 December 2015).

Edwards, C. (2016) 'Labour MP Ruth Smeeth: "I've never seen anti-Semitism in Labour like this, it's normal now"', *Business Insider UK*. Available: http://uk.businessinsider.com/mp-ruth-smeeth-ive-never-seen-anti-semitism-in-labour-like-this-2016-9?r=US&IR=T (accessed 9 October 2016).

Eisen, P. (2008) 'My life as a Holocaust denier'. *RighteousJews.org*. Available: www.righteousjews.org/article27a.html (accessed 6 October 2016).

Eissens, R. (2001) 'The morning after', *ICARE*. Available: www.icare.to/wcar/ (accessed 21 July 2016).

Ensel, R. (2014) 'Singing about the death of Muhammad al-Durrah and the emotional mobilization for protest', *International Journal of Media and Cultural Politics*, 10(1): 21–38.

EUMC (2014) 'Working definition of antisemitism'. Available: http://euro pean-forum-on-antisemitism.org/definition-of-antisemitism/english-english (accessed 24 August 2016).

European Monitoring Centre on Racism and Xenophobia (2004) 'Manifestations of antisemitism in the EU 2002–2003', *European Union Agency for Fundamental Rights*. Available: http://fra.europa.eu/sites/default/files/fra_uploads/184-AS-Main-report.pdf (accessed 27 July 2016).

Ezra, D. (2007) 'The abuse of Holocaust memory: the far right, the far left and the Middle East', *Engage Journal*, 4. Available: https://engageonline. wordpress.com/2015/11/04/the-abuse-of-holocaust-memory-the-far-right-the-far-left-and-the-middle-east-michael-ezraissue-4-engage-journal-february-2007/ (accessed 19 September 2016).

FA Staff (2014) 'Nicolas Anelka suspended for five matches and fined', *The FA*. Available: www.thefa.com/news/2014/Feb/27/nicolas-anelka-west-brom-five-match-suspension#SGK4M3UxhaWP2f2d.99 (accessed 13 November 2016).

Faludi, S. (2006) *Backlash: The Undeclared War Against American Women*, New York: Broadway.

Fanon, F. (1968) *Black Skins, White Masks*, trans. C. Markmann, London: Mac-Gibbon & Kee.

Field, F. (2015) 'I nominated Jeremy Corbyn to spark debate but I don't think he can win a General Election', *Mirror*. Available: www.mirror.co.uk/news/uk-news/nominated-jeremy-corbyn-spark-debate-6120291 (accessed 5 October 2016).

Fine, R. (2006) 'The lobby: Mearsheimer and Walt's conspiracy theory', *Engage*. Available: https://engageonline.wordpress.com/2006/03/21/the-lobby-mearsheimer-and-walts-conspiracy-theory-robert-fine/ (accessed 26 October 2016).

Fine, R. (2007) *Cosmopolitanism*, London: Routledge.

Fine, R. (2009) 'Fighting with phantoms: a contribution to the debate on anti-semitism in Europe', *Patterns of Prejudice*, 43(5): 459–479.

Fine, R. (2011) 'Cosmopolitan solidarity', in G. Delanty (ed.) *Handbook of Cosmopolitan Studies*, London: Routledge, pp. 376–386.

Fine, R. (2014) 'Book review: drawing fire: investigating the accusations of apartheid in Israel', *Fathom*. Available: http://fathomjournal.org/book-review-drawing-fire-investigating-the-accusations-of-apartheid-in-israel/ (accessed 12 November 2016).

Fine, R. (2015) 'Karl Marx and the radical critique of antisemitism', *Engage Journal*, 2. Available: https://engageonline.wordpress.com/2015/11/04/karl-marx-and-the-radical-critique-of-anti-semitism-robert-fine-engage-journal-issue-2-may-2006/ (accessed 27 July 2016).

Fine, R., and Davis, D. (1991) *Beyond Apartheid: Labour and Liberation in South Africa*, London: Pluto Press.

Fine, R., and Spencer, P. (2017) *The Left and Antisemitism: The Recurrence of the Jewish Question*, Manchester: Manchester University Press.

Finkelstein, D. (2013a) 'Surprised to find our Lord Ahmed Jews story not in BBC radio news summaries', *Twitter*, Online Posting. Available: https://twitter.com/dannythefink/status/312107941589315585 (accessed 5 October 2016).

Finkelstein, D. (2013b) 'Reply to Michael White', *Twitter*, Online Posting. Available: https://twitter.com/Dannythefink/status/312111162303074304 (accessed 5 October 2016).

Finkelstein, N.G. (2005) *Beyond Chutzpah: On the Misuse of Antisemitism and the Abuse of History*, New York: Verso.

Finkelstein, N.G. (2006) 'Kill Arabs, cry antisemitism'. Available: http://normanfinkelstein.com/2006/09/12/kill-arabs-cry-anti-semitism/ (accessed 12 November 2016).

Fisk, R. (2006) 'United States of Israel?', *The Independent*. Available: www.independent.co.uk/voices/commentators/fisk/robert-fisk-united-states-of-israel-6102654.html (accessed 26 October 2016).

Foot, P. (2003) 'Worse than Thatcher', *The Guardian*. Available: www.theguardian.com/politics/2003/may/14/labour.politicalcolumnists (accessed 26 October 2016).

Fraser, R. (2007a) 'Open Letter', *The Academic Friends of Israel*. Available: www.academics-for-israel.org/index.php?page=v6n8 (accessed 18 October 2016).

Fraser, R. (2007b) 'UCU boycott news', *The Academic Friends of Israel*. Available: www.academics-for-israel.org/index.php?page=v6n14 (accessed 18 October 2016).

Frazer, J. (2015) 'Jeremy Corbyn defends banned vicar Sizer who suggested Israel was behind 9/11', *Jewish News Online*. Available: http://jewishnews.timesofisrael.com/jeremy-corbyn-defends-banned-vicar-who-suggested-israel-was-behind-911/ (accessed 5 October 2016).

Frazer, J. (2016) 'Top historians take down Ken Livingstone's claim that 'Hitler supported Zionism'', *The Times of Israel*. Available: www.timesofisrael.com/top-historians-take-down-livingstons-claim-that-hitler-supported-zionism/ (accessed 19 September 2016).

Gardner, M. (2016) 'Corbyn and rent-a-mob: how to wreck an anti-racism event', *CST*. Available: https://cst.org.uk/news/blog/2016/07/01/

corbyn-and-rent-a-mob-how-to-wreck-an-anti-racism-event (accessed 9 October 2016).

Garrard, E. (2013) 'The pleasures of antisemitism', *Fathom*, Summer. http://fathomjournal.org/the-pleasures-of-antisemitism/ (accessed 26 October 2015).

Geras, N. (2008) 'Criticism of Israel or Israeli policy are not, as such, antisemitic – a commentary by Norman Geras', *Engage*. Available: https://engageonline.wordpress.com/2008/04/20/criticism-of-israel-or-israeli-policy-are-not-as-such-anti-semitic-a-commentary-by-norman-geras/ (accessed 27 November 2015).

Geras, N. (2009) 'Forgetting the Holocaust', *normblog*. Available: http://normblog.typepad.com/normblog/2009/01/forgetting-the-holocaust.html (accessed 9 October 2016).

Getchman, R. (2011) 'The debates on the national and Jewish questions in the second international and the Jewish labour bund 1889–1914', in A. Grabski (ed.) *Rebels against Zion*, Warsaw: Jewish Historical Institute.

Gidley, B. (2011) 'The politics of defining racism: the case of anti-semitism in the University and College Union', *Dissent*. Available: www.dissentmagazine.org/blog/the-politics-of-defining-racism-the-case-of-anti-semitism-in-the-university-and-college-union (accessed 21 July 2016).

Gilbert, A., Langleben, A., Bara, J., Rich, D., Nerva, N., and Stein, J. (2012) 'The letter to Ed Miliband from Jewish Labour supporters', *The Jewish Chronicle Online*. Available: www.thejc.com/news/uk-news/65426/the-letter-ed-miliband-jewish-labour-supporters (accessed 20 September 2016).

Gill, M. (2016) 'Watch: fury at anti-semitism event as Momentum vice chair Jackie Walker criticises Holocaust memorial', *HuffPost Politics*. Available: www.huffingtonpost.co.uk/entry/watch-anger-as-momentum-vice-chair-jackie-walker-criticises-holocaust-memorial-day-at-antisemitism-event_uk_57eb736de4b0e315f281c764 (accessed 7 October 2016).

Gilligan, A. (2015) 'Jeremy Corbyn, friend to Hamas, Iran and extremists', *The Telegraph*. Available: www.telegraph.co.uk/news/politics/labour/11749043/Andrew-Gilligan-Jeremy-Corbyn-friend-to-Hamas-Iran-and-extremists.html (accessed 5 October 2016).

Gilligan, A. (2016) 'Malia Bouattia elected NUS President after causing controversy over "anti-Semitism and refusing to condemn Isil"', *The Telegraph*. Available: www.telegraph.co.uk/news/2016/04/20/malia-bouattia-elected-nus-president-after-causing-controversy/ (accessed 7 October 2016).

Gledhill, R. (2008) 'Israeli ambassador Ron Prosor brands carol service anti-semitic', *The Times*. Available: www.thetimes.co.uk/tto/faith/article2099942.ece (accessed 22 September 2008).

Gold, R. (2016) 'Submission to the labour party enquiry on anti-semitism and other forms of racism', *Engage*. Available: https://engageonline.wordpress.com/2016/07/02/submission-to-the-labour-party-enquiry-on-anti-semitism-and-other-forms-of-racism-by-richard-gold-member-bury-south-clp/ (accessed 12 November 2016).

Goldberg, M. (2013) 'What does American Studies Association's Israeli boycott mean for academic freedom?' *The Nation*. Available: www.thenation.com/article/what-does-american-studies-associations-israel-boycott-mean-aca demic-freedom/ (accessed 1 November 2016).

Gordon, N. (2003) 'Against the Israeli academic boycott', *The Nation*. Available: www.thenation.com/article/against-israeli-academic-boycott/ (accessed 18 October 2016).

Gordon, N. (2009) 'Boycott Israel', *The Times*. Available: http://articles.latimes.com/2009/aug/20/opinion/oe-gordon20 (accessed 18 October 2016).

Grabski, A. (ed.) (2011) *Rebels against Zion: Studies on the Jewish Left Anti-Zionism*, Warsaw: Jewish Historical Institute.

Graham, D., and Boyd, J. (2010) *The Attitudes of Jews in Britain Towards Israel*, Institute for Jewish Policy Research. Available: http://jpr.org.uk/publication?id=94#.WAX1-5MrL_R (accessed 18 October 2016).

The Guardian Leader (2007) 'Neither balanced nor fair', *The Guardian*. Available: www.theguardian.com/commentisfree/2007/apr/20/pressandpub lishing.israel (accessed 18 October 2016).

Hakakian, R. (2004) *Journeys from the Land of No*, New York: Crown.

Hallé, C. (2007) 'Guardian editor condemns U.K. journalist's call to boycott Israel', *Haaretz*. Available: www.haaretz.com/news/guardian-editor-con demns-u-k-journalists-call-to-boycott-israel-1.218337 (accessed 18 October 2016).

Hari, J. (2009) 'Dupes? No, we were telling the truth', *The Independent*. Available: www.independent.co.uk/opinion/commentators/johann-hari/johann-hari-dupes-no-we-were-telling-the-truth-1649528.html (accessed 27 November 2015).

Harman, C. (2007) 'Building solidarity with Palestine', *Socialist Review*. Available: http://socialistreview.org.uk/316/building-solidarity-palestine (accessed 26 October 2016).

Harris, M. (2011) 'Holocaust memorial day in Lewisham', *BobFromBrockley*. Available: http://brockley.blogspot.co.uk/2011/01/holocaust-memorial-day-in-lewisham.html (accessed 8 October 2016).

Hartley, E. (2015) 'Jeremy Corbyn responds to Tony Blair: "I don't do personal abuse"', *HuffPost Politics*. Available: www.huffingtonpost.co.uk/2015/08/14/jeremy-corbyn-responds-to-tony-blair-i-dont-do-personal-abuse_n_7986782.html (accessed 6 October 2016).

Hartsock, N.C.M. (1997) 'The feminist standpoint: developing the ground for a specifically feminist historical materialism', in L. Nicholson (ed.) *The Second Wave: A Reader in Feminist Theory*, London and New York: Routledge.

Hattenstone, S. (2015) 'Jeremy Corbyn: I don't do personal', *The Guardian*. Available: www.theguardian.com/politics/2015/jun/17/jeremy-corbyn-labour-leadership-dont-do-personal (accessed 6 October 2016).

Henry, J. (2003) 'Outrage as Oxford bans student for being Israeli', *The Daily Telegraph*. Available: www.telegraph.co.uk/education/education news/3313901/Outrage-as-Oxford-bans-student-for-being-Israeli.html (accessed 17 October 2016).

Herf, J. (2010) *Nazi Propaganda for the Arab World*, New Haven: Yale University Press.

Herf, J. (2016) *Undeclared Wars on Israel: East Germany and the West German Far Left, 1967–1989*, Cambridge: Cambridge University Press.

Herman, E., and Chomsky, N. (1995) *Manufacturing Consent: The Political Economy of the Mass Media*, New York: Vintage.

Hirsh, D. (2003) *Law Against Genocide: Cosmopolitan Trials*, London: Glasshouse.

Hirsh, D. (2006a) 'Which camp are you in?', *The Guardian*. Available: www.theguardian.com/commentisfree/2006/may/11/israelandimperialism (accessed 26 October 2016).

Hirsh, D. (2006b) 'Openly embracing prejudice', *The Guardian*. Available: www.theguardian.com/commentisfree/2006/nov/30/anewmenacingcur rentisappe (accessed 13 November 2016).

Hirsh, D. (2007) 'Anti-zionism and antisemitism: Cosmopolitan reflections', *Working Paper*. Yale Initiative for the Interdisciplinary Study of Antisemitism (YIISA) Occasional Papers, New Haven. Available: http://eprints.gold. ac.uk/2061/1/Hirsh_Yale_paper.pdf (accessed 27 November 2015).

Hirsh, D. (2008a) 'Jenny Tonge believes in Jewish conspiracy', *Engage*. Available: https://engageonline.wordpress.com/2008/09/07/jenny-tonge-believes-in-jewish-conspiracy/ (accessed 18 November 2015).

Hirsh, D. (2008b) 'Half-truths cannot aid peace', *The Guardian*. Available: www.theguardian.com/commentisfree/2008/mar/06/halftruthscannotaidpeace (accessed 6 October 2016).

Hirsh, D. (2010a) 'Accusations of malicious intent in debates about the Palestine-Israel conflict and about antisemitism: the *Livingstone Formulation*, "playing the antisemitism card" and contesting the boundaries of antiracist discourse', *Transversal*, 1: 47–77. ISSN 1 607-629X. Available: http://eprints. gold.ac.uk/7144/1/hirsh_transversal_2010.pdf (accessed 27 November 2015).

Hirsh, D. (2010b) 'David Hirsh's talk at UCU', *Engage*. Available: http://enga geonline.wordpress.com/2010/01/18/david-hirshs-talk-at-ucu/ (accessed 27 November 2015).

Hirsh, D. (2011a) 'Live blogging from the UCU Congress: the EUMC Working Definition', *Engage*. Available: https://engageonline.wordpress.com/2011/05/30/live-blogging-from-ucu-congress-the-eumc-working-definition/ (accessed 20 July 2016).

Hirsh, D. (2011b) 'Instead of addressing its antisemitism, UCU proposes to change the definition of antisemitism', *Engage*. Available: https://engageonline.wordpress.com/2011/05/20/instead-of-adressing-its-antisemitism-ucu-proposes-to-change-the-definition-of-antisemitism/ (accessed 20 July 2016).

Hirsh, D. (2013a) 'Michael White, *Guardian* assistant editor, cries "Israel" in response to concern over Lord Ahmed's antisemitism', *Engage*. Available: http://engageonline.wordpress.com/2013/03/14/michael-white-guardian-assistant-editor-cries-israel-in-response-to-concern-over-lord-ahmeds-antisemitism/ (accessed 27 November 2015).

Hirsh, D. (2013b) 'Open letter to Claire Potter', *Engage*. Available: https://engageonline.wordpress.com/2013/12/17/open-letter-to-claire-potter-from-david-hirsh/ (accessed 1 November 2016).

Hirsh, D. (2013c) 'Hostility to Israel and antisemitism: toward a sociological approach', *Journal for the Study of Antisemitism*, 5: 23–44. Available: www.jsantisemitism.org/images/journals/jsa_5-1.pdf (accessed 20 September 2016).

Hirsh, D. (2015a) 'The Corbyn left: the politics of position and the politics of reason', *Fathom*, Autumn. Available: http://fathomjournal.org/the-corbyn-left-the-politics-of-position-and-the-politics-of-reason/ (accessed 28 November 2015).

Hirsh, D. (2015b) 'Jeremy Corbyn supports BDS', *Engage*. Available: https://engageonline.wordpress.com/2015/09/25/jeremy-corbyn-supports-bds/ (accessed 12 November 2016).

Hirsh, D. (2016a) 'How raising the issue of antisemitism puts you outside of the community of the progressive: the *Livingstone Formulation*', *Engage*. Available: https://engageonline.wordpress.com/2016/04/29/the-livingstone-formulation-david-hirsh-2/ (accessed 20 July 2016).

Hirsh, D. (2016b) 'David Hirsh's submission to the Labour Party inquiry into antisemitism', *Engage*. Available: https://engageonline.wordpress.com/2016/06/29/david-hirshs-submission-to-the-labour-party-inquiry-into-antisemitism/ (accessed 8 October 2016).

Hirshfield, C. (1980) 'The Anglo-Boer war and the issue of Jewish culpability', *Journal of Contemporary History*, 15(4): 619–631.

Historical Papers Research Archive (2013) 'The freedom charter'. Available: www.historicalpapers.wits.ac.za/inventories/inv_pdfo/AD1137/AD1137-Ea6-1-001-jpeg.pdf (accessed 25 October 2016).

Historical Research Department of the Nation of Islam (1991) *The Secret Relationship Between Blacks and Jews: The Jewish Role in Black Slavery*, New York: The Nation of Islam.

Hobsbawm, E. (1995) *Nations and Nationalism Since 1780: Programme, Myth, Reality*, Cambridge: Cambridge University Press.

Home Affairs Committee, Parliament Live TV (July 4, 2016). Available: http://parliamentlive.tv/event/index/89a8f38d-0676-4873-b388-46666415e8bf?in=17%3A25%3A25&out=17%3A26%3A04 (accessed 27 July 2016).

Home Affairs Select Committee (2016) 'Antisemitism in the UK: tenth report of session 2016–2017'. Available: www.publications.parliament.uk/pa/cm201617/cmselect/cmhaff/136/136.pdf (accessed 16 October 2016).

Howard, N. (2011) 'The Church of England must take action against Rev Stephen Sizer', *Harry's Place*. Available: http://hurryupharry.org/2011/12/27/rev-nick-howard-the-church-of-england-must-take-action-against-rev-stephen-sizer/ (accessed 6 October 2016).

Ingrams, R. (2003) 'I'm still on the train', *The Observer*. Available: http://observer.guardian.co.uk/comment/story/0,6903,997338,00.html (accessed 26 October 2016).

Ingrams, R. (2005) 'A futile pursuit', *The Guardian*. Available: http://politics.guardian.co.uk/backbench/comment/0,14158,1567455,00.html (accessed 16 November 2013).

Ingrams, R. (2007) 'It's about time someone spoke out', *The Independent*. Available: www.independent.co.uk/voices/columnists/richard-ingrams/richard-ingrams-week-sadly-brown-is-making-these-fatuous-tributes-too-464043.html (accessed 12 November 2016).

Innovative Minds (2007) 'Enough occupation: 40th anniversary of the occupation of large parts of Palestine', *Innovative Minds*. Available: www.inminds.co.uk/enough.occupation.9.june.2007.php (accessed 27 November 2015).

Irving, D. (2002) 'No title', *Action Report Online*. Available: www.fpp.co.uk/docs/Irving/RadDi/2002/110502.html (accessed 28 October 2016).

Jacobs, J. (2011) 'Bundist anti-Zionism in interwar Poland', in A. Grabski (ed.) *Rebels against Zion*, Warsaw: Jewish Historical Institute.

Jacobson, H. (2007) 'Those who boycott Israeli universities are doing intellectual violence – to themselves', *The Independent*. Available: http://spme.org/spme-research/letters-from-our-readers/howard-jacobson-those-who-boycott-israeli-universities-are-doing-intellectual-violence-to-them selves/3521/ (accessed 12 November 2016).

Jacobson, H. (2009) 'Let's see the "criticism" of Israel for what it really is', *The Independent*. Available: www.independent.co.uk/opinion/commentators/howard-jacobson/howard-jacobson-let8217s-see-the-8216criticism8217-of-israel-for-what-it-really-is-1624827.html (accessed 3 October 2016).

Jacobson, H. (2011) *The Finkler Question*, London: Thorndike.

Jacobson, H. (2015) 'Corbyn may say he's not anti-semitic, but associating with people he does is its own crime', *The Independent*. Available: www.independent.co.uk/voices/corbyn-may-say-hes-not-anti-semitic-but-associating-with-the-people-he-does-is-its-own-crime-10487318.html (accessed 6 October 2016).

James, L. (2010) 'How should the British left engage with Islamists?', *Progress: Labour's Progressives.* Available: www.progressonline.org.uk/2010/09/28/how-should-the-british-left-engage-with-islamists/ (accessed 20 September 2016).

Jewish Chronicle (2015) 'The key questions Jeremy Corbyn must answer', *The Jewish Chronicle.* Available: www.thejc.com/news/uk-news/142144/the-key-questions-jeremy-corbyn-must-answer (accessed 5 October 2016).

Jewish Chronicle Reporter (2015) 'Jeremy Corbyn responds to the JC's seven questions', *The Jewish Chronicle.* Available: www.thejc.com/news/uk-news/142656/jeremy-corbyn-responds-jc%E2%80%99s-seven-questions (accessed 6 October 2016).

Jewish Socialist Group (2006) 'Open letter to Scottish Palestine Solidarity', *www.JewishSocialist.org.* Available: www.jewishsocialist.org.uk/spscopenletter.htm (accessed 30 November 2006).

Jewish Tribal Review (2002) 'Ethics, antisemitism, the Palestinian cause and Israel: an email exchanged with Michael Neumann, Jewish professor of philosophy'. Available: www.jewishtribalreview.org/neumann2.htm (accessed 15 February 2007).

Johnson, A. (2012) 'Judith Butler: more Palestinian than the Palestinians', *World Affairs.* Available: www.worldaffairsjournal.org/blog/alan-johnson/judith-butler-more-palestinian-palestinians (accessed 6 October 2016).

Johnson, A. (2015a) 'An open letter to Jeremy Corbyn', *Left Foot Forward.* Available: http://leftfootforward.org/2015/06/an-open-letter-to-jeremy-corbyn/ (accessed 6 October 2016).

Johnson, A. (2015b) 'No, Jeremy Corbyn is not antisemitic – but the left should be wary of who he calls friends', *NewStatesman.* Available: www.newstatesman.com/politics/staggers/2015/09/no-jeremy-corbyn-not-antisemitic-left-should-be-wary-who-he-calls-friends (accessed 6 October 2016).

Johnson, A. (2016) 'Submission to Labour Party inquiry into antisemitism', *British Israeli Communications and Research Centre.* Available: www.bicom.org.uk/analysis/submission-labour-party-inquiry-antisemitism/ (accessed 12 November 2016).

Judgment of the Employment Tribunal Between: Mr R Fraser v. University and College Union, Case Numbers 2203390/2011 (25 March 2013). Available: www.judiciary.gov.uk/judgments/fraser-uni-college-union/ (accessed 21 July 2016).

Judt, T. (2007) 'In Defense of Academic Freedom', Chicago.indymedia.org. Available: http://chicago.indymedia.org/archive/usermedia/audio/6/af_tony_judt.mp3 (accessed 21 May 2017).

Julius, A. (2010) *Trials of the Diaspora: A History of Anti-Semitism in England*, Oxford: Oxford University Press.

Julius, A. (2011) 'UCU facing possible legal action', *normblog*. Available: http://normblog.typepad.com/normblog/2011/07/ucu-facing-possible-legal-action.html (accessed 2 November 2016).

Julius, A., and Dershowitz, A. (2007) 'The contemporary fight against anti-semitism', *The Times*. Available: www.timesonline.co.uk/tol/comment/columnists/guest_contributors/article1928865.ece (accessed 18 October 2016).

Kahn-Harris, K. (2014) *Uncivil War: The Israel Conflict in the Jewish Community*, London: David Paul.

Karmi, G. (2007) *Married to Another Man*, London: Pluto.

Kasrils, R. (2007) 'Israel 2007: worse than apartheid', *Mail & Guardian*. Available: http://mg.co.za/article/2007-05-21-israel-2007-worse-than-apartheid (accessed 25 October 2016).

Keogh, D., and McCarthy, A. (2005) *Limerick Boycott 1904: Antisemitism in Ireland*, Cork: Mercier Press.

King, L. (2016) 'Brent Council leader shared Facebook post calling Israel "a terrorist state like ISIS"', *Brent and Kilburn Times*. Available: www.kilburntimes.co.uk/news/brent_council_leader_shared_facebook_post_calling_israel_a_terrorist_state_like_isis_1_4516174 (accessed 7 October 2016).

Kirkup, J. (2015) 'Does Labour actually want to win the next election?', *The Guardian*. Available: www.telegraph.co.uk/news/politics/labour/11755437/Does-Labour-actually-want-to-win-the-next-election.html (accessed 6 October 2016).

Klaff, L. (2014) 'Holocaust inversion and contemporary antisemitism', *Fathom*, Winter. Available: http://fathomjournal.org/holocaust-inversion-and-contemporary-antisemitism/ (accessed 4 December 2015).

Kovler, A. (2009) 'Whatever did he mean by that?', *Fair Play Campaign Group*. Available: www.fairplaycg.org.uk/2009/05/ucu-whatever-did-he-mean-by-that/ (accessed 30 October 2016).

Kuhn, R. (2011) 'Jewish Anti-Zionism in the Galician Socialist Movement', in A. Grabski (ed.) *Rebels against Zion*, Warsaw: Jewish Historical Institute.

Küntzel, M. (2006) 'Hitler's legacy: Islamic antisemitism in the Middle East', *MathiasKuentzel.de*. Available: www.matthiaskuentzel.de/contents/hitlers-legacy-islamic-antisemitism-in-the-middle-east (accessed 26 October 2016).

Kuper, R. (2006) 'Singling out Israel', *Red Pepper*. Available: www.redpepper.org.uk/Singling-out-Israel/ (accessed 26 October 2016).

Lappin, S. (2005) 'Why I resigned from the AUT', *normblog*. Available: http://normblog.typepad.com/normblog/2005/04/why_i_resigned_.html (accessed 17 October 2016).

Lerman, A. (2009) 'Must Jews always see themselves as victims?', *The Independent*. Available: www.independent.co.uk/news/world/middle-east/must-jews-always-see-themselves-as-victims-1639277.html (accessed 28 October 2016).

Levick, M. (2013) 'The antisemitic reflex: a Jew-baiting tweet by *The Guardian's* Michael White', *UK Media Watch*. Available: http://ukmediawatch. org/2013/03/14/the-antisemitic-reflex-a-jew-baiting-tweet-by-the-guardians-michael-white/ (accessed 27 November 2015).

Lindbergh, C. (1941) 'Des Moines speech'. Available: www.charleslindbergh. com/americanfirst/speech.asp (accessed 12 November 2016).

Livingstone, K. (2006) 'An attack on voters' rights', *The Guardian*. Available: www.theguardian.com/politics/2006/mar/01/society.london (accessed 27 November 2015).

Livingstone, K. (2011) *You Can't Say That: Memoirs*, London: Faber and Faber.

Loach, K. (2016) 'UK: Ken Loach joins campaign for Labour in Birmingham', *YouTube*, Online Posting. Available: www.youtube.com/watch?v=9xeLj-F-Qqc (uploaded 1 October 2016) (accessed 13 November 2016).

Lowman, S. (2016) 'Desmond Tutu's warning shot: Zuma and ANC worse than apartheid govt', *Biznews.com*. Available: www.biznews.com/leader ship/2016/02/02/desmond-tutu-goes-360-jacob-zuma-and-anc-worse-than-apartheid-govt/ (accessed 25 October 2016).

Lucas, C. (2008) 'No green light for occupiers', *Jewish Socialist Magazine*, Spring. Available: http://socialistunity.com/jewish-socialistcaroline-lucas-on-boycott/ (accessed 12 November 2016).

Mackey, R. (2014) 'French court upholds ban on comedian who mocks Holocaust commemoration', *The New York Times*. Available: http:// thelede.blogs.nytimes.com/2014/01/09/french-court-upholds-ban-on-comedian-who-mocks-holocaust-commemoration/?smid=tw-thelede& seid=auto&_r=5 (accessed 28 October 2016).

Macpherson, W., advised by Cook, T., Sentamu, J., and Stone, R. (1999) *The Stephen Lawrence Inquiry: Report of an Inquiry*. Available: www.gov.uk/gov ernment/uploads/system/uploads/attachment_data/file/277111/4262.pdf (accessed 9 October 2016).

Marsden, C. (2003) 'Britain: Labour extends antiwar witch-hunt to Tam Dalyell', *World Socialist Web Site*. Available: www.wsws.org/en/articles/2003/05/ lab-m22.html (accessed 27 November 2015).

Martin (2007) 'UNISON: boycott before the boycott', *Workers' Liberty*. Available: www.workersliberty.org/node/8555 (accessed 18 October 2016).

Marx, K. (1994) 'The Jewish question', in J. O'Malley (ed.) *Marx: Early Political Writings*, Cambridge: Cambridge University Press.

Massad, J. (2003) 'The ends of Zionism: racism and the Palestinian struggle', *Interventions*, 5(3): 440–448.

Massad, J. (2006) 'Pinochet in Palestine', *Al-Ahram Weekly*, issue no. 819. Available: https://electronicintifada.net/content/pinochet-palestine/6525 (accessed 12 November 2016).

Matgamna, S. (2003) 'The last time we were heresy-hunted', *Workers' Liberty*. Available: www.workersliberty.org/node/997 (accessed 19 September 2016).

May, J. (2016a) 'Ken Livingstone on BBC Radio London: "Israel Lobby" tries to smear critics with "anti-semitism" tag', *Politics Home*. Available: www. politicshome.com/news/uk/social-affairs/discrimination/news/74365/ ken-livingstone-bbc-radio-london-israel-lobby-tries (accessed 19 September 2016).

May, J. (2016b) 'Jeremy Corbyn: my "grave concerns" over Ken Livingstone', *Politics Home*. Available: www.politicshome.com/news/uk/social-affairs/ discrimination/news/74392/jeremy-corbyn-my-grave-concerns-over-ken (accessed 19 September 2016).

McSmith, A. (2016) 'Khadim Hussain: former Lord Mayor of Bradford suspended by Labour Party over anti-Semitism', *The Independent*. Available: www.independent.co.uk/news/uk/politics/khadim-hussain-former-lord-mayor-of-bradford-suspended-by-labour-party-over-anti-semitism-a6948856.html (accessed 7 October 2016).

Mearsheimer, J., and Walt, S. (2006a) 'The Israel lobby', *London Review of Books*, 2(6): 3–12. Available: www.lrb.co.uk/v28/n06/john-mearsheimer/the-israel-lobby (accessed 26 October 2016).

Mearsheimer, J., and Walt, S. (2006b) 'The Israel lobby and US foreign policy', *Faculty Research Working Paper Series*, Harvard University and John F. Kennedy School of Government, Working Paper Number: RWP06–011. Available: http://ksgnotes1.harvard.edu/Research/wpaper.nsf/rwp/RWP 06-011 (accessed 26 February 2007).

Mearsheimer, J., and Walt, S. (2008) *The Israel Lobby and US Foreign Policy*, London: Penguin Books.

Mendes, P. 'Denying the Jewish Experience of Oppression: Australian Jews against Zionism and Annti-Semitisim (JAZA) and the 3CR Controversy', in A. Grabski (ed.) *Rebels against Zion: Studies on the Jewish Left Anti-Zionism*, Warsaw: Jewish Historical Institute, pp. 171–187.

Meyjes, T. (2016) 'Labour suspends a third councillor in a day over anti-Israel posts', *Metro*. Available: http://metro.co.uk/2016/05/02/labour-suspends-a-third-councillor-in-a-day-over-anti-israeli-posts-5854895/ (accessed 7 October 2016).

Miller, R. (2007) 'British anti-Zionism then and now', *Covenant*, 1(2). Available: www.covenant.idc.ac.il/en/vol1/issue2/miller.html (accessed 26 October 2016).

Milne, S. (2001) 'They can't see why they are hated', *The Guardian*. Available: www.theguardian.com/politics/2001/sep/13/september11.britainand911 (accessed 6 October 2016).

Milne, S. (2009) 'What credibility is there in Geneva's all-white boycott?', *The Guardian*. Available: www.theguardian.com/commentisfree/2009/apr/23/ un-race-conference-walkout-ahmadinejad (accessed 19 September 2016).

Milne, S. (2015) 'The demonization of Russia risks paving the way for war', *The Guardian*. Available: www.theguardian.com/commentisfree/2015/mar/04/demonisation-russia-risks-paving-way-for-war (accessed 6 October 2016).

Milosz, C. (2001) *The Captive Mind*, trans. J. Zielonko, London: Penguin Books.

Molyneux, J. (2008) 'More than opium: Marxism and religion', *International Socialism*, Issue 119. Available: http://isj.org.uk/more-than-opium-marxism-and-religion/ (accessed 13 November 2016).

Mulholland, H. (2009) 'Muslim Council of Britain boycotts Holocaust day', *The Guardian*. Available: www.theguardian.com/uk/2009/jan/26/5 (accessed 8 October 2016).

Neil, A. (2016) 'Daily politics', 'Transcript of Shami Chakrabarti interview with Andrew Neil', *Facebook*, Online Posting. Available: www.facebook.com/dhirsh1/posts/10153858718880918 (accessed 12 November 2016).

Nelson, C. (2014) 'The problem with Judith Butler: the political philosophy of the movement to boycott Israel', *LARB*. Available: https://lareviewofbooks.org/article/problem-judith-butler-political-philosophy-movement-boycott-israel/#! (accessed 18 October 2016).

Nelson, C. (2016) 'Academic freedom in Palestinian universities', *TELOS*. Available: www.telospress.com/academic-freedom-in-palestinian-universities/ (accessed 18 October 2016).

Neumann, M. (2002) 'What is antisemitism?', *Counterpunch*. Available: www.counterpunch.org/2002/06/04/what-is-antisemitism/ (accessed 26 October 2016).

O'Loughlin, E. (2007) 'US-backed Abbas risks being tagged "quisling"', *Theage.com*. Available: www.theage.com.au/news/world/usbacked-abbas-risks-being-tagged-quisling/2007/06/17/1182018936936.html (accessed 7 November 2016).

Organization for Security and Co-operation in Europe (1990) 'Charter for Paris for a New Europe'. Available: www.osce.org/node/39516 (accessed 21 July 2016).

Orwell, G. (1943) 'Looking back on the Spanish war', London. Available: http://orwell.ru/library/essays/Spanish_War/english/esw_1 (accessed 13 November 2016).

Orwell, G. (2004) *Nineteen Eighty-Four*, London: Penguin.

Oryszczuk, S. (2016) 'Baroness Royall: "no institutional anti-Semitism" at Oxford University Labour Club', *Jewish News Online*. Available: http://jewishnews.timesofisrael.com/baroness-royall-no-institutional-anti-semitism-at-oxford-university-labour-club/ (accessed 8 October 2016).

Osborn, M. (2005) 'Now mobilise for NATFHE boycott!', *Workers' Liberty*. Available: www.workersliberty.org/node/4219 (accessed 21 July 2016).

PACBI (Palestinian Campaign for the Boycott of Israel) (2006) 'The PACBI call for academic boycott revised: adjusting the parameters of the debate'. Available: http://pacbi.org/etemplate.php?id=1051 (accessed 25 October 2016).

Palestinian Solidarity Campaign (2016) 'Our patrons'. Available: www.palesti necampaign.org/about/patrons/ (accessed 4 November 2016).

Pappé, I. (2006) 'Genocide in Gaza', *The Electronic Intifada*. Available: https:// electronicintifada.net/content/genocide-gaza/6397 (accessed 8 October 2016).

Parliament UK (2016a) 'House of commons debate', 9 March 2016, vol. 607. Available: https://hansard.parliament.uk/commons/2016-03-09/debates/ 16030943000028/Engagements (accessed 7 October 2016).

Parliament UK (2016b) 'House of Commons Debate', 4 May 2016, vol 609. Available: https://hansard.parliament.uk/commons/2016-05-04/debates/ 16050453000018/Engagements (accessed 7 October 2016).

Paul, J. (2011) 'UK academic union rejects EU definition of anti-Semitism', *Jerusalem Post*. Available: www.jpost.com/International/UK-academic-union-rejects-EU-definition-of-anti-Semitism (accessed 27 November 2015).

Paul, J. (2013) 'British MP blames jail term on Jewish conspiracy', *The Jerusalem Post*. Available: www.jpost.com/International/UK-politician-blames-jail-sentence-on-Jewish-conspiracy (accessed 27 November 2015).

Payne, A. (2016) 'Jeremy Corbyn was paid by an Iranian state TV station that was complicit in the forced confessions of a tortured journalist', *Business Insider UK*. Available: http://uk.businessinsider.com/jeremy-corbyn-paid-iran-press-tv-tortured-journalist-2016-6 (accessed 4 November 2016).

Pike, J. (2006a) 'Wrong in principle, wrong in practice', *The Guardian*. Available: www.theguardian.com/commentisfree/2006/may/09/post76 (accessed 17 October 2016).

Pike, J. (2006b) 'Academic freedoms and the limits of boycotts: some Kantian considerations', *Engage Journal*, 1. Available: https://engageonline.wordpress. com/2015/11/04/academic-freedom-and-the-limits-of-boycotts-some-kantian-considerations-jon-pike-engage-journal-issue-1-january-2006/ (accessed 17 October 2016).

Pike, J. (2008) 'Antisemitism and testimonial injustice', *Engage*. Available: https://engageonline.wordpress.com/2008/01/31/jon-pikes-response-to-david-hirshs-paper-last-wednesday-antisemitism-and-testimonial-injus tice/ (accessed 18 November 2015).

Pike, J. (2013) 'The myth of the institutional boycott', *Engage*. Available: https:// engageonline.wordpress.com/2013/02/27/the-myth-of-the-institutional-boycott-jon-pike/ (accessed 17 October 2016).

Pogrund, B. (2015) 'Israel has many injustices. But it is not an apartheid state', *The Guardian*. Available: www.theguardian.com/commentisfree/2015/may/22/ israel-injustices-not-apartheid-state (accessed 25 October 2016).

Postone, M. (2006) 'History and helplessness: mass mobilization and contemporary forms of anticapitalism', *Public Culture*, 18(1): 93–110.

Potter, C. (2013) 'Blogging across the water: a response to David Hirsh about the ASA Revolution', *The Chronicle*. Available: www.chronicle.com/blog network/tenuredradical/2013/12/blogging-across-the-water-a-response-to-david-hirsh/ (accessed 1 November 2016).

Press Gazette (2007) 'Broadcasters call to end NUJ Israel boycott', *Press Gazette*. Available: www.pressgazette.co.uk/broadcasters-call-to-end-nuj-israel-boycott/ (accessed 18 October 2016).

Pugh-Jones, A. (2009) 'BRICUP's guest Bongani Masuku falls foul of Human Rights Commission', *Engage*. Available: https://engageonline.wordpress.com/2009/12/03/bongani-masuku-bricup-boycott/ (accessed 28 October 2016).

Quinn, B. (2013) 'Lib Dem MP David Ward defends remarks about Israel', *The Guardian*. Available: www.theguardian.com/politics/2013/jan/25/lib-dem-david-ward-israel (accessed 4 December 2015).

Ramadan, T. (2012) 'Behind the Toulouse shootings', *Tariq Ramadan*. Available: http://tariqramadan.com/english/behind-the-toulouse-shootings/ (accessed 7 October 2016).

Rashty, S. (2016) 'John Mann pledges to confront Ken Livingstone over "Hitler backed Zionism" comment', *The Jewish Chronicle Online*. Available: www.thejc.com/news/uk-news/158563/john-mann-pledges-confront-ken-livingstone-again-over-hitler-backed-zionism-comm (accessed 19 September 2016).

Reade, B. (2009) 'Douglas Alexander's Gaza aid pledge typifies Britain's cowardly subservience to US pro-Israel lobby', *Daily Mirror*. Available: www.mirror.co.uk/news/columnists/reade/2009/03/05/douglas-alexander-s-gaza-aid-pledge-typifies-britain-s-cowardly-subservience-to-us-pro-israel-lobby-115875-21173281/ (accessed 30 October 2016).

Readings, G. (2010) 'Livingstone: Al-Qaradawi is a "leading progressive voice" in Muslim world', *Left Foot Forward*. Available: http://leftfootforward.org/2010/09/livingstone-al-qaradawi-is-a-leading-progressive-voice-in-muslim-world/ (accessed 20 September 2016).

Reasons of the Regulatory Commission (2011) 'The Football Association and Luis Suarez'. Available: www.furd.org/resources/FA%20v%20Suarez%20Written%20Reasons%20of%20Regulatory%20Commission.pdf (accessed 12 November 2016).

Report of the Stephen Lawrence Inquiry (1999). Available: www.archive.official-documents.co.uk/document/cm42/4262/sli-06.htm (accessed 30 October 2016).

Reuters (2008) 'Ahmadinejad: Zionism has nothing to do with the Jewish people', *Ynetnews.com*. Available: www.ynetnews.com/articles/0,7340,L-3602437,00.html (accessed 27 November 2015).

Reynolds, P. (2007) 'Profile: David Miliband', *BBC News*. Available: http://news.bbc.co.uk/2/hi/uk_news/politics/6248508.stm (accessed 27 November 2015).

Rich, D. (2016a) *The Left's Jewish Problem: Jeremy Corbyn, Israel and Anti-Semitism*, London: Biteback Publishing.

Rich, D. (2016b) 'Gerry Downing's "Jewish Question"', *CST*. Available: https://cst.org.uk/news/blog/2016/03/10/gerry-downings-jewish-question (accessed 7 October 2016).

Rich, D. (2016c) 'The Left and the Holocaust', *Engage Journal*, 4. Available: https://engageonline.wordpress.com/2015/11/04/the-left-and-the-holocaust-david-rich-engage-journal-issue-4-february-2007/ (accessed 8 October 2016).

Ridley, L. (2016) 'Cathy Newman abused for Momentum Jackie Walker Interview, points out she's not Jewish', *The Huffington Post*. Available: www.huffingtonpost.co.uk/entry/cathy-newman-kevine-walcott-anti-semitic_uk_57ee249de4b0397f73b92a93 (accessed 8 October 2016).

Rose, J. (1996) *Mourning Becomes the Law*, Cambridge: Cambridge University Press.

Rose, J. (2004) *The Myths of Zionism*, London: Pluto.

Rose, J. (2007) *The Question of Zion*, Princeton: Princeton University Press.

Rose, J. (2009) 'Why Howard Jacobson is wrong', *The Guardian*. Available: www.theguardian.com/commentisfree/2009/feb/23/howard-jacobson-antisemitism-caryl-churchill (accessed 28 October 2016).

Rose, J. *et al* (2007) 'Let's have more boycott debate', *The Guardian*. Available: www.theguardian.com/news/2007/jun/15/leadersandreply.mainsection (accessed 17 October 2016).

Roth, P. (2004) *The Plot Against America*, New York: Vintage Books.

Royall, J. (2016a) 'I cleared Labour of anti-semitism – but it must make Jewish people more welcome', *The Guardian*. Available: www.theguardian.com/commentisfree/2016/may/18/labour-antisemitism-party-jewish-chakrabarti (accessed 8 October 2016).

Royall, J. (2016b) 'Allegations of anti-semitism: Oxford University Labour Club', *The Jewish Chronicle*. Available: www.thejc.com/images/Report_OUC_Final.pdf (accessed 9 October 2016).

Sacranie, I. (2005) 'Holocaust memorial day is too exclusive', *The Guardian*. Available: www.theguardian.com/world/2005/sep/20/religion.uk (accessed 26 October 2016).

Said, E. (1978) *Orientalism*, Harmondsworth: Penguin.

Samuel, H. (2015) 'Anti-semitic comedian Dieudonné accused of glorifying Paris killer', *The Telegraph*. Available: www.telegraph.co.uk/news/worldnews/europe/france/11391256/Anti-semitic-comedian-Dieudonne-accused-of-glorifying-Paris-killer.html (accessed 28 October 2016).

Searle, C. (2007) 'Interview: Gilad Atzmon', *The Morning Star*. Available: www.alterinfo.net/Chris-Searle-Forward-Groove-Jazz-and-the-real-world-from-Louis-Armstrong-to-Gilad-Atzmon_a26045.html (accessed 12 November 2016).

Seymour, D. (2007) *Law, Antisemitism and the Holocaust*, London: Routledge.

Shaw, M. (2008a) 'Antisemitism and the boycott: an exchange between Martin Shaw and David Hirsh', *Democratiya*, Autumn 2008. Available: www.dissentmagazine.org/wp-content/files_mf/1389809313d14ShawHirsh1.pdf (accessed 18 September 2015).

Shaw, M. (2008b) 'Yet more on Israel and antisemitism'. Available: http://theorypolitics.blogspot.com/2008/10/yet-more-on-israel-and-anti-semitism.html (accessed 18 November 2015).

Sherwood, H. (2016) 'Ken Livingstone: "I didn't say Hitler was a Zionist"', *The Guardian*. Available: www.theguardian.com/politics/2016/jun/14/ken-livingstone-i-didnt-say-hitler-was-a-zionist (accessed 19 September 2016).

Shiblak, A. (2005) *Iraqi Jews: A History of Mass Exodus*, London: Saqi.

Shindler, C. (2011) *Israel and the European Left: Between Solidarity and Delegitimization*, London: Continuum.

Simons, N. (2016) 'Ken Livingstone should be suspended for Hitler and antisemitism comments, say Labour MPs', *Huffpost Politics*. Available: www.huffingtonpost.co.uk/entry/ken-livingstone-should-be-suspended-from-party-for-hitler-comments-say-labour-mps_uk_5721d8f1e4b06bf544e14f19 (accessed 19 September 2016).

Sizer, S. (2007) 'Church's share sale is not anti-semitic', *The Independent*. Available: www.independent.co.uk/voices/letters/letters-black-musicians-and-the-media-5337155.html (accessed 18 November 2015).

Snowdon, K. (2016) 'Labour's anti-semitism row "cynical" attempt to challenge Jeremy Corbyn's leadership, Len McCluskey warns', *The Huffington Post*. Available: www.huffingtonpost.co.uk/entry/labour-anti-semitism-row-attempt-to-challenge-jeremy-corbyn-leadership-len-mccluskey_uk_57266218e4b0d6f7bed60632 (accessed 9 October 2016).

Socialist Worker Online (2006) 'Politics in store at cultures of resistance concert', Issue 2029. Available: https://socialistworker.co.uk/art/10036/Politics+in+store+at+Cultures+of+Resistance+concert (accessed 28 October 2016).

Sommers, J. (2016) 'Jeremy Corbyn responds to leadership challenge and Theresa May becoming PM by going to Cuban solidarity event', *The Huffington Post*. Available: www.huffingtonpost.co.uk/entry/jeremy-corbyn-responds-to-leadership-challenge-and-theresa-mays-coronation-as-pm-by-going-to-cuban-solidarity-event_uk_5783d4b1e4b07a99eadd0fcd (accessed 5 October 2016).

Sparrow, A. (2015) 'Maria Eagle says Corbyn's comment on not pressing nuclear button unhelpful', *The Guardian*. Available: www.theguardian.

com/politics/blog/live/2015/sep/30/labour-conference-jeremy-corbyns-morning-interviews-politics-live (accessed 6 October 2016).

Spencer, P. (2012) *Genocide Since 1945*, Oxon and New York: Routledge.

Srebrnik, H. (2011) '"An enemy of the Jewish masses": the ICOR and the campaign against Zionism', in A. Grabski (ed.) *Rebels against Zion*, Warsaw: Jewish Historical Institute.

Stern-Weiner, J., and Finkelstein, N. (2016) 'The American Jewish scholar behind Labour's "antisemitism" scandal breaks his silence', *Open Democracy*. Available: www.opendemocracy.net/uk/jamie-stern-weiner-norman-finkelstein/american-jewish-scholar-behind-labour-s-antisemitism-scanda (accessed 19 September 2016).

Stewart, H., Mason, R., and Parveen, N. (2016) 'Labour MP apologises to commons amid antisemitism row', *The Guardian*. Available: www.theguardian.com/politics/2016/apr/27/shadow-minister-calls-for-suspension-of-naz-shah-over-israel-posts (accessed 19 September 2016).

Stoll, I. (2006) '"Israel lobby" caused war in Iraq, September 11 attacks, professor says', *New York Sun*. Available: www.nysun.com/new-york/israel-lobby-caused-war-in-iraq-september-11/40629/ (accessed 26 October 2016).

Stoltzfus, N. (1982). *Resistance of the Heart: Intermarriage and the Rosenstrasse Protest in Nazi Germany*, London: Weidenfeld and Nicolson.

Strawson, J. (2005) 'Why I am against the boycott', *Engage*. Available: https://engageonline.wordpress.com/2005/05/05/why-i-am-against-the-boycott-by-john-strawson-18-may-2005/ (accessed 25 October 2016).

Sussex Friends of Israel (2016) *Facebook*, Online Posting. Available: www.facebook.com/521248807933259/videos/1135282233196577/ (accessed 7 October 2016).

Swaine, J. (2009) 'Lord Ahmed freed from prison after dangerous driving sentence suspended', *The Telegraph*. Available: www.telegraph.co.uk/news/4982260/Lord-Ahmed-freed-from-prison-after-dangerous-driving-sentence-suspended.html (accessed 18 November 2015).

Symons, L. (2010) 'UCU under fire for "institutional racism"', *The Jewish Chronicle Online*. Available: www.thejc.com/news/uk-news/26284/ucu-under-fire-institutional-racism (accessed 18 November 2015).

Totten, S., and Jacobs, S.L. (2013) *Pioneers of Genocide Studies*, New Brunswick: Transactions Publishers.

Transcript (2006) 'This is a transcript of the taped exchange between Ken Livingstone and Oliver Finegold outside of City Hall last year', *The Guardian*. Available: www.theguardian.com/society/2006/feb/25/localgovernment.politicsandthemedia (accessed 18 November 2015).

Traubmann, T. (2006) 'British professor confirms "silent" boycott of Israel', *Haaretz*. Available: www.haaretz.com/british-professor-confirms-silent-boycott-of-israel-1.188063 (accessed 17 October 2016).

Tutu, D. (2002) 'Apartheid in the Holy Land', *The Guardian*. Available: www.the-guardian.com/world/2002/apr/29/comment (accessed 8 October 2016).

U.S. Department of State (2008) 'Contemporary global anti-semitism: a report provided to the United States Congress', *U.S. Department of State*. Available: www.state.gov/documents/organization/102301.pdf (accessed 21 July 2016).

U.S. Department of State (2010) 'Defining anti-semitism', *U.S. Department of State*. Available: www.state.gov/j/drl/rls/fs/2010/122352.htm (accessed 24 August 2016).

UCU (2003) 'Motions'. Available: www.ucu.org.uk/index.cfm?articleid=527 (accessed 18 November 2015).

UCU (2007) 'Events'. Available: www.ucu.org.uk/index.cfm?articleid=2555 (accessed 18 November 2015).

Ungar-Sargon, B. (2013) 'Is Jewish control over the slave trade a nation of Islam lie or scholarly truth?', *Tablet*. Available: www.tabletmag.com/jewish-arts-and-culture/books/137476/slave-trade-black-muslim (accessed 7 October 2016).

Verso Press (2015) 'Publicity note on Reflections on Antisemitism', *Versobooks.com*. Available: www.versobooks.com/books/1110-reflections-on-antisemitism (accessed 30 October 2016).

Walker, J. (2016) 'Jackie Walker crowdfunds to bring legal proceedings against Iaian McNicol', *Free Speech on Israel*. Available: http://freespeechonisrael.org.uk/jackie-walker-crowdfunds-bring-legal-proceedings-iain-mcnicol/ (accessed 28 October 2016).

Wallis Simons, J. (2015) 'Jeremy Corbyn DEFENDS a controversial vicar who was banned from social media for sharing "clearly anti-semitic" material blaming Israel for 9/11 attacks', *Daily Mail*. Available: www.dailymail.co.uk/news/article-3191393/Jeremy-Corbyn-defended-controversial-vicar-banned-social-media-promoting-clearly-anti-Semitic-material.html (accessed 27 November 2015).

Watson, G. (2016) 'Statement on today's launch of the Chakrabarti report', *Ruthsmeeth.org.uk*. Available: www.ruthsmeeth.org.uk/statement_on_the_launch_of_the_chakrabarti_report (accessed 9 October 2016).

Watt, N., and Syal, R. (2013) 'Ed Miliband to review Labour's link with trade unions', *The Guardian*. Available: www.theguardian.com/politics/2013/jul/05/ed-miliband-trade-unions (accessed 5 October 2016).

Weber, M. (1978a) 'Class, status and party', in W.G. Runciman and E. Matthews (eds) *Max Weber: Selections in Translation*, Cambridge: Cambridge University Press.

Weber, M. (1978b) 'The nature of social action', in W.G. Runciman and E. Matthews (eds) *Max Weber: Selections in Translation*, Cambridge: Cambridge University Press.

Weisfeld, H. (2016) 'What hope the fight against antisemitism when Malia Bouattia leads the NUS?', *The Guardian*. Available: www.theguardian.com/commentisfree/2016/apr/22/antisemitism-malia-bouattia-nus-muslim-anti-zionist?CMP=share_btn_fb (accessed 7 October 2016).

Weissman, J. (2012) 'Ben White tries to save face about his racist tweet', *Harry's Place*. Available: http://hurryupharry.org/2012/05/30/ben-white-tries-to-save-face-about-his-racist-tweet/ (accessed 13 October 2016).

Wheatcroft, G. (2006) 'After the rhapsody, the bitter legacy of Israel and the left', *The Guardian*. Available: www.theguardian.com/commentisfree/2006/mar/24/israel (accessed 26 October 2016).

Whine, M. (2004) 'International organizations: combating anti-semitism in Europe', *Jewish Political Studies Review*, 16(3–4). Available: www.jcpa.org/phas/phas-whine-f04.htm (accessed 24 August 2016).

Whine, M. (2006) 'Progress in the struggle against anti-semitism in Europe: the Berlin declaration and the European Union Monitoring Centre on Racism and Xenophobia's Working Definition of Anti-Semitism', *Jerusalem Centre for Public Affairs*. Available: http://jcpa.org/article/progress-in-the-struggle-against-anti-semitism-in-europe-the-berlin-declaration-and-the-european-union-monitoring-centre-on-racism-and-xenophobias-working-definition-of-anti-semitism/ (accessed 21 July 2016).

Whine, M. (2010) 'Two steps forward, one step back: diplomatic progress in combating antisemitism', *Israel Journal of Foreign Affairs*, IV(5): 91–102.

White, M. (2013a) 'Reply to Daniel Finkelstein', *Twitter*, Online Posting. Available: https://twitter.com/michaelwhite/status/312110762552332288 (accessed 5 October 2016).

White, M. (2013b) 'Reply to Daniel Finkelstein', *Twitter*, Online Posting. Available: https://twitter.com/michaelwhite/status/312118251456954368 (accessed 5 October 2016).

White, N. (2016) 'Will someone point out to the idiots that latest anti-Semitism row was launched by Tory blogger Guido Fawkes & promoted by Mail on Sunday', *Twitter*, Online Posting. Available: https://twitter.com/michaelwhite/status/725950000962764800 (accessed 7 October 2016).

Whitehead, A. (2002) '"No common ground": Joseph Massad and Benny Morris discuss the Middle East', *History Workshop Journal*, 53(1): 205–216.

Wilkins, B. (2014) 'Desmond Tutu urges boycott of "apartheid" Israel', *Digital Journal*. Available: www.digitaljournal.com/news/world/desmond-tutu-urges-boycott-of-apartheid-israel/article/375545 (accessed 25 October 2016).

Wilkinson, M. (2015) 'David Cameron: a greater Britain with conservatives, not with terrorist-sympathising Jeremy Corbyn – as it happened', *The Telegraph*. Available: www.telegraph.co.uk/news/politics/david-cameron/11916178/david-cameron-speech-conservative-conference-live.html (accessed 6 October 2016).

Winstanley, A. (2015) 'Jeremy Corbyn backs boycott of Israeli universities involved in arms research', *The Electronic Intifada*. Available: https://electronicintifada.net/blogs/asa-winstanley/jeremy-corbyn-backs-boycott-israeli-universities-involved-arms-research (accessed 12 November 2016).

Wistrich, R.S. (1982) *Who's Who in Nazi Germany*, London: Weidenfeld and Nicolson.

Wistrich, R.S. (1994) *Antisemitism: The Longest Hatred*, New York: Shocken.

Woodward, W. (2003) 'Lecturers' union to debate boycott of Israel', *The Guardian*. Available: www.theguardian.com/uk/2003/may/05/internationaleducationnews.highereducation (accessed 17 October 2016).

Yudkin, M. (2007) 'Is an academic boycott of Israel justified?' *Engage Journal*. Available: https://engageonline.wordpress.com/2015/11/04/is-an-academic-boycott-of-israel-justified-michael-yudkin-engage-journal-special-issue-april-2007/ (accessed 12 November 2016).

Zimmer, Heidingsfelder and Adler (2010) 'Interview with Judith Butler', *Aviva-Berlin.de*. Available: www.aviva-berlin.de/aviva/content_Interviews.php?id=1427323 (accessed 26 October 2015).

Zoydo, V. (2008) 'Le Pen à 20minutes. Fr: je suis le parrain de la troisième fille de Dieudonné devant Dieu et devant les hommes', *20minutes*. Available: www.20minutes.fr/france/242082-20080716-pen-a-20minutesfr-je-parrain-troisieme-fille-dieudonne-devant-dieu-devant-hommes (accessed 28 October 2016).

Zucker, B. (2011) 'American Jewish communists and Palestine during the 1930s', in A. Grabski (ed.) *Rebels against Zion*, Warsaw: Jewish Historical Institute.

INDEX